LANDLORD
AND PEASANT IN
COLONIAL
OAXACA

LANDLORD
AND PEASANT IN
COLONIAL
OAXACA

WILLIAM B. TAYLOR

STANFORD UNIVERSITY PRESS
STANFORD, CALIFORNIA
1972

Stanford University Press
Stanford, California
© 1972 by the Board of Trustees of the
Leland Stanford Junior University
Printed in the United States of America
ISBN 0-8047-0796-0
LC 70-153819

To Lic. Luis Castañeda Guzmán
Lawyer, educator, gentleman,
and fellow student of Oaxaca's past

PREFACE

THIS IS a study of the relations between man and land in the Valley of Oaxaca, Mexico, during the Spanish colonial period. Land tenure is an especially good way to approach society in colonial Latin America, for except in the mining regions and the centers of trade, land was the main economic foundation of the social order. Landlords and peasants were at the base of colonial society. Other classes—artisans, merchants, and men of the pen and the sword—were superimposed on these groups.

The focus is on the system of tenure, on the changing social relations among the members of colonial society and the division of land among them. At all stages I have tried to go beyond the laws governing land use to the land regime in practice, the actual distribution of land over the three hundred years of Spanish rule. Although this study deals with the colonial period as a whole, the documentation is most complete for the eighteenth century. Because of the absence of notarial records before 1684, the discussion of land transfers for the sixteenth and seventeenth centuries should be considered tentative. It is frequently impossible to identify specific boundaries, especially for Indian lands. Still, although not always precise, the documentation is complete enough to establish a range of different kinds and sizes of landholdings, and to reveal changes in the relative importance of different forms of tenure. The Valley of Oaxaca is a significant and manageable area for such a study. All the major social and ethnic groups involved in the colonial experience were present: a permanent community of Spaniards, an active body of churchmen, small numbers of Negroes and *castas* (those of mixed ancestry), and a large Indian population with a hereditary elite.

The literature dealing with land tenure in colonial Latin America has several distinctive features. Before the work of François Chevalier the focus was clearly on land law. Historians have spent considerable energy compiling colonial land legislation and studying the legal history of land tenure. José María Ots Capdequí (*El régimen de la tierra en la América española durante el período colonial*) has long been a leading student of land law. Several other aspects of land tenure have been much debated in print. The *hacienda* receives considerable attention, usually in rather vague moral terms. Whether the hacienda was a "feudal" institution has been a topic of special interest. Recent research on the social history of land in New Spain usually draws on examples from widely scattered parts of the viceroyalty. There are general works on broad themes but virtually no monographs on which a solid synthesis can be based. Without a foundation of regional studies the composite treatment tends to homogenize the colonial experience and to blur important differences wrought by different geographical and human factors. The results obtained for Oaxaca confirm the need for other detailed studies of land tenure in diverse geographical settings. Large haciendas, debt peonage, and landless Indians—the familiar features of the colonial Latin American land system—were all found in the Valley of Oaxaca. But, significantly, these features did not predominate there. The physical setting and the indigenous population played an active part in shaping colonial society in general and land tenure in particular. This example suggests that the Spaniard did not and could not control land and society to the same extent that he controlled styles of art and architecture.

The principal archival source for colonial land tenure is the Archivo General de la Nación in Mexico City. I am especially grateful to Director Jorge Ignacio Rubio Mañé, Beatriz Arteaga Garza, Licenciado Eduardo Báez Macías, Francisco Javier Carreño Avendaño, and Miguel Saldaña of the Archivo for their assistance and good will. Other public archives in Mexico that proved valuable are the Archivo Histórico and the microfilm collection of the Instituto Nacional de Antropología e Historia, the archives of the Departamento de Asuntos Agrarios in Mexico City, the Archivo de Notarías in Oaxaca, and the Biblioteca del Estado de Oaxaca. Of the Spanish archives the Archivo General de las Indias in Seville and the Biblioteca Nacional and the Real Academia de Historia, both in Madrid, were especially useful. In the United States the libraries of the University of New Mexico and the University of Texas provided a small but important body of manuscripts on Oaxaca.

Not the least of my reasons for choosing to work in Oaxaca was the prospect of pleasant surroundings and lively associates. I was not disappointed. I am deeply indebted to several *oaxaqueños* for aiding me in the research, above all to Licenciado Luis Castañeda Guzmán, who graciously permitted me to use his large collection of hacienda and Church records. The many citations to this collection in the notes attest to its value. Licenciado Castañeda Guzmán also shared keen insights into Oaxaca's past and provided some important bibliographical references. The officials of Tlacolula kindly allowed me to rummage through the mountain of eighteenth-century and nineteenth-century documents housed under the bandstand there. These documents represent a unique source of information concerning the landholdings of individual Indians and the tensions in an Indian community. The officials of Mitla were equally generous in supplying land records and colonial land maps. During my stay in Mitla John Paddock and Cecil R. Welte offered much good advice and many fruitful leads to colonial materials. The maps in this book have been adapted from Welte's "Mapa de las Localidades del Valle de Oaxaca" (1965).

In the course of my work I have received the selfless help of many people. Dauril Alden, Woodrow Borah, Lewis Hanke, Jeffrey Parsons, Sylvia Thrupp, and Glen S. Waggoner brought their critical skills to bear on an earlier version of the study. Charles Gibson supervised my doctoral dissertation, which covered much of the same ground. His dedication and exacting but sympathetic criticism were sources of energy and inspiration.

Grants to carry out this study came from the University of Michigan, the American Philosophical Society, and the University of Colorado. I recognize a special debt of gratitude to Gabriele Von Munk Benton, Richard E. Greenleaf, and Clifton B. Kroeber, who did much to encourage my early interest in Latin America. Finally, Barbara E. Taylor contributed her secretarial skills and a wife's gentle understanding.

                                                              W.T.

CONTENTS

INTRODUCTION 1

I THE SETTING 9

II COLONIAL CACICAZGOS 35

III PUEBLO AND PEASANT LANDS 67

IV SPANISH ESTATES 111

V CHURCH ESTATES 164

CONCLUSION 195

Appendixes 205

Notes 229   Glossary 259

Bibliography 265

Index 279

APPENDIXES

A. Lands Rented Out by Indian Nobles   205

B. Land Disputes Among Indian Towns   209

C. An Emphiteutic Grant by the Marqués del
   Valle, 1618   211

D. Viceregal Land Grants to Spaniards   213

E. Hacienda Transfers   214

F. Mortgages of the Convent of Santa Catalina de Sena   221

G. Eighteenth-Century Land Documents of the
   Convent of Santa Catalina de Sena   222

H. Eighteenth-Century Land Transactions
   Involving Secular Priests   224

ILLUSTRATIONS

Maps

1. The Valley of Oaxaca   25
2. Cacicazgo Lands   58
3. Indian Towns Suffering Damage from Spanish Cattle in the Sixteenth Century   118
4. Spanish Secular Estates in the Eighteenth Century   125
5. Church Estates in the Valley of Oaxaca, 1660   175
6. Church Estates in the Valley of Oaxaca, 1760   177
7. Dominican Landholdings, 1600–1810   178

Figures

1. Tributaries in Three Valley Jurisdictions, 1570–1810   32
2. Eighteenth-Century Cuatro Villas Tributaries   33
3. Livestock on Three Valley Haciendas   129
4. Value of Livestock According to Hacienda Inventories   130
5. Debts of Debt Peons in the Valley, Eighteenth Century   150

Plates

I. The Lands of Santo Domingo Jalieza and Santa Cecilia Jalieza, 1798   76
II. The Lands of Tlacochahuaya, 1760   86
III. The *Labor* of Don Matheo Delgado, 1730   136

TABLES

1. The Population of Antequera, 1526–1826   18

2. The Population of Antequera in 1792   19

3. Sujetos Granted Licenses to Elect Their Own Officials   30

4. Tributary Population in the Cuatro Villas Jurisdiction   31

5. Summary of Eighteenth-Century Cuatro Villas Tributary Figures   33

6. Tributaries in the Valley of Oaxaca in the Late Eighteenth Century   34

7. Land Grants to Indian Towns   80

8. Livestock on the Marquesado Estate, 1549–1636   114

9. Regular Clergy in Antequera, 1777 and 1792   167

10. Sales of Land by Regular Orders   172

11. Houses in Antequera Owned by Monasteries and Convents, 1792   173

LANDLORD
AND PEASANT IN
COLONIAL
OAXACA

INTRODUCTION

WHEN Fernando Cortez and his hearty followers pushed inland from Veracruz in 1519, they encountered a vast and richly varied terrain. Mountains dominate the Mexican landscape, dividing the interior of the country into sharply contrasting regions. Two great mountain chains jut southward from the United States to the Isthmus of Tehuantepec, enclosing a high, semi-arid central plateau. Only about one-third of the country's land surface is reasonably level. These natural barriers and the distribution of the Indian population fostered the growth of distinctive pockets of settlement rather than a uniform, integrated colony. The Valley of Oaxaca, on the mountainous southern fringe of the central highlands, was one of the important regional centers of colonial life.

By air from Mexico City the soft hues of the fertile Valley appear quite suddenly and in sharp contrast to the stark, rugged expanse of the Mixteca Alta. The high mountain slopes surrounding the Valley were never great obstacles to the movement of people, but they did form a boundary that tended to differentiate Indians living in the Valley from those in adjoining areas. The dense settlement of the Valley from pre-Spanish times through the colonial period suggests that the surrounding mountains discouraged movement away from the area, and that the level plain and rich soils attracted Indians and Spaniards alike. The Valley was especially well suited to an agrarian Indian culture that lacked both the wheel and draft animals. Because the various regions of the Valley were flat and accessible, peasants tended to buy town products instead of depending entirely on what they could produce at home. In Oaxaca, as in other inte-

rior Indian centers, the ease of transportation and the abundance
of good farmland encouraged large Indian markets and the spe-
cialization of crafts and other skills. The Valley's isolation from
other basins of similar size and its agricultural potential gave it
a special attraction. It is little wonder that virtually all of the
Valley has been put to some productive use for nearly a millen-
nium.//

Geography had a direct influence on the character of colonial
life in Mexico. Colonial centers developed in areas with the largest Indian populations and the richest agricultural and mineral
resources. The Chichimec frontier, an imaginary line along the
northern borders of the states of Mexico, Querétaro, and Hidalgo,
separated a densely populated Indian settlement from natives
with a more transient, rudimentary style of life. A shifting cultural boundary, the Chichimec frontier does not correspond ex-
actly to well-defined geographical features. Although the area
just north of the frontier proved to be decent farmland, in general the area south of the frontier was better suited to Indian
agriculture and intensive farming. Central Mexico's abundant
rainfall, rich soils, and lakes and rivers made it the most promising location for settlement. On the eve of the Spanish conquest,
there may have been as many as 25 million natives in the area
between the Chichimec frontier and the Isthmus of Tehuantepec.[1] The native population was concentrated in regional centers: the Valley of Mexico, the Huasteca, the Mixteca-Puebla
zone, the Lake Pátzcuaro area, and the Valley of Oaxaca. This
settlement pattern did much to shape the pattern of Spanish
colonization.

The great energy of the few thousand Spaniards engaged in
the early exploration and conquest of Mexico was awesome. By
1550 Spaniards in search of precious metals and unredeemed
souls had traversed most of modern Mexico. The Spanish colonists were not so adventurous as the early explorers, however.
They preferred town living, and although some brave souls settled in remote parts of the viceroyalty, most grouped together
in central Mexico. From the early years of conquest to the 1540's,

the colonists and missionaries were attracted to the centers of native population, reinforcing the regionalism that had been the Indians' response to local geography. Mexico City quickly became the capital and the major urban center of the viceroyalty. At the same time small bands of conquistadores and other early colonists cast their lot with regional centers outside the Valley of Mexico, in the states of Tlaxcala, Morelos, Puebla, Michoacán, Jalisco, Mexico, Hidalgo, Yucatán, and Oaxaca.

During the sixteenth century most of the provincial centers were loosely tied together in a trading network. Oaxaca became the important link between Mexico City and Guatemala to the south. Cacao and wine merchants in the Guatemala trade frequently used Antequera (the city of Oaxaca) as their home base.[2] Locally produced hides and wheat were shipped to Guatemala, Puebla, and Mexico City; and for a time Oaxaca supplied wheat for the west-coast shipping fleet.[3] The silk industry that flourished in the Mixteca Alta in the mid-sixteenth century also brought Oaxaca into international commerce.[4] As intracolonial trade declined in the seventeenth century, regional centers like Oaxaca became more isolated. The silk industry collapsed and distant markets for wheat, cloth, and hides evaporated, with the result that the Spanish city of Antequera and the regional Indian markets became centers of a more localized trade.

The Spaniards brought a variety of new influences to central Mexico. They introduced new crops, notably wheat and sugar cane, and they denuded many of the forested mountain slopes. They introduced livestock, thus adding grazing land to the land used by the Indians—forests, arable fields, orchards, and townsites with vegetable plots. A disdain for manual labor and the association of livestock raising with noble rank predisposed many Spanish colonists to a career in ranching. The discovery of great silver mines in Hidalgo, Zacatecas, and Guanajuato in the 1540's increased the demand for hides, tallow, meat, and draft animals— all the more incentive to ranch. Much of the Spaniards' energy and attention, therefore, was quickly devoted to that enterprise; and cattle, sheep, goats, and pigs took hold wherever they set-

tled. The northern part of Mexico, with its vast expanses of unoccupied grassland and brushland, was especially well suited to
cattle. But even in a good agricultural region like the Valley of
Oaxaca, European livestock quickly took over much of the untilled land. By the 1540's the number of animals had risen im-
pressively, and the destruction of agricultural lands by livestock
was a growing problem. Consequently, the Crown began to make
specific land assignments to individual ranchers as a means to
control and stabilize the growth of the ranching industry. The
effect was to formalize the use of much land for grazing and to
set the stage for a Spanish interest in land ownership.

The Spanish commitment to carry the faith to the millions of
unredeemed souls in America made priests an important part
of the land regime. The "spiritual conquest" brought many
churchmen to America in the early colonial period, especially to
Mexico. Central Mexico was divided into jurisdictions under the
religious authority of bishops and the regular orders. The Dominicans were assigned the province of Oaxaca and very quickly
turned to land ownership and ranching to support their religious
activities. Many of the earliest ranches and orchards in the Valley
were owned by the Dominicans, and their holdings increased
right up to the end of the colonial period.

Indian landholding was respected in early colonial law, for
Indian agriculture supported the first Spanish colonists. As long
as Indians were willing to produce the foodstuffs needed by Spanish towns and cities, the European colonists and their descendants
took little interest in owning and farming arable land, beyond
cultivating an occasional orchard plot or growing crops for ex-
port, especially sugar cane. To ensure Indian sources of production, the Crown confirmed native title to all lands worked prior
to the conquest and assessed a large portion of royal tribute in
corn. Indians living in areas suited to wheat were sometimes required to pay their tribute in that grain. Despite these efforts,
however, there seems to have been a chronic gap between the
Spanish demand for wheat and the Indian supply. The Indians
of central Mexico adjusted to the material culture of the Spaniards in many ways, adopting the ox and the plow, various cloth-

ing styles, and Hispanic law; but they usually resisted radical changes in diet, ignoring the abundant meat supply and refusing to produce many European foods.[5] It was not uncommon for an Indian community whose tribute was levied in wheat to buy it from outside sources rather than turn over part of its cropland to Spanish cereals. As a result some Spaniards were encouraged to take up wheat farming to meet the demand. Nevertheless, it is safe to say that the Spaniards relied on Indian farming whenever possible in the early colonial period. This was just part of a more general and extravagant reliance on Indian labor. The *encomienda* (a grant of one or more Indian towns to a Spaniard, usually with the right to exact tribute) and the *repartimiento* (a labor draft), the most important colonial institutions bearing on Indian life in the sixteenth century, were essentially coercive labor institutions.

A catastrophic decline in the Indian population reduced the total population of central Mexico to about two million by the 1630's and hastened changes in the pattern of landholding. The discrepancy between Spanish demands for food and the Indian supply became greater, for while the Indian population was declining precipitously, the number of Spaniards and *mestizos* (persons of mixed white and Indian ancestry) was growing. A striking response of the colonial society to the food shortages, the loss of Indians, the decline of mining, and the growth of the non-Indian population was the emergence of the *hacienda* in the late sixteenth and early seventeenth centuries. The hacienda was a new kind of large colonial estate, distinct from the early ranches, although apparently growing out of them in many cases. It combined the traditional Spanish interest in livestock with labor-intensive agriculture. Capital investments were small and operating costs low. The tools and materials for production were rudimentary and largely produced right on the estate. The only important capital investments were in the compound and living quarters of the owners, an imposing set of permanent buildings, and in the debts owed the estate by resident workers. Debt peonage went hand in hand with the development of the hacienda. The Spaniards met their new demand for farm workers primarily by advancing money to residents of nearby communities, who were then obliged to pay off their debts in the form of labor. The bond of indebtedness tied most laborers to the hacienda, although the comprehensive responsibility assumed by the estate for its residents ultimately gave the arrangement a paternalistic flavor.

The hacienda, then, signified a growing Spanish interest in land ownership. The conditions that prompted this turning to the land make the hacienda seem to be an institution of retrenchment. It grew up in what has been called "New Spain's century of depression," a period of declining Indian population, sluggish trade, and sharply reduced mining production. For many observers the hacienda has become the essence of colonial Mexico, a symbol of the country's backwardness and an impediment to national progress before the Revolution of 1910. Drawing largely from examples in northern Mexico, François Chevalier describes the colonial haciendas as immense estates that, in pursuit of self-sufficiency and on an inexorable course of expansion, gradually engulfed Indian communities and turned them into tiny islands in a sea of under-used estate property. Expansion without much attention to use does seem to be characteristic of late colonial estates. The seeds of this striving for independence and growth may well be found in the Spanish temperament. Chevalier has called the hacienda a reflection of "the psyche of the Spanish Golden Age . . . which sought to dominate without developing."[6] To say that Spaniards were predisposed to acquire large estates and to use them inefficiently does not make the hacienda a feudal or medieval institution, however, as many have suggested.[7] The Spaniards did not bring the hacienda to America. Instead, it developed in response to the special economic and social circumstances of a maturing colony.

The North Mexican hacienda had certain striking features that point to a stabilization of the land regime and rural colonial society, with vast stretches of territory held by Spanish estates. Size and the idea of continuous ownership in one family, sometimes with the legal sanction of entailment, gave the hacienda an aura of permanence. The *composiciones de tierras* (the legaliza-

tion of land titles) in the 1640's is clearly an important bench-
mark in the history of the Mexican hacienda. These composiciones confirmed title to many pieces of land that had been acquired informally by estates without written title. From this
point on, the history of the hacienda seems to be one of uninterrupted growth. Large numbers of landless peasants were brought
to the estates as permanent residents and workers; individual
families became long-term estate owners; and the hacienda began
to fulfill virtually all of its own needs. During the colonial period
the hacienda gradually acquired an all-encompassing kind of
authority and special political rights. Hacienda chapels established separate religious jurisdictions for the residents; jails were
constructed on the estates; and the *hacendado* (the owner of an
hacienda) became the dispenser of local justice. All these developments define the hacienda as a separate unit of colonial society as well as a new kind of economic institution. As one French
traveler saw it, the hacendado represented a "little king" within
his territorial domain.[8]

It is generally agreed that immense rural estates dominated
northern Mexico, and it is also generally thought that haciendas
controlled most of central and southern Mexico in the colonial
period. But the spread of haciendas throughout Mexico has been
understood as through a glass darkly. Isolated examples of large
rural estates in southern Mexico are occasionally mentioned,
and recently a survey of haciendas and ranches in Tlaxcala in
1712 was published. But even this important document resolves
few of the nagging questions about land tenure and the real importance of the hacienda in central and southern Mexico, since
it does not include the lands of Tlaxcalan Indians and small
farmers. The editor's conclusion that large haciendas dominated
land tenure in the late colonial period rests heavily on the un-
spoken assumption that the Spaniard could and did impose his
will wherever he went, and that regional differences in Indian
population and in geography and climate were not decisive factors in the process of colonization.[9]

The development of Indian tenure and the hacienda in colonial Oaxaca stands in striking contrast to the land regime in

northern Mexico, which is often taken as a rough model of late colonial land tenure. The transition from Spanish ranches to more complex estates was not accompanied by a widespread disintegration of Indian towns or the confinement of towns to little more territory than the *fundo legal* (townsite). Native communities were usually self-sustaining and held more than enough land to escape the paternalism and peonage of hacienda life. Curiously, late colonial Oaxaca did not experience a dramatic expansion of Spanish landholdings. Relatively little land was added to the Valley estates founded in the sixteenth and early seventeenth centuries. The increases in Spanish holdings that did occur in the eighteenth century resulted primarily from the establishment of small new estates, which fragmented the pattern of Spanish tenure.

The colonial land regime of New Spain was a complex intertwining of Spaniards seeking the good life, Spanish law and its enforcers, the Church, mixed races, Indian communities, and the native nobility. To understand the importance of any landholding group, we must compare it with all other groups. There *were* large, entailed haciendas in Oaxaca and there *were* landless Indians; but the important question is whether or not they were as typical as the North Mexican model suggests. In the case of Oaxaca, as we shall see in this study, the answer is clearly no. The haciendas there bore only a pale resemblance to the great rural bastions of northern Mexico, and most Indian communities preserved their territorial integrity and economic independence throughout the colonial period.

I

THE SETTING

THE VALLEY of Oaxaca, tucked into the rugged southern highlands of Mexico, is a wide alluvial plain roughly 700 square kilometers in area. Mountain ranges divide the Valley into three regions, with the city of Oaxaca (Antequera) at the hub. The Valley of Etla extends 20 kilometers to the northwest, the Valley of Tlacolula some 29 kilometers to the southeast, and the Valley of Zimatlán some 42 kilometers to the south. The southern reaches of the Valley are less clearly delimited than the other two regions, since the plain extends as far south as the town of Miahuatlán. For this study the Valley will be defined by the Atoyac River basin, as it was in colonial times.[1] The southern border will be drawn at the narrow neck of the principal plain near Magdalena Ocotlán, where the Atoyac and "Y" rivers meet.

Each of the three regions is somewhat different in geography and climate. Elevations on the Valley floor average 1,550 meters, ranging from 1,530 in the south at Ocotlán and 1,563 at the centrally located city of Oaxaca to 1,620 in the southeast at Tlacolula and 1,640 in the northwest at Etla.[2] Rainfall varies considerably from region to region and from year to year, although the Valley as a whole has a seasonal rhythm of wet weather in the period of high sun (May to August) and dry weather in the period of low sun (November to March). The southeastern region, with an annual average rainfall of 492 millimeters in the period 1940–60, is consistently the driest. Oaxaca had an average of 650 millimeters in the same period, Etla 662, and Ocotlán and Zimatlán more than 720. Since localized thundershowers account for most of the rainfall, there may be wide variations even within one section of the Valley. Valley farmers today cannot always depend on high rainfall during the rainy season, and references in colonial records to periodic droughts and floods confirm a history of erratic precipitation. Temperatures averaging between 66.7 and 70.2 degrees and the lack of strong seasonal contrasts make year-round cultivation possible in the Valley. Frosts occur only rarely and are generally restricted to the higher regions.[3]

In short, the Valley has a tropical highland climate—temperate, warm, and fairly dry—with some sectional variations. Using the Koeppen system of classification, José L. Lorenzo describes Tlacolula as having a semi-arid climate, Ocotlán a somewhat more temperate climate with seasonal rains, Etla and Oaxaca a climate between these two types, and Zimatlán, southwest of Ocotlán, a tropical savanna climate with a marked seasonal rhythm of rainfall.[4]

The Atoyac River drains the Valley, flowing southward through the Etla and Zimatlán regions.* In some areas the river was an asset to colonial agriculture; in others it represented a destructive force. In the Etla plain, where the river channel was deep, there was little danger of flooding. Etla was the most productive section of the Valley during the colonial period, extensive irrigation permitting some towns to harvest two or three crops annually. One section of the Atoyac near Soledad and Nazareno Etla was elevated enough for irrigation canals to be tapped off the main artery,[5] and a number of tributaries feeding into the river in the Etla region provided additional sources of water. Because the river channel was shallower in the central and southern areas, they were vulnerable to flooding. In the 1560's corvée laborers diverted the river south and west of Antequera to lessen the danger of urban floods.[6] Flood damage to farmlands was reported at Tlapacoya in 1581, San Agustín de las Juntas in 1648 and 1652, San Jacinto Amilpas in 1761, and various parts of the southern arm in 1789.[7] In the case of San Agustín de las Juntas, the swollen Atoyac deposited a layer of sand up to ten feet deep

---

* The Atoyac River is said to have lain underground for a considerable distance below Zimatlán in the sixteenth century. ENE, 4: 142.

on the rich, moist bottomland, converting it into less productive
temporal (unirrigated cropland). There are fewer tributaries in
the southern arm, and colonial records for this area mention
irrigation less frequently than Etla records do. Cuilapan is one
southern community noted as having irrigated lands (ca. 1580).[8]

Often dry during part of the year, the Salado River, a tributary
of the Atoyac, is the major source of water for the Tlacolula valley. Fast-flowing streams come to life during the rainy season on
the steep slopes surrounding this valley, but there are few streams
suitable for irrigation during the dry months. The small number
of irrigated fields during the colonial period were concentrated
at Tlalixtac, San Juan Guelavia, and San Juan Teitipac.[9]

In addition to the natural flow of rivers and streams in the
Valley, several man-made water diversions affected the agricultural capabilities of individual communities. There were at least
two major projects to divert water for household and agricultural
use. The Jalatlaco River was banked and channeled directly into
Antequera from San Felipe del Agua in the early eighteenth century, and an irrigation canal four miles long was under construction near Zimatlán in 1719.[10]

Parts of the Valley's arable land were naturally moist because
of the high water table. These bottomlands, known as *tierras de
humedad*, were especially common in the southern arm of the
Valley. Colonial records mention them near Zimatlán, Ocotlán,
Cuilapan, Zaachila, and San Pedro Ixtlahuaca in the south, and
Tlacochahuaya and Tlacolula in the southeast.[11] In some cases
the bottomlands were veritable swamps, but most could be put
to productive use. Near Cuilapan they served as orchards. Near
Zimatlán and Tlacochahuaya they had become overgrown with
grass, providing year-round pastureland. Tierras de humedad
made superior farmlands, frequently yielding two annual crops.*

The average width of the Valley is six to eight kilometers, with
the Etla arm being generally narrower than the other two. A
cross-section profile of the Etla arm indicates these physiograph-
ic zones: a low alluvial surface, a higher alluvial surface, a piedmont zone with a section of fluvial fan gravels, and mountain

---

* Pot irrigation as practiced today is not mentioned in colonial records.

slopes.[12] The extensive flat areas and gentle undulation of the Valley floor have kept soil erosion from becoming a serious problem. In both the low and high alluviums, the water table is close to the surface, providing easy access to enough well water for household needs and small-scale irrigation.

Soil types in the Valley vary somewhat from town to town, but again there are sectional distinctions. The reddish clay of the Valley of Tlacolula is derived from limestone, slate, and volcanic material, and is generally more porous than soil in the other two arms.[13] Soils in the southern arm, mostly derived from materials of basaltic origin, are somewhat heavier and more humid. Etla lands are described in colonial records as "rich, moist, and black."[14] Cultivable alluvium, rich in mineral nutrients but poor in organic matter, encompasses roughly 10,000 hectares in the Valley of Tlacolula, 20,000 in the Valley of Etla, and 40,000 in the Valley of Zimatlán (including a portion of the area south of the Valley).[15]

Colonial Oaxaca was much like Oaxaca today in terms of climate and physiography. Bartolomé de Zárate, writing in 1544, found the Valley to be temperate and rarely subject to frost, with the southeast arm somewhat warmer and drier than the other two.[16] The *Relación del obispado de Oaxaca* (1569) and the *Relaciones Geográficas* for Tlacolula, Mitla, Macuilxóchitl, Teitipac, Tlalixtac, and Huitzo (1579–1581) echo these observations. The average rainfall of the Valley may have been slightly higher and the average temperature slightly lower during the colonial centuries, if the trend toward drier and warmer weather noted by José L. Lorenzo for the last 50 years is a long-range one.

Travelers in colonial Mexico frequently noted the Valley of Oaxaca's fertility and lushness. Motolinía called it a "rich and most fertile valley."[17] In the late eighteenth century Thièry de Menonville praised the area in these terms:

Nothing can be conceived more magnificent than the site of Guaxaca. From San Juan del Rey to this town, opens a plain two leagues in breadth, which extends the length of five or six to the environs of the town. It is amply furnished with cereal products, and fruit of all kinds from the plain; the foot of the slope on which it is built is bathed by a beautiful river; and well-planned aqueducts supply it with abundance of water of the utmost excellence. Finally, magnificent and highly ornamented prospects, excellence of soil, profusion of fruits as well European as American which succeed each other in unremitting continuance, would make an actual paradise of Guaxaca, were it only possessed by a more industrious and active race of men.[18]

Because of the Valley's temperate climate, broad alluvial plain, perennial rivers, and high water table, it could support a dense colonial population dependent on farming. The alluvial plain in the Etla region and the northern half of the Zimatlán valley were the most intensively cultivated areas during the colonial period. The extent to which Valley towns cultivated surrounding hillsides cannot be determined, since there is only one recorded example of terrace agriculture: a 1798 map shows cultivated hillsides in the Tlacolula valley near Santa Cecilia Jalieza (Plate I, page 76).[19] The variety of European and native crops grown reflects the variety of ecological niches in the Valley and their general suitability for agriculture. Native crops harvested in the colonial period were maize, *maguey* (agave), beans, squash, various kinds of chile, tomatoes, *tuna* cactus (which nurtures cochineal insects, from which a red dye is obtained), *zapotes*, nuts, sweet potatoes, avocados, herbs, and fodder. European crops grown were white and yellow varieties of wheat, chick-peas, sugar cane, grapes, lettuce, cabbage, onions, garlic, radishes, apples, pomegranates, peaches, melons, figs, oranges, lemons, grapefruit, and pears.[20]

The Valley of Etla was best suited for the cultivation of wheat, and early in the colonial period wheat fields abounded there.[21] Tribute records for the Cuatro Villas del Marquesado (the political jurisdictions of Etla, Cuilapan, Tlapacoya, and the Villa de Oaxaca) dating from the 1570's show that Etla's tribute in kind was exclusively wheat, whereas the other three villas were assessed in maize.* The cultivation of wheat was attempted elsewhere in the Valley with limited success; in the sixteenth century it was occasionally raised in the southeastern region and on sev-

---

* Wheat production appears to have increased markedly in the Etla arm during the second half of the sixteenth century. Woodrow Borah ("Collection," p. 408) indicates that the tithe collected on wheat from Etla rose from 99 pesos in 1568 to 900 pesos in 1599.

eral haciendas south of Antequera. But in the early seventeenth century documentary sources speak of Etla as by far the major source of wheat for Antequera and the Valley.[22] It even supplied the market of Tehuantepec with wheat at this time. Most communities on the Etla plain produced many other crops in addition to wheat, as suggested by this 1777 list for Huitzo: "In this head town and all of its subject towns, one finds *anonas* [custard apples], *chirimoyas, nanches, guayabas* [guavas], peaches, *pitayas*, corn, wheat, beans, chick-peas, maguey, and cacti."[23]

Sugar cane was grown in small quantities in the Valley of Zimatlán and near Huitzo in the Etla area during the colonial period.* The success of the crop in the southern arm around Cuilapan, Zimatlán, and Tlapacoya was probably due to the somewhat higher rainfall and warmer temperatures there. Eighteenth-century hacendados from the Tlacolula region grumbled that they were impoverished because their lands, unlike the Marquesado sections of the Valley, were not suited to sugar-cane production.[24] Production of the dyestuff cochineal, which supported the economic prosperity of Oaxaca in the late eighteenth century, was also centered in the southern end of the Valley.† In addition, the southern arm produced pomegranates, oranges, quinces, and figs.

The *Relaciones Geográficas* for Tlacolula, Mitla, Teitipac, and Macuilxóchitl list a variety of Spanish fruits and vegetables found in the Valley of Tlacolula—notably quinces, oranges, wheat, garlic, onions, cabbage, turnips, radishes, lettuce, and grapes—as well as such native fruits as zapotes and avocados. Maguey was a specialty of this area. Most of the Valley's producers of *pulque* and *mezcal* (liquors derived from maguey) were located there. A few towns in the Tlacolula arm were also reported to be harvesting small amounts of cochineal in the eighteenth century: San Francisco Lachigolo, San Marcos Tlapazola, San Juan Guelavia, San Bartolomé Quialana, Santa María Guelaxe, Tlacolula, Tlacochahuaya, and Tlalixtac.[25]

* CCGG, fols. 35r–40r; AGNT 123, exp. 1. Production increased in the nineteenth century.
† Between 1745 and 1854 cochineal production was limited to the bishopric of Oaxaca. Dahlgren de Jordán, *La grana cochinilla*, p. 10.

Turkeys, bees, and dogs were among the few domesticated animals raised in the Valley before the conquest. Wild game found there were deer, mountain lions, rabbits, birds, mud turtles, and peccaries.[26] Hunting was an important source of meat at that time, and although the need for wild meat decreased after the introduction of European livestock, hunting continued during the colonial period. It has been suggested that before the conquest only the Indian nobility ate meat, and that hunting was practiced primarily to supply their larders.[27] A colonial remnant of this dietary distinction between nobles and commoners is mentioned in a 1576 document from Tlacolula. Among the privileges enjoyed by the *cacique* (native chieftain) of Tlacolula was an annual celebration in which everyone in the community spent one day hunting game for his benefit.[28] Much hunting was done in the Valley of Tlacolula, and a number of towns in the other two arms also supplemented their diet with wild game. Sixteenth-century references to hunting mention the towns of Macuilxóchitl, Teotitlán del Valle, Teitipac, Tlacolula, Mitla, and Tlalixtac in the southeast, and Cuilapan, Chichicapa, Santa Cruz Mixtepec, Zaachila, and Huitzo elsewhere in the Valley.[29]

The introduction of European livestock into the Valley in the sixteenth century modified the traditional pattern of land use: many unused grassy areas were turned over to grazing cattle, horses, sheep, goats, and swine. *Ganado mayor* (cattle and horses) were introduced in large numbers during the first half of the century. Damage to Indian crops by untended Spanish cattle became so extensive that in 1549 Viceroy Antonio de Mendoza issued an edict prohibiting cattle ranching in the Valley and requiring sheep ranches to employ guards.[30] Mendoza's edict had only a transitory impact; by the 1560's large Spanish *estancias de ganado mayor* (cattle ranches) were in operation.[31] The discovery of mines in the mountains separating the Tlacolula and Zimatlán valleys created new markets for hides and meat in the late sixteenth century and led to larger concentrations of cattle in the southern arm, where much good farmland was converted into pastureland. Cattle were also raised in the Valley of Tlacolula during the colonial period, although *ganado menor* (sheep and goats) were predominant there, in contrast to the Valley of

Zimatlán. Ganado mayor and ganado menor were present in smaller numbers in the Valley of Etla. All in all, there were some 260,000 head of cattle in the Valley in 1826, somewhat fewer than in the mid-eighteenth century. A general decline in the number of cattle on Spanish estates had occurred in the late eighteenth century and probably continued during the revolutionary period after 1810.[32]

Animal diseases, wheat blights, and climatic changes affected the productivity of Valley estates in the colonial period. Since the Valley's residents relied heavily on agriculture and livestock before the cochineal boom of the late eighteenth century, these natural disasters created serious hardships. The combination of droughts, frosts, wheat blight, and a fatal epidemic among cattle and sheep in the early eighteenth century had especially far-reaching effects on the local economy. As production declined many Spanish estates decreased in value; several were mortgaged and eventually sold. Rental and interest payments of all kinds were often long overdue; the religious orders suffered losses in income; and local trade in non-agricultural goods and services diminished.

The Valley and its immediate surroundings had other natural resources in addition to farming and grazing land. Eight *salinas* (salt deposits) are mentioned in colonial records: one southeast of Tlacochahuaya on the Hacienda Santo Domingo Buenavista; one in the Etla arm near San Juan del Estado, on land belonging to the cacique of Magdalena Apasco; one on the rancho Xabiogo near San Pablo Etla; one near Tlacolula; one on the San Blas estate east of San Pedro Ixtlahuaca; and three near San Juan Teitipac, Mitla, and Teotitlán del Valle. With the exception of those at San Juan del Estado and Mitla, the deposits were described as small; and they may not have been exploited in pre-Hispanic times, since the *Relaciones Geográficas* mention Tehuantepec as the principal source of salt for the Valley in the early colonial period.* In the 1820's merchants from San Miguel

---

* See BEOB, fol. 115r, AGNT 415, exp. 3, tercera numeración, fol. 4v, AGNT 155, 2:4v, and AGNT 1049, 11:81–94 for Valley salinas. The *Relacion Geográfica* for Miahuatlán states that the Tehuantepec salt deposits were heavily exploited after

Mixtepec still traveled to Tehuantepec to obtain salt.[33] The forested mountains surrounding the Valley provided wood for fuel, construction beams, and utensils. Quarries of green rock supplied building material for colonial cities. Lime, used in the preparation of corn meal, was mined south of Antequera near San Agustín and San Antonio de la Cal. The Spaniards mined the precious metals found in nearby mountains. Placer gold was worked in the Etla area in the first decades of the colonial period, and in later years there were rumors of gold elsewhere in the Valley.[34] Silver and copper mines were discovered near Chichicapa in the 1570's and were worked until the late seventeenth century.[35]

In sum, the Valley consisted of an extensive plain with a temperate climate and enough water to support a dense native population capable of using small-scale irrigation techniques. The surrounding piedmont and mountain zones provided pastureland, firewood, and wild game. A variety of native and European crops were cultivated, though maize and beans remained the staples of the native diet. Wheat cultivation was centered in the Etla arm, and orchards were common in the central and southern regions. Livestock was widely dispersed, with heavy concentrations in the Valley of Tlacolula and the southern end of the Zimatlán arm.

During the colonial period Indians, Spaniards (peninsulars and creoles), and small numbers of Negroes, mestizos, and mulattoes lived in the Valley. Using tributary figures for 1569* and Borah and Cook's formula for the rate of decline between 1519 and 1568, we arrive at 350,000 as an estimate of the Valley's native population on the eve of conquest.[36] By 1568 the native population had probably dwindled to about 150,000, and at its lowest

---

the conquest, so perhaps they were not an important source for the Valley in pre-Hispanic times. Paso y Troncoso, *Papeles*, 4: 130. In short, written records do not answer the question of salt supply before the conquest, but judging from the estimated population of the Valley in 1519, local salinas would not have been adequate to meet the demand.

* Tribute was a capitation tax paid by the Indians to the King. It was charged according to the adult male population, with exemptions for such groups as invalids and the nobility. A married male represented one tributary, a widower or an unmarried male usually one-half tributary.

point in the 1630's to perhaps 40,000–45,000. Although it is hard
to determine the total population of the Valley at any one time
(especially for the seventeenth century, because of poor statistics),
the Indian population always represented the overwhelming majority. In the first half of the seventeenth century, the Valley
probably had fewer than 50,000 inhabitants (2,000 in Antequera
and roughly 40,000 elsewhere), or less than 71 people per square
kilometer. By 1740 the total had risen to nearly 70,000, and by
the 1790's to some 110,000. In 1959 the Valley had some 290,000
inhabitants, or 414 people per square kilometer.[37]

Changes in the Spanish population can be estimated by population figures for the city of Antequera, the only large Spanish
community in the Valley. As Table 1 indicates, Antequera's pop-

TABLE 1

The Population of Antequera, 1526–1826

Date	Households (*vecinos*)	Census or popu- lation estimate	Source
1526	30	120	Gay, tomo 1, vol. 2, pp. 390, 389
1541[a]	130	650	RAHM 68, fol. 29
1544	30	150	Gay, tomo 1, vol. 2, p. 501
1569	—	980	AGII 1529
1579	500	2,500	Barlow, "Descripción," p. 135
1595	—	1,740	Cook and Borah, *Indian Population*, p. 83
1626	—	2,000	Gay, tomo 2, vol. 1, p. 221
1646	500	2,500	Gay, tomo 2, vol. 1, p. 221
1660[b]	—	3,000	Portillo, fol. 145
1777	—	19,653	AGIM 2591
1792[c]	—	18,241	AGNTr 34, exp. 7
1797	—	19,062	Portillo, fol. 145
1804	—	18,626	Cook and Borah, *Population of the Mixteca Alta*, p. 77
1808	—	17,000	Humboldt, 2: 242
1810	—	17,056	Humboldt, 2: 242
1815	—	15,704	Esteva, "Copias"
1826	—	18,118	Murguía y Galardi, "Extracto general," fol. 20v
1960	—	60,000	Tamayo, *Oaxaca*, p. 8

[a] Adult men.
[b] Burgoa gives a figure of 2,000 vecinos.
[c] Two other figures for 1792 have been located. Humboldt estimates 24,000 and Portillo 22,113. These higher figures probably include the population of the adjoining Villa de Oaxaca.

ulation fluctuated in the sixteenth century, increased during the seventeenth in response to the city's growing commercial role, and peaked in the second half of the eighteenth. (Unfortunately, population figures for the first half of the eighteenth century have not been located.) The total tapered off from 1792 to 1815, before beginning to rise again in the early national period. Throughout most of the colonial period Antequera was the third largest city in New Spain, following Mexico City and Puebla.

The sixteenth-century figures for Antequera give a fairly reliable idea of the Spanish population in the entire Valley, since the city was the only major Spanish settlement at that time and since the figures refer exclusively to Spanish residents. Later statistics for Antequera are less accurate indicators of the total Spanish population. After the discovery of the Chichicapa mines in the 1570's, a number of Spanish families moved to the Valley town of Ocotlán and the mining town of San Baltazar Chichicapa.[38] Late colonial records indicate that small numbers of Spaniards also resided in many other Valley towns, notably Huitzo, San Juan Teitipac, Ayoquesco, Zimatlán, Tlapacoya, Tlacolula, and Jalatlaco.[39] Further, after the mid-sixteenth century, figures for Antequera include significant numbers of mestizos, Negroes, and Indians. By 1569 roughly one-third of the city's inhabitants were mestizos and mulattoes. Of the 18,241 residents of Antequera in 1792 (Table 2), 7,143 were mulattoes and Indians, and an unknown number were mestizos.[40]

The size of the mestizo population is particularly difficult to determine, since mestizos were not included in the tribute rolls

TABLE 2

The Population of Antequera in 1792

Group	Families	Men	Women	Boys	Girls	Total
Spaniards and mestizos	2,957	3,033	4,060	2,028	1,383	10,504
Mulattoes	679	673	917	424	356	2,370
Indians	1,513	1,468	1,577	1,084	644	4,773
Clerics and their servants	——	285	309	——	——	594
TOTAL	5,149	5,459	6,863	3,536	2,383	18,241

or listed as a separate category in the figures for Antequera. They seem to have been most prevalent in the immediate vicinity of Antequera and on the Spanish rural estates. Between 20 and 200 mestizos lived in Zaachila, Ocotlán, Tlapacoya, Coyotepec, the Villa de Oaxaca, San Antonio de la Cal, and Jalatlaco by 1777.[41] Valdeflores and Santa Gertrudis, two southern haciendas, had large mestizo populations by the same year, 148 and 138, respectively.[42] Population information for Indian towns suggests that relatively little racial mixing went on there; thus there were few mestizos in the outlying areas of the Valley. A 1686 investigation to identify non-Indians living in Indian towns in the Etla arm located only 16 in an area with more than 850 Indian tributaries.[43] No more than five of these 16 resided in any one *pueblo* (community). Even in the late eighteenth century, many of the largest communities in the Valley were entirely Indian. A 1777 census lists non-Indians in only 42 of the 88 towns surveyed; and in 1804 the towns of Azompa, Cuilapan, San Pedro Apostol de Etla, Xoxocotlán, and Asunción Etla, which represented 805½ tributaries, recorded only seven Spanish and mestizo residents.*

Because racial mixing was especially common near Antequera, the colonial experience of towns in this area was very different from the experience of more remote communities. The town of Jalatlaco, on the eastern edge of Antequera, underwent the most radical racial and economic changes. Composed of Indians from the Valley of Mexico, this post-conquest community was placed under the political control of Antequera early in the colonial period; it paid tribute to Antequera and was governed by the city's *cabildo* (municipal council).[44] As Antequera grew Jalatlaco was gradually engulfed, losing its farmland and water resources. The residents of Jalatlaco thus became increasingly tied to the economy of the city. As early as the 1630's men from Jalatlaco were known as the bakers of Antequera. Other residents of the town worked as tailors, hatters, and cobblers in the city.[45] Jalatlaco's location and its political and economic dependence on

* AGNH 63, *passim*; AGNT 485, primera parte, 1:12v. In 1725 Mitla petitioned its *alcalde mayor* (district official) to appoint a *procurador* from the native nobility to oversee the local treasury "because there is no Spaniard in the town."

Antequera encouraged an intermingling of ethnic groups that gradually undermined the Indian character of the community. In the 1630's Indians in Jalatlaco complained of Negroes and mulattoes moving in and abusing the residents. By 1777 Jalatlaco was no longer a predominantly Indian community, 162 of its 294 residents being non-Indians.[46]

Negroes and mulattoes composed a small but identifiable part of the Valley's population. Negro slaves were present in small numbers from the first decades of the sixteenth century, serving as cowpunchers, laborers in sugar mills, and household servants for the Spanish in Antequera and for a few Indian caciques.[47] There were still a number of slaves in Antequera and in the mills in the eighteenth century. Notarial papers from that century record five to ten sales and manumissions of household slaves in Antequera annually. By the 1790's 16,767 free Negroes and mulattoes had been identified in the province of Oaxaca, 2,436 of whom lived in the Valley of Oaxaca.[48] Of the Negroes and mulattoes in the Valley, 1,670 (68 per cent) lived in the jurisdiction of Antequera, 416 (17 per cent) in the mining and sugar areas of Chichicapa and Zimatlán, 211 (9 per cent) in the Cuatro Villas jurisdiction, and 139 (6 per cent) in the southeastern jurisdiction of Teotitlán del Valle. Several of the free Negroes living in the Cuatro Villas are known to have owned small farms.[49]

The ethnic composition and the settlement pattern of the Valley's native population underwent changes during the nearly 300 years of Spanish rule. The ebb and flow of total numbers was accompanied by shifts in the distribution of various Indian groups. Ancient communities disappeared, new towns sprang up, and other communities moved. In the sixteenth and early seventeenth centuries, Spanish civil and religious authorities attempted to consolidate the Indian population by combining scattered settlements into larger communities called *congregaciones*. The trend was reversed in the eighteenth century, however, as growing *barrios* (neighborhoods) and *sujetos* (politically subordinate towns) split away from their *cabeceras* (head towns) to become separate communities.

In the years immediately preceding the Spanish conquest, three ethnic groups lived in the Valley: Zapotecs, Mixtecs, and Nahuas (Aztecs). According to sixteenth-century sources the Zapotecs were predominant in all three extremities of the Valley, and Mixtec and Aztec communities were clustered in the central region around Antequera (see Map 1). There were also several Mixtec settlements in more distant sections of the Etla and Zimatlán arms. Zapotec speakers were the most numerous; but judging from sixteenth-century tribute data for the Mixtec communities, there were more Mixtec speakers than has generally been supposed.* The Aztec community, essentially a garrison based at the intersection of the three valleys, represented a very small minority. The Aztecs' influence was considerably greater than their strength in numbers, especially at the upper levels of native society. The Zapotec nobility in particular seems to have adopted elements of Aztec culture and to have mixed with the Aztec nobility. Dominican friars in the Valley found that Zapotec caciques and *principales* (lesser nobles) were fluent in Nahuatl.[50] Much early evangelism was conducted in Nahuatl with Zapotec nobles serving as interpreters. There is some indication that pre-conquest acculturation involved marriages between Zapotec nobles and Aztec women. The *Relación de Guaxolotitlán* (Huitzo) notes that the Aztecs used intermarriage as a means of incorporating subordinate Zapotec leaders into their political and social hierarchy.[51]

The distribution of the three ethnic groups shifted somewhat in the early colonial period. At the instigation of Fernando Cortez, who as the first Marqués del Valle controlled much of the Etla and Zimatlán arms, many Mixtec speakers were grouped together during the 1520's and 1530's at Cuilapan, 15 kilometers south of Oaxaca.† Cuilapan was the largest native community in

---

* Mixtec is apparently no longer spoken in the Valley, even at Cuilapan. It has disappeared during the last 150 years, since documents indicate that it was still in use in the late eighteenth and early nineteenth centuries. A 1774 document, for example, mentions that a Mixtec-speaking priest lived at the Cuilapan monastery (AGNT 2386, 1:53v); and surveys of the Valley in the 1740's, 1770's, and 1820's refer to Cuilapan's population as Mixtec speakers. Villaseñor y Sánchez, 2: 119–21; AGII 107; AGIM 2589–91.

† Cuilapan was once thought to have been the only Mixtec settlement in the Valley before the conquest (*Handbook of Middle American Indians*, 3: 965). But evidence that other Mixtec communities were relocated at Cuilapan shortly after the con-

the Valley of Oaxaca throughout the colonial period. Although many Mixtec hamlets probably lost some inhabitants to Cuilapan during this period, they remained identifiable as Mixtec communities to the end of the colonial era. Mixtec towns included San Juan Chapultepec, Xoxocotlán, San Pedro Ixtlahuaca, San Andrés Ixtlahuaca, Azompa, San Jacinto Amilpas, and San Lucas Tlanechico.[52] In addition, Tlapacoya, Santa Ana Zegache, and Zaachila each contained a Mixtec barrio.[53] There were also Mixtecs in the Etla region at Huitzo, Santiago Suchilquitongo, and Tenexpan in the seventeenth and eighteenth centuries; they were probably newcomers who had left the poor farming conditions in the mountains to become sharecroppers in the fertile Etla valley.[54] Finally, San Lorenzo Albarradas, a community in the mountains east of Mitla that no longer speaks an Indian language, may have been founded by Dominicans in the sixteenth century and populated by reed weavers from the Mixteca Alta.[55]

The arrival of Nahua soldiers and laborers in the Valley in the sixteenth century considerably increased the Aztec population, which remained centered around Antequera. As many as 4,000 Nahuas may have come to the Valley as native allies of the first Spanish troops, establishing communities at the Villa de Oaxaca and the nearby towns of Jalatlaco, Ixcotel, San Martín Mexicapan, and Santo Tomás Xochimilco.[56] Ringing the Spanish city of Antequera, these towns may have been part of Cortez's efforts to prevent rival Spanish colonists from acquiring nearby lands.[57] Some Indians from Tlaxcala also settled in the Valley as Spanish allies. The cacique of Jalatlaco in 1718 claimed direct descent from the "Tlaxcalan conquerors."[58] After the discovery of silver in the mountains southeast of Antequera in the 1570's, Indians from the Valley of Mexico were brought in as mine laborers, some 10,000 according to one source.[59] Cortez also brought in small numbers of Indian slaves from the Valley of Mexico before 1550.[60]

quest, as well as the identification of other colonial Mixtec towns, suggests a wider distribution of Mixtecs in the Valley before 1521. John Paddock (*Ancient Oaxaca*, pp. 367–85) brings together a number of published materials dealing with this topic.

KEY TO MAP 1

1. Antequera
2. Villa de Oaxaca
3. San Pedro Ixtlahuaca
4. Cuilapan
5. San Andrés Huayapan
6. San Sebastián Tutla
7. Santo Domingo Tomaltepec
8. San Agustín de las Juntas
9. San Bartolo Coyotepec
10. Zaachila (Teozapotlan)
11. San Lucas Tlanechico
12. Santa Catarina Quiané
13. San Lorenzo Zimatlán
14. Santa Ana Zegache
15. San Pablo Huistepec
16. San Juan Chilateca
17. Santo Domingo Ocotlán
18. Santa Catarina Minas
19. San Pedro Apostol
20. Santa Ana Tlapacoya
21. Santa Cruz Mixtepec
22. Magdalena Mixtepec
23. San Felipe del Agua
24. San Miguel Tlalixtac
25. Santa María del Tule
26. San Gerónimo Tlacochahuaya
and San Sebastián Abasolo (San
Sebastián Tlacochahuaya)

27. San Sebastián Teitipac
28. San Juan Teitipac
29. Santo Domingo Jalieza
30. Santa Cecilia Jalieza
31. San Juan Guelavia
32. Macuilxóchitl
33. Teotitlán del Valle
34. Santa Ana del Valle
35. Tlacolula
36. Mitla
37. Santiago Matatlán
38. Santa María Azompa
39. San Jacinto Amilpas
40. San Felipe Tejalapan
41. San Pablo Etla
42. San Sebastián Etla
43. Guadalupe Etla
44. Soledad Etla
45. San Andrés Zautla
46. Villa de Etla
47. Reyes Etla
48. Magdalena Apasco
49. San Juan del Estado (San
Juan del Rey)
50. Huitzo (Guaxolotitlán)

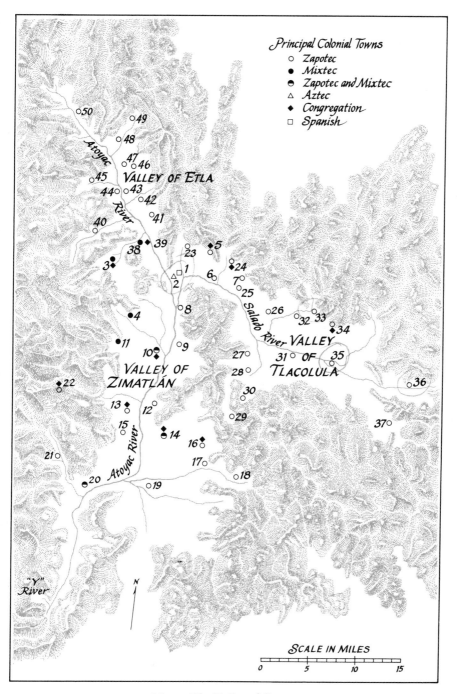

Map 1. The Valley of Oaxaca

The Dominicans, attempting to facilitate both administration and evangelism, were responsible for regrouping various Indian hamlets into larger communities during the sixteenth century. Zimatlán was the most ambitious of the Dominicans' congregaciones, for it involved the formation of a large town on previously unoccupied territory. According to Burgoa the Zimatlán townsite was not inhabited at the time of the conquest because of its vulnerability to attack from the surrounding mountains.[61] Tlalixtac, about eight kilometers east of Antequera, may have been another community sponsored by Dominicans, with the help of some Zapotec caciques from the mountains.[62] One abortive eighteenth-century ecclesiastical congregación has been identified. In 1716 the priest of Mitla tried without success to compel the natives of Santa Catarina Saneya, San Miguel de la Sierra, and Santo Domingo to reside in Mitla.[63]

Civil congregaciones account for other important, if often temporary, shifts in the native population from 1595 to 1605. Although only one example for the Valley of Oaxaca is listed in the manuscript "Libro de congregaciones," references to nine civil congregaciones have been located for this period. San Andrés Huayapan and Santo Domingo Tomaltepec were consolidated at Huayapan, and San Gerónimo Tititlán, Asunción Mixtepec, and Santo Domingo (Santa Catalina Mixtepec?) at Tepezimatlán (Magdalena Mixtepec).[64] Santa Catarina Minas was combined with San Juan Chilateca, San Francisco Tutla with San Sebastián Tutla, Santa Cecilia Jalieza with Zaachila, and San Gerónimo Zegache with Santa Ana Zegache.[65] San Blas, Soledad, and San Sebastián became barrios of San Pedro Ixtlahuaca.[66] The towns of Santa Ana del Valle and San Jacinto Amilpas were apparently created as congregaciones.[67] In addition to the stated goal of creating manageable units in a shrinking native population, the Spanish apparently considered their labor needs in relocating Indians.[68] Repartimientos were frequently tied to the establishment of congregaciones. Several disillusioned recipients of these drafts complained that the laborers refused to serve.[69] The removal of Indians from their lands to a congregación did not automatically mean the Indians lost their holdings; congregación records generally stipulated that abandoned lands were to remain in the possession of the Indian owners.[70] In fact, however, some abandoned lands adjoining Spanish estancias or cultivated fields of other towns were lost by their legitimate owners.

Congregaciones in the Valley of Oaxaca were remarkably short-lived. Most had broken down into their constituent communities by the end of the seventeenth century. The Chilateca, Tepezimat-lán, and Huayapan consolidations failed almost immediately, the *congregados* either fleeing the Valley altogether or insisting on returning to their former towns. Residents of Santa Cecilia Jalieza split away from Zaachila in 1634; and San Sebastián Tutla and San Gerónimo Zegache were reestablished in the 1680's by descendants of the congregados, whose demands for separation grew with their numbers. The San Pedro Ixtlahuaca congregación was still intact in 1734, although the constituent communities retained the separate status of barrios and remained antagonistic toward each other.

Despite the general trend toward consolidation after the 1590's, the pattern of dispersion that seems to have characterized the late pre-Hispanic period continued in some areas.[71] Cuilapan, for example, was composed of six distinct, widely scattered barrios throughout the colonial period. The area of a settlement does not seem to have been related to the number of Indians living there. Plate I, on page 76, shows two towns with similar populations, Santo Domingo Jalieza and Santa Cecilia Jalieza; Santo Domingo was spread out and Santa Cecilia was compact.

Population losses and congregaciones brought the extinction of several Indian towns in the Valley during the sixteenth century. Among the abandoned towns mentioned in colonial records are San Gerónimo near Zimatlán, Santa Ana near Azompa, San Pablo near San Agustín de las Juntas, Santiago el Viejo on the Etla plain, San Jacinto near Azompa, and San Sebastián, which became a barrio of San Pedro Ixtlahuaca in the civil congregation period.[72] During the eighteenth century some towns died, oddly enough, because of population increases. Santo Domingo Suaina, northwest of Tlacochahuaya, was abandoned before 1715, apparently because Tlacochahuaya, under the pressure of providing for a growing population, had usurped nearly all of Santo Domingo's land.[73] Santa Anita, a barrio of San Juan Chapultepec, disappeared in the third quarter of the eighteenth century under similar pressure from San Martín Mexicapan.[74]

The decline in the population of Indian towns in the Valley was not totally attributable to death.* Pressures within a community or excessive demands by the colonial authorities often forced Indians to choose between flight and active resistance, and many chose to abandon their homes. Residents of even the largest and most affluent towns demonstrated great mobility when faced with involuntary service in the mines or a tyrannical native leader. Large numbers of able-bodied men and their families left Macuilxóchitl, Tlacolula, and Ejutla in the first half of the seventeenth century, for example, to avoid serving in the repartimiento for the Chichicapa mines. Several other mass exoduses from Indian communities are known. In 1590 natives were reported to be abandoning Zaachila, perhaps because of the community's chronic land shortage. Rather than work for the Spaniard who held the encomienda for their town, a large group of Tlacochahuayans left in the 1630's and established a new town, Santa Ana, located "above Antequera." After a disputed election in San Juan Teitipac in 1701, the barrio of Loyuxe was completely abandoned. And in 1796 the entire community of Soledad Etla temporarily disappeared into the hills when the *alcalde mayor* (Spanish district official) threatened reprisals after a disturbance at a boundary measurement of the Hacienda Guadalupe.[75]

Shifts in the Indian population during the colonial period created new towns as well as causing old ones to disappear. Several new towns have already been mentioned: Santa Ana; the Aztec towns of Jalatlaco, Mexicapan, Ixcotel, and Xochimilco; the congregación towns of Zimatlán, Tlalixtac, San Jacinto Amilpas, and Santa Ana del Valle; and the Mixtec town of San Lorenzo Albarradas. Five other Indian towns of post-conquest origin

---

* Epidemics seem to have led to greater population losses in Indian communities than the actual number who died of disease. Perhaps it was common for many who were not stricken to flee the community in the hope of saving their own lives. Cuilapan in 1609 is a case in point. AGNT 2964, exp. 123.

began as settlements of landless peasant sharecroppers on private lands. Eight families established San Antonio de la Cal in 1580 on lands belonging to a *principal* (Indian noble) of San Juan Chapultepec. Guelatoba was formed on lands belonging to the Hacienda Valdeflores, and San Francisco Lachigolo in the sixteenth century on lands of the cacique of Tlacochahuaya. San Lucas Tlanechico became a separate town with its own lands in 1699, after beginning as a community of sharecroppers on lands belonging to Cuilapan. And Santísima Trinidad became an independent town in 1716, after purchasing Dominican lands that the town residents had occupied as sharecroppers since the 1650's. A sixth town, San Pablo Huistepec, was formed in the sixteenth century by a group of squatters from various Zapotec mountain communities on an abandoned estancia of the Marqués del Valle.[76]

Indian towns in the Valley generally declined in size from 1520 to 1630; then the population began to swing upward again, fostering the growth of larger communities throughout the rest of the colonial period. Population increases resulted in fragmentation as well as expansion. Communities with over 50 Indian tributaries were eligible to apply to the Crown for recognition as pueblos, which carried the privilege of electing a town council independent of the cabecera. The *Ramo de Indios* of the Archivo General de la Nación (Mexico) records a number of licenses granted to sujetos to elect their own officials (Table 3). In most instances growing sujetos, sometimes larger than their cabeceras and driven by a strong sense of community identity, seized the opportunity for political separation. San Andrés Zautla, for example, began to elect its own officials over the objections of its cabecera (Huitzo) several years before seeking royal permission to do so. Exploitation of sujeto citizens, particularly in the form of labor demands, was frequently a factor in these political separations. The residents of three sujetos, San Agustín de las Juntas in 1648, San Pablo Etla in 1699, and Santa Cruz La Chizalana, stated that they sought political independence in order to avoid involuntary labor on the farmlands and the public works projects of the cabeceras.[77]

Data about the size of the Valley's Indian population in the

TABLE 3

Sujetos Granted Licenses to Elect Their Own Officials

Date	Sujeto	Source
1638	San Felipe Tejalapan and San Andrés Zautla	AGNI 11, exp. 53
1640	Xoxocotlán	AGNI 12, segunda parte, exp. 75
1648	San Agustín de las Juntas	AGNI 15, exp. 2
1697	Guadalupe Etla	AGNI 33, exp. 244
1698	Santa María Ixcotel	AGNI 33, exp. 322
1699	San Pablo Etla	AGNI 34, exp. 37
1700	Three barrios of San Juan Teitipac	AGNI 34, exp. 200
1701	Santa Cruz Papalutla	AGNI 35, exp. 87
1706	Santísima Trinidad	AGNI 35, exp. 318
1714	Santa Cruz (jurisdiction of Huitzo)	AGNI 39, exp. 61
1719	Santiago Mixtepec	AGNI 42, exp. 160
1728	San Blas and Soledad (barrios of San Pedro Ixtlahuaca)	AGNI 51, exp. 246

colonial period are fragmentary. The most complete figures come from tribute records for the Cuatro Villas jurisdiction, which are continuous only for the eighteenth century. Population and tribute figures for a number of towns have been found but are too random to establish detailed patterns of change over time and across locations. Tables 4 and 5 summarize the population data available for the Cuatro Villas.[78] Figures 1 and 2 are graphic depictions of the same data.

I have multiplied tribute figures for the sixteenth century by 2.9 to obtain equivalents to population estimates in Borah and Cook's study "The Population of Central Mexico in 1548."[79] (I have included the original tribute figures in cases where this conversion is made.) Tribute figures for the seventeenth, eighteenth, and early nineteenth centuries are not converted into population estimates because reliable multiplying factors have not been determined. The widely accepted multiplier of 5.0 for eighteenth-century New Spain is inappropriate for the Valley of Oaxaca.[80]

TABLE 4
Tributary Population in the Cuatro Villas Jurisdiction

Date	Tributaries	Population estimate	Date	Tributaries	Date	Tributaries
		NORTHWEST ARM: ETLA JURISDICTION				
1568	——	4,696	1718	1,195	1771	883
1570	1,600[a]	4,640	1729	1,156½	1775	883
1584	761	2,207	1734	1,156½	1777	910½
1595	——	3,210	1740	765½	1783	855
1597	1,138	3,300	1748	896½	1791	855
16??	633½	——	1750	1,107	1793	925½
1664	859	——	1753	1,015½	1805	998
1716	1,154	——	1769	875½	1808	993
		SOUTHERN ARM: VILLA DE OAXACA JURISDICTION				
1568	——	1,129	1716	387	1769	474
1582	661	1,917	1718	442	1771	495½
1587	721	2,091	1729	496	1777	578½
1591–99	617	1,789	1734	496	1783	648½
1600	511	1,482	1740	448½	1793	741½
1602	465	1,349	1748	455	1800	745½
1630	291½	——	1750	490	1805	693
16??	198½	——	1753	548	1808	693½
1664	214	——				
		SOUTHERN ARM: CUILAPAN JURISDICTION				
1526	15,000[b]	43,500	16??	1,377	1769	2,176
1568	——	20,246	1664	1,569	1771	2,274
1570	6,000[a]	17,400	1716	2,268	1775	2,264
1582	3,012	8,735	1718	2,373	1777	2,420
1584	2,539	7,363	1729	2,397	1783	2,248
1587	3,097	8,981	1740	1,859	1790	2,258
1595	3,210	——	1748	2,255	1793	2,359
1591–99	3,001	8,703	1750	2,339	1805	2,684
1600	2,372	6,879	1753	2,468	1808	2,669
1630	1,624½	——				

SOURCES: All figures are from AGNH except as follows. For the Etla jurisdiction, the 1568 and 1595 figures are from Cook and Borah, *Indian Population*, the 1570 figures from *Relación del obispado de Oaxaca*, in Luis García Pimentel. For the Villa de Oaxaca jurisdiction, the 1568 figure is from Cook and Borah, *Indian Population*. For the Cuilapan jurisdiction, the 1526 figures are from Gay, the 1568 figure is from Cook and Borah, *Indian Population*, the 1570 figures are from García Pimentel, and the 1595 figure is from Cook and Borah, *Population of the Mixteca Alta*.

[a] These numbers are questionable, since the *Relación del obispado de Oaxaca* gives two different figures for each community.

[b] Number of families. The *Relación Geográfica* for Ixtepejí estimates Cuilapan's maximum population at 10,000 to 12,000 families, whereas Burgoa gives a figure of 14,000 families.

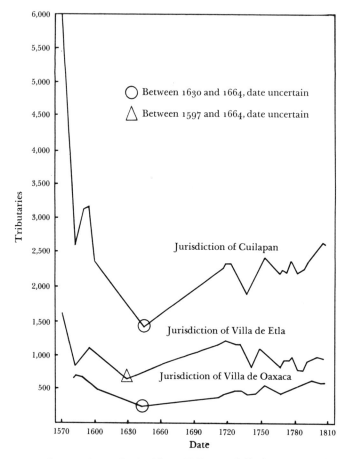

Fig. 1. Tributaries in Three Valley Jurisdictions, 1570–1810

A *Hospital de Jesús* survey that counted both tributaries and individual family members (including unweaned infants) for seven
Marquesado towns in 1804 yielded multiplying factors ranging
from 4.3 to 4.83, with a combined average of 4.48.[81] This figure
is probably fairly accurate for the late eighteenth century, but
there is no indication that it can be projected back to the early
eighteenth century or to the seventeenth. The eighteenth-century
tribute figures at least give a general idea of demographic
changes, although the earlier figures probably represent a somewhat smaller ratio of tributaries to total population than the
later ones.

TABLE 5

Summary of Eighteenth-Century
Cuatro Villas Tributary Figures

Year	Tributaries	Year	Tributaries	Year	Tributaries
1716	3,986	1748	3,792	1780	(epidemic)
1718	4,180	1750	4,007	1783	3,947
1725	4,007	1753	4,228	1790	4,136
1729	4,216	1759	4,426	1793	4,234
1734	4,590	1769	3,703	1800	4,234
1738	(epidemic)	1771	3,832	1805	4,604
1739	4,215	1777	4,124	1808	4,582
1740	3,252				

Little can be said with certainty about native population changes in the Valley during the sixteenth century and the first decades of the seventeenth, except that the decline was steep, generally continuous, and primarily the result of epidemic disease. The early post-conquest decline must have been great, judging from the estimated losses for towns included in the *Relaciones Geográficas* for 1579–81. Fernando Cortez is said to have found 15,000 families in Cuilapan in 1526. By 1570 Cuilapan's total population had fallen to about 20,000 individuals, by 1582 to less than 9,000, and by 1600 to about 7,000. The available tribute figures indicate that the first half of the seventeenth century was the final period of demographic contraction. This was fol-

Fig. 2. Eighteenth-Century Cuatro Villas Tributaries

TABLE 6

Tributaries in the Valley of Oaxaca
in the Late Eighteenth Century

Jurisdiction	Caciques	Town governors (*gobernadores*)	Tributaries
Zimatlán (1800)	4	113	4,462
Antequera (1794)	6	76	7,840
Cuatro Villas (1793)	10	44	4,270
Teotitlán del Valle (1797)	2	65	2,803½
TOTAL	22	298	19,375½

lowed by slow expansion during the rest of the colonial period, interrupted by occasional epidemics that swept away large numbers of natives. A rough estimate of the number of Indians in the Valley in the 1790's can be derived from an 1805 AGN *Ramo de Tributos* table (Table 6), which gives 19,375½ as the total number of tributaries for the jurisdictions of Zimatlán, Antequera, Cuatro Villas, and Teotitlán del Valle. Multiplying this figure by 4.48 (the average multiplier for seven Marquesado towns in 1804), we get 86,802 as the total Indian population.[82]

In summary the population of the Valley in the colonial period changed more in terms of location and absolute numbers than in terms of racial composition. In spite of the great losses suffered by the Indian population during the sixteenth and early seventeenth centuries, when the white and mestizo groups were on the increase, it remained by far the largest racial group in the Valley. Negroes and mestizos were present only in fairly small numbers. During the late colonial period, from the 1670's to 1810, the population of the Valley as a whole rose significantly, although the population of the Etla valley fell by approximately 13.5 per cent. By the 1790's the population of the Valley approached 110,000, or 157 people per square kilometer. About 18,000 lived in the city of Antequera, where the white and mestizo groups were concentrated, and about 90,000 in the outlying communities, which were predominantly Indian.

II

COLONIAL CACICAZGOS

Rᴇᴄᴇɴᴛ sᴛᴜᴅɪᴇs about the impact of Spanish rule on native cultures in America have demonstrated the selective survival of Indian institutions and customs. The most durable features of Indian culture were those strongly held traditions that proved consonant with Spanish moral and religious beliefs and did not threaten the colonies' security and economic potential.[1] As a major center of native population in southern Mexico, the Valley of Oaxaca is a promising region for the study of acculturation and continuity. This chapter deals with the hereditary nobility—how they persisted as important landholders and leaders of Indian society, and how their position was modified during the three centuries of Spanish rule.

Titles, Estates, and Succession

The retention of substantial landholdings and high social status by the hereditary native chieftains is a distinguishing feature of colonial society in the Valley of Oaxaca. Land grants, wills, and property disputes provide solid evidence of the magnitude of *cacicazgos* (estates of native chieftains). Heated disputes in the seventeenth and eighteenth centuries over the succession to Valley cacicazgos—especially bitter and protracted in the cases of Cuilapan, Etla, and Magdalena Apasco—further testify to the enduring wealth and prestige of the caciques.[2] The survival of large cacicazgo landholdings in the Valley of Oaxaca after 1550, when the native nobility was generally in decline elsewhere in Spanish America, is closely related to two factors: the strength of the caciques before the conquest and the significant role they played in the peaceful transition to Spanish domination. Within these two broad areas, a number of specific developments in the 1520's and 1530's help to account for sizeable cacicazgo estates.

By submitting peacefully to the conquistador Francisco de Orozco in 1521, the Valley's Zapotec and Mixtec caciques paved the way for special grants and rewards from the Spanish. Orozco himself is said to have promised to defend the caciques' traditional "rights and prerogatives" in exchange for their support.[3] Peaceful conquest spared the Valley of Oaxaca the loss of life and the grave social and psychological dislocations experienced by the Aztecs in the Valley of Mexico. Further, thanks to Fernando Cortez, the Valley of Oaxaca avoided another development that radically modified the caciques' status elsewhere in central and southern Mexico: the proliferation of encomiendas (grants of Indian towns, usually carrying the right to assess tribute). In 1529 Cortez received the Marquesado del Valle, a royal grant encompassing most of the Valley. As Marqués, Cortez had the authority to grant encomiendas in this area, and he was careful to preserve his own power by granting only a few. Unlike smaller encomenderos of the early sixteenth century, he apparently limited his interest in the Valley to the collection of tribute. (Throughout the colonial period the Marqués del Valle had only one official representative in the Valley. This administrator, later titled the alcalde mayor de las Cuatro Villas, supervised the local cacique or *principal* who collected the tribute.) So far as we know, Cortez did not exercise his de facto prerogatives to mobilize a force of involuntary laborers or to appoint his favorites as caciques and *principales*.[4] By the 1540's, when the size and power of the Marquesado were considerably reduced (owing to the consolidation of royal authority in Mexico and bitter disputes between Cortez and rival colonists), the Crown had all but ceased to assign new encomiendas. Thus Valley encomiendas were limited to ten towns outside the Marquesado's Cuatro Villas jurisdiction. By 1559 half of these grants had been reclaimed by the King.*

---

* The ten Valley encomiendas were Tlalixtac, Coyotepec, Ocotlán, Teitipac, Tlacochahuaya, Tenexpan, Zimatlán, Mixtepec, Mitla, and Macuilxóchitl. The Tla-

The recognition of the native elite was a practical expedient in early colonial administration. The nobles' loyal service in the years immediately after the conquest ensured a peaceful transition to colonial rule and kept the native social structure largely intact.[5] There is good evidence that Valley caciques were crucial in the consolidation of Indian towns in the early sixteenth century—a process the Spaniards saw as essential to political control and mass religious conversion. Because of their leadership in the formation of congregaciones, the caciques won the firm support of the Dominicans, who led the religious thrust into the Valley. The Dominicans' first step in disseminating Christianity was to convert the Indian nobles, who then served as examples for their people, bringing them together in towns for Christian ministration.[6] Later, in the seventeenth century, the Dominicans supported the caciques in the face of popular movements for separate cabeceras and the participation of *macehuales* (Indian commoners) in local government.[7]

Caciques were also valuable as tribute collectors and military leaders in Oaxaca.[8] Spanish officials willingly turned to the caciques as straw bosses and tax collectors. Juan Peláez de Berrio, Oaxaca's first alcalde mayor, set the precedent by gathering the Indian nobles together, announcing that he was their lord, and ordering them to organize labor drafts and to collect gold.[9] In the late sixteenth century various nobles even received grants of special labor drafts (repartimientos) to supplement their shrinking pool of retainers and to allow them to devote full attention to the collection of tribute.[10] With respect to military service, three nobles from Cuilapan served as commanders in Spanish military expeditions in 1525, 1526, 1547, and 1549; and in later years other Valley caciques served with the Spaniards at their own expense.[11] In the 1620's, for example, Felipe Garcés, the ca-

lixtac, Zimatlán, Mitla, Macuilxóchitl, and Mixtepec grants were revoked before 1550. The other five were still in effect in 1579, but only the Tlacochahuaya encomienda continued into the seventeenth century. It ended in 1639 with the death of Diego de Cepeda. Zavala, *La encomienda indiana*, p. 316; Iturribarría, *Oaxaca en la historia*, p. 99; AGNI 11, exp. 160. At least 18 encomiendas outside the Valley were held by residents of Antequera: Miahuatlán, Ejutla, Sola, Estayula, Coixtlahuaca, Nexapan, Coatlán, Molongas, Teposcolula, Tejupan, Tamazulapan, Atoyac, Cuicatlán, Tehuacán, Teocuicuilco, Atepec, Petapec, and Suchitepec.

cique of Huitzo, financed and led a small cavalry unit against a
Dutch pirate vessel based at Puerto Escondido on the coast of
Oaxaca.[12]

The nobles' loyalty to their Spanish rulers was accompanied
by a ready acceptance of Spanish ways. Caciques considered themselves aristocrats on the Spanish model. In many respects they
had more in common with the Spanish society of Antequera than
with the people of their own jurisdictions. This aloofness early
became a matter of physical as well as psychological distance:
by 1600 most caciques who could afford it lived permanently in
Antequera and only occasionally visited their towns.[13] From the
first years of colonial rule, Valley caciques were fluent in Spanish
and dressed as Spaniards. The exquisite signatures of caciques,
which contrasted greatly with those of their fellow natives, suggests a familiarity with the written as well as the spoken word.
Certainly the many documents confirming noble titles and landholdings indicate that the Valley's caciques quickly grasped the
importance of written law and the niceties of Spanish legality.
AGN *Ramo de Indios* and *Ramo de General de Parte* contain numerous licenses to nobles permitting them to display the traditional symbols of nobility, a sword and a mount.[14]

Although most caciques preferred Antequera to their native
communities, the likelihood of chronic absenteeism was greatest
when the cacicazgo passed to a female heir, because of a strong
tradition of patrilocality. In the 1740's, for example, the cacica
of Etla lived in the Mixteca Alta with her husband, the cacique
of Acatlán and Teposcolula.[15] Likewise, the cacicas of San Sebastián Tutla, San Pablo Guaxolotitlán, and the Villa de Oaxaca
in the second quarter of the seventeenth century lived in the cabeceras of their husbands' cacicazgos.[16] An exception to the patri-
local tradition was Gerónimo de Lara II, who spent part of each
year at his inherited estate, the cacicazgo of Cuilapan, but established his permanent residence at Tejupan in the Mixteca Alta,
where his wife was cacica.*

* AGNH 69, bk. 2, fol. 173r, 1618. Nobles might be absent from their communities
for reasons other than marriage or a preference for Antequera. At the insistence
of the Spanish authorities, Domingo de la Cruz, a particularly able *principal* of
Huitzo, moved to Zaachila to serve as *juez-gobernador* there. AGNI 6, segunda

Cacique lineages in the Valley of Oaxaca were not greatly diluted by racial mixing. Thus the Valley is an exception to Magnus Mörner's conclusion that "the efforts of the Crown to maintain the exclusively Indian character of the native leadership had failed completely."[17] In my research I have found only five clear instances of marriages between native nobles and non-Indians: in 1712 the cacica of Santa Cruz Mixtepec married the lieutenant of Oaxaca's alcalde mayor, in the 1730's a *principala* of Cuilapan married a Spanish militia officer and a *principala* of Tlalixtac a mulatto, and in the 1770's the cacique of Santa Cruz Mixtepec married a mestiza and the cacica of Huitzo a Spaniard.[18] Mestizos participated only rarely in Indian cabildos in the Valley of Oaxaca. Racial mixing at all levels of society was largely restricted to communities in the immediate vicinity of Antequera and the Chichicapa mines, especially the towns of Oaxaca and Ocotlán; more distant pueblos like Mitla, Etla, and Tlacolula showed considerable ethnic continuity.

Native caciques who embraced the faith were recognized by the Crown as legitimate local leaders with legitimate property rights. As the King stated in 1557: "Before the advent of Christianity, some natives of the Indies were caciques and lords of towns. Since it is just that having converted to our Holy Catholic Faith they should continue to enjoy their former privileges, and having pledged allegiance to us they should not be made to occupy a lower position, we order our Royal Audiencias to hear these caciques or *principales*, descendants of the first lords, with utmost dispatch if they seek justice in successfully holding and inheriting their cacicazgos."[19]

The King backed up his commitment by making numerous grants of unoccupied lands to nobles and by confirming cacicazgo rights and lands held at the time of conquest. The nobles understood the importance of asserting their claims; indeed the royal grants were a response to petitions that they initiated. In this way many nobles secured clear title to Valley lands at an early

parte, exp. 311. Trading interests in the southern arm explain why a late seventeenth-century *principal* of Macuilxóchitl lived in San Martín Tilcajete. CDChO, rollo 7.

date, before the Europeans became interested in land ownership. These early rights proved invaluable in later land disputes with Spaniards and Indian communities. Without a doubt, clearly confirmed titles gave a solid legal base for the maintenance of cacicazgo lands in the seventeenth and eighteenth centuries.

Individual nobles enlarged their estates by petitioning the King for title to unused lands. Of the 25 known sixteenth-century grants made to nobles of the Valley of Oaxaca, 24 were for ranches. Domesticated animals requiring large areas of pastureland were not indigenous to America, and cacicazgo lands traceable to ancient times had been confined to arable tracts or woodlands. The new grazing lands accordingly had to be acquired under colonial law.[20]

Royal confirmation of the caciques' pre-conquest privileges and holdings crystallized many of the larger estates of the native nobility. Whereas most of the *mercedes* (royal and viceregal grants) to Indian nobles date from the second half of the sixteenth century, the known confirmations of existing cacicazgo lands cluster in the first three decades of the colonial period: San Juan Chapultepec, 1523; Tlalixtac, 1543; Cuilapan, pre-1550; Tomaltepec, 1551; Mitla and Tlacolula, 1553; Jalatlaco, pre-1555; and Tlacochahuaya, 1564.[21]

In the case of San Juan Chapultepec, a sujeto of the Indian Villa de Oaxaca and a present-day suburb of the city of Oaxaca, a Mixtec manuscript and map submitted in a 1696 land dispute may be the original 1523 cacicazgo title or a copy. The document describes an estate of considerable size with carefully marked boundaries. According to the manuscript the first cacique, baptized Don Diego Cortez Dhahuyuchi, wisely chose to accept the Christian faith and to establish friendly relations with members of the first Spanish *entrada* (expedition) into Oaxaca. In exchange for his loyalty Don Diego received title to his cacicazgo and to the town lands of the three barrios in his domain. Don Diego was careful to affirm the hereditary nature of the cacicazgo lands: "I give my lands to my children so that they and their descendants may keep and inhabit them forever."[22] This document describes the cacicazgo lands and the town as an integral unit. Accordingly, any of Don Diego's descendants who attempted to take exclusive control of the land title would be fined 300 *pesos de oro común* because it also belonged to the town. By underscoring this connection the title made the lands less vulnerable to seizure by the Crown or by private land-grabbers in the event that heirs to the cacicazgo could not be found. In a similar situation in Tlalixtac in 1663, the community did incorporate cacicazgo lands when there was no legitimate heir to a barrio estate.[23]

Another early title gave the nobles of Tomaltepec their traditional estates and also a blank check to take whatever unoccupied lands they needed: "Don Domingo de Aguila, Don Pablo de Aguila, Don Pedro de Zárate, and Don Domingo de Zárate y Velasco, these four native caciques of this town of Santo Domingo Tomaltepec shall be granted the lands that they may request."[24] Apparently some caciques were also granted the tribute payments of their subjects. The cacicazgo title for Jalatlaco, another modern barrio of Oaxaca, was said to include "the tribute, salt deposits, and lands of several towns."[25] The caciques of Mitla had the same kind of control over tribute in their jurisdiction as that entailed in an encomienda grant, and the sixteenth-century caciques of Huitzo were entitled to an annual tribute of thirty pesos from their community.[26]

The numerous pieces of land clearly owned by nobles without colonial grants and worked by hamlets of tenant farmers provide indirect evidence of the size and complexity of pre-Hispanic cacicazgos. The serf-like status of entire barrios within the jurisdiction of a colonial cacique suggests that the residents were descendants of the *mayeques* (Indians of a subordinate class, below macehuales) who lived on these lands in pre-Hispanic times. *Terrasguerro*, the term frequently used in colonial records to identify the occupants of cacicazgo lands, had a broader meaning than its modern definition, a laborer who pays rent to the lord of the manor for the land that he occupies. In colonial usage, terrasguerro status did not denote an exclusively financial relationship and might include obligations to cultivate a plot of land for the cacique and to perform other unspecified services.

The cacique's terrasguerro had obligations similar to those of the *solariego* peasant of late medieval Spain, who was bound to the lord's land and received usufruct rights in exchange for labor services that were rarely spelled out in detail.*

The large cacicazgo of Cuilapan had the most highly developed network of terrasguerro communities in the Valley during the colonial period. According to the 1717 will of the cacica, Juana de Lara, terrasguerros occupied two barrios, Miniyuu and Adamni, and the subject town of Xoxocotlán. The cacica specified that in recognition of its status "each [community] must sow a tract of land for me and do service."[27] Numerous other examples of this kind of arrangement have been located. In 1618 residents of a barrio of San Raimundo Jalpan served on surrounding lands attached to the cacicazgo of Cuilapan.[28] Two *principales*, Luis de San Juan and Juan de Rojas, received rent and labor services from terrasguerros in Citidzicucu and Aticuto, barrios of Cuilapan; indeed the nobles were even called *dueños* (owners) of the barrios.[29] Another *principal* of Cuilapan, Pedro de Sosa, was said to have terrasguerros "who serve him and recognize him as their lord."[30]

Records of the cacicazgos of Oaxaca and Etla indicate that they were also served by entire barrios of terrasguerros. In 1743 the Oaxaca estate included five barrios of San Pedro Ixtlahuaca, each of which paid the cacique ten pesos annually and cultivated a field of corn.[31] In 1576 the Etla cacicazgo had 150 terrasguerros. The labor demands of the repartimiento system in the late sixteenth century resulted in the transfer of terrasguerros from Etla to other parts of the Valley and thus undercut the control of the Etla caciques. In 1580 the cacique applied for a 12-man repartimiento on the grounds that his terrasguerros no longer had time to serve him.[32] Still, as late as 1640 the barrio of Nativitas Etla was composed of terrasguerros who worked on the estates of the Etla cacique.[33] Terrasguerros on noble estates seem to have

---

* The fourteenth-century *Libro del Becerro* contrasts the status and open-ended obligations of the *solariego* in the Kingdom of Castile with the position of the *behetría* peasant, whose contractual arrangement with the lord designated duties of a more specific, less onerous nature and allowed for more freedom of movement. *Becerro.*

been less common in the Tlacolula arm. Only two examples are known: five plots of land belonging to the cacique of Tlacochahuaya were worked by terrasguerros in 1591, and residents of Santa María del Tule served as terrasguerros to the cacique of Tlalixtac in the seventeenth century.[34]

The case of San Antonio de la Cal provides a glimpse of how terrasguerro communities were formed. Though the town is of post-conquest origin, the example has implications for pre-Hispanic times as well. In 1580 the cacique of San Juan Chapultepec allotted a tract of land to eight native families "because they are poor and have been refused permission to settle on the plain of Xoxocotlán." The allotment was made on the condition that "they recognize the Marqués del Valle as their lord and render to me, their cacique, service in my house."[35] By the late seventeenth century some cacicazgos secured labor by debt peonage or wages, like the conventional colonial estates, and no longer used terrasguerros. A *principal* of San Pedro Apostol in the southern section of the Valley, for example, paid the annual tribute of five Indians who lived and worked on his land, and gave them a monthly wage as well.[36] Nobles from San Sebastián Teitipac and Tlapacoya advanced 339 pesos and 67 pesos, respectively, to various natives in the eighteenth century, on the condition that these debts would be repaid in labor services on the nobles' lands.[37] The *principales* had trouble retaining laborers by debt, an experience shared by the Valley's hacendados, as we shall see. The San Sebastián *principal* complained that the five natives who took advance payments from him refused to work.[38]

Cacicazgo holdings may have been somewhat larger in the early years of the colonial period than they were in pre-Hispanic times. According to François Chevalier, after the conquest Valley caciques and *principales* appropriated lands formerly set aside for local religious cults.[39] Cacicazgos were probably not greatly expanded in this way, however, since many caciques were major religious figures in ancient Oaxaca and thus probably already controlled these lands. The position of cacique included priestly functions, such as presiding over the marriage ceremony, well into the sixteenth century.[40] Without a doubt, caciques enlarged their estates by taking over vacant lands, by obtaining land assignments from the Marqués del Valle in 1617–19, and by seizing land outright. Still, disputes over land allegedly taken by caciques represent only a very small part of all land litigation in colonial records for the Valley. This of course does not prove that usurpation was limited, for we have no way of knowing how many cases of this type failed to reach the courts.[41]

Colonial cacicazgos were considered entailed estates modeled after the Spanish *mayorazgo*. Laws treating cacicazgos draw a clear parallel between the two. "The succession of caciques is to be from father to son after the manner of the Spanish mayorazgos, with preference given to the oldest male heir," wrote Solórzano Pereira in the early seventeenth century.[42] By equating cacicazgos with mayorazgos Spanish colonial legal practice tended to standardize the succession to cacicazgos, which to that time had been quite variable. Spanish law also tended to preserve cacicazgos by making them inalienable. The colonial cacicazgo of Magdalena Apasco is a good example, having been inherited intact from father to son into the eighteenth century. In 1682 the cacique succinctly described how the new process worked: "After the conversion of my ancestors to the Holy Catholic Faith, following the example and form of the mayorazgos of Spain, inheritance of the cacicazgo has been by blood relation, with preference given to males in the order of lineage."[43]

Legal entailment helped preserve some of the larger cacicazgos in the Valley. Before selling a piece of land, the owner had to prove that it was held as private property, not as part of a cacicazgo; further, it was necessary to make a *pregón* (public announcement) of all sales of Indian-owned property. Several sales of Etla estate lands were revoked because they failed to conform to the principle of mayorazgo.[44] Many of the cacicazgo lands rented to Spaniards in the eighteenth century might have been sold were it not for the formal entailment of these estates.

Still, most cacicazgos show considerable deviation from the Spanish legal model. A good deal of cacicazgo land was undoubtedly sold under the guise of private property. Hasty sales transactions in the early seventeenth century were apparently approved with no attempt to determine whether or not the property was part of the cacicazgo. Then, too, the law was often stretched to permit the division of cacicazgos. In 1599 the cacica of San Sebastián Teitipac sold a piece of her estate on the condition that as part of her cacicazgo and therefore inalienable, it could never be resold. If the buyer or his descendants lacked heirs, the land was to revert to the cacicazgo.[45] Another legal fiction used to divide cacicazgos was the grant of estate lands for one or more generations.[46] Encountering no legal opposition nobles became bolder about dividing up their estates. In the early seventeenth century, for example, the cacica of San Andrés Ixtlahuaca distributed her land equally among her three children.[47]

Like mayorazgos colonial cacicazgos generally favored male succession, but some leeway was allowed to accommodate local custom. Inheritance of cacicazgos by female descendants was not uncommon, even when potential male heirs were at hand. A number of cacicas can be identified, including the Señora de Cuilapan, Petronilla de León and Isabel Ramírez de León of Etla, Beatriz de Montemayor of San Sebastián Teitipac, Magdalena de Velasco of San Andrés Ixtlahuaca, and Catalina de San Pedro of San Lorenzo Cacaotepec.[48] Records specifically mention the presence of male successors in two cases: Catarina de Cervantes, the cacica of the Villa de Oaxaca in the early eighteenth century, had a younger brother who was to succeed her should she be childless, and Juana de Lara shared the cacicazgo of Cuilapan with her brother, Gerónimo, until assuming full control on his death in the 1680's.[49] (Later the Audiencia honored Juana's decision to pass the cacicazgo on to her adopted son, Miguel de los Angeles y Lara, rather than to her nearest relative, the cacica of Etla, which further revised the rules of mayorazgo.[50])

Unlike cacicazgos the lands of *principales*, or lesser nobles, were apparently not tied to rules of primogeniture and inalienability.[51] Many such estates were openly divided at the whim of the noble. For example, Joseph Ruiz, a *principal* of Matatlán, divided his 12 plots equally among his wife and four grandchildren.[52] Juanito López, a *principal* of San Sebastián Teitipac, devised a more complicated plan for distributing his estate, perhaps in order to provide an economic incentive for family solidarity. He divided ten pieces of land among four sons and one grandson in an intricate arrangement based on the sharing of plots, and gave one piece to the parish church.[53] The lack of an institutionalized method of transferring *principal* estates intact helps explain why many *principales* fell into the category of macehual, whereas many caciques remained prominent throughout the colonial period. Macehuales were even challenging the *principales'* control of the Indian cabildo, their last stronghold of status.

The *principales* of Cuilapan were an exception: they remained important landowners throughout the colonial period. Judging from the independent authority wielded by Cuilapan *principales* in the early colonial period, they were probably more powerful than other Valley nobles before the conquest, which helps explain their continuing importance. Several Cuilapan nobles are called "caciques" of various sujetos and barrios, and at least two families controlled barrios of terrasguerros.[54] Since there are no inventories for Cuilapan *principales*, evidence is limited to incomplete records of grants, sales, and rentals. The Zúñiga-Guzmán family stands out in these records as one of the most prominent noble lines. Diego de Zúñiga, referred to as "the cacique of Cuilapan," received a sheep-ranching grant and two *caballerías* (210 acres) in 1566 and another ranch in 1599.[55] His son, Juan de Zúñiga, owned properties near Huitzo and lands surrounding the 1566 estancia. Presumably the family had other holdings as well: when Juan's son, Gerónimo de Guzmán, sold two ranches and a large plot of cropland in 1658 and 1659, he claimed to own "many other lands."[56] Two other notable Cuilapan families were the San Juans, whose early-eighteenth-century estate included a barrio of Cuilapan, a nearby farm, and "various lands on the outskirts of Xoxocotlán," and the Cruz y Fonsecas, caciques of San Juan Chapultepec, whose holdings included at various times a rancho, a canyon, and an estancia de ganado menor.[57] The latter family was responsible for founding the terrasguerro community of San Antonio de la Cal.

Several *principales* in the Etla region were also virtual hacendados. One *principal* of San Pablo Guaxolotitlán owned two large plots of arable land totaling some 420 acres and 17 small tracts totaling some 11 acres.[58] Joseph de Silva, a *principal* of Santo

Domingo Etla, owned 26 tracts of land near Santa Marta, Santo Domingo, and Santiago Etla, and a *labor* (farm) near Santa Marta. The *labor* was rented to a free Negro, and most of the smaller pieces were worked by sharecroppers and debt peons.[59] In Etla, as elsewhere in the Valley, the holdings of *principales* dwindled in the eighteenth century, and sales became more frequent. Examples indicate that Valley *principales* at that time normally owned five to ten small farming plots, one or two house sites, a team of oxen, and perhaps a few head of cattle or sheep.[60]

The actual use of cacicazgo lands varied considerably from one estate to another. Cattle raising was an important interest of the native nobility. In addition to the ranching grants acquired by various nobles in the 1570's and 1580's, a number of caciques and *principales* successfully sought permission to graze sheep on land they already owned. Often an Indian noble would acquire herds and flocks before obtaining royal grants to graze them.[61] Evidence indicates that the livestock enterprises of the nobility were roughly the same size as contemporary Spanish estates. Juan de Mendoza of Ocotlán owned two estancias in 1600; on one he grazed 3,671 sheep and on the other he bred horses, cows, and more sheep.[62] In 1691 Diego de Rojas, a *principal* of Magdalena Apasco, owned 2,573 sheep, 44 head of cattle, 35 horses, 8 mules, 3 goats, and a burro.[63] Grazing livestock was attractive to the native elite for several reasons. Cattle required very little care, and consequently ranches needed only a few laborers. Ranching was an eminently acceptable occupation to the Spanish nobles, whom the status-conscious caciques were quick to imitate. Cattle raising may also have been fairly lucrative; the Indian markets in the Valley obtained their meat supplies from native sources, and caciques raised a large proportion of Indian cattle.[64] Cochineal-bearing cacti and maguey were two other lucrative products raised on cacicazgo lands during the colonial period. Both are mentioned frequently in cacicazgo inventories.

Caciques reaped other economic benefits from land in addition to those of agriculture and stock raising. The cacique of Etla owned a stone quarry near San Agustín Etla, and the chieftains of Tlacolula and Magdalena Apasco owned salt deposits.[65] The cacique of San Felipe del Agua was considered the owner of the woods near his community and of the stream that supplied potable water to Antequera.[66] Wheat mills, especially in the Etla arm, were another resource of the nobility. The caciques of the Villa de Etla and *principales* from San Juan Guelache, San Miguel Etla, and the Villa de Etla all owned and operated wheat mills.[67]

Many, perhaps most, cacicazgo lands in the late colonial period were not directly used or supervised by caciques. One form of indirect tenure involved the occupation of the nobility's lands by terrasguerros. From the cacique's viewpoint this arrangement provided what amounted to a perpetual rent, as well as rights to certain personal services from the tenants. Numerous rentals of cacicazgo lands to Spaniards, mestizos, and Indian communities are recorded in eighteenth-century notarial records or are mentioned in land disputes. The landed caciques of the late colonial period, then, were content to receive a fixed money rent and to forgo the direct use of their lands. The majority of rentals went to Spaniards, although sharecropping arrangements with mestizos and free Negroes are occasionally mentioned.[68] Such rentals were validated by a contract specifying the length of time, usually nine years, and the annual fee. Leases for periods of five and eight years were also common. A few rentals were made for indefinite periods, to be terminated when the cacique repaid certain debts. There were also occasional cases of perpetual rents, similar to the *censos perpetuos* of the Marqués del Valle.[69]

The Political Role of the Nobility and Its Effects on Land Ownership

A growing physical and psychological distance between the native nobility and the macehual class resulted in smaller cacicazgos and less efficient land use in the late colonial period. The declining political position of hereditary nobles in the Valley made their lands more vulnerable to indirect use, disputes over ownership, and abuse by other natives. However, some caciques who accepted the inevitability of reduced political influence retained sizeable landholdings.

In the densely settled portions of central Mexico in the six-

teenth century and the first half of the seventeenth, the Indian
nobility dominated the political affairs of their communities.
Caciques regularly held the position of *gobernador*, the highest
elected office on the Indian cabildos established during the viceregency of Antonio de Mendoza in imitation of Spanish town
government. Since only nobles could vote, it was a foregone conclusion that the other cabildo posts would go to *principales*. At
the close of the sixteenth century, however, the Indian nobles
of New Spain began to lose their political power. The judicial
role of caciques in their cabeceras (head towns) and sujetos (subject towns) was assumed by Spanish *corregidores de indios* (local
representatives of the King). By 1650 the influence of the nobility was definitely on the decline. Macehuales were elected to
municipal offices; and through commercial enterprise, marriage
with *principales*, and the division of *principal* estates, many commoners rose to a position of wealth equal to that of most nobles.
The macehuales' newly acquired wealth and rising aspirations
brought increasing conflicts with the *principales*, who continued
to monopolize cabildo elections in the eighteenth century.[70]

Although the political influence of nobles in the Valley of
Oaxaca generally declined in the late colonial period, tensions
between the macehuales and the nobility varied considerably
from town to town, and some interesting compromise solutions
were fashioned. In Oaxaca, as elsewhere, a select group of official
electors called *vocales* was responsible for the yearly selection of
a new cabildo. Most frequently, the vocales were the *principales*
of the Indian cabecera and its sujetos. Sometimes, as in Tlacochahuaya in 1606, the *principales* obtained legal licenses to restrict electors to the nobility.[71] Another method of selection,
practiced in Zaachila before 1700, gave outgoing cabildo officials
the right to choose their own successors.[72] Sujetos normally did
not have cabildos of their own, but resident nobles did partici-
pate in the selection of cabecera officials. The number of vocales
varied from less than 20 in the least populous sections of the
Valley to more than 50 in Cuilapan.[73]

The macehual class gained more and more political control
as the colonial period played out. One group of historians has
discerned a "democratization" of native elections in the eigh-

teenth century, implying that suffrage for macehuales was another aspect of Bourbon reform. Gonzalo Aguirre Beltrán states that "all resolutions favorable to the macehuales, by which the common man was granted the right to vote, date from the reign of the House of Bourbon."[74] In fact, examples of viceregal support for the enfranchisement of macehuales in the Valley date from the early seventeenth century, well before the rise of the reform-minded Bourbon monarchs in Spain. As early as 1628 the macehual class of Zimatlán was permitted to elect several cabildo officers; in the 1640's macehuales of Coyotepec selected two *alcaldes*; and in 1699 the commoners of Santiago (jurisdiction of Ocotlán) were permitted to elect one representative.[75]

The macehuales' increasingly insistent demand for political power, given substance by their wealth and numbers, seems a more direct reason than Bourbon reform for their growing role in local government. The positions taken by the colonial government in the eighteenth century on the election of Valley cabildos lack the consistency of a reform program. Viceregal policy, repeated in decrees of 1742 and 1768, favored the restriction of voting rights to *principales*.[76] And this policy was applied to specific cases, such as the Valley towns of Tlalixtac in 1734 and Santiago Huitzo in 1714.[77] Still, macehuales were given a voice in electing officials in Tlacochahuaya in 1704 and in the Villa de Oaxaca in 1709, as well as in the towns already mentioned in the seventeenth century.[78]

The legal extension of voting privileges to macehuales in the Valley of Oaxaca took the form of compromise solutions aimed at placating both the traditional electors and the aspiring commoners. Thus, although macehuales in a number of towns gained the right to elect several cabildo officials, no instance of an entire cabildo elected by the native community as a whole has been found.*

---

* The make-up of Indian cabildos in the late colonial period varied from the relatively small slate of San Juan Teitipac—one *tequitlato*, four *topiles*, one *juez de sementeras*, one *alguacil de doctrina*, one *escribano*, and two *topiles de la iglesia*—to the more elaborate hierarchy of Macuilxóchitl, actually a smaller community than San Juan—one gobernador, two alcaldes, six *regidores*, six *alguaciles mayores*, one *alguacil de comunidad*, one *juez de sementeras*, one *escribano*, one *mayordomo*

Native cabildo posts generally were for a one-year term with reelection possible only after an intervening period of three years.[79] Yearly elections were held in the Valley of Oaxaca, but there are several recorded cases of individuals who were repeatedly reelected to the same posts. Alonso de Mendoza, a *principal* of Teotitlán del Valle, was elected gobernador for 11 consecutive terms, and Domingo de Mendoza of Tlacolula for 15, to the dismay of the townspeople.[80] In certain cases the Crown granted permission for especially able native leaders to continue in office.[81]

Generally, the towns in which macehuales held offices were those in which they had at least a limited voice in electing cabildos, although in the mid-eighteenth century macehuales of Tlacochahuaya could be elected as alcaldes and regidores without enjoying voting privileges.[82] Macehuales served as regidores in Santiago (Ocotlán jurisdiction), Zimatlán, Tlacochahuaya, and Coyotepec.[83] There are two known cases in which non-natives held cabildo offices: a mestizo bullied his way into the office of alcalde for Santa Ana Zegache, and a mulatto was elected gobernador of Tlalixtac after marrying a local woman of noble birth.[84] In both instances the colonial government moved quickly to nullify the elections.

The caciques' hold on the influential office of gobernador in the Valley was weakened considerably in the seventeenth and eighteenth centuries. Only one cacique is known to have held the office after 1725.[85] Sometimes caciques were forbidden to hold any office, as in Ocotlán in 1616, but most lost control because of waning prestige, hostile electors, or the procedural requirement of yearly elections. Francisco de Burgoa, who knew the caciques of Huitzo over a period of 43 years, attributed the seventeenth-century decline of this cacicazgo to a series of inept rulers:

The caciques [of Huitzo] nowadays are half as intelligent and twice as wicked as their predecessors. All the old caciques have died, and with them have gone their esteemed reputation and courage, as well

del rey, one *mayordomo de estancia*, one *alguacil de la Santa Iglesia*, and one *alguacil menor de la Santa Iglesia*. AGNI 35, exp. 25, 1701; AGNI 38, exp. 116, 1713.

as the cattle estates they once possessed. Their heirs, more absent-minded than vigilant, find themselves poverty-stricken. Their habits are corrupt; and when they lack outsiders with whom to quarrel, they stir up disputes and misunderstandings within their towns.... To sustain their petulant excesses they even usurp the *capellanías* [benefices] that were granted to the convent by former caciques.[86]

Caciques who forced confrontations on the issue of political power ultimately reaped the whirlwind. In the 1690's the cacique of Zimatlán, Hipólito Vásquez, informally made himself perpetual gobernador in a community that had already granted macehuales a role in electing officials. His high-handed seizure of power united both the *principales* and macehuales against him. After long litigation Vásquez was forbidden to hold office and his estate was confiscated.[87]

The caciques contributed to their own political demise by stubbornly maintaining the attitude that any position other than gobernador was beneath their dignity. For example, the cacique of Coyotepec was insulted by his election as regidor in 1710 and refused to serve.[88] The gradual political changes of the late colonial period were leading to a dual hierarchy within native society—one status group based on hereditary privileges and entailed estates and another based on political officeholding, commercial wealth, and recently acquired lands.*

Although caciques generally dropped out of the formal political hierarchy, strong-willed nobles could still exert much indirect influence. The cacique of Matatlán in the 1720's, Diego de los Angeles Aguilar y Velasco, was such a man. Here is how the frustrated gobernador of the community described Don Diego's influence over the townspeople in 1722: "He is a captious, bold, and shameless man whose only interest is in stirring up the rustic temperament of the natives of this town. He constantly arouses them against their priests and ministers, the alcaldes mayores, and the other representatives of justice."[89]

---

* This dual social hierarchy, recognized by Pedro Carrasco, adds a subdivision to his concept of a civil-religious hierarchy in native society in Middle America. In contrast to Carrasco's general impression the social hierarchy in the Valley of Oaxaca did not become homogeneous, with only one ladder of prestige. The nobility was not eliminated as a separate group with special privileges. Carrasco, "Civil-Religious Hierarchy."

According to the records we have, tensions between macehuales and nobles over municipal elections and officeholding in
the Valley of Oaxaca began in the second half of the sixteenth
century and became increasingly frequent in the late seventeenth
and eighteenth centuries.[90] Of 18 known disputes, 11 fall in the
period 1699–1765. In five of these cases macehuales used, or
threatened to use, force. In 1590, for example, macehuales in
Zaachila disrupted the annual elections, leaving the town temporarily without officials. Later in the colonial period macehuales
used force in attempts to oust unacceptable officials, a goal that
suggests a growing political sophistication. The townspeople of
Macuilxóchitl forcibly turned the hated gobernador out of office
in 1670, replacing him with their own favorite. Similarly, an
ambitious pretender supported by macehuales ousted the gobernador of Zaachila in 1719.

Still, 14 of the 18 Indian communities with grievances ultimately took their cases to the Audiencia or the Juzgado de Indios
rather than seizing power. These suits involved demands by macehuales for representation on cabildos or complaints against cabildo members for malfeasance in office. In 1590, 1594, 1616, and
1714, for example, nobles of Zaachila, Ocotlán, Etla, and Santiago (jurisdiction of Ocotlán) were accused of using their offices
to exact involuntary labor from their communities. The Indians'
frequent recourse to litigation, often at great expense, is one of
the most striking aspects of their adjustment to colonial rule.
The later importance of the Mexican president as the nation's
greatest *patrón* can be explained in part by the paternalism of
the colonial administration and the Indians' ready acceptance
of this avenue of redress.

The declining political influence of caciques in the last 150
years of colonial rule was accompanied by increasing numbers
of land disputes between nobles and their communities.[91] This
development is still more evidence of a growing lack of respect
for the nobility. In 1689 Francisco Ramírez de León, the cacique
of Etla, was openly opposed by the townspeople: "The people of
the Villa de Etla have declared themselves my enemies."[92] (The
peasants' wrath was warranted in this case, since Ramírez de
León had given away community lands to the Church.) A spirit

of disobedience and rejection of the caciques' authority arose among terrasguerro communities in the late seventeenth and eighteenth centuries. Inhabitants of these communities began to assert their right to own the land they occupied, and disavowed usufruct rights that carried obligations to the noble. In 1741 terrasguerros of the Villa de Oaxaca cacicazgo refused to pay rent or cultivate the customary plot, claiming that the land belonged to them.[93] Terrasguerros at Nativitas and Soledad took similar action against the caciques of Etla in 1701 and 1730, and terrasguerros at Xoxocotlán refused to do service for the cacique of Cuilapan in 1717 because "the lands are ours."[94] The earliest known case of a refusal by cacicazgo terrasguerros to perform the duties of *terrasgo* is that of Tlalixtac in 1663.[95]

Colonial records of land disputes blame about half on commoners and half on nobles, which suggests that the resentment of macehuales toward nobles was both a cause and an effect of land encroachments. The Audiencia ruled on 12 disputes between caciques and macehuales over land in the Valley of Oaxaca, seven of which involved infringements by natives. The cacique's only recourse in cases where his authority and ownership were flouted was to the colonial judicial authorities. Still, all in all, the small number of seizures of cacicazgo lands recorded in AGN *Ramo de Tierras* indicates that the landed wealth of the native nobility was not challenged to the same extent as its political monopoly.

Indian usurpation was one of several ways in which colonial caciques lost effective control of land. Encroachments by Spaniards account for a few losses. For example, in the late 1640's Juan de Veracruz and Alonso de Céspedes apparently moved onto lands of the cacicazgo of Cuilapan.[96] Such acts were discouraged, however, by the heavy fines levied in cases brought before the Audiencia. In the first quarter of the seventeenth century, the revenue-minded Pedro Cortez, the fourth Marqués del Valle, made a concerted effort to locate and claim unoccupied lands in the Valley of Oaxaca. His action prompted the transfer of various lands belonging to the caciques of Cuilapan and Etla. A few plots were successfully claimed by the Marqués, who immediately parceled them out in exchange for perpetual rents.[97]

More important, several caciques resolved to sell unoccupied lands to which they held valid title rather than face costly litigation with the Marqués over possession. The cacique of Cuilapan in 1618, Gerónimo de Lara, complained that "because the said lands seem to be idle and uncultivated, representatives of the Marqués del Valle have tried to divide and sell them in my absence, and it has cost me a great sum of money to defend my rights." To avoid an imminent clash with the Marqués, Lara claimed to own much more land than he needed or could use, and began to sell sections of the cacicazgo, including arable land and grazing estancias.[98] *Principales* in Cuilapan and the Etla arm followed Lara's example. Many of the Spanish estates listed in a 1644 composición de tierras include tracts purchased from these natives during the height of the Marqués del Valle's attempts at expansion.

Debts were clearly an immediate cause of diminishing cacicazgo estates in the late colonial period. Sometimes the debts resulted from profligate spending by nobles, as in the case of Francisco Ramírez de León of Etla; but more often they were incurred in costly litigations over cacicazgo succession or land boundaries. Several caciques surrendered the use of the land and the income from it to obtain loans and mortgages from Spaniards, although the nobles still had a tenuous hold on the actual titles. The same rationale behind debt peonage was often applied to these transactions; that is, liens on cacicazgo properties often gave the lender usufruct rights until the debt was repaid or until the rent lost by the cacique was equal to the debt. Recorded liens on cacicazgo lands range from 80 to 1,000 pesos, or roughly 8 to 100 years' use for a piece of land with an annual rent value of 10 pesos.[99] One kind of modified lien allowed the lender to use lands for virtually unlimited periods of time: caciques borrowed a sum of money on the condition that the lender could rent a tract of cacicazgo land for a fixed annual fee until the entire debt had been repaid. A loan of 2,000 pesos to Francisco Ramírez de León, for example, ensured the lender perpetual use of a fertile *labor*.[100] Debts also forced certain nobles to sell lands that were not part of their entailed estates. A case in point is the cacique of Ocotlán, who sold two ranches with 2,000 sheep for 2,000 pesos to meet "many debts."[101] In short, though nobles often claimed that they rented cacicazgo lands because they had more land than they could use, isolated examples suggest that they did so because of debts as well.[102]

Lands of the Major Cacicazgos

Despite the examples of sales and rentals we have just discussed, generally speaking the declining political position of caciques in the late colonial period was not accompanied by a corresponding decline in cacicazgo wealth. The entailed nature of cacicazgo properties and the confirmation of cacicazgo titles in the early colonial period help account for the persistence of sizeable estates. Two great Valley cacicazgos were located at Cuilapan and Etla.

The extent of the cacicazgo lands at Cuilapan can be inferred from the land cases and the composiciones de tierras of the seventeenth and eighteenth centuries. According to these descriptions, nearly every land site between Zaachila to the south and Azompa to the north was bordered on at least one side by lands of the cacique (see Map 2). The important role of the caciques in relocating the Valley's Mixtec peoples at Cuilapan and their participation in early Spanish entradas into southern Mexico helped to preserve and enlarge this cacicazgo. Another reason for the long-term power of the caciques of Cuilapan was their singular aggressiveness. In 1717 the natives of Cuilapan complained that the cacica, Juana de Lara, had forcibly usurped "many lands belonging to the community as well as those of some individuals."[103] A similar complaint over a house and an orchard was lodged in 1723 against Juana's successor.[104] Also, records for Cuilapan in the 1640's state that the caciques regularly increased their holdings by appropriating the lands of Indians who had died without wills.*

An inventory of the Cuilapan cacicazgo contained in the will

---

* AGNH 69, bk. 1, fols. 200r–204r. The dogged contentiousness of Cuilapan's caciques is illustrated by a 1760 land map of San Pedro Ixtlahuaca, which shows that the cacique was disputing nearly all the town boundaries. Land disputes involving Spaniards and the caciques of Cuilapan were common in the seventeenth and eighteenth centuries. One dispute with the Ramírez de Aguilar family continued for over 50 years. AGNH 348, exp. 9.

of Juana de Lara (1717) provides a detailed picture of the estate's size and the distribution of its holdings in the early eighteenth century. By adding the cacicazgo properties sold before 1717, we can also estimate the cacicazgo's size at its peak in the late sixteenth century. Juana de Lara's will lists 36 tracts of land: 7 *solares* (house plots), 5 *labores* encompassing 12 caballerías, 7 plots totaling another 12 caballerías, 5 orchard plots, 2 ranchos, and 10 *suertes* (plots) of unknown size.* Recorded sales before 1717 amount to 4 estancias and 21.5 caballerías.[105] Adding together the definite figures we have, we get this minimum estimate for the holdings of the Cuilapan cacicazgo: 6 estancias, 45.5 caballerías, 5 orchards, and 7 solares, or more than 4,775 acres of cropland and 11,568 acres of pasture.

The Cuilapan estate was rich in productive arable land, large segments of which were worked by permanent retainers and sharecroppers. The inhabitants of entire barrios of San Agustín de las Juntas, Cuilapan, and Xoxocotlán served as terrasguerros on surrounding cacicazgo lands.[106] The properties of the cacicazgo were distributed over much of the central portion of the Valley, from Antequera south to Zaachila and from Cuilapan west into the *sierra* (mountains) toward San Miguel de las Peras. Despite the fragmented appearance of the Cuilapan holdings (some 45 separate pieces of land), most of the tracts were large, workable units. Of the 22 arable plots listed in the 1717 inventory, 12 were at least 100 acres in size.

The pattern of land tenure in the Cuilapan cacicazgo changed significantly in the eighteenth century: rentals became the dominant form of land use. Lands once managed by the cacique were now rented out for a fixed annual sum. Between 1734 and 1799, 16 rentals of Cuilapan cacicazgo lands were recorded, whereas only one pre-1700 rental is known. (See Appendix A for a summary of rentals of all cacicazgo lands.) This change in the caciques' relationship to the land coincides with two related developments: the growing scarcity of cacicazgo retainers and the accumulation of debts by several dissolute caciques.[107]

The limited information available on other cacicazgos in the

---

* *Suerte* was the standard term for one-quarter caballería, but it was also used to identify any tract of land smaller than a caballería. Carrera Stampa.

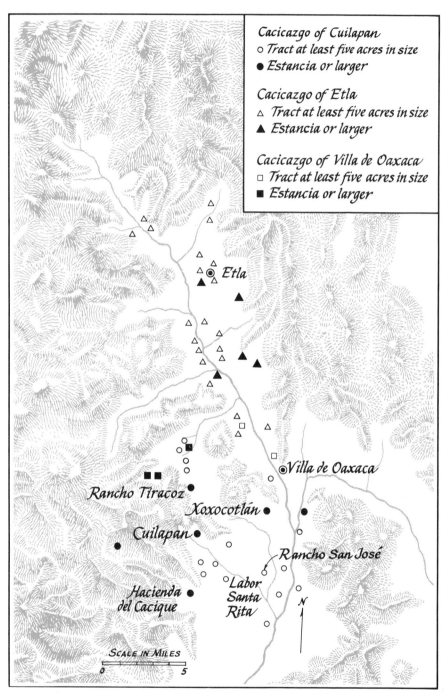

Map 2. Cacicazgo Lands

southern arm suggests that several nobles held smaller but substantial amounts of land. The cacicazgo of Zimatlán received three sheep ranches by royal grant in the late sixteenth century, complementing the arable lands it already owned.[108] The demise of this cacicazgo in the early eighteenth century resulted directly from the greed of the cacique, Hipólito Vásquez, rather than from the more common cause of debts. Vásquez earned the enmity of Zimatlán's citizens as early as 1676, when he ignored the voting rights of macehuales and had himself elected gobernador by a group of handpicked *principales*. In 1697 Vásquez again forced his way into office, this time alienating a large group of *principales* by refusing to let them vote.[109] He then proceeded to abuse every other group in the community. He usurped two ranches and three caballerías of community land as well as many individual plots, and sold them for his own personal profit; he assaulted and seriously wounded a *principal*. Even the Church could not escape the cacique's rapacity: in 1702 and 1708 he seized Dominican and *cofradía* (sodality) lands.[110] The coup de grace for Vásquez came after he ejected the parish priest from the church during mass: "As alcalde, this foolhardy native was so impudent as to remove the parish priest from the altar just as the service was about to begin. He did so, shoving the priest into the sacristy and telling him that this was not the time to celebrate Mass."[111]

In 1718 Vásquez's estate was confiscated and sold in order to restore the property he had pirated.[112] The cacicazgo, discredited and landless, was held by the Vásquez family into the nineteenth century. Apparently having regained some respectability, the cacique in 1819, Bernardo Vásquez, owned a small ranch near Santa Inéz del Monte and served as alcalde in Zimatlán's cabildo.[113]

The cacicazgo of Ocotlán was also in a state of decline by the early eighteenth century. It had acquired three sheep ranches in 1570, 1571, and 1592,[114] and in 1600 the cacique owned over 3,500 sheep. In 1695, however, two of the ranches were sold to meet various debts. The third ranch, with 600 sheep, 20 horses, 20 cows, and 12 mules, was still owned by the cacique in 1708.[115] The cacicazgo of Coyotepec included a large cattle ranch and a farm some 12 kilometers away, near San Andrés Ixtlahuaca.[116] Chronic encroachment by San Andrés in the seventeenth century eventually led the caciques to sell these lands, which became the nucleus of the Hacienda Jalapilla in the eighteenth century.[117] The Coyotepec cacicazgo also owned lands south and west of San Agustín de las Juntas.

Evidence points to the cacicazgo of Etla in the northern portion of the Valley as the largest native estate. Rentals, sales, and boundary descriptions specifically identify 5 *labores* totaling over 20 caballerías, 4 estancias, 2 wheat mills, and 11 other tracts of land—in all, at least 7,712 acres of pasture and 2,000 to 3,000 acres of cropland.[118] In addition to these large tracts, the cacicazgo possessed numerous small plots scattered throughout the Etla arm, presenting a contrast to the more compact holdings of the cacicazgo of Cuilapan. A brief report in 1725 on land distribution in the Etla area indicated that the cacique's lands pervaded the entire region:

There is a very pernicious cacicazgo in that jurisdiction of the Valley known as the Villa de Etla. This Valley is about five leagues in length, and 15 towns subject to the Marquesado del Valle are located there. Most of these towns are without lands, even the 600 *varas* to which each is entitled by Royal decree. This is because the said cacicazgo is in control of almost the entire five leagues, as follows: in each of the above-mentioned towns the cacique owns one, two, three, or four separate pieces of land; and on town borders he owns various haciendas and ranchos. These miserable towns are in a state of great distress. There is no place where they can be given more land, for they are completely surrounded by the said cacicazgo.[119]

Identifiable lands of the Etla cacicazgo were all located within the Etla arm and were heavily concentrated on the rich alluvial lands adjoining the Atoyac River. The 1725 report estimated the value of these lands at 80,000 pesos, or about twice the value of the largest hacienda in the Etla arm, including the hacienda's cattle, buildings, and other improvements.[120] The cacicazgo of Etla had other important resources as well. It owned a valuable stretch of land along the Atoyac River near the towns of Soledad, Guadalupe, and Nazareno, where irrigation canals could be tapped off the main river. The three communities sponsored an annual fiesta in honor of the cacique and paid him a regular fee to obtain water from his *toma de agua* (source).[121] The cacicazgo also owned two mills near San Juan de Dios and a limestone quarry near San Agustín Etla.[122]

The Etla lands were apparently not seriously affected by the Marqués del Valle's efforts to claim unused lands in the 1620's. One sales transaction of ten caballerías of unoccupied cacicazgo land is recorded for 1619, but few of the Spanish estates in the Etla arm that underwent composición in the 1640's included lands previously belonging to the cacique.[123] The wealth and influence of the Etla cacicazgo declined sharply during the era of Francisco Ramírez de León (1689–1730). Having a keen interest in city life and gentlemanly vices, Ramírez de León cared little for rural properties. His decision to trade a fertile *labor* to a Spaniard for houses in Antequera in 1709 is suggestive of his priorities.[124] Looking back on the first 35 years of Don Francisco's tenure, the alcalde mayor of the Cuatro Villas in 1725 lamented the repeated instances when Spaniards encroached on cacicazgo lands or deceived the cacique into selling various tracts for the pocket change needed to sate his thirst.[125] Since most of these lands were illegally alienated, the formal records do not yield information on the extent of the loss. However, the recorded rentals of Etla cacicazgo properties provide graphic evidence of the wholesale surrender of usufruct rights by Francisco Ramírez de León. He initiated 19 of the 27 Etla rentals during the colonial period, usually on the grounds that the land was not being used for other productive purposes and that it was in danger of encroachment. "The cacicazgo is so large he cannot cultivate all the lands. As a result, they are of no productive use to the cacique, and without guards, they are frequently encroached on."[126] Debts ranging from 300 to 2,000 pesos, owed to various Spaniards, led Ramírez de León to rent the cacicazgo's larger properties prior to 1708.[127]

The state of the Etla cacicazgo at the turn of the eighteenth century was in part the legacy of the previous cacique, Sebastián Ramírez de León. Don Sebastián waged a costly dispute over succession to the cacicazgo of Magdalena Apasco in the 1680's and then played havoc with his own estate by stipulating in his will that the properties be divided among all his heirs. Thus, in addition to his own extravagant expenses, Francisco Ramírez de León was burdened with debts accumulated during a lengthy and unavoidable struggle over the indivisibility of the estate. A 1692 petition by Ramírez de León for permission to rent two large sections of the cacicazgo to a creditor provides a clear picture of the cacique's dilemma and the expedient measures he resorted to:

Captain Antonio de Abellán y Carrasco, [now] deceased, stirred up a lawsuit in an attempt to divide the . . . cacicazgo [that I inherited as the eldest son]. I have answered every phase of the prosecution and personally traveled to the Audiencia of this kingdom various times. To defend my interests and pay for these expenses, Captain Jacobo Barba de Figueroa lent me 1,000 pesos. I won my case and am today in possession of the said cacicazgo, which would have been lost had it not been for the said Captain Jacobo, *alcalde ordinario* of Antequera. Because the said captain justly asks me to repay the loan and I find myself without the means to do so, and do not expect to be able to do so for many years, I have offered to turn over to the captain certain arable lands of the said cacicazgo, named Xanabitobi Xaguanigola, as security until the debt is paid. These lands are to remain with the said captain as long as I delay in repaying the said 1,000 pesos, with the right to cultivate them and to enjoy the fruits as his own. If he should construct buildings or make other improvements, these also must be paid for by me and my heirs.[128]

Subsequent land disputes with Indian communities and Spanish hacendados further cut cacicazgo land revenues.[129] Open antagonism between the Etla caciques and their subjects over labor and lands added to the problems.[130] The difficulties of managing such a large, fragmented estate were considerable, since small properties were especially subject to plunder by Indians and Spaniards alike. The expense of hiring guards made it more economical to rent such lands.[131] Relations with the Indians in Etla were further aggravated in the late period by the cacique's preference for life in Antequera and the persistent demands of subject towns for political autonomy from the cabecera and the hereditary nobility.

Francisco Ramírez de León's successors, his daughter Isabel

and later her cousin Juana Faustina Pimentel, attempted to re-
vive the cacicazgo by collecting rents more efficiently and by
leasing out other properties. Seven nine-year rentals were drawn
up between 1737 and 1739, yielding an annual income of 540
pesos.[132] And the caciques of Etla owned and operated at least
one hacienda in the Valley as late as the 1790's.[133]

The nobility in general seems to have fared well in the Etla
arm during the colonial period. Other cacicazgos preserved sizeable holdings composed of numerous small plots into the eighteenth century. The cacique of San Juan Guelache in mid-cen-
tury owned 3 houses, 5 house plots, a half interest in a wheat mill,
and 32 arable plots scattered about the towns of San Juan, San
Miguel, Santo Domingo, San Agustín, and La Asunción. Only
about half of the lands were inherited, the rest having been purchased from individual Indians. Twenty-eight of the plots were
choice irrigated lands varying in size from 1 to 15 *medidas* (0.5
to 7.5 acres) and from 3 *almudes* to 3 *fanegas de sembradura* (0.5
to 9 acres). A rough estimate of the cacicazgo's total landholdings
is 192 to 247 acres.[134] The cacique of San Juan Guelache also had
at his disposal a number of lands near Cuilapan that were held
by his wife, a noble of the Mixtec cabecera.[135]

Magdalena Apasco represented another large and vigorous cacicazgo of the eighteenth century. The following properties, listed in the 1683 will of Diego de Rojas, were still intact in 1723:
one rancho; one hacienda with 2,658 sheep, 35 horses, 30 cows,
and 3 teams of oxen; 12 arable plots ranging in size from 0.5 to
5 fanegas de sembradura; a millstone quarry; and a salt deposit.[136]
Only two plots were rented out: a piece of irrigated land in 1714
and a section of the hacienda in 1723.[137] The rancho was worked
by eight mulatto slaves, the hacienda relied on debt peons, and
the other arable tracts were let out to various residents of Magdalena Apasco on shares. The cacicazgo of Huitzo as of 1650 was
somewhat more compact. Its estate was composed of 20 tracts of
land, including one *labor*, five caballerías, and pieces ranging in
size from 2 to 50 medidas.

The landholdings of caciques in the Valley of Tlacolula were
generally smaller than the cacicazgo properties in the Valley of

Etla. These holdings were frequently based on late sixteenth-century mercedes and suffered more severely from late colonial disintegration. The few sizeable estates included large amounts of unproductive land suitable only for cattle grazing. The apparent lack of a substantial terrasguerro group in the early colonial period and the caciques' limited control of arable lands made cattle ranching the natural endeavor of those few nobles in the Tlacolula arm who took an interest in landholding.

The cacicazgo of Tlacolula enjoyed considerable prosperity until 1576, when the cacique, Don Domingo de Mendoza, was charged with hiding 140 tributaries, demanding involuntary services from the community, and usurping Indian lands. Found guilty, Mendoza was forced to give up a part of his estate in 1607, including most of his livestock.[138] Prior to the 1576 investigation, Mendoza's holdings consisted of a sitio de ganado menor with 2,600 sheep and 610 goats; a sitio de ganado mayor with 80 horses, 8 oxen, and 8 mules; several houses in Tlacolula; and a piece of arable land that the community was obliged to cultivate for him. Clear titles to the ranches had been established in a 1553 boundary agreement with *principales* of Mitla, who possessed an adjacent estancia east of Tlacolula.[139] In 1588 a third estancia was added to the cacicazgo.[140] The estate was reduced in the seventeenth century, one estancia and half of another being sold between 1611 and 1620.[141] The 1701 will of the cacique Gerónimo de Velasco shows that one and one-half estancias still pertained to the estate. The will also lists eight tracts of arable land, all surrounded by property of natives of Tlacolula; but these were apparently private lands, since Mendoza had earlier divided them among five different relatives.[142] The half estancia was mortgaged to a Spaniard, Dionicio de Abellán, in 1712. The community of Tlacolula later paid off the mortgage on the condition that it could rent the grazing land and an additional 300 acres belonging to the estate. This arrangement was still in effect in 1804, thus limiting the cacique's holdings to one sheep ranch.[143]

Other caciques in the eastern arm were virtually indistinguishable from ordinary peasants by the end of the colonial period. In 1809 Clemente Velasco, the cacique of Teotitlán del Valle, possessed only a small rancho, which he was compelled to rent in order to meet personal debts.[144] The cacicazgo of Tlalixtac was incorporated into the community's holdings in 1663, after the last cacique died without issue.[145] By the eighteenth century certain *principales* and macehuales in the Valley of Tlacolula overshadowed local caciques in wealth and lands. For example, Joseph Ruiz, a macehual of Matatlán, owned a large ranch with 900 sheep, 7 teams of oxen, 4 mules, and 16 cows; 13 tracts of arable land; and several plots of maguey and cochineal-bearing cactus. The cacique of Matatlán by contrast had only five small arable tracts.[146]

Conclusion

The position of a hereditary cacique was still a rank of prestige and authority at the end of the eighteenth century, despite a general decline in wealth and formal political power. There were still unwritten sumptuary laws distinguishing nobles from commoners in some communities at the end of the eighteenth century, and caciques remained the largest Indian landowners in Oaxaca throughout the colonial period.[147] Although the documentation on cacicazgos is too sparse to allow an estimate of the total area of landholdings, the cacicazgos of Cuilapan and Etla were the largest individual estates, Indian or Spanish, in the Valley of Oaxaca. Each encompassed more land than the largest Spanish hacienda in the Valley. This late colonial prominence in landholding was closely related to the caciques' power and authority before the conquest and to the early and explicit confirmation of entailed cacicazgos.

The ability of caciques in Oaxaca to retain large estates is quite remarkable, considering the dispersed character of these holdings and the social and political developments in the late colonial period that threatened the traditional role of hereditary leaders. Such fragmented holdings presented a myriad of problems of labor and utilization and were extremely vulnerable to encroachment. The trend toward political decentralization and a broader electoral base in native society bred tensions between nobles and macehuales that reduced the supply of Indian laborers for cacicazgo lands and led to costly land disputes.

Although the prestige and influence of many caciques outside the political hierarchy remained intact, social position was not a guarantee of continuing wealth. In response to pressures from Indian communities that threatened the profitable use of cacicazgo lands, caciques let out many properties at very low annual fees in the eighteenth century—a significant change in land tenure throughout much of the Valley. Caciques who attempted to force their way back into the political hierarchy ultimately lost both their influence and their estates. Those caciques who accepted the informal role assigned to them by the changing political climate generally fared much better.

The fate of colonial cacicazgos has been well known only for areas of central and northern Mexico, where the conquest and the rise of the hacienda were accompanied by a thorough disintegration of cacicazgos. López Sarrelangue and Gibson have shown that by the mid-seventeenth century caciques in Tarascan Michoacán and the Valley of Mexico were indistinguishable from macehuales in status and wealth. The Valley of Oaxaca in southern Mexico witnessed a much less complete disintegration of cacique status and wealth. The dense occupation and subdivision of Valley lands by natives before the conquest, the relatively peaceful conquest of Oaxaca, and the less impressive growth of haciendas there help explain the survival of Valley cacicazgos. Further investigation may well indicate that a vigorous native nobility was not confined to Oaxaca in the late colonial period, but was also present in similar regions of southern Mexico and highland Guatemala.

III

PUEBLO AND PEASANT LANDS

THE LANDS of the native population in Spanish America were protected by a long series of royal and viceregal laws. The general policy of the Crown on Indian lands was summarized in a 1532 *cédula real* (royal order): "The Indians shall continue to possess their lands, both arable tracts and grazing lands, so that they do not lack what is necessary."[1] Later enactments formulated royal policy more specifically. A law of 1573, repeated several times, declared that Indian towns were entitled to an *ejido* (community pasture) of one league, meaning one square league or a circular area with the radius of a league.[2] A cédula of 1713 gave the most complete description of the lands to which an Indian town was theoretically entitled: "Indian towns shall be given a site with sufficient water, arable lands, woodlands, and access routes so that they can cultivate their lands, plus an ejido of one league for the grazing of their cattle."[3] Laws of 1588 and 1598 ordered that no land grants prejudicial to Indian pueblos could be conferred; such grants already made were to be revoked.[4] Other laws authorized minimum townsites for all Indian communities, and various towns received grants for specific lands in the Valley of Oaxaca.

Types of Holdings

Few of the Valley's Indian communities in the colonial period fitted into the land system prescribed by royal law. The types of Indian land tenure were numerous and complex, and the size of community lands varied considerably. Some communities possessed only the minimum townsite, whereas many others had holdings that greatly exceeded one square league in area. Excluding cacicazgo estates we can distinguish six types of Indian lands in the Valley of Oaxaca: (1) the fundo legal, or townsite, (2) communal lands worked collectively to support religious festivities and to meet other community expenses, (3) communal woods and pasturelands for the private use of all townsmen, (4) communal barrio lands, often divided into plots and worked separately by individuals and families of the neighborhood, (5) communal tracts that were allotted to landless townsmen and "servants" of the community, and (6) privately owned tracts.

The laws on townsites were the only colonial laws relating to Indian lands that were consistently enforced and regularly reexamined.* As the Marqués de Falcés, the Viceroy of New Spain, declared in 1567, all Indian towns were entitled to a townsite of 500 *varas* (1,375 feet) in each of the four cardinal directions. No one else, including Spaniards, could own cultivated fields within this zone, and no ranches could extend to within 1,000 varas (2,750 feet) of an Indian community.[5] The fundo legal was to be divided into house plots measuring 25 varas (69 feet) on a side;† unused portions were to be set aside for cultivation by landless citizens.[6] In 1687 the fundo legal was enlarged to 600 varas (1,650 feet), measured from "the last house" of the town. This enactment was qualified by a clause that allowed for a larger townsite under certain conditions: "If the town is more populous than usual and the townsite appears inadequate, I order you, my Viceroy of New Spain, and you, my Royal Audiencia of Mexico, to distribute to the said town all the additional land

---

* Two leading *indigenistas*, Lucio Mendieta y Núñez and Gonzalo Aguirre Beltrán, agree that the fundo legal was preserved among Indian communities in New Spain. Both see it as "an island of communal property in a sea of great estates." Aguirre Beltrán, *El señorío de Cuahtochco*, p. 196; Mendieta y Núñez, *El problema agrario*, p. 47. Indian communities in the Valley of Oaxaca were generally more fortunate than the isolated, landless towns the two find characteristic of colonial Mexico.

† Provisions for new towns, such as the congregaciones of the late sixteenth and early seventeenth centuries, also called for the division of the fundo legal into plots of 25 varas on a side. AGNT 71, 9:416v, 1603, San Andrés Huayapan. The settlement pattern of pre-conquest towns, however, rarely conformed to the 25-vara rule.

that is necessary to support the Indians, enabling them to farm without scarcity or want."[7]

Spanish landowners offered loud and prolonged opposition to the 1687 provision. Measuring the fundo legal from the edge of town gave many Indian communities a much larger area of land than the law intended. These settlements were generally not compact units, and the last house might be several kilometers from the center of town. Apparently some towns took advantage of the 1687 law by intentionally spreading out their dwellings to encompass more land within the fundo legal.[8] In response to the landowners' complaints, colonial authorities promulgated another law relating to the fundo legal in 1695. Although 600 varas remained the basic measurement, it was now to be stepped off from the parish church, which was taken to be the center of town, rather than from the outskirts.[9] The law further provided that cattle estancias were to be at least 1,100 varas from the town center.

The fundo legal laws were enforced in the Valley through periodic inspections and prompt attention to complaints of encroachment on the townsite. General inspections were made in the Cuatro Villas jurisdiction in 1760 and 1818 and in the *corregimiento* (local district) of Antequera in 1776.[10] Of the 28 native communities included in the 1776 survey, seven occupied a townsite smaller than the fundo legal: San Agustín Amatengo, San Andrés Ixtlahuaca, Trinidad de las Huertas, Jalatlaco, Santa María Ixcotel, Santa María del Tule, and Santísima Trinidad. The other towns exceeded the 600 varas by a comfortable margin.* Of the four towns for which records of the 1760 survey have been found, only San Juan Chapultepec possessed less than its rightful fundo legal. The other three had townsites considerably larger than the area prescribed by law; San Pedro Ixtlahuaca's site measured 12,274,581 square varas, over eight times the fundo legal; San Jacinto Amilpas's, 4,993,613 square varas, over three times the fundo legal; and the Villa de Oaxaca's, 2,872,797 square

---

* Several towns wisely reported only that they possessed the fundo legal. San Pedro Apostol, for example, stated that it owned lands of unknown dimensions extending beyond the 600 varas: "We find ourselves well endowed." AGNT 997, 1:11r.

varas, or twice the fundo legal. Because of its larger population, the Villa de Oaxaca needed still more territory.

The Spanish response to complaints of encroachment on Indian townsites demonstrates that the fundo legal took precedence over other land titles. After the 1760 survey determined that San Juan Chapultepec possessed only half its fundo legal, adjoining lands were taken from the town of San Martín Mexicapan and from several individuals to make up the difference.[11] Colonial courts likewise settled other cases in which a town lacked its fundo legal by restoring the 600 varas: Santa Cruz Amilpas, 1658 and 1720; Santa Lucía, 1719; Guadalupe Etla, 1730; San Pedro Guaxolotitlán, 1731; San Jacinto (near San Juan Teitipac), 1776; Santa María Guelaxe, 1788; Soledad Etla, 1797; and Santa María Albarradas, 1815.[12]

Still, the enforcement of the fundo legal regulations was generally less flexible than the spirit of the law allowed. Strict interpretation prevailed. The 600 varas were allotted and preserved for nearly all Valley towns, but apparently the colonial government did not allow for circumstances that might require more than this minimum. The 1687 provision that a town should have more than 600 varas if its population or the limited resources of its site warranted it was not implemented. When the Villa de Etla sought more land because most of its fundo legal was rocky and unsuited to farming, the Audiencia refused to make an adjustment, stating flatly that 600 varas was a fixed measurement and could not be altered because the town was situated in an undesirable spot.[13] In another case, a 1692 dispute between a pueblo and an hacendado over land to which neither had clear legal title, the corregidor of Antequera ruled in favor of the hacendado because the Indian community "already has much more than its 600 varas."[14] Some flexibility in the fundo legal provisions, however, resulted from misinterpretations by local officials. The corregidor of Antequera in 1719, for example, mistakenly measured Santa Lucía's 600 varas from the outskirts of the town rather than from the churchyard.[15]

 Communal lands worked collectively by the townspeople were of several types. During the sixteenth and early seventeenth cen-

turies, when much royal tribute was still collected in kind rather
than in specie, some towns set aside one or more tracts of land
to be worked to pay the annual tribute assessment. Even when
the tribute was collected in specie, some towns used communal
lands to defray the cost. Mitla, for example, paid part of its royal
tribute with the income from a small herd of cattle that grazed
on community pasturelands.[16] A community tribute, or *tributo
de comunidad*, was required of Indian townspeople in addition
to the royal tribute.[17] Tributo de comunidad was usually paid
in service on communal farmlands during the sixteenth century.
According to *El libro de las tasaciones de pueblos de la Nueva
España* (1549), the citizens of all towns in the bishopric of
Oaxaca "must each year collectively work a field of corn for the
benefit of the community."[18] In the 1550's in the Valley of Oaxaca, lands used for community tribute were divided into plots of
ten *brazas* on a side (about .07 acre), one such plot to be worked
by each tributary male.[19] This became the standard obligation
of tributaries throughout Spanish America in 1582 as a result
of a royal law.[20]

Presumably, when New Spain's royal tribute came to be demanded exclusively in cash in the early seventeenth century, the
community tribute followed suit, reducing the need for communal *sementeras* (cultivated plots).[21] But farmlands worked collectively to support town projects did not disappear altogether
in the Valley of Oaxaca during the colonial period. Two eighteenth-century examples are known: San Pablo Guaxolotitlán
(1730) and San Jacinto Amilpas (1760).[22] Land to support the
religious festivities of an Indian community was also collectively
owned and operated. Property set aside for cofradías, or religious
brotherhoods, in the Valley of Oaxaca was less often farmland
than small cattle ranches, which required little from the community in the way of labor.[23] Of the 11 late-eighteenth-century
Indian cofradías whose sources of financial support are known,
nine relied on livestock, one owned a wheat mill, and one owned
four pieces of arable land. The cofradías with livestock had an
average of 55 cattle and 213 sheep.[24]

Other lands that Indian communities owned or had the right

to work were set aside for the personal use of the inhabitants. In addition, individual natives and communities alike had the benefit of *tierras realengas*—the royal woodlands, rivers, hunting areas, and lime deposits. A 1551 cédula allowed Indians to breed livestock, including cattle and horses in limited numbers. Before the end of the sixteenth century, many Indian households owned a team of oxen and a few sheep, goats, or cows, which they grazed on tierras realengas or the community pasture (ejido).[25]

Barrio land was a type of communal property separate from the Indian town as a whole. Barrios, neighborhoods within an Indian town, usually divided such land into inalienable family plots similar to the Aztec *calpullalli*.[26] That a barrio had exclusive right to its land is demonstrated by the disparate holdings of different barrios within one town. The Villa de Oaxaca in the early eighteenth century is one example. In 1710 the barrio Santa Cruz complained to the alcalde mayor of the Cuatro Villas that it possessed no farmlands at all, whereas the barrio Santa Lucía owned nearly one league of land, most of which it could not use and thus rented.[27] Two other clear references to separate barrio lands have been found: in 1699 the principal barrio of Santa Catalina Quiané sold a part of its land to another barrio, Xaguia Abilana, and in 1686 the barrio San Blas of San Pedro Ixtlahuaca was reported to possess over 200 acres of arable land.[28]

Some communities designated tracts of arable land for use by citizens who had no lands of their own. These landless Indians might enter into a terrasguerro relationship with the community, by which they performed certain services in exchange for the use of these lands. In the town of San Sebastían Teitipac, native nobles willed tracts of land to the community specifically for this purpose. Juan López, for example, bequeathed 15 medidas (about 7 acres) in 1624 with the stipulation that the land become "the property of the community for [the use of] the servants of the town."[29] Also, a town might distribute unused portions of the fundo legal to landless peasants, as did San Pablo Guaxolotitlán in 1730, when it gave each of four married citizens an arable tract holding two *almudes* of seed (about one acre).[30]

Not all lands possessed by Indian communities were inalienable. Of the various holdings mentioned above, only lands classed as *primitivo patrimonio* (dating from pre-conquest times) could not be sold.[31] To sell a tract of land acquired by grant or purchase, the community had to secure permission from the Viceroy or a representative designated by him. Sales made without this permission or without a public announcement of the intent to sell at least 30 days in advance were voided. Indians were further restricted in selling land by the condition that any transaction could be revoked if the alcalde mayor decided the price was unfair. Lands sold by Indian communities included sheep ranches by Cuilapan in 1617, Tlacolula in 1592, and Zimatlán sometime before 1734.[32]

The importance of privately owned Indian lands in colonial Mexico (excluding cacicazgos) has not yet been carefully examined. Opinions range from Gonzalo Aguirre Beltrán's impression that there was no private ownership of land in native communities to Emilio Rabasa's notion that private ownership was the predominant form of tenure.[33] Documentation for the Valley of Oaxaca tends to support Helen Phipps, who claims that the colonial period witnessed a gradual acceptance of private ownership by individual natives.*

The introduction of domesticated animals into the Valley, which led to the division of previously unused areas and to the sale of some cacicazgo lands, promoted private ownership. Certainly the concept of private property developed early among the native nobles and was encouraged by Spaniards anxious to acquire lands of their own. The hallmark of private ownership, in contrast to the communal ejido forms of tenure prevalent in many Mexican communities today, is the power to buy and sell or otherwise alienate land. Under the type of modern ejido tenure that most closely approximates private ownership, a family

* Phipps, p. 29. Although not referring specifically to Oaxaca, a letter to the King from the Audiencia of Mexico in 1532 suggests that in the early colonial period most Indian land in central Mexico was communally owned: "In most communities few [citizens] have private lands except the native lords or their descendants. Very few commoners or tributaries own land. Most land is communally owned and worked. Communal lands serve to maintain the native nobility, to support their churches and celebrations, and now to pay tribute to Your Majesty." RAHM, vol. III, fol. 124.

has the use of a particular piece of land and can will it to relatives within the community but cannot sell it.

Nobles began to sell lands shortly after the conquest, despite
the legal inalienability of many noble estates. As early as 1529
Cortez's administrator in the Valley of Oaxaca bought a large
tract of land from the cacique of Tlapacoya.[34] At first the claim
that such lands were privately owned must surely have been a
ruse used to legalize the sale of entailed cacicazgo lands; but by
1600 many cacicazgos included lands that had been acquired
since the conquest by purchase or grant, and that were acknowl-
edged as private property by both the Indian and white communities. Grants for cattle ranches conferred the rights of private ownership on the recipient so long as the grant was actually
used for the grazing of specified kinds of livestock. Some grants
to Valley caciques and *principales* were legally sold as private
property in the early seventeenth century. In 1619, for example,
Andrés de Mendoza sold the estancia de ganado menor that he
had received in the 1590's.[35]

The nobility's notion of private property gradually filtered
into the macehuales' system of land tenure. Eighteenth-century
records of land purchases and sales by macehuales are numerous.
Occasionally utter necessity forced the sale of lands that might
otherwise have been retained. Sales in the first half of the seventeenth century were sometimes made in order to pay the annual
tribute, which weighed especially heavily on towns that had suffered a loss of population between census counts.[36] In other cases
lands were sold to meet extraordinary expenses, such as the cost
of a burial or marriage festivities.[37] Most of the sales were made
to other Indians, as in one case of a plot of irrigated land 72 by
32 varas that Pascual Martín of San Felipe Guaxolotitlán sold to
his fellow townsman Favián de Mendoza in 1718.[38] The individual Indian's ability to own land, reflected in his ability to dis-
pose of it, was limited by the fact that Indians were legally wards
of the Crown and therefore had to petition the King's representative for permission to sell their lands. A number of sales made
after petitioning the Crown are found in AGN *Ramo de Indios*.
When the property was worth less than 30 pesos, the Audiencia

usually authorized sale and waived the usual requirement of a
30-day public announcement.[39] In the eighteenth century natives
frequently rented land out or let it out on shares, which provided
a partial solution to local imbalances in property ownership without forcing landless townsmen to abandon their homes. Most of
these transactions were between individuals, but in one instance
a native rented a piece of land to his village for communal purposes.[40]

Two late-eighteenth-century land disputes further illustrate
that private ownership was a distinguishable type of Indian land
tenure in the Valley of Oaxaca. In 1784 the wife and two sons of
Francisco Raymundo, a native of Mitla, quarreled over the house
and land he had left them; the dispute was settled by selling the
property to two other residents of Mitla and dividing the proceeds among the three heirs.[41] The second case involved a conflict between the community of Xoxocotlán and Andrés Fernández, a macehual, over title to the land he worked. The town
claimed that Fernández had sold it the land and would therefore
have to pay rent if he planned to continue to cultivate it. When
Xoxocotlán was unable to present written proof of sale, full title
to the land was awarded to Fernández.[42]

Ownership and Land Use

An individual Indian in colonial Oaxaca had much more freedom in disposing of his lands than the modern ejido tenure al-
lows. Wills from the sixteenth and early seventeenth centuries
reveal that macehuales and *principales* distributed land at their
personal discretion, implying at least an incipient form of private ownership. As well as to members of the nuclear family,
lands were willed to cousins, uncles, nephews, in-laws, servants,
the Church, and even non-relatives living outside the community.*

* See AGNT 256, exp. 2, and AGNT 388, exp. 1, for representative wills. The
ability to mortgage a piece of land is also an important aspect of ownership. In
three of the four cases in which lands were mortgaged by individual Indians, the
lender was another Indian. AMT, docs. 5, 6, 30. In one case the use of land as loan
collateral carried the stipulation that the lender was entitled to usufruct rights
until the loan was paid off.

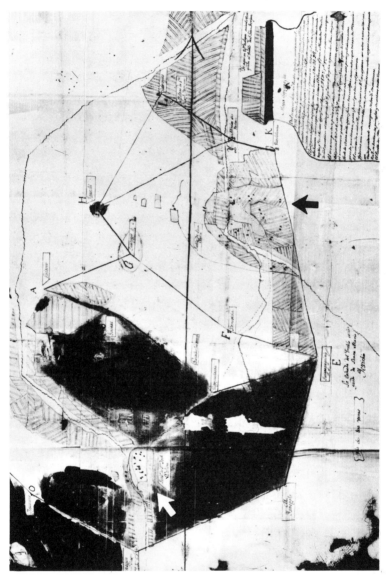

I. The Lands of Santo Domingo Jalieza and Santa Cecilia Jalieza, 1798 (AGNT 1864, exp. 2). Santo Domingo, in the upper left-hand section (white arrow), is a compact settlement; Santa Cecilia, in the lower right (black arrow), is dispersed. Note that many of the plots on this colonial map, one of the few showing cultivated areas, are plowed crosswise.

A deceased's properties were regularly divided among various heirs, but at least during the colonial period the result was not classic *minifundio*, in which tracts of land are eventually divided into sections so small that they cannot be effectively used. Even in the late eighteenth century an Indian's land almost always bordered on land of non-relatives, suggesting that though individual tracts of land were rarely passed on intact to one heir, they were not in the process of being divided into tiny parcels.* The average individual plot of Indian land in the late colonial period was large enough to be worked as a unit. Based on a sample of 124 arable plots in the Valley documented for the seventeenth and eighteenth centuries, the average size was in the range of 5.6 to 8.5 acres per plot.[43] This is about twice the size of the average present-day Indian holding.

The distribution pattern of individual native landholdings was a mosaic of scattered, irregularly shaped plots. Despite the widespread use of oxen, cultivated plots were not uniformly long and narrow, and even the ones that were might be plowed crosswise instead of lengthwise (see Plate I). (Twentieth-century peasant farmers in the Valley continue to plow carefully even the smallest triangular ends of their plots.) Commonly, an Indian peasant had the use of three or more separate pieces of land, some of which might be over five kilometers from his barrio and completely surrounded by lands belonging to natives of another community. In one case during the eighteenth century, several natives of Guadalupe Etla and Jesús Nazareno owned lands that bordered only on lands owned by residents of Soledad Etla.[44] Taking two as a conservative estimate of the number of plots owned by a Valley Indian and using the average plot size calculated from the 124-plot sample, we can figure that the average native farmer had the use of 11 to 17 acres.

Very little land unwittingly slipped away from Indian towns in the Valley of Oaxaca. Individual Indians or communities oc-

* Often one individual had the use of lands in several locations. The probable explanation for this fragmented pattern is that, in the Valley as in other agricultural societies, land was divided on the basis of fertility; this generally precluded large consolidated holdings, which would normally include some inferior land. Marc Bloch (pp. 39–40) has described a similar practice in medieval France.

casionally sold lands, but intestate property legally belonging to
the King or the Marqués del Valle was virtually non-existent. A
1644 survey for intestate Indian property instigated by the Marqués turned up unclaimed lands only in towns that had been
completely abandoned.[45] The reason for the absence of intestate
property in spite of a declining population was that Indians always made wills; those few who died without settling their affairs
had relatives who were entitled to inherit. Even communities
that lost all their lands sometimes found alternatives to complete
abandonment of the townsite or incorporation into a rural hacienda. Residents of Zaachila, for example, sharecropped on surrounding lands belonging to the town of Cuilapan and to Spanish hacendados. In 1660 the people of Santa María Ixcotel, find-
ing themselves without arable land, became terrasguerros for the
town of Santa Lucía; this arrangement lasted until 1686, when
the residents of Santa María acquired lands of their own.[46]

The Indians' ownership of lands in the Valley of Oaxaca during the colonial period rested on several bases: evidence of ownership at the time of the conquest, mercedes, composiciones de
tierras (title inspections and land measurements) during the seventeenth and eighteenth centuries, purchases, and bequests. Colonial authorities applied these criteria for ownership throughout
most of New Spain. Primitivo patrimonio, ownership at the conquest, was most important in areas with sedentary cultures, like
Oaxaca, where the Spaniards knew that natives had occupied the
same lands for many years. Primitivo patrimonio carried less
weight in colonial law in the areas of northern Mexico traversed
by hunters and gatherers, where Indian settlement was often temporary and ephemeral.

Possession in pre-Hispanic times was a claim frequently voiced
by Indian communities in the Valley of Oaxaca during the sixteenth century. Their petitions were generally affirmed by the
Spanish courts, since Spanish colonists were only mildly interested in owning arable land at that time, and they help account
for the Indians' reasonably secure hold on large areas of the Valley in the late colonial period. The so-called lands of Huichilobos, tracts used to support the pre-conquest priesthood, were

the only primitivo patrimonio lands legally vulnerable to Spanish confiscation. In the 1530's the cabildo of Antequera and Juan
López de Zárate, the first bishop of Oaxaca, successfully petitioned the Crown for title to such lands.[47] "Lands of Montezuma," cropland acquired by the Aztecs in the course of conquest,
were apparently returned to the local communities and set aside
for paying royal tribute.[48] Ancient ownership declined as a legal
argument in the seventeenth century, when the composiciones de
tierras initiated by the Crown confirmed what were considered
to be valid titles of primitivo patrimonio.[49] Afterwards, evidence
of composición served as a substitute title, and in most cases
claims of primitivo patrimonio were no longer accepted.

Purchases and bequests from caciques and non-Indians con-
stitute another source of Indian lands in the colonial period. Purchases of 11 cattle ranches and one mill by Indian communities
are known: Tlalixtac, 1537; Cuilapan, two ranches, 1552 and
1560's; Zimatlán, 1554; Mitla, pre-1610; San Pedro Apostol,
1612; San Juan Guelache, mill, 1695; Santa Catalina Quiané, pre-
1710; Tlacolula, 1712; San Andrés Ixtlahuaca, 1717; San Sebastián Teitipac, 1720; and San Pedro Ixtlahuaca, 1799.[50] Several
bequests from caciques to Indian towns have already been mentioned, but only one important legacy from a Spaniard to an Indian town has been found: Bishop Zárate left two mills and a
large section of arable land to the town of Tlalixtac in the
1550's.[51]

Royal mercedes were the third important source of land for
Valley Indians in the sixteenth and early seventeenth centuries.* Mercedes were royal licenses for the use of specific lands.
In practice they amounted to limited grants of ownership. Provided that the lands were used in the manner specified by the
merced, the recipient retained full ownership rights, including
the right to sell or otherwise alienate the property. If the lands
were not used in accordance with the merced, they could be reclaimed by the Crown. For example, a merced granted to an Indian community for the grazing of ganado menor could be re-

---

* Some mercedes to individual natives and communities did not grant new lands
but merely authorized cattle grazing or mill construction on lands already owned.

TABLE 7
Land Grants to Indian Towns

Date	Town	Type of grant[a]	Source
1555	Villa de Oaxaca	GM	AGNMer 4
1556	Villa de Etla	HM	AGNMer 4
1561	Villa de Etla	GM	AGNMer 5
1561	Coyotepec	GM	AGNMer 5
1561	Tlacolula	GM	AGNMer 5
1565	Mitla	GM	AGNMer 8
1567	Azompa	GM	AGNMer 9
1571	Zimatlán	GM	AGNH 85, exp. 5
pre-1579	Santiago Ixtaltepec	GM	AGNG 2, exp. 155
pre-1579	Tlalixtac	GM	AGNG 2, exp. 378
pre-1581	Huitzo	GM	Paso y Troncoso, *Papeles*
pre-1581	Magdalena Apasco	GM	Paso y Troncoso, *Papeles*
1582	Zimatlán	GM	AGNH 85, exp. 5
1582	Sta. Ana Zegache	GM	AGNT 203, exp. 6
1583	Huitzo	2 HM	Cruz Caballero
1584	San Pablo Huistepec	GM	AGNH 85, exp. 5
1585	Magdalena Apasco	GM	AGNT 415, exp. 3
1586	Huitzo	2 GM	Cruz Caballero
1587	Cuilapan	GM	AGNMer 14
1588	Macuilxóchitl	GM	BEOB
1588	Sto. Domingo del Valle	GM	ADAA, exp. 276.1
1588	Zimatlán	GM	AGNT 241, exp. 7
1591	Coyotepec	GM	CCGL, 1591
pre-1592	Ocotlán	GM	CCGSJ, 1592
1592	Villa de Etla	HM	AGNMer 18
1593	Zaachila	CB	AGNT 1045, exp. 5
1593	Cuilapan	2 CB	AGNMer 19
1594	Mitla	GM	Schmieder
1599	Cacaotepec	GM	CCGG, 1599
1599	Zaachila	GM	AGNT 2784, exp. 1
15??	Sta. Catarina Minas	GM	AGNH 380, exp. 9
15??	San Andrés Ixtlahuaca	GM	AGNH 69, bk. 2
1607	Cuilapan	GM	AGNH 69, bk. 2
pre-1612	Teotitlán del Valle	GM	BEOB
1613	Villa de Etla	GM	AGNMer 28
1615	Sta. María del Tule	GM	AGNT 2922, exp. 1
1623	San Andrés Ixtlahuaca	GM	AGNI 33, exp. 177
1698	San Martín Tilquiapan	CV	AGNI 33, exp. 304
1717	Zimatlán	C	AGNI 40, exp. 146

[a] GM = Sitio de ganado menor. HM = *Herido de molino* (mill site). C = *Ciénega* (swamp). CB = Caballería. CV = *Cría de vacas* (breeding cattle).

voked if the community used the land for grazing ganado mayor or for farming.

Table 7 and the grants to cacicazgos discussed in Chapter 2 represent an incomplete inventory of mercedes to Indian towns and individuals in Oaxaca. Significantly, almost all of these grants were for sheep ranches; only individual nobles received cattle ranches.[52] Documents consulted by José Miranda, who has studied native cattle ranching in the Mixteca Alta north and west of the Valley of Oaxaca, suggest that it was viceregal policy to restrict Indian grazing grants to ganado menor (sheep and goats).[53]

Although they did not receive grants for ganado mayor, Indian towns and individuals were not restricted from buying cattle enterprises, as we have seen, or from obtaining special licenses to own a few mules or horses.[54] Occasionally, Indian communities possessed herds of cattle and horses without a license, as did Teotitlán del Valle in the 1580's.[55] Early in the eighteenth century the policy against cattle breeding in Indian communities was liberalized, and licenses to raise ganado mayor were granted to at least three Valley towns: San Miguel Tilquiapan, Ocotlán, and San Andrés Zautla.[56] Colonial authorities openly promoted Indian cattle ranching in the eighteenth century by limiting the meat supply for large Indian markets like Ocotlán to native sources.[57]

Individual natives also owned small numbers of ganado mayor. At least as early as 1551, Philip II granted permission for Indians to own European livestock.[58] Most ganado mayor owned by Indians were draft animals, principally oxen, as an 1826 census in the Valley of Oaxaca clearly indicates. Of the 28,285 ganado mayor in Valley towns included in that census, 13,349, or 47.2 per cent, were oxen.[59] Native farmers in the Valley seem to have abandoned the digging stick in favor of the plow early in the colonial period. Burgoa, writing in the mid-seventeenth century, was much impressed with the widespread use of the plow. He claimed that "in all of New Spain one cannot find Indians with so many teams of oxen."[60] A peasant farmer was likely to own his own team of oxen, but only in exceptional cases did he own other livestock. Of the 57 households in San Bartolomé Quialana in 1826, 37 owned one team of oxen, one family two teams, and another three teams. Ten individuals owned the remaining livestock in the community—226 sheep, 4 pigs, and 2 horses.[61]

The Indians' traditional use of cropland in the Valley puzzled the Spanish colonists. Many complained that the natives were satisfied with maize and beans when the soil would yield all kinds of grains and vegetables. Certainly few Indians had any desire to produce many different kinds of crops on their lands. The Spaniards had to assess Indian tribute in flour in the sixteenth century to induce natives to plant wheat. The 1777 *Relaciones Geográficas* for the Valley frequently mention the limitation of crops. As the Mixtepec chronicler put it, "These lands are so fertile they yield every sort of seed and vegetable in great abundance. Even though experience shows that peas, chick-peas, and cotton grow very well, the Indians avoid them. They plant only maize, wheat, and beans in the head town and only maize in the other villages."[62] Judging from the number of taverns in the Valley in the early eighteenth century, much Indian land must also have been devoted to maguey. A survey of Indian drinking houses in 1726 turned up 513 public and private taverns for 46 Valley towns.

The Defense of Indian Lands

Oaxaca's Indian communities defended their lands from usurpation through legal channels and by force. The most acceptable means of settling land disputes from the Spanish government's point of view was an appeal to the colonial courts, first to the local corregidor de indios, from whom appeals might be then made to the Audiencia and to Spain. Indians in the Valley of Oaxaca were notoriously litigious. As one representative of the cathedral church learned, the Indians might be all too aware of their rights: when he tried to collect the tithe on lands worked by terrasgueros for their own benefit near Tule in 1799, the representative was startled by one Indian who "insolently" quoted from the *Recopilación* to support his exemption from such taxes.[63]

Even though an appeal often went unconsidered for several

years and a final verdict might be delayed as much as a century, with great expense to all parties, taking a grievance to the highest court apparently helped raise Indian morale. It was not uncommon for groups of humble oaxaqueños to make the long trip to Mexico City on foot in order to defend their rights to a small piece of land before the Audiencia.[64] One proud native from Mitla in the 1790's even mortgaged all his belongings to sail to Spain to appeal directly to the King on behalf of his town.[65] Villages in Oaxaca were not alone in their appetite for litigation. In a circular of October 19, 1799, the Viceroy deplored the endless stream of Indians descending on Mexico City and the provincial seats of justice from all parts of the colony:

> The following is a well-known public abuse: Indians in growing number are traveling to the viceregal and provincial capitals, remaining there for many days on the pretext of engaging in lawsuits or entering petitions on behalf of their towns. Serious problems have resulted. There is a shortage of agricultural labor; residents of the countryside are growing accustomed to the laziness and vices of the cities; small towns are burdened with supporting their representatives; and there is a growing shortage of supplies in the capitals. I have found it advisable to order that no Indian town can send more than one or two representatives to engage in litigation or for any other purpose. *Subdelegados*, alcaldes ordinarios, and judicial officials are to take care that no more than two Indians from any town in their jurisdiction leave as representatives to a capital or city. Magistrates in the capitals are to recognize only two such representatives and should order others to leave. So that this order reaches the attention of everyone and is duly obeyed, I order that it be published in this capital and in other cities, towns, and settlements of this viceroyalty.[66]

The Indians' use of colonial courts was by no means an eighteenth-century development. In the second half of the sixteenth century, Viceroy Martín Enríquez complained that land disputes were the greatest source of trouble from the Indians.[67] However, the greater frequency of litigation in Oaxaca in the eighteenth century indicates that disputes over Indian lands became more intense in the late colonial period.

In light of the widely accepted notion that haciendas engulfed

Indian towns, it is surprising that even in the eighteenth century, when haciendas in the Valley were expanding, the great
majority of land disputes pitted one Indian town against another
(see Appendix B). Of the 52 known land disputes involving Indian towns, 37 were between two or more Indian towns and 13
between Indian towns and Spanish haciendas. (Two pitted an
Indian town against an individual Indian.) Roughly 62 per cent
of the exclusively Indian disputes took place in the Valley of
Tlacolula, 24 per cent in the Valley of Zimatlán, and 14 per cent
in the Valley of Etla. Five of these disputes between Indian towns
wore on for nearly a century, despite several supposedly definitive boundary measurements.

In part the difficulty in solving Indian disputes stemmed from
the "obscurity of Indian land titles," as one Spanish judge lamented.[68] The Indians' concept of boundaries further complicated disputes. They associated boundaries with physical features
of the terrain, such as swamps, hills, and rivers. These *parajes*
(boundary markers) were themselves sizeable land areas, or per-
ishable or moveable features such as trees and rocks. Conflicts
frequently arose when the Spaniards attempted to make boundaries more precise. Two towns might agree that a marsh divided
their lands, but when colonial officials established a definite
boundary line either through or along one side of the marsh,
endless disputes were almost inevitable. Haciendas and towns
seem to have fared better in their boundary relations, often because hacendados were willing to draw the boundary line at the
limit of the paraje acceptable to their Indian neighbors. San Juan
Lachigalla (near Chichicapa) is a graphic example: although the
town had boundary disputes with all its Indian neighbors, it had
none with the adjacent Hacienda San José.[69]

When legal channels of complaint were too slow or unprofit-
able, Indians had little hesitation in resorting to encroachment
and violent interference with boundary measurements and possession rites. *Vistas de ojos* (surveys) almost invariably provoked
resistance by residents of Indian towns. Although their fears were
not always justified, Indians assumed that a vista de ojos would
mean a loss of land. As one sympathetic alcalde mayor explained,

"What they fear most is losing the peace and tranquillity in which they live, and the lands that each individual and his community peacefully possess."[70] Large, menacing crowds of Indians often turned out for vistas de ojos. Occasionally they would throw rocks at the officials or steal the measuring rope. In several cases a community massed in front of the inspectors and refused to let them proceed with the measurement. A frightened alcalde mayor of the Cuatro Villas jurisdiction reported the following scene at a boundary survey east of Antequera in 1720:

When we had reached the boundary of a plot of land belonging to Gabriel Martín, a native of the pueblo of Santa Cruz . . . , many Indians from Santa Cruz appeared, joining others who had assembled there. Massing together in a crowd, they sought, in disobedience of the Royal Order and Royal justice, to stop the proceedings, shouting that we would not be allowed to go beyond the said boundary. At the same time, the Indians picked up stones and threw three; they aimed one at Your representative, but it struck one of the Indian officials instead.[71]

Similar demonstrations took place at San Juan Teitipac in 1692, Tlacochahuaya in 1692 and 1788, San Marcos (a sujeto of Teotitlán) in 1705, Santa Lucía (a sujeto of Antequera) in 1710, San Pedro Ixtlahuaca in 1716, Cuilapan in 1725, Zimatlán in 1740, Macuilxóchitl in 1747, Mitla in 1792, and Soledad Etla in 1796.[72]

Land disputes between Indian towns could erupt into violence. A four-sided boundary dispute involving Tlacolula, Tlacochahuaya, Teotitlán del Valle, and Macuilxóchitl in 1726 led to a short-lived pitched battle, in which natives wielded clubs, spears, knives, and firearms against each other.[73] A common tactic used by Valley towns to force quick settlements was to kidnap a number of leading citizens from the rival town and imprison them until an agreement was reached. San Juan Guelavia used this technique in a dispute with San Marcos (jurisdiction of Cuilapan) in 1705, as did Zimatlán against San Pedro Apostol in 1709.[74]

Indian land encroachments ranged from the creeping expansion of a town's cultivated fields onto adjoining fallow lands to armed invasions that literally drove the owners off large tracts of

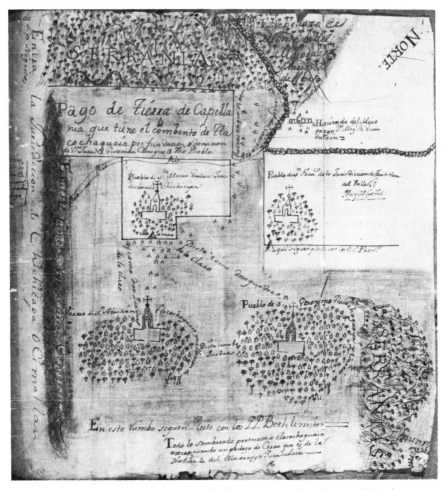

II. The Lands of Tlacochahuaya, 1760 (AGNT 867, exp. 9). Tlacochahuaya's lands, represented by the shaded area, border San Francisco Lachigolo on two sides and completely surround Santa María Guelaxe.

land. In the southern valley San Pedro Apostol resorted to expansion by force in 1563, burning down the fences of a neighboring Spanish ranch and occupying the land.[75] Mitla also burned fences along its border with the Hacienda Xaagá in 1792, and residents of San Marcos, brandishing machetes, took over a cornfield from San Juan Guelavia in 1705.[76]

A recurrent theme of eighteenth-century disputes is the aggressiveness of larger towns toward smaller villages of different political jurisdictions. Beginning in the late seventeenth century and continuing without pause into the early nineteenth, Tlacochahuaya, a sujeto of Antequera, waged a fierce campaign against two neighboring hamlets in the jurisdiction of Teotitlán del Valle, Santa María Guelaxe and San Francisco Lachigolo. The effect of Tlacochahuaya's territorial expansion is shown on a 1760 map (Plate II). Santa María Guelaxe was completely surrounded by lands of the larger community. The map shows Tlacochahuaya's lands on two sides of San Francisco Lachigolo; the text of the document says that Tlacochahuaya bounded the pueblo on three sides, with the Hacienda de Guendulain on the fourth.[77] At any rate San Francisco did not have its rightful 600 varas. Santa Domingo, another nearby town whose lands had been isolated by Tlacochahuaya, was completely abandoned.

By 1765 Guelaxe was reduced to less than its fundo legal.[78] San Gerónimo Tlacochahuaya and its barrio San Sebastián, the modern town of Abasolo, appropriated the area south of Guelaxe by cultivating fields there and erecting adobe huts right next to the hamlet's outermost buildings. Guelaxe had only 62 tributaries to Tlacochahuaya's 506. Residents testified that they had not been able to resist the incursions "because of the number of people who live in the said town of Tlacochahuaya, and because later [when Guelaxe tried to defend its lands] they attacked us and took our animals."[79] Small pieces of land were later ceded to Guelaxe by the Hacienda de los Negritos and the Dominican monastery at Tlacochahuaya, but as of 1791 Guelaxe still held less than the minimum 600 varas.

The many land cases pending in the eastern section of the Valley in the late eighteenth century reflects the chaos created by

Tlacochahuaya. The prolonged dispute with Guelaxe lasted to the end of the colonial period. Tlacochahuaya was also involved in two land suits with the Bethlemites, who owned the Hacienda Santo Domingo Buenavista to the south, two with San Francisco, and two with the Hacienda de los Negritos to the west.[80] (These were only the latest in a long history of disputes. For example, Tlacochahuaya had quarreled over boundaries with San Juan Teitipac in 1558 and with Macuilxóchitl in 1579 and 1709–12.[81]) The town's quest for new lands continued into the early nineteenth century with a fresh invasion of San Francisco's territory in 1816.[82] By this time, however, Tlacochahuaya had suffered several major setbacks. The loss of one dispute with Guelaxe in 1803 brought court costs of 6,500 pesos; and a violent dispute erupted in 1800 between the town's two principal barrios over encroachments on lands belonging to the parish church of Tlacochahuaya.[83]

Tlalixtac's expansion at the expense of Santo Domingo Tomaltepec, documented for the period 1801 to 1809, followed the same pattern as Tlacochahuaya's exploitation of its smaller neighbors. Tomaltepec, a sujeto of the Villa de Oaxaca with 600 to 700 residents in the 1820's, barely extended beyond its fundo legal; Tlalixtac, a sujeto of Antequera with about 2,400 inhabitants, claimed most of the surrounding territory.[84] The reputation of Tlacochahuaya and Tlalixtac as lawless land-grabbers was well established among eighteenth-century residents of the Valley. When Indians from San Antonio de la Cal encroached on lands of the Jesuit *labor* San Miguel in 1754, the resident friar accused them of "seeking to follow the example of Tlacochahuaya and Tlalixtac."[85] Other instances of encroachment by large towns on smaller neighbors include Macuilxóchitl against San Marcos in the 1680's, San Juan Teitipac against San Marcos in the 1690's Tlacolula against San Juan Guelavia in 1814, and Zimatlán against Magdalena Ocotlán and Santa Inés Yatzechi in the early nineteenth century.[86] Intrusion by one town could set off a chain reaction of land disputes, as when Zaachila, increasingly hemmed in by its larger neighbor Cuilapan, responded by usurping territory from Santo Domingo Ocotlán and Coyotepec.[87]

Population pressures as well as long-standing hatreds seem to have been at the root of these intrusions. If we may assume a fairly even birthrate for all Indian communities, larger towns had more new mouths to feed.[88] In the case of Tlacochahuaya, lands acquired by force were quickly put to use. According to a corregidor who made an inspection in 1760, Tlacochahuaya was using all the land at its disposal, which implies that population pressures motivated the community's expansion. The corregidor found that to restore Guelaxe's 600 varas would require taking land from Tlacochahuaya, and in his words, "It would be impossible for Tlacochahuaya to endure the loss of land in any direction."[89] Usually the will of the larger town prevailed in spite of appeals to Mexico City. The colonial government did little more than pledge to protect the smaller town from extinction and increase its holdings to the meager area of the fundo legal.

Land Distribution in the Valley

The size and distribution of Indian landholdings are difficult to discern for any one town and its citizens. Communal lands received considerable attention in the colonial records, but references to private lands and the barrio tracts divided up among individuals are too incomplete in most cases to give an accurate picture of a community's total landholdings. Detailed information is generally limited to communities involved in land disputes, that is, primarily the larger communities. Still, by examining each arm of the Valley as a unit, the distribution pattern of Indian lands can be clarified.

Before beginning a description of Indian lands in the three major sections of the Valley, we should note two factors that affect the importance of the size of landholdings to a community's economic well-being. First, since not all lands in the Valley were (or are) equally fertile, size alone does not provide an accurate picture of productivity. For example, one acre of irrigated land in the Etla arm, where two or three crops could be harvested each year, was obviously more productive than one acre in the drier Tlacolula arm, where only one annual crop was harvested. Second, a town with other sources of income would not need so much land as a neighboring town whose sole economic activity was farming. Weekly markets and local industries such as hat making, pottery, charcoal production, and weaving were the most common supplementary activities. When the documentation permits, I will consider these complicating factors.

Valley of Etla. Etla, the most fertile section of the Valley, was an area of general land shortage for Indian communities in the late seventeenth and eighteenth centuries. A 1687 survey of Etla lands made by the Marqués del Valle confirmed that few towns held more than the fundo legal, and that many were limited to even smaller areas. The sorry condition of San Pedro Apostol de Etla especially impressed the surveyor: Since the town was located on a hillside and was surrounded by gravel deposits, the natives had no farmland.[90] The survey could not find one single plot of unclaimed land in the Etla arm; nowhere in the Valley of Oaxaca was the land divided into so many pieces, with virtually every square foot accounted for.

The surprising decline in population in the Etla arm during the eighteenth century (see Table 4), when the rest of the Valley was growing, is another indication of a fixed or decreasing supply of land, insufficient to sustain the population. The considerable size of the Etla cacicazgo and the expansion of private estates in the seventeenth and eighteenth centuries aggravated the land shortage. In 1725 the alcalde mayor of the Cuatro Villas was moved to remark, "There is no reason why so many tributaries should perish when there are enough lands for the caciques as well as everyone else."[91] Later in the eighteenth century an inspector of cofradías described the Etla region as a land of "pestilence, hunger, shortage of water, continuous land usurpation, and other afflictions."[92] The increasing unrest among Etla Indians in the late eighteenth century is also symptomatic of a desperate land and food problem.* The possibility of regaining land by litigation or force was remote; Etla's population pressures could only be relieved by voluntary abandonment of the land or by epidemic disease.

* There are three known instances of mass violence in Etla over official land ceremonies in the second half of the eighteenth century. AGNH 307, exp. 18, 1755; AGNT 1271, exp. 2, 1796; AGNT 1877, exp. 2, 1797.

Generally without local industries, communities in the Etla arm depended on irrigation and the fertility of the soil to compensate for small landholdings. The soil did yield an abundant variety of crops, including maize, beans, chile, chick-peas, tomatoes, onions, maguey, melons, pitayas, a small amount of sugar cane, and much wheat. Some communities specialized in one particular commercial crop, such as San Sebastián Xochimilco, which supplied onions to the Oaxaca market, and San Andrés Ixtlahuaca, which supplied tomatoes.[93] The woodlands of the surrounding mountains were an important supplementary source of income for several Indian communities in the Valley of Etla. San Pedro Ixtlahuaca, San Andrés Ixtlahuaca, and Huitzo regularly brought charcoal and rough-hewn wood to Antequera. When the tax on pulque became burdensome in the early eighteenth century, San Andrés Zautla abandoned its maguey fields in favor of charcoal and firewood.[94] Most Etla towns successfully preserved their integrity as separate communities against the encroachment of caciques and hacendados, although few were able to accommodate a growing population.

In terms of land use Etla communities had two important advantages over the Indian towns of the southern and eastern valleys: irrigation and community-owned flour mills. Twelve mills belonging to eight communities have been located: two belonging to San Juan Guelache, two to the Villa de Etla, two to Huitzo, two to San Juan del Estado, one to San Gabriel, one to San Agustín, one to San Miguel Etla, and one to San Pablo Etla.[95] Six mills whose origins can be traced were obtained by royal grants or purchase during the late sixteenth and early seventeenth centuries: the Huitzo mills by merced in 1583, one Villa de Etla mill by merced in 1556 and the other by purchase from a noble in 1619, the San Gabriel mill by merced in 1592, and the San Agustín mill by merced in 1630.

Although these mills were an important source of income for the Etla communities, they were not always an unmixed blessing. The Indians' control over their mills was vulnerable to attack from several sides. In the 1590's Spaniards took over the principal mill at the Villa de Etla to grind their own wheat, leaving the Indian harvests to rot.[96] Mill-owning communities of Etla lodged a collective complaint again Spanish wheat farmers for the same abuse in the late eighteenth century.[97] A second threat to Indian mills was the loss of water power. Water for most of the community mills came from tributary streams originating in the mountains that abutted the Valley floor. The supply of running water for the town mill was at the mercy of the party upstream who controlled the source. Before 1686 the cacique of Etla sold a canyon supplying water to one of the Etla mills to a Spaniard, who first diverted the stream, completely shutting off Etla's water supply, then later agreed to rent the town water at the exorbitant rate of six pesos per day.[98] The San Agustín mill was forced to shut down in the mid-seventeenth century, when the owner of the Molinos de Lazo estate closed off the stream that operated the mill. By 1686 an agreement similar to that in the Etla case was reached: San Agustín paid the estate six pesos daily for four months of the year and three pesos daily during the remaining eight months.[99]

Despite the interest of Spaniards and Indians alike in owning and operating the mills, some shut down for long periods in the seventeenth and eighteenth centuries. The San Pablo mill lay idle from 1650 until 1714, when the town obtained a license to rebuild it. In 1781 it was reported that the San Gabriel mill had not been in working order for many years.[100] One of the Etla mills was rented out after 1744, as was the San Agustín mill in 1781. Two of the mills were completely lost to the Indian communities. One, belonging to Guelache, was sold in 1695; the second, belonging to Huitzo, was given to the local Dominican monastery.[101]

Water for irrigating Indian wheat and corn in the Valley of Etla was equally uncertain. Towns located on the alluvial plain, far from the headwaters of the mountain streams, were the most likely to lose their water supply. Eight Etla towns are known to have relied on other communities for their water. In several cases water was completely cut off; but in most the community worked out a rental or distribution agreement with the party closest to the source. The towns of Soledad Etla and San Juan Guelache obtained water for irrigation from sources belonging to the cacique of Etla, to whom they paid an annual rent. Guelache's water supply was temporarily shut off in 1669, when the cacique rented the toma de agua to Juan de Santaella, the owner of a nearby mill. Guelache solved its water problem in 1695 by purchasing the mill.[102] As already mentioned, the Villa de Etla and San Agustín Etla were obliged to pay as much as six pesos per day to the Spanish and creole landowners who controlled their feeder-streams. Santo Domingo Etla was in the same predicament.[103] Rental records for the town run from 1634 to 1799, when a renter of the Molinos de Lazo arbitrarily blocked off the stream to Santo Domingo's fields and refused to renew the rental. On petitioning Santo Domingo learned that the non-Indian owner was not bound to renew contracts with landowners downstream.*

Where two or more Indian towns using the same source of water for irrigation disagreed over rights, the royal guideline of "reparto de aguas por días como le parece," or distributing water by days, was applied.[104] One such dispute, lasting from the 1690's to the 1770's, involved a toma de agua of Soledad Etla that diverted water from the Atoyac River to fields of Soledad, Nazareno, and Guadalupe Etla on the western bank. In a 1703 ruling that was repeated in 1774 the judge apportioned 14 days of irrigation to Soledad because it owned lands nearest the toma, 9 days to Guadalupe, and 7 days to Nazareno.[105] A 1631 dispute between Reyes and Nativitas Etla over the use of the Magdalena River was resolved in favor of Nativitas because the stream was the town's only source of water, whereas Reyes was said to be able to irrigate from other sources.[106]

Huitzo and its subject towns at the northern end of the Etla arm seem to have fared better than towns to the south. Huitzo possessed two wheat mills and three ranches, all in the immediate vicinity of the townsite.[107] Although Huitzo reportedly lost arable land in the late seventeenth and early eighteenth centuries as a result of irresponsible sales by caciques, sharecroppers still

---

* CDChO, rollo 64, libro 4, cuaderno 8, 1799. Both Santo Domingo and San Agustín had experienced the uncertainty of renting stream water from the Spaniards before. (San Agustín had also rented water from the Molinos de Lazo at least as early as the 1630's.) In 1634 the Molinos de Lazo shut off the water supply originating on its lands.

came down from the mountains east of the Valley to work surplus community lands.[108] Huitzo rented two of its ranches from the 1690's on, which also suggests that the community owned more than enough land for its own use. Magdalena Apasco was another community in the northern end of the Etla valley with larger holdings than towns further south, including at least two ranches as well as irrigated farmland.*

Valley of Zimatlán. Lands in the Zimatlán valley were generally less productive than those in Etla. The area south of Antequera contained fewer tributary streams suitable for irrigation, and as a result most Indian lands yielded only one annual crop. The Atoyac River was more of a liability than an asset to native agriculture in the south. Few examples of irrigation off the Atoyac have been located; moreover, on several occasions floods deposited a thick layer of sand on lands adjoining the river and rendered them useless.

Indian towns of the southern valley produced one important commercial crop, cochineal, which did not require a great deal of first-rate farmland. Cochineal helped offset the problem of land shortage for a number of communities. Villaseñor and Murguía y Galardi (compilers of statistical surveys in the late eighteenth and early nineteenth centuries) indicate that nearly all communities south of Antequera tended stands of cactus that hosted the dye-rich cochineal insect.†

* AGNT 415, exp. 3, primera numeración, fol. 1r. The Indian holdings in the northern end of the Etla arm were larger, partly because the rolling terrain there was less suitable for the cultivation of wheat and the Spaniards were thus less interested in the area. Another reason for these large consolidated tracts is that since the jurisdiction of Huitzo lay outside the purview of the cacique of Etla, it was not divided up by extensive cacicazgo holdings.

Several communities closer to Antequera received mercedes for cattle estancias but were increasingly hemmed in by private estates during the late colonial period. San Andrés Ixtlahuaca received a merced for an estancia de ganado menor in 1623, as had Azompa in 1567. San Pedro Ixtlahuaca owned two estancias in the eighteenth century, one very near the Villa de Oaxaca.

† Villaseñor y Sánchez, 2 (book 4): 123; Murguía y Galardi, "Extracto general," segunda parte, partido de Zimatlán. Cochineal was produced in Ayoquesco, Quiechapa, Santa Cruz Mixtepec, and the Villa de Oaxaca, according to the *Relaciones Geográficas* of 1777. The quality of Valley cochineal was said to be inferior to that produced in the mountains and in the area to the south around Miahuatlán. BN 2450.

Native communities in the Valley of Zimatlán varied more widely in terms of population and landholdings than those in the Etla region. Most of the southern communities had good farmland, and some had access to irrigation.[109] But inequalities in landholdings brought serious problems of food supply, even to some fairly large Indian towns. Boundary tensions, small holdings, and fluctuating populations were characteristic of those parts of the southern arm where there were large Spanish haciendas or large, expanding Indian communities.

Cuilapan, the most populous Indian community in the Valley of Zimatlán, controlled the largest land area. A 1701 report described Cuilapan as having "more than four leagues of canyons, arable rolling hills, woodlands, pastures, and streams."[110] More precisely, we can identify seven sheep ranches (about 21 square miles), one cattle ranch (about 7 square miles), about 800 acres of cropland, and a large area of mountainous woodlands, in addition to an unknown expanse of arable fields and orchards lying just outside the community. All of the ranches appear to have been acquired in the sixteenth century. Two were located directly north of Cuilapan; two more, San Cristóbal and Manzano, were near San Pedro Ixtlahuaca; the fifth adjoined the Antequera–San Pedro road; the sixth spread along the fringe of the mountains between San Pedro and Cuilapan; and the seventh was located to the south, near San Lucas Tlanechico. The cattle ranch bordered on San Jacinto Amilpas, northwest of Antequera. Two ranches were sold by the community: one of the sheep ranches near San Pedro in 1575 and the cattle ranch in 1617. Cuilapan's lands also extended west at least six miles into the mountains to the borders of San Miguel de las Peras, San Pablo Cuatro Venados, and Santa María Peñoles.[111] In the late sixteenth century Cuilapan's farmlands stretched southward for a considerable distance. The *Relación Geográfica* for Teozapotlan (Zaachila) states that the town, five kilometers southeast of Cuilapan, was completely encircled by Cuilapan's lands.

Cuilapan produced a number of marketable commodities. Moist bottomlands were used for vegetable gardens and orchards of zapote and nut trees. The community obtained firewood and charcoal from its woodlands to the west.[112] Irrigation, enabling two annual crops, is mentioned in two colonial sources, one in the seventeenth century and one in the eighteenth, but water resources were apparently not plentiful enough for widespread irrigation.[113]

Cuilapan had a long history of boundary disputes and encroachments against neighboring Indian communities.[114] There were chronic troubles with Zaachila; and Cuilapan reportedly usurped land from the small Aztec towns near Antequera in the sixteenth century, and carried on a running, occasionally bloody dispute with its mountain neighbors to the west.* Cuilapan lost little land during the seventeenth century despite a considerable decline in population between 1570 and 1630, but by 1700 five Spanish estates had taken over Indian lands along the town's borders. Spanish estates grew in the area by buying cacicazgo lands and by occupying unclaimed territory.

Cuilapan enjoyed a surplus of good land to the end of the colonial period; the extent of its unused land, as determined by rental records from the eighteenth century, was unmatched in the Valley.[115] The San Cristóbal and Manzano ranches were rented from 1716 to 1808, the ranch near San Lucas was rented in 1786, a grazing site north of town in 1798, the ranch west of San Pedro Ixtlahuaca in 1774, and the ranch on the San Pedro–Antequera road as early as 1618.[116] The great expanse of Cuilapan's lands was noted by the early nineteenth-century geographer and hacendado José María Murguía y Galardi, who suggested that too much good land had bred indolence and insolence among Cuilapan's citizens.[117]

Whereas Mixtec Cuilapan enjoyed abundance, neighboring Zaachila, the former Zapotec capital, suffered a chronic shortage of land from the sixteenth century into the 1920's. Zaachila did receive two viceregal grants in the 1590's, one for a sheep ranch, the other for a piece of arable land.[118] The arable grant is itself a sign of land shortage, since nearly all other grants to Indian

---

* AGNT 395, exp. 1; AGNT 2941, exp. 96. Legal investigations into the dispute with the western mountain towns were initiated in 1586, 1721, and 1782, but the disagreement was never satisfactorily settled. Steininger and Van de Velde report that tensions between Cuilapan and San Pablo Cuatro Venado have survived into the twentieth century.

towns were for previously unused pastureland. According to the 1593 title the grant was made because Zaachila could not support its large population on existing community lands—even though the arable lands Zaachila did possess were fertile bottomlands.[119] These grants, combined with continuing population losses in the early seventeenth century, still did not relieve Zaachila's land problems. The town's attempt to expand its territory during this period runs counter to the general trend in the Valley toward sales and the contraction of community lands. Residents of Zaachila moved onto two ranches belonging to Santo Domingo Ocotlán in the late 1630's and unsuccessfully attempted to claim lands belonging to Coyotepec in 1664.[120]

Zaachila's land problems persisted into the eighteenth and nineteenth centuries. The only major change was that by 1750 the town was bordered by Spanish estates instead of by lands of Cuilapan: on the north by the Hacienda San José, on the east by the Haciendas Zorita and Mantecón, on the south by the Haciendas Tlanechico, Coronación, and Cortabarría, and on the northwest by the Hacienda de Noriega. In 1792 a petition on behalf of Zaachila complained that the community's lands were continually shrinking because of encroachments by neighboring haciendas: "Various hacendados daily encroach on our fields (some up to the very edge of our homes) to such an extent that we are hemmed into the townsite without any land to plant our crops."[121] A number of Zaachila's able-bodied men could not meet their annual tribute payments and were thus forced to serve on the haciendas or were put in jail.

Zaachila's predicament did not improve in the first years of Mexican independence. As Carlos María Bustamante observed in the 1820's, "This is a large community, but it does not possess the lands needed to sustain itself."[122] In the late nineteenth century, citizens of Zaachila had at their disposal only 1,782 hectares of land, including a 187-hectare townsite.[123] Zaachila's strong support for the agrarian movement in the 1920's, which met with only scattered enthusiasm elsewhere in the Valley, is understandable in view of this long history of land shortage.*

* Velasco, p. 133. The government subsequently transferred expropriated property to Zaachila, increasing its holdings to 4,922 hectares in 1926.

The landholdings of other Indian communities and their citizens in the southern arm range from less than the fundo legal to more than ten square leagues. Zimatlán and San Pedro Apostol at the southern end of the Valley rank with Cuilapan as leading landholders. As of 1717 Zimatlán possessed a swampy area obtained in 1715, an unknown amount of arable land, and five ranches: Quialana, Tres Ríos, Lobenisa, Segoba, and Lubixui.[124] One of the ranches was purchased from a Spaniard in 1554, and three others were secured by viceregal grant in 1571, 1582, and 1588. The Quialana site was sold in 1734, but by that time Zimatlán had purchased another ranch from Ocotlán bordering on the Atoyac River. Judging from community rentals in the eighteenth century, Zimatlán owned an excess of both arable land and pastureland: in 1721, 105 acres of the town's farmland were rented for nine years at 24 pesos annually; in 1708 the town's only cattle ranch was rented to a cofradía; the sheep ranch Tres Ríos was rented in the first decade of the eighteenth century; and Quialana was rented continuously from 1610 to 1734.[125] Records for San Pedro Apostol are less detailed but do suggest that the community had sizeable holdings. One 1709 document mentions a cattle estancia; and an inspection of San Pedro's fundo legal in 1776 records more than 600 varas in all directions, and quotes Indian witnesses as testifying that "we are well supplied with land."[126]

In contrast the relatively large towns of Santa Catarina Minas, Santa Ana Zegache, and Tlapacoya owned less, generally poorer land, and were plagued with tense boundary relations and with crop destruction by cattle from neighboring ranches.[127] Tlapacoya had at least two ranches, but both were rented because the community did not own enough livestock to keep them in use.[128] Some of Tlapacoya's arable land was periodically rendered useless by sands deposited along the Atoyac River. Maize, beans, and chile were produced on most of the town's farmland, though small quantities of wheat and sugar cane were also cultivated.[129] Santa Catarina Minas was in much the same situation as Tlapacoya, except that it was a major producer of cochineal.[130] The town owned three ranches, two of which were rented in the eighteenth century, but it had limited arable land and nowhere to expand. By 1644 there were no unclaimed lands in the southern valley, and Spanish estates had acquired much of the area in the mountains around Minas after the discovery of silver there in the late sixteenth century.[131]

Santa Ana Zegache also owned several grazing sites but little arable land. One ranch, obtained in a 1582 grant, was given to the local church in 1603; another, Lachigubicha, was rented out in 1708.[132] The fact that 39 householders of the community sharecropped for the local Dominican convent suggests a shortage of arable land. According to one eighteenth-century source cotton was grown in Zegache; but other records mention only that the town grew maize, beans, and chile, and had a small herd of swine.[133]

Coyotepec owned two ranches obtained by grant in the sixteenth century. Both were used for grazing sheep and goats and for cultivating maguey, the community's major cash crop. Firewood from the mountains east of town was another important source of income for the local Indians. Coyotepec's shortage of arable land was aggravated in the 1640's, when Gaspar de Espina, the owner of a neighboring hacienda, took over a section of the community's best land and used it to graze his cattle. These lands were returned to the town in 1647.[134] The southern towns of Guegorexe and Chilateca also relied on firewood and maguey for income, although Chilateca had the advantage of a *tianguis* (weekly market), which promoted such money-making activities as the vending of beverages and prepared food.[135]

Ocotlán had the most desirable holdings of all the southern communities below Cuilapan. These holdings probably did not exceed those of Tlapacoya or Minas in total area, but they included more farmland, which even though unirrigated, produced a large annual crop of maize.[136] Then, too, a popular weekly market was held on Fridays at Ocotlán during the colonial period. Ocotlán's two cattle ranches were apparently the major, if not the only, source of meat for the tianguis.[137] Ayoquesco, south of Ocotlán, also held a weekly market in the eighteenth century and owned much good farmland.[138] Part of Ayoquesco's arable land was let out to sharecroppers from the Mixtepec valley to the west.*

San Pablo Huistepec, as a post-conquest community, experienced a more radical change in its landholdings than other towns in the southern valley. Huistepec was established in the midsixteenth century by a small group of sharecroppers on the Hacienda Valdeflores. In 1584 they received title to a sheep ranch bordering on lands belonging to the Marqués del Valle, which became the townsite. In 1639 Huistepec acquired about 600 acres of arable land located two miles east of town; and when the Marqués del Valle's lands were left unattended in the 1640's, Huistepec laid claim to nearly the entire estate of four estancias. Between 1677 and 1699 the Marqués reclaimed his lands in court, but Huistepec could still afford to rent out a large plot holding 15 *fanegas de sembradura* (some 132 acres) in 1719.[139]

Judging from an inspection of the fundos legales of Indian towns in the southern arm in 1776, smaller communities near large Spanish estates were hard-pressed for land. The town lands of San Agustín Amatengo, Santa Lucía, San Pedro Mártir, San Lucas, Santiago Apostol, San Jacinto Ocotlán, San Andrés Ixtlahuaca, and Santísima Trinidad barely measured 600 varas and were surrounded by ranches and haciendas.† Many residents of San Raimundo Jalpan and San Antonio de la Cal are known to have worked as day laborers or sharecroppers on nearby haciendas, owing to the shortage of community lands.[140]

The Indian towns surrounding Antequera urgently needed land in the eighteenth century. The populous Villa de Oaxaca, separated from Antequera on the east by only the width of a street, bounded on the west by the Atoyac River, and hemmed in by private *labores* on the north and south, had insufficient farmland and no room for expansion. One of the few stretches

---

* Méndez, pp. 180–84. Many Mixtepec towns lacked farmland because of the swampy conditions along the Quelobigoa River. The inhabitants of several of these towns turned to other pursuits, such as gathering firewood and pine sap and making amole, a kind of soap. Residents of San Miguel Mixtepec were said to have engaged in trade, principally bringing salt to their district from Tehuantepec. BN 2450, fol. 18v.

† AGNT 997, 1:1–38. San Andrés Ixtlahuaca, however, is known to have owned two ranches. AGNG 24, exp. 326.

of open land at the Villa's disposal was a small ranch west of the river, rented from San Pedro Ixtlahuaca.[141] This land shortage meant that most residents of Oaxaca could not depend on agriculture for their livelihood. Some townspeople remained in the Villa as hat makers, and many others probably found employment in Antequera as vendors, servants, and textile workers. (As many as 500 looms may have been in use in the city's *obrajes*, or textile workshops, at the end of the eighteenth century.[142]) The neighboring towns of San Juan Chapultepec and Jalatlaco also suffered shortages of land. Chapultepec controlled even less than its fundo legal of 600 varas in 1760. Owing to population pressures the entire barrio of Santa Anita was abandoned between 1760 and 1778, which left just enough land for the barrio of San Juan to remain intact.[143] The somewhat larger community of San Martín Mexicapan, the village primarily responsible for Chapultepec's loss of land, owned three ranches and a number of small plots; but because of debts accumulated in various lawsuits, it was forced to rent out all but enough arable land to support the community.[144] Jalatlaco, on the eastern fringe of Antequera, also barely included the 600-vara townsite. It had rented land from Antequera as early as 1533.[145] The author of Jalatlaco's 1777 *Relación Geográfica* blamed the gradual abandonment of the town on water shortages and diminishing community lands.[146] By the eighteenth century residents of this early post-conquest village relied more on small family enterprises than on farming to support themselves. They made hats, produced charcoal and lime, mined clay, and collected mineral water for sale to other natives and Spaniards.[147]

Xoxocotlán, southeast of Antequera, possessed little community land because of its long terrasguerro relationship with the caciques of Cuilapan. Later in the colonial period private farms grew up to the south and west, lying within 600 and 1,900 varas of the town.[148] Some 200 acres of community land, located a kilometer to the east between the Atoyac and Jalatlaco rivers, was lost to the Hacienda San Miguel when the Atoyac suddenly changed course.[149] A long period of fruitless litigation ensued. Still, if limited by terrasguerro status and the proximity of private estates, many residents of Xoxocotlán had the use of fertile lands, which produced maize, beans, other vegetables, some sugar cane, maguey, and fruit trees. Xoxocotlán had no special crafts or industries, but the women contributed to the community's income by supplying *tortillas* to Antequera.[150]

Valley of Tlacolula. The division of land between Indians and non-Indians in the Tlacolula valley had crystallized by the first half of the seventeenth century, with Indian communities controlling large sections of arable land and grazing land. The fact that most Indian tracts bordered on other Indian tracts rather than Spanish estates is a striking characteristic of the eastern arm of the Valley. According to colonial records most eighteenth-century land disputes there were among Indian pueblos, suggesting that the area escaped the major changes in land tenure experienced by the northwestern and southern arms. In contrast to the extensive land claims and transfers recorded in the 1644 composiciones de tierras for Etla and Cuilapan, the first half of the seventeenth century saw only the founding of the Mayorazgo de Guendulain in the Tlacolula valley. The prevalence of Indian sharecroppers around Santa María del Tule, the center of the Guendulain estate, does indicate a shortage of community lands in this area, but elsewhere in the eastern valley debt peonage and landless natives were rare. A 1553 agreement on an exact boundary between two of the larger communities, Mitla and Tlacolula, helps to explain how Indian lands were preserved. The early date of this document gave the two communities clear title to the land before Spanish cattlemen could overrun it. Consequently no Spanish estancias bordered on this land, although there were several in the area between Teotitlán del Valle and Mitla in the sixteenth century. The boundary settlement did not, however, prevent serious land disputes among Tlacolula, Teotitlán del Valle, and Macuilxóchitl in the eighteenth century.[151]

The size of Indian holdings in the Valley of Tlacolula must be considered in light of their relative infertility. Owing to the arid climate and limited opportunities for irrigation, Indian towns needed more land to meet their basic needs. Maize, beans, and chile were about the only food crops that could be successfully grown, although tomatoes were found at Santa María Guelaxe and wheat fields at San Francisco Lachigolo, San Marcos Tlapazola, and Teotitlán del Valle.[152] In many areas sizeable holdings and relative infertility promoted extensive rather than intensive land use. Sheep raising and the cultivation of maguey were important activities. Maguey was grown in nearly all eastern towns, the following being the major producers in the first decade of the nineteenth century: Tlalixtac, 8,000 plants; Matatlán, 6,000; Tomaltepec, 5,000; Tlacochahuaya, 4,000; San Sebastián Teitipac, 4,000; San Juan Teitipac, 3,100; Santa Cruz Papalutla, 3,000; and Macuilxóchitl, 3,000.[153] Much of the maguey was apparently grown by individuals rather than by communities; two residents of Tlacochahuaya, for example, owned 1,130 plants.[154] Sheep were raised in Macuilxóchitl, Tlacolula, Santiago Ixtaltepec, Mitla, Teotitlán del Valle, San Lucas Quiavini, and Santo Domingo del Valle.[155]

Both major agricultural products, maguey and sheep, promoted local industries that supplemented community revenues. Several distilleries in Tlalixtac and Tlacolula produced pulque and mezcal from maguey juice. Both towns supplied liquor to Antequera and maintained local taverns. Sheep raising provided wool for weaving blankets and serapes, a craft confined to the Tlacolula valley. Residents of Santo Domingo del Valle (Díaz Ordaz), Tlacolula, Mitla, Macuilxóchitl, and Teotitlán del Valle were weavers in the eighteenth century.[156]

Several other towns also developed local industries. Santa Cecilia produced wooden spoons; San Lorenzo Albarradas and San Baltazar, in the mountains east of the Valley, wove *petates* (palm leaf mats); San Andrés Huayapan was a pilgrimage site in the colonial period; and Mitla held a weekly market on Thursdays during the eighteenth century.[157] Towns located near the edge of the Valley gathered firewood from the surrounding mountains and made charcoal to sell in the local and regional markets. Residents of Santa Cecilia, San Felipe del Agua, Tlacochahuaya, Magdalena Teitipac, Tlacolula, and San Sebastían Teitipac earned money in this way. Many of the Valley's itinerant Indian merchants were apparently from the Tlacolula arm. Several

1576 documents mention that Teotitlán del Valle, Macuilxóchitl, Mitla, Tlacolula, and San Juan Teitipac had "many trad-
ers and merchants."[158]

As in the Zimatlán arm landholdings of Indian communities
in the Valley of Tlacolula varied greatly in size. Generally, the
larger communities controlled considerably more land than the
smaller ones, owing both to original disparities and subsequent
encroachments. Tlacochahuaya in the eighteenth century is the
classic example, reducing San Francisco Lachigolo, Santa María
Guelaxe, and Santo Domingo to their fundos legales. Without
irrigation or local industries, these three towns suffered greatly
from the shortage of productive land. By 1788 Tlacochahuaya
controlled 19,649,000 square varas around the town; in addition
its residents privately owned woods and arable land as far west
as the mountains above Coyotepec.* Since Tlacochahuaya was
located in a particularly dry part of the Valley and was considered to be "one of the most sterile towns in this region," it under-
standably needed more land to support its residents than did
communities working the humid, black soil of the Etla arm.[159]

The landholdings of Tlalixtac, eight kilometers east of Antequera, were considerable, and the town prospered at the expense
of its smaller neighbors, Santo Domingo Tomaltepec and Santa
María del Tule. Tlalixtac's lands came to within 600 varas of
Tule on three sides and within 600 varas of Tomaltepec on two
sides.† In addition to arable lands, some of which were irrigated,
Tlalixtac owned at least two sheep ranches. The town's prosperity, reflected in her fertile lands and well-kept houses with
tile roofs, was undiminished throughout the colonial period. Bustamante was moved to remark in the 1820's that Tlalixtac was
"a large and beautiful town, the result of fertile lands and abundant waters."[160] Various lands not used by members of the community, including the ranches, were rented. A 1695 incident indicates that Tlalixtac had more land than it desired to use. When

---

* AGNT 1206, 1:14r, 1788. Tlacochahuaya also claimed to own community land
near Coyotepec. ADAA, exp. 276.1, p. 1370.
† AGNT 997, 1:35v. Tule received a merced for an estancia de ganado menor in
1615, but by the eighteenth century most of its residents were terrasguerros on
the Hacienda de Guendulain. AGNT 2922, 1:10v.

several *principales* illegally rented out a tract of community land, the cabildo demanded payment rather than the return of the land.[161]

San Sebastián Tutla and San Juan Teitipac were two other towns with sizeable holdings amidst smaller towns complaining of shortages. Two early-eighteenth-century records report that San Sebastían rented out several pieces of unused land, whereas the nearby towns of Santa Lucía and Santa Cruz Amilpas possessed only a little more than the fundo legal.[162] San Juan Teitipac enjoyed the same advantage over its neighbor San Jacinto, whose lands measured about half of the fundo legal and were completely surrounded by the larger town's fields.[163] San Juan's lands stretched southward to Santa Cecilia Jalieza. Plate I (page 76), dated 1798, shows that residents of San Juan planted cornfields only a few hundred meters northeast of Santa Cecilia; the rest of the land between the towns was apparently used strictly for grazing. San Juan experienced the usual run of boundary disputes with its Indian neighbors, principally with Santa Cruz Papalutla, San Sebastián Teitipac, and Tlacochahuaya in the eighteenth century.*

San Sebastián's lands included two sheep ranches, one of which was bought from the local cacique in 1769 for 1,100 pesos.[164] Many residents of the town gathered firewood and cultivated maguey, which were traded with other communities for maize, salt, and chile.[165] Several early-seventeenth-century wills help explain the need to trade for corn and other basic foodstuffs. These documents reveal that seven individuals owned more than 550 medidas of arable fields (at least 322 acres). Many of the tracts were classified as moist bottomlands, the most productive of San Sebastián's lands.[166]

The community of Tlacolula, located in the eastern portion of the arm, where towns were farther apart, early laid down a solid base for its land claims. In 1553 the town concluded an agreement with Mitla on an eastern boundary; in 1561 it received the title to a sheep ranch; and in 1565, on orders from

* AGNT 185, 16:1–2. Land disputes between Tlacochahuaya and San Juan Teitipac go back to the 1550's. ENE, 8: 228.

the Viceroy, it distributed all vacant lands in the vicinity among its citizens.[167] In the eighteenth century Tlacolula's lands extended approximately three-quarters of a league west to a border with San Juan Guelavia, one to two leagues north and northwest to borders with Santa Ana and Macuilxóchitl, and about one league south and southeast to borders with San Juan Teitipac, Mitla, and the Hacienda Tanibé.[168] The community took over half an estancia from the cacique of Tlacolula in 1717 and also bought houses from individual town residents as investments.[169]

San Juan Guelavia, to the west of Tlacolula, owned at least one grazing site and two large tracts of arable land bordering on lands of San Marcos Tlapazola. Because of costly boundary disputes with San Marcos and Tlacolula, Guelavia had to borrow 400 pesos from Spaniards, who in return secured rights to certain community lands while the debt remained unpaid. Irrigation from the Salado River was a mixed blessing to Guelavia, since there were internal wranglings over the distribution of the water. In 1807 jealous citizens with small holdings shut off the canal that supplied water to other Indians, thus destroying their crops.[170]

Although owning sufficient lands, Mitla was the one large community of the eastern section of the Valley frequently in conflict with Spanish estates. In the eighteenth century the town was bordered on the east by the Hacienda Xaagá, on the north by the rancho del Fuerte, on the northwest by the sitio de Don Pedrillo, and on the southwest by the Hacienda Tanibé. The extremely bitter land disputes between Mitla and the Hacienda Xaagá started in the mid-sixteenth century over water rights; a ranching tract that later became part of the hacienda contained one of Mitla's two principal sources of water. A 1791 land map indicates that the dividing line drawn by Mitla and Tlacolula in 1553 (1549, according to the map) was still intact, although Don Pedrillo and del Fuerte had since been established on Mitla's side of the line. The map does not show Mitla's two sheep ranches, obtained by merced in 1565 and 1594, but it does show arable land and pastureland south and west of the town. By 1791 Mitla had lost the extensive community lands to the north described

in the *Relación Geográfica* of 1581,[171] owing not to Spanish encroachment but to the splitting away of Santa Catarina and San
Miguel, which became separate towns with their own lands.

The limited information on Teotitlán del Valle, Macuilxóchitl, and Santiago Ixtaltepec suggests that these towns also had
sizeable holdings. A 1782 boundary description identified the
mountains to the north and west as far as Santa Catarina de Sena
as belonging to Ixtaltepec. Burgoa described Teotitlán del Valle's
lands as fertile, though without irrigation. The community had
received a merced for an estancia de ganado menor by 1612, and
several individuals are known to have owned small ranches and
distant tracts of arable land. Macuilxóchitl owned three ranches,
one of which was sold in 1597.[172]

Conclusion

The Indians of Oaxaca were not an inactive element in the complex, changing colonial society. Native peasants and communities were important landholders throughout the period. They
worked the best of the Valley's cropland in the sixteenth century and in general were still self-sufficient farmers on the eve
of the independence movement in 1810. Only a handful of communities became dependent on lands they did not own. Three
or four towns relied on Spanish haciendas for their basic needs,
and the residents of several others sharecropped. The Indian
peasant actually had more communal and personal land at his
disposal in the colonial period than he has today, owing to the
recent growth of Oaxaca's population and the limited possibilities for land redistribution after the Revolution of 1910. The
reasons for the persistence of Indian lands in the Valley of Oaxaca are implicit in the foregoing discussion, but they merit a
more direct statement.

The Indian element. The large Indian population was orga-
nized into distinct communities occupying specific and sizeable
areas of land. The Indians had a well-developed sense of property ownership, which was reflected in the grants, title confirmations, and boundary agreements they obtained by request in the
sixteenth century, before many Spaniards acquired Valley lands.

The Indians' appreciation of the importance of formal wills left very little Indian property intestate despite great population losses. Oaxaca's Indians quickly learned the legal options open to them in seeking new lands and in preserving title to old ones. Their initiative and endurance in litigation is certainly impressive.

The colonial government. The interest of the royal government and the Marqués del Valle in collecting Indian tribute tended to protect Indian lands. A seventeenth-century instruction from the Marqués to his alcalde mayor charged him to "preserve and protect the Indians. . . . Where not disputed, let them own the lands they cultivate."[173] Tribute established a sensitive and continuous connection between the colonial government and Indian communities, serving to check usurpation. In 1647, for example, after Coyotepec was unable to pay its annual tribute, the Audiencia immediately ordered an inquiry that resulted in the restoration of community lands illegally taken by Gaspar de Espina, one of the leading hacendados in the southern arm.[174]

The legal system. The Spanish system of justice tended to protect Indian lands in the Valley. The colonial courts provided an avenue of redress that the Indians came to know well. The Audiencia and the Juzgado de Indios in particular heard many disputes involving Valley Indians. Although decisions were often delayed for many years, the records of these land cases suggest that the judges made an honest effort to rule fairly on the basis of the facts available to them. Even when facing a Spanish opponent in court, the Indians often won.

The legal doctrine that colonial authorities were to recognize as legitimate the Indians' claims to land held *de inmemorial tiempo* (that is, at the time of the conquest) was the vehicle for the confirmation of much Indian land in the Valley. At the local level heavy fines were levied on Spaniards who attempted to monopolize the meat supply to Indian markets. Sales and rentals of Indian lands were revoked when the price agreed on was not just, or when the procedure of obtaining government permission and publicly announcing sales had not been followed.

Still, in the final analysis, the legal system had an inherent bias in favor of Spaniards. The following commentary, written by a corregidor of Antequera who had just ruled for an hacendado in a land dispute with San Pedro Etla, reveals that the criteria for evaluating evidence placed Indian communities at a definite disadvantage. The corregidor assumed that the testimony of an Indian could not carry as much weight as that of a Spaniard, ignoring the possibility that vested interests might have colored the hacendados' testimony:

[In reaching a verdict] it is essential to review the number, quality, and circumstances of the witnesses, as well as the other evidence submitted by the parties involved.... As for the evidence of the said natives, we find that it is presented by twelve witnesses: one Spaniard, three mulattoes, and the rest Indians—whose testimony does not completely agree.... [It is] defective in comparison with [that of] the Spanish witnesses, *gente de razón*, who affirm the contrary. Even though the evidence of don Pedro de la Vega is presented by fewer witnesses, we find that only one of these is a mulatto. The nine Spaniards, men of quality, have a clearer and firmer knowledge of the disputed lands because several of them are owners of the said San Joseph and El Vergel haciendas, others are their overseers and administrators, and others rent or live on or near these lands. Most of the said Spaniards are well known as men of truth, integrity, and esteem. Therefore, the evidence of the said don Pedro, in regard to the boundary violation in which the two parties are opposed, is better and more worthy of credit.[175]

Undoubtedly the legal system was twisted or circumvented entirely by some of the Indians' opponents. But the colonial legal system cannot be dismissed as totally irrelevant in the shaping of land tenure in Oaxaca. It is absurd to think that the pattern of land distribution would have been the same if Spanish policy had sanctioned the usurpation of Indian lands and denied the Indians any legal means of redress.

Spanish residents of the Valley. There were only a small number of Spaniards in Oaxaca in the sixteenth century, and they were preoccupied with mining and cattle ranching; thus the Indians had a period of grace in which to learn about the Spanish judicial system and to acquire written evidence of their ownership of specific lands. The Spanish cabildo of Antequera, representing the white society, issued decrees in the sixteenth century encouraging Indian communities to expand their holdings and farmlands in order to meet the demand for foodstuffs among the city-dwelling Spaniards.[176] If we can believe Burgoa and his disciples, the Church, particularly the Dominicans, defended the Indians' right to their lands and educated them to the necessity of securing valid titles.

It is difficult to say which, if any, of these factors could have been eliminated without greatly affecting the pattern of Indian land distribution. The importance of each is so closely dependent on one or more of the others that they can be separated only artificially. For example, could the legal system have protected Indian lands if the Indians themselves had not been disposed to appeal their grievances? Could the Indians have secured possession of such a large portion of the Valley's arable land through legal channels if the Spaniards in Antequera had not been dependent on them for food in the sixteenth century? All of the factors mentioned above are crucial, and the absence of any one of them might account for meager Indian holdings elsewhere in New Spain.

IV

SPANISH ESTATES

THE HISTORY of Spanish estates in the Valley of Oaxaca does not parallel the growth of the Spanish community. The acquisition of land by Spaniards was minimal up until 1570, when the population of Antequera had already reached 3,000. This delay was partly because of Cortez's efforts to shield the Valley from Spanish colonists, and partly because of the limited interest in land ownership shown by those Spaniards who did penetrate his domain.

The first Spanish settlement in the Valley was a garrison of 120 soldiers who remained after the military expedition of Francisco de Orozco in 1521. Situated at the hub of the three arms of the Valley, the garrison was to grow into the colonial city of Antequera. In 1526 the Spanish community there, now consisting of 50 families, received formal recognition from the King and the royal title of "villa." The early colonists were apparently attracted by the large supply of native labor and the discovery of gold in the Etla region.[1] The movement of Spaniards into the Valley slackened at the end of the decade, as Cortez sought to protect his claims from interlopers by means of a legal action against the permanent community at Antequera. His original 1529 title to the Marquesado del Valle de Oaxaca afforded him jurisdiction over almost the entire valley;[2] and as of 1531 he seemed to be winning the court case to preserve his authority. Meanwhile, approximately 4,000 Aztec and Tlaxcalan Indians who had served in the Spanish entrada into Oaxaca settled in small towns on the outskirts of Antequera: the Villa de Oaxaca,

Santo Tomás Xochimilco, San Martín Mexicapan, Jalatlaco, and Santa María Ixcotel. These and other nearby towns effectively hemmed Antequera in, making it impossible for the Spanish community to acquire adjacent pastureland, except for a narrow stretch to the southeast.*

In 1531 and 1532 the Spanish residents of Antequera gained the upper hand in their struggle with Cortez. The Audiencia had illegally but permanently stripped him of 16 Indian districts in the southern and eastern portions of the Valley.† Then in 1532 Antequera's emissary to the King, Diego de Porras, returned with a royal decree granting Antequera the privileges of a city and the right to use royal lands as communal pastures.[3] The Crown was now fully committed to a Spanish settlement in the Valley. The decision in favor of Antequera hinged on several factors, notably the presence of a representative of the community at court, a growing royal suspicion of Cortez's independent power, and perhaps most important, reports of large gold deposits in the Chichicapa area in 1531.[4]

Cortez's power in the Valley was limited in 1533 by a cédula real that redefined the terms of the 1529 Marquesado del Valle title.[5] The cédula stated clearly that the Marquesado grant did not include title to lands within the Valley of Oaxaca but was essentially an encomienda grant for the Cuatro Villas of Oaxaca, Cuilapan, Etla, and Tlapacoya and their sujetos. A 1538 decree further limited the Marqués del Valle's control over land in the Valley by forbidding him to reserve woodlands and vacant royal lands within the Marquesado for his own use.‡

---

* Gay, tomo 1, vol. 2, p. 448. The residents of Antequera were uneasy about the encirclement of the city by Indian towns and requested the Viceroy's permission to build a fortress. *Instrucciones que los vireyes*, pp. 239–40. In a letter to the King dated February 25, 1552, Viceroy Luis de Velasco referred to the city's predicament: "Cuilapan has the city of Antequera surrounded. The residents have no place to farm or graze their livestock, except in the jurisdiction of the Marqués del Valle." RAHM, vol. 113, fol. 137.
† The disputed districts were Macuilxóchitl, Teotitlán del Valle, Chichicapa, Ocotlán, Mixtepec, Tepezimatlán, Peñoles, Tlacochahuaya, Mitla, Tlacolula, Teitipac, Zaachila, Zimatlán, Tlapacoya, Coyotepec, and Huitzo. AGIJ 224, 117, 192.
‡ Chevalier, *La formation*, p. 107. In 1532 Valley Indians testified that they were well treated by Cortez and wished to remain in the Marquesado. AGIJ 117.

Spanish Land Tenure in the Sixteenth Century

Although students of the period disagree about whether the Marqués owned the land within the Marquesado by right, the holders of the grant in the sixteenth century did not act as if they had private property rights over the area. The two Valley estates owned by the Marquesado before 1600 were both acquired by purchase and with royal approval. A large cattle estate in the southern end of the Valley, composed of five estancias de ganado mayor and menor, was originally purchased in 1529 by Diego de Guinea, Cortez's administrator for the Cuatro Villas jurisdiction, from the cacique of Tlapacoya for one piece of gold. Guinea then ceded this property to Cortez in 1539.[6] The other Marquesado holding consisted of arable land and a wheat mill in the Etla arm at the present site of the Molinos de Lazo estate. Guinea also purchased this property from two natives of Etla in 1543.[7]

Interest in the ownership and operation of the two Valley estates was greatest in the 1540's and 1550's, when Fernando Cortez and then his son Martín served as Marqués. The cattle estancias held the *abasto de carne* (monopoly on the meat supply) for Antequera at that time, and 4,500 mulberry trees were planted on the Etla estate in an effort to develop the silk industry in the Valley.[8] Waning interest in the Valley lands is first apparent in 1564, when Martín Cortez rented one of the estancias with 200 ganado mayor.* By 1572 all five estancias had been let out, and rentals continued until the 1630's, when the estate lapsed into complete disuse. The decreasing attention to the cattle properties in the southern arm is also illustrated by the falling number of livestock on the Marquesado estate from 1549 to 1636 (see Table 8). The abasto de carne continued at least until 1576, however, since a rental agreement in that year stipulated that the tenant supply 1,000 steers to Antequera annually.[9]

The Marquesado's mill at Etla was rented in 1590 and sold

---

* AGNH 404, exp. 2. Earlier, in 1552, the Marqués had attempted to rent out Indian lands near Ocotlán. The rental was voided and the lands returned to the native owners. AGNH 85, exp. 6.

TABLE 8

Livestock on the Marquesado Estate, 1549–1636

Date	Cattle	Horses	Sheep	Pigs
1549	1,406	348	—	2,760
1569	2,000	438	8,144	—
1578	—	765	9,515	—
1590	—	130	9,000	—
1598	—	297	7,500	—
1615	—	—	2,630	—
1632	—	—	2,643	—
1636	—	—	—	—

SOURCE: AGNH 146, 430:329–45.

the following year to Rafael Pinelo.[10] The cattle estate, abandoned from 1636 to 1734, was invaded by neighboring Indian towns, notably San Pablo Huistepec. After a long period of litigation in the late seventeenth and early eighteenth centuries, the Marqués recovered much of the lost land; but the estate lay in ruins throughout the eighteenth century.[11] Even at the height of their productivity, the Marqués did not make a concerted effort to expand the cattle estate and the mill site. By the late 1560's loans to local Spaniards, which totaled 15,961 pesos, were the principal Marquesado investment in the Valley.[12]

The declining interest of the Marqueses in land ownership in the Valley of Oaxaca after the late sixteenth century was related both to viceregal restrictions and to the unprofitability of the Valley properties, especially in comparison with the Marquesado's sugar plantations near the Valley of Mexico. The silk-raising venture, not mentioned after 1550, apparently failed completely. The cattle estancias were hurt by the viceregal decrees of Antonio de Mendoza, Luis de Velasco I, and Martín Enríquez that limited ganado mayor in the Valley. As a result the estate's livestock enterprise became centered in the Bajío-Aguascalientes region north of Mexico City. By the early eighteenth century at least ten haciendas in the Bajío were attached to the Marquesado. Two of these holdings, Las Mesillas and Los Molinos, controlled some 1,500 square kilometers and over

83,000 head of cattle and sheep.[13] Since the limited holdings in Oaxaca were more than 300 kilometers over rough terrain from the core of the Marquesado's wealth in the area of Morelos and the Valley of Mexico, it is not surprising that they received little attention.

The question of the Marqués del Valle's ownership of lands within the Marquesado jurisdiction of the Valley was clearly settled in the sixteenth century: the Marqués did not *ipso facto* own any lands in the Valley. Who had the power to grant lands within the Marquesado—the Crown or the Marqués—was less certain. Although no mercedes authorized by the Marqués del Valle have been found for the Valley of Oaxaca, Fernando Cortez apparently allotted lands near San Martín Mexicapan and San Juan Chapultepec to Nahua immigrants.[14] In the early seventeenth century the Marqués del Valle laid claim to various unoccupied lands within the Cuatro Villas jurisdiction and granted these lands to individuals in *censo perpetuo* contracts. With some exceptions the Crown accepted these grants as valid. Since all the territory the Marqués is known to have claimed was immediately assigned to others, it is unlikely that he kept any of these *baldíos* (vacant lands) for his own use. Like the *donatarios* who held proprietary grants in sixteenth-century Brazil, he apparently could make land grants in his domain but could not, in effect, grant the same lands to himself.[15]

Censos perpetuos were very nearly full grants of ownership. (See Appendix C for an example of such a grant.) There were four principal restrictions on the ownership of lands received from the Marqués del Valle in censo perpetuo: (1) the recipient had to pay a fixed annual rent, and under no circumstances could he request a lower one; (2) the land could not be sold without the permission of the Marqués del Valle, although in practice approval seems to have been automatic; (3) within 30 days after the transfer of property, the new owner had to acknowledge his obligation to pay the censo; and (4) a 5 per cent fee, the *veintena*, was to be paid by the new owner at the time of transfer.[16]

The revenue-conscious Pedro Cortez was the father of censos perpetuos in the Marquesado portion of the Valley. (Such grants

were also common elsewhere in the Marquesado at this time.[17])
Between 1618 and 1623 he made 22 grants, yielding an annual
income of 847 pesos. Thereafter, the income from censos declined rapidly. On September 23, 1623, the Audiencia of Mexico
voided all censo perpetuo grants made to Indians, apparently
allowing the Indians to keep the lands. This cut the number of
Valley censos to 12 properties, which returned 316 pesos in annual rent. Two more of the original censos were canceled before
1635, when it was found they rightfully belonged to Indians.
By 1657 there were only six Marquesado censos left in the Valley,
with a total annual rent of 93 pesos. Between 1657 and 1828 one
more censo was lost and seven others were added; thus the Marquesado was still collecting perpetual rents on 12 Valley properties in the 1820's.[18]

Although the existence of Antequera was assured by the royal
decisions of 1532 and 1533, the community still did not have
enough land. In the 1540's and again in 1551, 1558, and 1562,
Antequera initiated lawsuits to force the Villa de Oaxaca and
other nearby Indian towns to withdraw so that it could use
adjacent lands for pasture.[19] These actions were unsuccessful,
since the viceregal government was reluctant to seize Indian
lands in the first half of the sixteenth century.[20] Antequera existed as a parasite in the 1540's and early 1550's. Reduced to 30
families in 1544, the Spanish population of the "city" subsisted
almost entirely on Indian tribute and salaried government ap-
pointments. The citizens were described as "all very poor and
needy people."[21]

Antequera's quest for pasture was not accompanied by a similar demand for cropland. The Spaniards preferred to rely almost
exclusively on Indian sources for foodstuffs. Petitions submitted
to the King by the cabildo of Antequera in 1532 urged him to
order Indians in the district to sell food to Spaniards in the city.
Bishop López de Zárate complained on behalf of the city in
1538 that Valley natives were not cultivating all the lands available to them, and that as a result there was a shortage of wheat
and corn. In 1551 the cabildo again urged the Crown to order
Indians to produce wheat, silk, and other commodities for the

Spaniards, arguing that otherwise the natives would produce only what they needed for the royal tribute and would become lazy and quarrelsome.[22] Antequera's dependence on the Indians for food is further reflected in recurrent pleas that more Indian towns be brought into its political jurisdiction, and in a 1551 order by the cabildo that more Indian lands be cultivated to meet the cereal needs of the city.[23]

The late 1550's represent an important turning point in the economic development of Antequera. From this point on, the city's landholdings slowly expanded, as did its population. A 1554 letter from Fray Bernardo de Albuquerque to the Council of the Indies helps explain why this happened: the Indian population around the city was declining at a noticeably faster rate than elsewhere in the Valley, leaving nearby lands vacant.[24] Royal mercedes for cattle estancias in 1555 and 1563 also helped to alleviate Antequera's shortage of pastureland.[25] Land shortage remained a problem in the late sixteenth century, and impoverished Spanish residents continued to seek political office as a substitute for the landed wealth beyond their reach. Nevertheless, the early-seventeenth-century traveler Thomas Gage could describe Antequera as a thriving community.[26] By the end of that century Antequera's ejidos extended west across the Atoyac River and south to the junction of the Atoyac and the Jalatlaco. Community pastureland was still scarce, however, because the Indian towns were now growing again, and because available ejido lands had been divided into small, private orchards and grazing sites as early as the 1540's. In 1722 Antequera could not find a meat supplier because it did not have enough grazing land for the number of cattle annually required for slaughter.[27]

In the sixteenth century Spaniards used Valley lands primarily for grazing cattle. The Spanish custom of moving livestock between mountain and lowland pastures, and the principle of common pasturage, whereby unoccupied lands were open for all private cattle, meant that Spanish holdings were fluid and without specific boundaries. Often they were not confirmed in writing for a number of years. For example, Cristóbal Gil, a regidor of Antequera, and Rodrigo Pacheco grazed cattle on two estan-

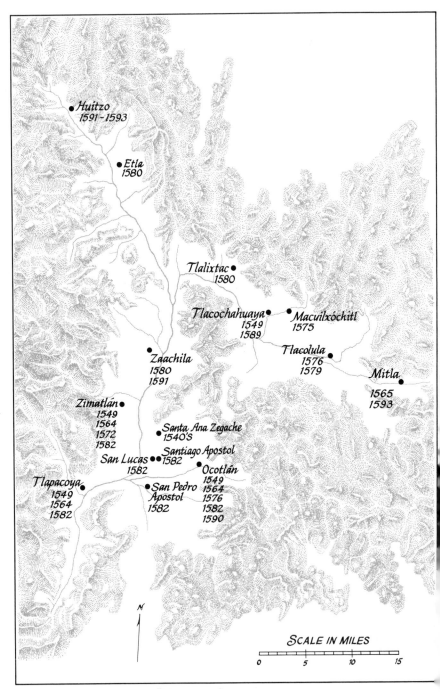

Map 3. Indian Towns Suffering Damage from Spanish Cattle
in the Sixteenth Century

cias near Tlacochahuaya as early as 1523, but these holdings were not formalized until 1538 by mercedes from the cabildo of Antequera.[28] The Spanish cabildo made other grants of cattle estancias in the late 1530's and early 1540's before the power to issue mercedes was limited to the Viceroy. We know of at least three others: a grant to Bartolomé Sánchez in 1539 for an estancia de ganado mayor near San Juan Guelavia, and grants dated 1541 and 1544.[29] These were canceled by later viceregal mercedes.

The known viceregal land grants to Spaniards in the Valley of Oaxaca during the sixteenth and early seventeenth centuries are listed in Appendix D. Of the 25 mercedes 21 fall between 1560 and 1605, with nine in the decade 1560–70 and eight more in the decade 1590–1600. Only one of these mercedes was granted for the Valley of Etla; 11 were granted for the Valley of Zimatlán and 13 for the Valley of Tlacolula.

Indian complaints of encroachment by Spanish cattle are another source of information about Spanish-occupied lands in the Valley. Like the records of mercedes they show that sixteenth-century Spanish ranches were concentrated in the southern portion of the Zimatlán arm and in pockets of the Tlacolula arm (see Map 3). The five large Marquesado del Valle ranches accounted for recurrent damage to the towns of Ocotlán, Zimatlán, and Santa Ana Zegache. Other towns south of Cuilapan reporting one or more incidents of damage by Spanish cattle were Ayoquesco, Tlapacoya, San Pedro Apostol, Santiago Apostol, San Lucas Ocotlán, Zaachila, Santa Catarina Minas, and Chichicapa. In the southeastern arm Tlacochahuaya, Macuilxóchitl, Teotitlán del Valle, Tlalixtac, Tlacolula, and Mitla filed complaints. The number of complaints in the southeast was small considering the number of estancias there. This was probably because the Indian population was smaller and more concentrated than in the Zimatlán valley, leaving much unoccupied land for pasture.

From the evidence we have of mercedes, sales, and Indian complaints, we can identify 15 estancias in the southern arm and 12 in the southeastern arm in the sixteenth century. In the south, in addition to the five Marquesado estancias, there were four near Cuilapan and Xoxocotlán, two east of San Pedro Apostol, and four north of Tlapacoya. In the southeast, there were three estancias near Tlacochahuaya (the two formalized by the cabildo of Antequera in 1538 and one belonging to the encomendero of Tlacochahuaya), one near Tlalixtac in 1592, one west of San Juan Teitipac in the 1580's, one south of Teotitlán del Valle in 1604, two near Macuilxóchitl before 1565, and four east of Mitla, granted in 1564, 1571, 1583, and 1591.

In contrast to the south and the southeast, the Etla region did not have many Spanish cattle estancias in the sixteenth century. Only three mercedes are known, one near San Andrés Zautla in 1549 and two near Huitzo in 1591 and 1593, and only the earliest one went to a Spaniard. One other ranch is known: Indians are reported to have encroached on an estancia in the 1530's, planting it with corn.[30] Etla's position as the main supplier of wheat, corn, and vegetables for Antequera probably spared its lands from foraging cattle. Only there did the early Viceroys encourage Spanish ownership of arable land. To promote a Spanish source of wheat, Viceroy Mendoza had unused swampland drained and allotted it to Spaniards.[31] As a further inducement labor repartimientos were assigned to wheat-producing estates. These attempts to encourage Spanish farming had little effect in the sixteenth century. Spaniards were likely to use the repartimientos assigned for wheat production in the Etla arm to tend their cattle elsewhere in central Oaxaca.[32]

The royal dilemma—how to promote the colonial livestock industry and at the same time protect Indian agriculture—is reflected in the ebb and flow of cattle raising in the sixteenth century. After attempting to ban cattle from the Valley entirely at one point in the 1540's, then to restrict them to the Zimatlán arm and part of the Tlacolula arm in the 1580's,[33] the viceregal government tried to forge a compromise by allowing ranching, but not on Indian lands. Based on incompatible goals, this vague policy proved impossible to implement, as the case of Antequera's pasturelands clearly demonstrates. In 1532, to regulate the spread of cattle, a royal cédula granted Antequera pasture rights to land within one league of the city and the use of untilled land up to 15 leagues away.[34] However, to protect Indian lands, the 1532 ejido grant stipulated that private property within the one-league radius was exempt. Since Indian towns encircled Antequera this rider reduced the ejido to small, isolated patches of territory. The following year, in an effort to carry out the spirit of the 1532 grant, the Crown ordered that the city could purchase Indian lands within one league for its ejido.[35] Legal rights to the one-league pasture were reaffirmed several times in the sixteenth and seventeenth centuries, but complaints by nearby Indian villages prevented the ejido title from ever being realized. Seventeenth-century records confirm that the city was virtually without grazing lands.[36]

The colonial government's attempts to balance the needs of Indian farmers and Spanish ranchers, punctuated by frequent Indian complaints about damage by Spanish cattle, culminated in clearly defined Spanish landholdings in the Valley by about 1600. To protect Indian fields and prevent future discord, the government laid out boundaries, and in some cases forced estancia owners to fence in part of their land. Cattle estancias were becoming specifically marked territories to which the holder possessed full ownership rights as long as he kept a certain number of livestock on the property. A distinguishable pattern of land distribution was now beginning to form.

The Development of the Hacienda

Several important developments affecting Spanish landed estates in the Valley of Oaxaca took place in the early seventeenth century. By 1630 the hacienda, a more complex estate than the estancia, had begun to develop; in 1643 colonial records for the Valley of Oaxaca listed 41 estates as haciendas.[37] The term "hacienda," meaning "property" in the generic sense, acquired a specialized meaning in late-sixteenth-century Spanish America. It defined a new economic entity devoted to supplying local markets with both grain and animal products. This new interest in agriculture created a greater demand for permanent and transient labor than had the cattle ranches of the sixteenth century.

Spaniards often met the need for more workers through a system of debt peonage. Haciendas were labor intensive rather than capital intensive. The equipment needed to operate such an estate was often valued at under 200 pesos, whereas the cost of labor, even at the going rate of two *reales* per man-day, often totaled 1,500 pesos or more annually. An imposing group of permanent buildings, the *casco* or *casa grande*, was usually an integral part of the hacienda. By the construction of the casco the owner established a permanent presence on the estate. He himself resided there for part of the year, usually during the planting and harvest seasons; the rest of the time he was represented by his *mayordomo* (overseer).[38]

The term hacienda is most often associated with the immense rural estates of northern Mexico. Although size was certainly a distinguishing feature of an hacienda, scholars cannot agree on a minimum for the purpose of definition. Suggestions range from 2,500 to 22,000 acres.[39] The hacienda in New Spain is thought to have approached economic and administrative independence, furnishing most of its own subsistence needs and building materials and meting out justice to those who lived within its borders.

Many Valley estates denoted as haciendas by the colonial records did not have all these characteristics. Valley haciendas varied considerably in size. Most of the 41 documented for 1643 consisted of one estancia and a few tracts of arable land, certainly much smaller than the 22,000-acre minimum proposed by Helen Phipps. The casa grande was often of very modest proportions, and few of the estates showed economic self-sufficiency or political independence. The features that all Valley haciendas did have in common and that did distinguish them from other Spanish-owned properties were the economic activities they engaged in and the means by which they secured labor. Valley haciendas were mixed ranching and agricultural enterprises relying on debt peonage for permanent labor.

Valley estates that did not share these features were called estancias, ranchos, and *labores*. To insist on including other characteristics in a definition of hacienda—such as administrative independence, an imposing casa grande, or a larger minimum size—would be to exclude most Valley estates actually called haciendas. Clearly, then, hacienda must be defined here in colonial terms. A more elaborate twentieth-century definition, such as the one used by Wolf and Mintz, is no less valid for studying Spanish American land tenure.[40] But it cannot be applied arbitrarily to colonial haciendas, which in Oaxaca were in fact less developed. (Map 4 shows Spanish estates in the Valley except for those held continuously by the Church; Maps 5–7 in Chapter 5 show Church estates. In addition, colonial documents locate 14 other Spanish estates by jurisdiction only: five *labores* and one rancho in the jurisdiction of Tlalixtac; three ranchos in Zimatlán; one rancho, one orchard, and one hacienda in Antequera; one *labor* in Jalatlaco; and one rancho in Santa Ana Zegache.*)

A few estates in the Valley, notably San José, El Vergel, Valdeflores, Xaagá, Guadalupe, the two San Isidros (one in the Etla arm and one in the Zimatlán arm), and Santo Domingo Buenavista, approached the larger definition of hacienda. Independence in the administration of justice, a crucial feature of the modern hacienda, began for these estates when the Crown granted licenses allowing mass to be said in their chapels. This privilege severed the last connection between nearby Indian towns and peasants residing on hacienda lands. The Indians were no longer religious and political subjects of the *doctrina* (parochial head town), which housed the local priest. Communication with Indian towns was also reduced because hacienda Indians

---

* Certain Valley estates are classified differently in different colonial documents. For the sake of clarity, however, I have generally used one label for each estate throughout the text. In most cases in which the change of labels reflects the growth of an estancia or a *labor* into an hacienda, I have used "hacienda" consistently, pointing out the origins of the estate in the discussion. (Occasionally I have retained the different labels to indicate estate growth; Xuchitepec, which developed from a rancho into an hacienda, is an example.) When documents use different designations for an estate but there is no other indication of a change in status, I have chosen the label most consistent with the available evidence. Thus I have used "sitio de Don Pedrillo" throughout because only one of the several sources that mention the estate calls it an hacienda, and because there is no evidence that it had a casa grande or cultivated crops in addition to raising livestock.

KEY TO MAP 4

Z1. El Vergel
Z2. San José
Z3. Guelavichigana
Z4. Guegonivalle (rancho)
Z5. La Chilayta (rancho)
Z6. Santa Rosa
Z7. Buenavista
Z8. Valdeflores
Z9. Maia
Z10. San Nicolás Gasé
Z11. San Isidro
Z12. Ortega
Z13. Xuchitepec
Z14. El Colector
Z15. Ortega
Z16. Mantecón
Z17. Los Reyes
I18. San Nicolás Obispo (Noriega)
I19. Tlanechico
I20. Estancia Ramírez de Aguilar
I21. Carrizal
I22. Zabaleta
I23. Díaz
I24. Espina
I25. Aguayo
I26. Santa Cruz
I27. San Juan
I28. San Isidro
I29. Jesús Nazareno
I30. San Javier
I31. San Joseph
I32. Ramírez de Aguilar
I33. Zauze
I34. *Labor* de Benito Merino

I35. La Quinta
I36. Candiana
I37. Cinco Señores
I38. Guadalupe
I39. Palma
I40. San Luis
I41. San Luis
T42. Aranjuez
T43. La Asunción
T44. Los Negritos (Santa Rosa Buenavista)
T45. San Antonio Buenavista
T46. San José Guelaviate (rancho)
T47. Santo Domingo Buenavista
T48. Alférez
T49. Tanibé
T50. Xaagá
I51. Carrión
I52. Arrasola
I53. San Blas
E54. San Cristóbal
E55. Jalapilla
I56. Varela
I57. Escovar
E58. Cantón
I59. Montoya
I60. Panzacola
E61. Santísima Trinidad
E62. Blanca (San Nicolás?)
E63. Guadalupe
E64. Molinos de Lazo
E65. Alemán (Santa Cruz)
E66. San Isidro
E67. San Isidro

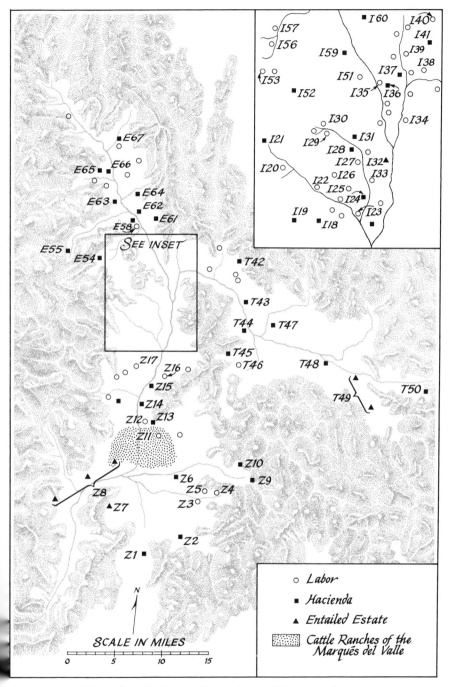

Map 4. Spanish Secular Estates in the Eighteenth Century

no longer left the estate to hear mass on Sundays. Licenses for mass for two large haciendas have been located: San José, 1616, and Santo Domingo Buenavista, 1630.[41]

The casa grande was the main feature distinguishing the larger haciendas in the Valley from the smaller ones. The Hacienda Guadalupe in the Etla arm had one of the more elaborate cascos, consisting of a main house, a chapel, a stable, and a granary.[42] The main house (all of whose rooms were covered with timbers and bricks, and the corridors with bamboo) consisted of a vestibule, a carriage house, a patio, a main living room, four bedrooms, an oratory, a kitchen, three other rooms, and two miradors. The casa grande represented one of the few signs of greater capital investment by the largest Valley estates. Significantly, it was not an investment designed to increase productivity. Large and small estates shared the same rudimentary agricultural technology. Various hacienda inventories from the seventeenth and eighteenth centuries indicate that the variety of tools and supplies was limited on all estates. The larger estates did have more tools in terms of absolute numbers, but even so equipment represented a very small part of their value. The Hacienda Guadalupe, worth 24,385 pesos in 1797, had only 1,435 pesos invested in farm equipment, draft animals, and building supplies.[43] The basic equipment of this hacienda included the following:

36 hoes	49 iron fittings for plows
31 sickles	6 saddles
1 large lock	1 branding iron
37 plows	2 augers
several iron tongs	31 axes
1 iron brick mold	2 chisels
12 leather buckets	1 hammer
2 handsaws	1 one-quartilla corn measure
1 adze	1 one-almud corn measure
7 plowshares	11 fetters
2 carts	1 anvil
5 lassos	2 *barretas* (iron-tipped staffs)
11 pitchforks	11 cart axles

A composite list of other buildings and equipment found on Valley haciendas is also quite limited in variety:

cheese presses and molds	*metates* for grinding salt
mason's rules	carriages
carpenter's benches	harnesses
mattocks	*norias* (irrigating wheels)
willow baskets	*jagueyes* (reservoirs for rain water)
cowbells	brick kilns
plumblines	barrels
wheelbarrows	poles
corn sieves	planes
copper ladles and pots	leather cinches
machetes	huts for servants and slaves
iron tips	chicken coops
earthen jars	saddles
horse blankets	

Corn and wheat were the principal crops grown on haciendas. Corn was more important everywhere except in the north; still, nearly every hacienda did attempt to grow wheat, despite small yields and poor quality outside the Etla arm. The Hacienda San Nicolás, for example, harvested 1,000 fanegas of corn, 25 fanegas of wheat, and 5 fanegas of beans in 1782.[44] Besides these staples Valley haciendas usually experimented with small plots of other crops. In 1791 San Juan Bautista produced 1,700 fanegas of corn, 140 fanegas of wheat, and small amounts of beans, fodder, watermelon, and cochineal.[45]

Sugar cane appears from time to time in inventories of Valley haciendas. Hacendados attempted to grow sugar cane in every part of the Valley at some time during the colonial period. In 1643 estate owners in the Tlacolula valley blamed their poverty on the fact that the crop did not flourish there.[46] Nevertheless, it was raised on the Hacienda San Bartolo in the mountains east of the Valley as early as 1555. In 1697 San Bartolo had six plots of land planted to sugar cane in spite of the danger of frost, which had ruined the hacienda's entire crop three years before. Burgoa mentions sugar in the Etla arm, and one fully equipped *trapiche* (sugar mill) was in operation near Huitzo in the eighteenth century. Like other sugar mills it was a much more capital-intensive operation than the hacienda. An outlay of nearly 15,000 pesos for slaves, copper caldrons, other metal implements, and building equipment was made for this relatively small mill.[47]

Small plots of sugar cane were often found on haciendas in the southern arm of the Valley. San Juan Bautista had 18 furrows of cane planted·in 1694 and 2 in 1702; San Nicolás Obispo, 9 furrows in 1708; San José Guelatoba, in the extreme south, 323 furrows in 1711; and San Isidro, 330 furrows in 1786.[48] The southern arm also had two licensed trapiches: La Soritana, which had 272 furrows of sugar cane in 1786 and 2,350 in 1808, and San José, east of Cuilapan, which was started by Gaspar de Espina in the 1650's but which operated only intermittently during the colonial period.[49] Before 1810 the largest producers of sugar cane in the general area lay south of the Valley in the jurisdictions of Ejutla and Miahuatlán.[50] More land was given over to sugar cane in the Zimatlán arm after independence. Estates with little or no interest in sugar during the colonial period began to develop cane fields. The Hacienda San Nicolás increased its planting from 9 furrows in 1708 to 960 in 1876 and San Juan Bautista from 2 furrows in 1702 to 50 in 1848. A list of sugar-cane producing estates in the Valley at the end of the nineteenth century includes 15 estates south of Oaxaca City and another 12 in the immediate vicinity of the city.[51]

Grazing livestock was a principal form of land use on Valley haciendas. Some had evolved from sixteenth-century ranching grants, including San José (a cattle grant in 1563), Xaagá (a grant for cattle and horses in 1564 and grants for sheep and goats in 1571 and 1583), San Bartolo (1591 and 1596 grants), Santo Domingo Buenavista (1538 grant), and San Joaquín (1561 grant).[52] Such haciendas usually continued to raise the kind of livestock specified in the original grants throughout the colonial period, although there were a few shifts: Xaagá changed from cattle and horses to goats; San Bartolo from cattle and horses to sheep and goats between 1652 and 1697, and then back to cattle and horses by 1723; and Guadalupe from sheep and goats to cattle in the last two decades of the colonial period. Inventories of livestock on haciendas in the mid-eighteenth century indicate that ranching was more developed in the Zimatlán and Tlacolula arms than in Etla, and that cattle and horses were most numerous south of Antequera.

Some of the available data on livestock raising in Oaxaca is depicted in Figures 3 and 4. Figure 3, which plots changes in the number of ganado mayor and menor on three Valley haciendas from 1580 to 1820, suggests that Valley estates did not enjoy uninterrupted expansion. Figure 4 plots price evaluations of three kinds of livestock obtained from hacienda inventories for the seventeenth and eighteenth centuries. It shows a slight down-

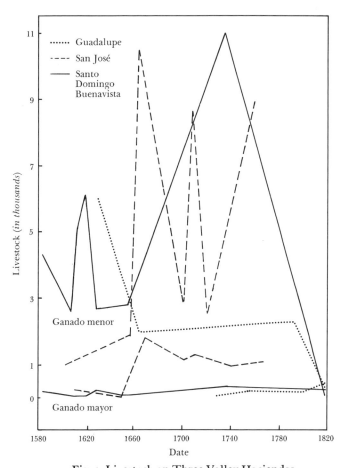

Fig. 3. Livestock on Three Valley Haciendas

ward trend in the first half of the eighteenth century, which is consistent with a general economic decline in the Valley at this time. However, a more striking conclusion suggested by this figure is that the price of livestock varied more from one year to the next than it did over a hundred years. (I have assumed that the animals inventoried were generally of equal quality, and that officials evaluated their worth fairly.) A team of oxen, for example, was valued at 25 pesos in 1699 and 35 pesos in 1703; but it was generally valued at 25 pesos throughout the period 1710

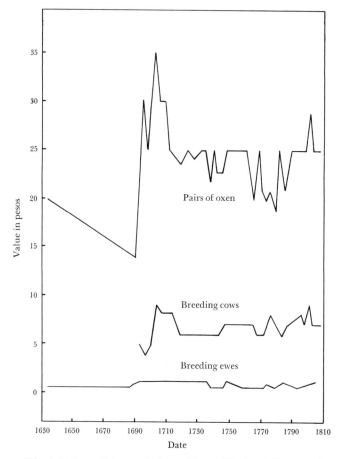

Fig. 4. Value of Livestock According to Hacienda Inventories

to 1810. This then was a base price from which yearly values fluctuated. Significantly, before 1780 the deviations from 25 pesos were invariably downward, whereas after 1780 the price tended to rise. The value of cows and ewes in the eighteenth century followed the same general pattern of a slow decline interrupted by considerable yearly fluctuations.

In addition to the direct use of their land, hacendados also let out arable plots to Indian or mestizo sharecroppers, who gave the Spaniards over half of their harvests in return. Sharecroppers who were not bound by debt peonage worked sections of the Haciendas Tanibé, Valdeflores, San Isidro (Zimatlán), Guendulain, and La Soritana at various times during the colonial period.[53] Hacendados also rented unused sections of their estates. The Guendulain mayorazgo, for example, rented a ranch attached to its hacienda in 1734 to Domingo de Zamora and a section of grazing land in 1743 to the Bethlemites, who had recently acquired the nearby Hacienda Santo Domingo Buenavista.[54]

As we have noted, some haciendas had their origins in sixteenth-century grants for estancias. But since the cultivation of crops was an essential part of the hacienda economy, estancias that did not have, or could not obtain, arable land remained ranches throughout the colonial period. Conversely, some haciendas grew from small tracts of arable land. Valdeflores, Molinos de Lazo, and Montoya, for example, began on tracts obtained in the sixteenth century from Indian communities and Indian nobles, who held a virtual monopoly on Valley farmland at that time.[55] The development of the hacienda as a combined agricultural and ranching enterprise was greatly facilitated by the drastic decline in the Indian population. In particular, cacicazgo lands worked by terrasguerros were sometimes completely abandoned after an epidemic.

As a result of the Marqués del Valle's quest for property in the seventeenth century, Spaniards acquired several arable tracts abandoned by Indians in the central and northern portions of the Valley. A number of Valley haciendas began on Indian land made available by the Marqués. The Haciendas Guadalupe, San

Miguel, and San Juan Bautista, for example, started with emphiteutic (perpetual use) grants from the Marqués between 1617 and 1619.[56] Also, rather than face costly litigation with the Marqués, various Indian nobles sold their unoccupied land during this same period. These tracts were the nuclei of other estates in the jurisdiction of Cuilapan: Jesús Nazareno, 1618; San Jacinto, 1633; Los Naranjos, 1633; San José, 1616; San Nicolás Obispo, 1615; San Javier, 1618; and Escovar, pre-1644. A number of other rural estates not identified by name in seventeenth-century records also began at this time.

Haciendas expanded their boundaries in several ways. Buying land from individual Indians was the most common means. Four haciendas in the Etla arm, Alemán, Santa Rita, San Isidro, and Guadalupe, grew almost exclusively by this means during the seventeenth and eighteenth centuries.[57] Rentals from Indian communities and nobles were also a common source of new land for Valley haciendas and *labores*. We know of 29 such rentals during the seventeenth and eighteenth centuries, involving these estates: Guadalupe, Escovar, Tanibé, Montoya, San Isidro (Etla), Arrasola, Jesús Nazareno, San Javier, La Quinta, Poblete, and Santo Domingo Buenavista. One hacendado, Cosmé Sánchez, made a verbal agreement to rent land from a *principal* of Huitzo. After occupying the land for a number of years, Sánchez tried to claim ownership on the basis of squatter's rights, since no written rental contract had been drawn up and the *principal* did not have written title to the land. The hacendado's devious attempt failed, however, and the *principal* was confirmed as the rightful owner.[58] Indian communities occasionally complained of Spanish intrusion, but there is little evidence that a significant amount of land was added to Valley haciendas by encroachment. Two clear cases of expansion by force, Zorita in the 1770's and El Vergel in 1695 suggest that such aggression was more likely when a new owner purchased an estate.[59]

Loans and mortgages were another means by which hacendados gained the use and sometimes the ownership of Indian lands. In several instances loans to Indians were based on the condition that the lender could use a particular piece of land until the debt was repaid.[60] In others the lender received the right to part of the crop harvested on a piece of land until the debt was repaid.[61] Several hacendados invested heavily in loans to Indian landowners, doubtless with a covetous eye on the land. In 1722 the Hacienda San Nicolás Obispo held liens totaling 556 pesos on five pieces of Indian land; in the 1790's Diego González Cataneo held liens on seven pieces belonging to Indians of Santa Marta Etla.

Rentals between Spaniards accounted for some expansion. These usually involved entire estates, although occasionally a landowner might rent a single tract to an adjoining hacienda. In 1734 and 1743, for example, Miguel de Guendulain rented a rancho and other grazing land from his Hacienda La Asunción to the Hacienda Santo Domingo Buenavista and to Domingo de Zamora. The Church also rented land out. Finally, some haciendas, notably San José, expanded as a result of sales between Spaniards.[62]

Few haciendas added large blocks of land to their original holdings, but many did expand slowly by the acquisition of small adjacent plots. These include Santa Rita, which obtained 15 pieces of land, all smaller than one acre, and Guadalupe, which added at least 15 small plots in the years 1655–87 and 1738–39.[63] In the 1780's and 1790's Diego Gonzáles Cataneo made a concerted effort to enlarge the Hacienda San Isidro (Etla) by the same method.[64] Two exceptions to this general pattern of gradual, limited expansion are San José and San Nicolás Obispo. San José was established in 1615 with the purchase of two ranches and a tract of farmland. In 1651 the hacienda obtained three more estancias and a *labor*. Another estancia de ganado menor was purchased in 1660, another *labor* in 1675, and the estancia La Garzona in 1701. San Nicolás began as a *labor* in 1615. A second *labor*, Santa Marina, was added in 1708, two ranches in 1711 and 1719, and three acres of arable land in 1727.[65]

In the seventeenth century a great deal of land was concentrated in the hands of a few families. (Several haciendas did not reach their maximum size until later, near the end of the colonial period, but by that time an individual or a family rarely owned more than one rural estate.) Some families, notably the

Guendulains, the Ramírez de Aguilars, and the Bohórquezes, converted their largest haciendas into entailed estates. Among the other families whose names appear regularly in seventeenth-century lands records, the Espinas are the most conspicuous. Their holdings included the Hacienda San Bartolo in the mountains east of the Valley, three ranches composing the Hacienda Xaagá near Mitla, two *labores* near Cuilapan (one of which was converted into a trapiche in 1658), and a mill with 200 acres adjoining Magdalena Ocotlán. The Espinas also gained respectability through marriage. Pedro de Espina, who had acquired the family's first holdings in the 1590's, married the daughter of a prominent family in the Valley, the Pachecos;* and their son married the daughter of a member of the Order of Santiago. The dispersed rural estates gradually slipped from the family's grasp, however. The two *labores* near Cuilapan passed to the Carmelite house in Antequera in the early eighteenth century, San Bartolo was sold by the executors of Gaspar de Espina's estate before 1693, and the Xaagá estancias were sold in 1728.[66]

Haciendas were heavily concentrated in the southern section of the Valley, where 39 have been identified by name for the colonial period. Most of these still existed in 1810, although some, including San Jacinto, Los Naranjos, and El Hijo, were absorbed into other haciendas before then. Haciendas in the eastern region, 15 in number, were generally larger in size than those in the south; few of them bordered on one another. Etla, the smallest arm of the Valley, had 13 haciendas, as well as a number of *labores*.

Valley haciendas in the late eighteenth century generally encompassed two or three cattle estancias and about five caballerías of farmland (roughly 4,500 acres). Haciendas in the southern valley whose size we know include San Nicolás Obispo, two estancias and two *labores* (4,200 acres); San Nicolás Tolentino, two estancias and 6⅓ caballerías (4,000 acres); and San Javier, one estancia and nine caballerías (2,900 acres). In the east Santo Domingo Buenavista had three estancias (6,000 acres) and Los Negritos four estancias and 1½ caballerías (8,000 acres). Spanish

---

* As of 1644 Francisco, Pedro, and Joseph Pacheco each owned one hacienda in the jurisdiction of Antequera.

estates were generally smaller in the Etla arm but encompassed proportionately more arable land. The Hacienda Guadalupe, for example, owned one estancia de ganado menor and at least ten caballerías of arable land (3,000 acres); Jalapilla owned two estancias, three caballerías, and two wheat mills (4,300 acres); and San José had one estancia and about five caballerías of rented farmland (2,500 acres). The largest haciendas were located in the southern portion of the Valley of Zimatlán and in the Valley of Tlacolula: San José and Valdeflores each encompassed seven estancias de ganado mayor y menor and two *labores* (20,000–30,000 acres); Xaagá, seven estancias; and San Bartolo, six estancias and two *labores*.

Size alone did not determine the assessed value of an hacienda. Several of the smaller estates in the Etla and Zimatlán arms were among the most valuable: Guadalupe, 24,385 pesos (1797); Soledad, 30,000 pesos (1737); Santísima Trinidad, 30,500 pesos (1793); Santa Cruz, 33,799 pesos (1729); and San Juan Bautista–San Jacinto–Los Naranjos, 60,000 pesos (1743). In contrast, San Bartolo and Los Negritos in the east were valued at 7,990 pesos (1745) and 12,000 pesos (1712), respectively. The most important factors determining an hacienda's worth were the amount of arable land and the number of cattle it owned, and the amount of money advanced to resident peons. With few exceptions the larger haciendas relied more heavily on livestock than the smaller ones.

Labores

Small rural estates distinct from haciendas were an important type of colonial Spanish landholding in the Valley of Oaxaca. There were several small cattle ranches, measuring one or two estancias (some 7–14 square miles), in the southern and eastern arms in the eighteenth century, well after the Valley's major haciendas had been established. Four ranches in the south belonged to creoles who apparently owned no other estates: Guegonivalle and San Cristóbal, northeast of San Pedro Apostol; El Capitán, east of the Hacienda San José, which later acquired it; and La Soledad, near Zimatlán.[67] The sitio Duhuatia, near San Pedro Ixtlahuaca, passed through many hands in the eighteenth cen-

III. The *Labor* of Don Matheo Delgado, 1730 (AGNT 41, exp. 1). The estate, shown in the lower left-hand corner, consists of the owner's house, a corral, a well, an orchard, cultivated fields, and pastureland.

tury, but it was not permanently tied to any larger estate. In the east the ranchos del Fuerte and Lope were owned separately until the 1740's, when they were absorbed by the Hacienda Xaagá.[68]

The rancho has long been recognized as a characteristic type of small Spanish estate in late colonial Mexico. Another, less familiar type of small, privately owned estate found in the Valley of Oaxaca was the *labor*, which usually consisted of one to four caballerías of arable, sometimes irrigated land.[69] Because of its small size and the nature of its holdings, a *labor* was viable only when cultivated intensively. Several crops were grown on Valley *labores*, including maize, wheat, beans, fodder, maguey, cactus, and various fruits and vegetables. Although *labores* emphasized farming, many combined it with other kinds of land use. Plate III depicts one *labor* in the 1730's, the *labor* of Don Matheo Delgado, north of Antequera near San Felipe del Agua. Delgado's house is shown on the southern edge of his estate. The land east and west of the house was apparently cultivated to the limits of the property. To the north a well and orchard are depicted. The corral northeast of the house indicates that the estate owned some cattle, which were probably grazed on the unplowed land north of the orchard.

The following 1733 inventory of Joseph del Castillo's *labor*, located on the Jalatlaco River about a mile south of Delgado's estate, is probably typical:[70]

3 caballerías of irrigated land (315 acres)
19 oxen
21 horses
1 mule
9 sheep
1 buggy drawn by two mules
various plows, hoes, and other farm implements
80 fanegas of corn
150 *zontles* of fodder (60,000 bundles)
2 fanegas of corn sown
4 fanegas of beans
637 pesos, 6 *reales* owed to the owner by "various servants"
95 pesos, 5 *reales* paid in advance to rent water from
    the Jalatlaco River

A *labor* had the appearance of a small family farm, but its system of labor resembled that of an hacienda. The inventories of *labores* in the Valley of Oaxaca indicate clearly that the Spanish owners performed little if any of the physical labor on their estates. Debt peons and transient workers prevailed there just as they did on haciendas. Then, too, the number of cattle on some *labores* suggests that the owners considered their estates miniature haciendas rather than farms. The *labor* San Isidro near Santa Ana Zegache, for example, grazed 219 sheep, 159 goats, 46 cows, 30 oxen, and 9 horses on its 315 acres of land. Only four small plots were planted to corn and beans.* The fact that many *labores*, like haciendas, were repeatedly mortgaged and sold is probably a matter of inefficient use. Unless it was intensively farmed, a *labor* could not support its owner. Although many *labores* were sold, few fell into the hands of hacendados to become small pieces of a large estate. This is partly because few *labores* bordered on large estates; most were surrounded by Indian lands.

Labores were especially numerous within a seven-kilometer radius of Antequera. Map 4 (page 125) shows those that can be clearly identified. Several grew from mid-sixteenth-century grants of orchard plots in the ejidos southeast of the city. Many *labores* near Antequera are mentioned in seventeenth-century records, and most, perhaps all, of those mentioned in eighteenth-century records date from an earlier period. It is difficult to estimate how many *labores* there were in the Valley. Unlike haciendas they did not usually carry a special name but were known only by the name of the current owner—"el *labor* de Diego de Benites Merino," for example. Thus, without detailed boundary descriptions, it is difficult to know whether or not the *labor* of Joseph Ramos "just outside Antequera" mentioned in a 1710 document is the same estate known as "el *labor* de Joseph del Castillo" in 1733.

If we count only *labores* that are clearly distinct from others,

---

* AN 1789, primera parte, fol. 77v. In contrast, the only livestock on six *labores* mentioned in the 1777 *Relación Geográfica* for Oaxaca were the oxen, mules, and horses needed for cultivation and transportation. BN 2450, fol. 7.

our best estimate for the early eighteenth century is 24 within seven kilometers of Antequera and at least 42 in the entire Valley. Five were known by name and can be identified as separate estates: San Antonio, south of Azompa; San Miguel, owned by the Jesuits; Sangre de Cristo, north of Xoxocotlán; La Noria, immediately south of Antequera; and La Quinta, north of Sangre de Cristo. A sixth *labor*, known as the *labor* of Joseph Ramos in 1708, bordered on San Juan Chapultepec west of Antequera. Several other farms were strung out along the eastern edge of the city near the Jalatlaco River: the *labores* of Diego de Benites Merino, Joseph del Castillo, and Luis Ramírez de Aguilar, all mentioned in 1725, and the *labor* of Matheo Delgado, cited in the 1760's. Two *labores* east of the river are noted in the 1740's: San Luis and San José. Another group of *labores* was clustered near San Pedro Ixtlahuaca, seven kilometers west of Antequera. In the 1690's these included the *labores* of Nicolás de Torres, Pedro de Escovar, Clemente del Pozo, and Francisco de Lara. Another group of *labores* were scattered south of Antequera, including in the late seventeenth century the *labor* Jesús Nazareno and those owned by Juan Barranco, Juan de Aragón, Gaspar de Espina, and Nicolás Feria. And by 1718 three other *labores* in this area had been mentioned, belonging to José Sarmiento, Juan de Almogabar, and Tomás Varela de Figueroa. One or more of these may duplicate *labores* mentioned in late-seventeenth-century records.[71]

Away from Antequera the number of *labores* diminished considerably. In the dry eastern arm, where it would have been difficult for small farms to be self-supporting, there were only a few. Two estates referred to as *labores*, the *labor* de Guadalupe and the *labor* de Soriano, were actually small cattle ranches rather than farms.[72] Five *labores* north of Azompa in the Etla arm are mentioned in eighteenth-century records: San Nicolás, near San Lorenzo Guaxolotitlán (1710); a *labor* near Santo Domingo Etla owned by Antonio de las Heras y Thorres (1718); a *labor* near Santiago Guaxolotitlán owned by Andrés de Palacios (1725); a *labor* near San Andrés Zautla owned by Juan de Santaella (1764); and Santa Rita, near San Sebastián Etla (1780).[73]

At least 11 *labores* can be found in the Valley of Zimatlán south of Cuilapan. Six of these were grouped around Santa Ana Zegache, San Gerónimo Zegache, and Santa Catalina Quiané: the *labores* San Isidro and Soledad, and four unnamed farms less than two caballerías in size. The *labores* San Juan and Tlanechico, as well as a farm belonging to Juan Morales in 1717, were located between Cuilapan and Zimatlán. Two others, Santa Rosa del Peñol and the *labor* of Diego Díaz de Ordaz, were situated near Ocotlán.[74]

Instability of Spanish Ownership

One of the most striking features of Spanish land ownership in the Valley was its instability. Although many rural estates grew noticeably, they did so in spite of a weakness in hereditary succession not usually associated with Mexico or other parts of Spanish America. Spanish landowners in the Valley showed no strong preference for primogeniture in the transfer of non-entailed estates; thus many estates were divided up among several relatives, especially those consisting of various holdings scattered throughout the Valley. Haciendas that were divided include San José and San Isidro, both near Zimatlán, in 1711 and Taniche, Arriba, and Abajo, all near Ejutla, in 1676.[75] Further, hacendados often found it expedient to sell their multiple estates rather than pass them on to relatives. In 1737 Tomás López Lozano sold all three of his haciendas, Las Monjas (near Miahuatlán), Comitlán (near San Baltasar Chichicapa), and Santa Rosa (near Ocotlán), and divided the proceeds equally among his children.[76] Joint inheritance of a single estate by several family members often led to sales. When Juan Díaz willed equal portions of the Guelavichigana and La Gachupina estates to his seven children, sale was the only means of settlement acceptable to the heirs.[77]

The history of the eight non-entailed haciendas for which we have fairly complete records—San José, San Bartolo, Guadalupe, San Juan Bautista, San Jacinto, Santo Domingo Buenavista, Xaagá, and San Nicolás Obispo—confirms that sale was a more common means of transfer than inheritance (see Appendix E).

During the colonial period these eight estates changed hands a total of 89 times. Only 13 of the 89 transfers were by inheritance; the remaining 76 (over 85 per cent) were by sale. Sales were especially frequent in the years 1699 to 1761, when the eight estates were sold a total of 36 times, including seven each for San José and San Bartolo and six each for Guadalupe and San Nicolás. Seventy-three other sales records of haciendas and *labores* have been located in the eighteenth-century notarial records for the Valley. Although fragmentary, these records suggest recurrent sales for other estates. The Hacienda Santa Rita, for example, was sold four times between 1740 and 1780, Aranjuez four times between 1710 and 1712, and the sitio Duhuatia five times between 1749 and 1799.[78] The lack of notarial records before 1684 makes it difficult to judge the frequency of hacienda sales in the seventeenth century. The eight haciendas with complete transfer records were sold 29 times during the seventeenth century and 42 times during the eighteenth, suggesting that sales were more frequent in the late colonial period.

The sales records contradict the notion that colonial haciendas were characterized by stable ownership and transfer by inheritance. Hacienda transfers in other parts of Spanish America must be examined before a balanced evaluation of sales versus inheritances will be possible. Mario Góngora's work on the Puangue Valley in central Chile during the colonial period is one source of comparison. The 15 haciendas in his study were sold a total of 44 times, considerably fewer than the eight Valley haciendas.[79]

The growth of mortgages, or *censos*, on rural estates in the late seventeenth century and the eighteenth, both in terms of value and in terms of numbers, helps explain the frequency of sales.[80] The Church was the major source of credit, normally charging 5 per cent interest. Because monasteries, convents, and priests generally considered interest payments a desirable fixed annual income, they did not encourage estate owners to pay off the principal. In fact, most borrowers could not afford to do so anyway. Heavily mortgaged estates paid as much as 1,000 to 1,500 pesos in annual interest, which might exceed the hacienda's income in a year of poor harvests or animal disease. Foreclosure occasionally followed a failure to meet interest payments, but more often a debt-ridden hacienda was sold when the owner died. Buyers could be found more readily for heavily mortgaged estates, since the initial capital investment, or the difference between the estate's assessed value and the principal of the mortgage, was small. The larger the mortgage, the less capital the new owner needed. However, a vicious circle of sales had probably been initiated, for the hacienda was quite likely to be sold again if the profits still did not exceed the interest by a safe margin.

Mortgages on rural estates were common throughout New Spain in the late colonial period, but their effect on land transfers was especially great in an area like the Valley of Oaxaca, where the value of mortgages was already high and was rising. Of 27 eighteenth-century estates for which sufficient information is available, 20 were mortgaged to over 80 per cent of their value, ten to over 90 per cent. The mean average was 76.79 per cent for 25 of the 27 estates and 66.92 per cent for all 27.[81] The sample shows a relationship between large mortgages and sales. All 20 estates mortgaged to over 80 per cent of their value were sold on or before the death of the owner.

The economic decline in Oaxaca in the first half of the eighteenth century helps explain the increase in mortgage values in the late colonial period. Many haciendas increased their indebtedness substantially between 1700 and 1750, and notarial records for the Valley during this period are filled with new mortgage contracts on haciendas and *labores*. The Hacienda San Bartolo, for example, which had no debts in 1640, was mortgaged for 5,000 pesos in 1712; the Hacienda Santo Domingo Buenavista, not indebted in 1731, had a 9,400-peso mortgage in 1765. During the second half of the eighteenth century, mortgages tended to level off and several owners made payments on the principal: the Mimiaga family, who acquired the Hacienda San José in 1766 with a mortgage of 30,040 pesos, reduced the debt to 14,000 pesos by 1770; and the owners of Jalapilla paid off one-fourth of its 8,000-peso mortgage between 1770 and 1786.[82]

Labor Supply

An adequate labor supply was crucial to the economic success of Spanish estates in the Valley of Oaxaca, and in turn to the survival of the Spanish population, who came to depend heavily on these estates for food. Though the Crown had a commitment to defend the native population from abusive labor practices and to support a voluntary system of labor, this was over-shadowed by the concern for maintaining the colony. In many cases Spanish administrators invoked the principle of "public utility" to allow labor institutions that had long been formally abolished to continue in practice.[83] Still, the seventeenth and eighteenth centuries saw a chronic labor shortage, another factor contributing to the relative weakness of Spanish haciendas in the Valley.

Encomiendas and Indian slavery, two major sources of labor elsewhere in New Spain during the first half of the sixteenth century, were of little importance in the Valley. The Marqués del Valle, on whose estancias six Indian slaves from the Valley of Mexico resided in 1549, is the only individual known to have held Indian slaves in the Valley; and the Marqués in 1590 no longer owned any.[84] Along with the absence of documentary evidence, the relatively peaceful conquest of central Oaxaca suggests that the enslavement of Indians was not a significant source of labor in the Valley. Neither were encomiendas widespread there. And the fact that several landowning encomenderos received labor repartimientos in the 1590's suggests that the 1549 law forbidding an encomendero to exact labor service from the Indians under his authority was enforced.[85]

In the sixteenth century Valley Indians paid the royal and Marquesado tributes in kind and thus kept the Spanish community supplied with cereals. The few Spanish estates in the Valley concentrated on raising livestock, which required only a few permanent laborers, and left the more labor-intensive farming activities to the Indian communities. In the second half of the century, the Spaniards met their minimal needs in part with Indian labor, retained legally in repartimientos of from one to

12 workers, or illegally by various other methods. Also, Spanish estates frequently employed Negro slaves. The large Valdeflores estate relied on 12 Negro slaves to look after its cattle and horses in the second half of the sixteenth century, for example, and the Jesuit farm near San Antonio de la Cal had Negro slaves as permanent laborers until it passed into secular hands in 1770.[86] In 1655 a slave even managed an estate near Macuilxóchitl consisting of two estancias and a *labor*.[87]

The drop in native population and the gradual shift from a tribute in kind to a money tribute in the seventeenth century meant that new sources of food were needed to supply the urban market of Antequera. The *labor* and the hacienda, which developed to fill this need, required more permanent and seasonal laborers than they could retain by the traditional methods. The increased demand for labor, never fully satisfied in the Valley, led to new kinds of labor institutions.

The repartimiento, a system whereby Indians were drafted to serve on public works projects, in the mines, and on estates, provided most of the agricultural labor needed by the Valley's Spanish landowners in the late sixteenth century and the early seventeenth. The period of service and the number of Indians required to work at any one time varied greatly throughout Spanish America. In parts of New Granada 4 per cent of the tributary males of an Indian community served together for a term of six months; in Guatemala the term was only one week, but 25 per cent of a community's tributaries served at once.[88] In the Valley of Oaxaca the normal period of service was one week, and 4 per cent of the tributary males were expected to work at one time. Based on the 4 per cent standard, an estate owner was assigned a fixed number of Indians, ranging from one to 12 in the examples found.[89] Indians were to be paid for this service, though in practice they often were not.

Repartimientos had a long history in the Valley. Mining repartimientos date from the 1530's and became widespread in the 1570's, after the discovery of the Chichicapa mines in the mountains dividing the eastern and southern arms of the Valley.[90] The dramatic population declines in the towns supplying mining repartimientos, particularly San Juan Teitipac and Ocotlán, suggests that harsh labor practices and mass Indian exoduses compounded the loss of population by disease. Mining repartimientos declined in the first half of the seventeenth century, when most of the nearby mines closed down; but some Spaniards still claimed to operate mines and secured repartimientos that they then used for agricultural work or rented out to hacendados.[91]

Agricultural repartimientos were occasionally awarded to cattle ranches in the sixteenth century. But after a cédula real legally ended repartimientos for agriculture in 1609, labor drafts were generally limited to wheat-growing estates.[92] The continuation of repartimientos for wheat production was justified on the grounds of "public utility," since wheat was a staple of the Spanish community. Several unscrupulous Spaniards got around this restriction by petitioning for repartimientos for their wheat fields and then using the Indians to tend their cattle.[93] Estate owners in Etla, the wheat center of the Valley, received most of the agricultural repartimientos after 1600. Towns in the Etla and Tlacolula arms continued to supply these drafts for perhaps 20 years after the repartimiento was abolished by law in 1629.[94] Allotments were usually made at the request of a landowner who could demonstrate that he had not been able to hire sufficient laborers. Francisco de Jaúregui Pinelo, for example, was granted a repartimiento of 12 Indians from Mitla in 1604 after submitting a sworn statement to the alcalde mayor of Antequera that he could find no day laborers to operate his mill.[95] Although conceived as temporary measures, such repartimientos were frequently renewed in routine fashion.

Abuses of agricultural repartimientos were common. Records from AGN *Ramo de Indios* indicate that often more than the fixed quota of Indians were compelled to serve. Many were forced to work seven days rather than the usual six, an interesting example of obedience to the letter of the law rather than its spirit, since seven days was within the stipulated maximum of one week. Other laborers were never paid for their service.[96] Population losses through the 1620's made repartimientos particularly burdensome to Indian communities, since downward adjustments in the quotas were often delayed by ten years or more.[97]

Several factors contributed to the decline of repartimientos. One was the royal commitment to a free labor system, a policy encouraged by the increasing dissatisfaction of Indian laborers and the recipients of repartimiento grants alike. Repartimientos had a markedly disruptive effect on Indian life. As population declines made the supply of repartimiento workers increasingly inadequate, Spanish landowners forced laborers into longer periods of service with little or no pay.[98] Indians complained in the late sixteenth century that they had no time left to work the lands from which they paid the royal tribute—a fact that the Crown could hardly ignore. Residents of entire towns openly flouted local authorities by refusing to serve in repartimientos, and other individuals avoided service by claiming exemptions as members of the native nobility.[99] From the white landowners' viewpoint, repartimientos were not a very satisfactory source of labor. The number of workers provided was never sufficient. Further, the survival of a repartimiento was precarious, since it depended on regular renewals by the royal government.[100] Finally, it was difficult to maximize the productivity of repartimiento laborers. With the gangs of Indians changing every week, tasks had to be reassigned and individuals retrained.

Although temporary agricultural repartimientos were unsatisfactory to all parties, they persisted in the Valley of Oaxaca to the last quarter of the eighteenth century for the sake of "public utility." This principle was specifically applied to wheat and cochineal production, and to occasional service for a parish priest or a local Spanish official. Repartimiento grants for wheat cultivation have been found for 1648, 1694 (two), 1710, 1714, 1732, and 1772.[101] Grants often went to haciendas facing utter ruin from a shortage of voluntary laborers. In 1694 Pedro de Espina Pacheco voiced a standard lament used by Spanish hacendados to obtain such grants: "The current high price of wheat is due to a shortage resulting from the laziness of Indians in the Valley, who refuse to work on my hacienda."[102] The temporary, stopgap nature of eighteenth-century repartimientos in the Valley is indicated by the fact that termination dates were clearly stated in the grants.[103]

In one case a labor shortage justified a repartimiento to an hacienda that did not produce wheat. After the flight of its debt peons in 1772, the Hacienda San Nicolás Obispo received direct support from the Audiencia in Mexico City. The Audiencia instructed the alcalde mayor to assign free Indians to the hacienda if the peons were not found. The Indians were to be "available for work whenever needed."[104] In 1787 Esteban Melgar, the corregidor de indios for Tlacolula, used a temporary repartimiento for another purpose. In order to implement royal decrees calling for increased corn production, Melgar had 25 Indians from Tlacolula and San Juan Guelavia clear a tract for a Spanish resident of Teotitlán del Valle. Each laborer was to receive "the customary cash wage."[105] Repartimientos to alcaldes mayores and priests for cochineal production were more frequent and permanent. According to a 1714 document from Tlacochahuaya, "It is accepted and customary that each week Indians serve the priest and the alcalde mayor of this jurisdiction. . . ."[106] Detailed records of cochineal repartimientos have not been located, but the parish priest of Tlalixtac in 1810 suggested that such repartimientos were widespread, at least until 1780.[107]

Spanish alcaldes, parish priests, and hacendados also exacted unpaid labor from Indians in the late sixteenth and seventeenth centuries. A directive from the Audiencia to the alcalde mayor of Antequera in 1591 noted that ranchers in that jurisdiction had been forcing local Indians to work for them without pay.[108] A viceregal cédula of December 2, 1654, ordered that Valley Indians were not to be taken from their towns and forced to perform "voluntary" service; this suggests that the practice was a fairly common one.[109]

A system of debt peonage, under which landless peasants were permanently bound to an estate by economic and legal ties, prevailed on Spanish estates in the late colonial period.* Rural

---

* Zavala, "Orígenes coloniales," p. 311. Debt peonage is generally thought to have been a coercive labor system based on advances of money and goods to peasants who could never afford to repay their creditors. Students of the period, however,

estates in Oaxaca were no exception to the general trend, although the situation there bore little resemblance to the extravagant use of residence laborers on the classical haciendas of the north. The difficulties of a labor system that depended on the individual's willingness to work persisted in the Valley;[110] and evidence suggests that the refusal of Indians to serve on haciendas often made debt peonage a coercive institution there.

The majority of resident servants on Valley haciendas in the late eighteenth century were Indians, although there were also significant numbers of mulattoes and mestizos. Of 1,499 non-Spanish residents on Valley haciendas recorded in 1777, 966 were Indians, 411 were mulattoes, and 122 were mestizos.[111] These records indicate that haciendas and *labores* in Oaxaca had modest numbers of peons indebted to them during the eighteenth century, ranging from one to 91. Of the 56 Valley estates included in a 1777 census, 12 had no resident servants, 33 had one to three servants, and only 4 had more than 50 servants. The mean average of resident laborers on Valley estates in 1777 was 11; the median was three. Not surprisingly, there were more debtors and peons on haciendas that emphasized agriculture, such as Montoya, Cinco Señores, San Blas, and the largest haciendas in the Zimatlán valley, Valdeflores and Santa Gertrudis. The record of accounts for the Carmelite Hacienda San Juan Bautista during the 1790's indicates that most Indian laborers there were hired on a seasonal basis and cannot be considered permanent residents. During 1793, 58 individuals worked at San Juan Bautista for an average of 4.3 days each.

Colonial regulations designed to prevent the spread of debt peonage set reasonable limits on the amount of money that could be advanced to a native laborer. The maximum in 1589, one

---

are now questioning and modifying this generalization. According to some, the colonial hacienda supplied certain material needs of the peasants that might not otherwise have been met. Further, evidence suggests that labor on haciendas was perhaps not so harsh or abusive as generally thought. Charles Gibson, for example, has found that in the Valley of Mexico some debts were small enough to be repaid, and that some peasants were apparently willing to move from their towns to haciendas (*Aztecs Under Spanish Rule*, pp. 255–56). In short, at this stage of research it would be a mistake to equate all colonial estates with the most exploitive haciendas of the late nineteenth century.

peso, represented 16 working days for a laborer earning one-half *real* a day. Later Viceroys changed this standard. In 1600 the Conde de Monterrey ordered that advance payments should not exceed six pesos, or about three months' wages. In 1619 the Marqués de Guadalcázar declared that advances were illegal except when used to pay the tribute of penniless Indians; this restriction was abandoned in 1629, however, when the Viceroy reverted to the standard of three months' wages. Figures are not available for the years 1643 to 1755, but Silvio Zavala suggests that three months' wages continued to be the maximum legal advance.[112] This amounts to from nine to 18 pesos, assuming a daily wage of one to two *reales*.[113] In 1755 a viceregal order set six pesos as the limit on loans to Indians; and a proclamation from the Audiencia on March 23, 1785, cut the maximum to five pesos.[114] Spanish law did allow for exceptions, however. The 1785 order permitted additional advances for the payment of tribute or other expenses of "extreme necessity." Further, the regulations on debts applied specifically to Indians; presumably unlimited advances could be made to non-Indians.[115]

Apparently advances to laborers in the Valley exceeded legal maximums to the extent that debt peonage can be said to have existed there in the eighteenth and early nineteenth centuries. In a sample of debts for 475 peons on 14 Valley estates during this period, the average debt was 35.5 pesos.[116] With monthly wages generally set at 3.2 pesos, this represents roughly 11 months' work. Individual debts ranged from one *real* to 425 pesos, with 79.6 per cent of them exceeding the 1755 limit of six pesos (see Fig. 5). Although debt peonage in Oaxaca clearly had coercive overtones, the large debts may actually indicate that Oaxaca's rural laborers had a strong bargaining position. Certainly 35.5 pesos was much more than was necessary to perpetuate a laborer's indebtedness. Hence the natives' reluctance to serve permanently on Spanish estates apparently had financial benefits. Large debts and the hacendados' efforts to discourage repayment suggest that the peon could and did demand special advances and luxuries from his master.[117] When the Audiencia enforced the five-peso rule for peons on the Hacienda Guadalupe in 1791, the owner

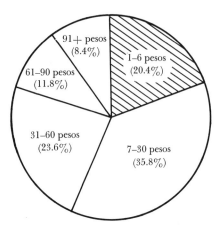

Fig. 5. Debts of Debt Peons in the Valley, Eighteenth Century
(sample of 475 debts from 14 haciendas). Shaded area shows debts
within the legal limit of six pesos.

complained bitterly that he would not be able to find Indians to
work for him regularly if he could not advance them more than
this.*

By law agricultural laborers, including debt peons, were free
to move from one estate to another. In fact, peons rarely left
Valley haciendas without a commotion. To move to another
estate, a peon had to pay off his current debts or find another
hacendado who would pay for him. Judging from the few recorded instances of debts being repaid or transferred, hacendados went to extremes to prevent peons from freeing themselves
from the obligations tying them to the hacienda. (No examples
of debts being transferred from one hacienda to another have
been found.) In the eighteenth century viceregal policy placed
limitations on the peons' freedom of movement. Especially in
cases involving haciendas with no other source of labor, peons
were ordered to work off their debts on the estate where they
had been accrued. This was true even if the peon was willing to

* AGNT 1216, 1:1r–2r. A late-eighteenth-century report on the state of agriculture
declared that the five-peso limit was the greatest threat to productivity in New
Spain. AGI *Papeles de Estado* 40, fol. 12v.

recognize the debt and to repay it by working on another estate.[118]

Spanish rural estates suffered labor shortages throughout the late colonial period, despite the gradual recovery of the native population. In an appeal to the Viceroy in 1732, one hacendado made the problem explicit:

Owing to a shortage of laborers and servants, I am able to cultivate only a very small plot of land on my hacienda. My profits are greatly diminished, and at times I have had to operate at a loss. The causes of my plight are the unwillingness of the Indians to work outside their communities and the lack of ways to oblige them to do so.

This sad state of affairs is also related to the flight of debt peons from the haciendas. They take refuge in the towns, from which they cannot be removed.[119]

The Indians' attitude toward hacienda labor gives us an important clue to why haciendas were starving for labor in the midst of an abundant supply. Several petitions on behalf of native towns in the eighteenth century refer to hacienda peons as "slaves" and "la gente misera."[120] In the 1790's an elder from Coyotepec provided a remarkable commentary on what he considered the degeneration of working conditions on Spanish estates. He noted that although a voluntary system of labor had remained inviolable since the conquest, there had been important changes: "Labor in former times, because of its mildness, the punctual attendance of the Indians, [and] their loyalty and love for the haciendas, cannot be compared with what we see now. We have no solace except to decry our unhappy fate. The Indians have completely abandoned the haciendas, returning to the towns where vice, drunkenness, and laziness reign."[121]

Indebted Indians found several means of escaping hacienda service. A few paid off their debts; others recognized their obligations but absolutely refused to do service on the hacienda in repayment.[122] The most common solution was to flee the hacienda and to hide at home or in the mountains. The Indians fled with a guilt-free conscience. After the flight of some laborers from the Hacienda Guadalupe in 1791, one Indian witness explained simply, "They fled from service that was exacted by force or compelled by the local authorities."[123] For Indians who did not escape, drunkenness was a common way to relieve the tensions of hacienda life. It was also often used as an explanation for criminal acts. According to eighteenth-century records from the municipal archives of Tlacolula, Indians charged with assault, murder, or attempted flight from haciendas frequently claimed that they had been drunk and did not remember what they had done.

Many estate owners relied on temporary help to ease the labor situation or else limited production. Others resorted to coercion to obtain more laborers. Some hacendados refused to allow debts to be repaid and attempted to make them hereditary. In contrast to nineteenth-century practice, debts could not legally be passed on to heirs in the colonial period. This principle was affirmed by the Audiencia: an Indian woman successfully regained custody of two young grandchildren taken from her by an hacendado who claimed they were responsible for the debts of their deceased father.[124] Peons might be threatened with physical harm if they attempted to leave, as several workers from Coyotepec learned while serving on the hacienda of Pedro de Espina Pacheco Calderón. In a practice reminiscent of the *reparto de efectos* (the monopoly of the Spanish corregidor de indios on certain goods in his jurisdiction), some hacendados literally forced money and goods on reluctant Indians in order to establish a legal bond of obligation.[125] At the local level the Spanish government supported involuntary hacienda labor in several ways. During the 1790's natives of Zaachila who were unable to pay their tribute were either put in jail or forced to work on various haciendas.[126] Native lawbreakers might also be sent to haciendas. For example, Indians from the rebellious town of Soledad Etla who tried to sell goods at the market in Antequera were arrested and sent to the Hacienda de Guendulain.[127]

Entailed Estates

In many respects it is the entailed estates, or mayorazgos, of Oaxaca that resemble the large haciendas found in other parts of Spanish America. The lack of a strong tradition of primogeniture (or any other means of transferring landed estates intact to one's heirs) meant that only when formally entailed did estates in the Valley of Oaxaca remain in the hands of one family for many years. Most mayorazgos in New Spain emerged in the second half of the sixteenth century or the first half of the seventeenth.[128] Five of the Valley's six mayorazgos fall into this period: Ramírez de Aguilar, established in 1565; Jaúregui Pinelo, about 1591; Maldonado, before 1623; Bohórquez, 1624; and Lazo de la Vega, 1625. The sixth, Guendulain, was founded in 1677. In two areas of colonial South America that have been studied, central Chile and the Colombian highlands, mayorazgos appeared later, apparently because primogeniture operated successfully without legal enforcement.*

Through entailment an estate, meaning buildings, livestock, and land, was declared inalienable and not to be mortgaged. The specific conditions of entailment in New Spain usually included primogeniture or in the absence of a legitimate son, succession by the nearest blood relation, with preference given to males; the exclusion of clerics and mentally deranged heirs from the line of succession; and the retention of the founder's family name.[129]

The Valley's mayorazgos flourished during the seventeenth century. Under the direct supervision of the owners, mayorazgo haciendas made large profits; new lands were acquired, generally outside the Valley; and families firmly established their social positions with knighthoods, perpetual seats on the cabildo, and opulent homes in Antequera. Mayorazgos were not, however, exempt from the economic slump of the early eighteenth century. Urban and rural properties began to deteriorate, urban rentals lapsed, and the production of cereals and livestock declined. To raise the money needed to maintain their standard of living and keep their most important properties in operation,

---

* A deterrent to the establishment of mayorazgos in the Valley of Oaxaca in the eighteenth century was the fact that mortgaged property could not be entailed. As we have seen, most of the Spanish-owned estates were heavily mortgaged by the 1730's.

the holders of mayorazgos resorted to nearly every means except the outright sale of entailed haciendas. Lands that had been acquired since the mayorazgos were founded and were not entailed were sold. Owners sought special licenses to sell entailed urban property, and many mayorazgo haciendas were rented out.[130] Land-poor mayorazgos even took out liens on their haciendas in the eighteenth century, an act expressly forbidden in most contracts of entailment. A cédula real of June 22, 1695, had empowered colonial courts to permit owners to mortgage deteriorated urban property that they could not afford to restore;[131] in practice, the law was interpreted to include any entailed property in need of repair. José de Guendulain, for example, was allowed to secure a lien of 36,400 pesos from the Cathedral of Oaxaca on his haciendas near Santa María del Tule and Cuicatlán; and the sitio de Don Pedrillo, belonging to the Ramírez de Aguilar mayorazgo, was mortgaged to the Dominican Monastery of Santo Domingo for 1,000 pesos.[132] The mortgaging of entailed property seems to have been common elsewhere in New Spain at this time as well.[133]

The earliest mayorazgo to include Valley lands was founded by Luis de Aguilar and María Ramírez for their eldest son, Cristóbal, in 1565.[134] A complete list of the property in this entail has not been located, but we do know that it included two ranches in the Valley of Tlacolula, together forming the nucleus of the Hacienda Tanibé.* By the 1590's Cristóbal Ramírez de Aguilar had obtained two other grazing sites in the Tlacolula arm, Don Pedrillo and Quiabejo. Luis de Aguilar also established an entailed estate for his second son, Juan, in 1571, which consisted of a house plot in Antequera, four garden plots east of the city bordering on the Jalatlaco River, and a rancho with two Negro slaves near Guamelula (Huamelulpan?) in the Mixteca Alta.[135] Juan purchased an estancia de ganado menor near Cuilapan in 1630, but he resold it two years later.[136] The third son of Luis de Aguilar also had an entailed estate, but it included no Valley lands. The fourth son received three estancias

---

* Other lands owned by Luis de Aguilar, which were not entailed and which he sold in 1579, became part of the Hacienda Xaagá.

near the estancia Xuchitepec in the southern arm on the death of his father in 1615; these were not entailed and were sold before 1700.

We can trace the history of Cristóbal Ramírez de Aguilar's mayorazgo with some certainty. Cristóbal died without issue and was succeeded by his brother Marcos in 1634. Marcos's son Nicolás followed in 1644, and his son, Luis Ramírez de Aguilar, inherited the entail in the late seventeenth century. In 1693, while serving as alcalde mayor of Cuicatlán, he purchased the trapiche San José near Coscatlán in the jurisdiction of Tehuacán. Luis, who had returned to Antequera by 1700, was not able to escape the hard times suffered by other landowners. In 1716 he was forced to sell the estancia Quiabejo because he could not meet overdue interest payments. At the time of his death in 1724, the ten buildings in Antequera owned by the estate were sadly in need of repair. A costly litigation over the succession to Luis's estate followed between the heirs to the other two family mayorazgos. Fernando Ramírez de Aguilar, the son of Luis's brother Félix, was eventually selected to succeed his uncle. Fernando's cousin, Enrico Buenaventura de Angulo, administered the mayorazgo for several years during Fernando's minority, and several of the houses in Antequera were repaired at his expense. After taking over the estate Fernando was obliged to give his cousin usufruct rights to two of the houses in repayment. The Don Pedrillo estate was sold before 1782, leaving Tanibé the mayorazgo's only rural property in the Valley.[137]

The Mayorazgo de Guendulain was founded in 1677 by Pedro de Guendulain, who served as *alférez real, alcalde ordinario*, and *alguacil mayor del Santo Oficio* for Antequera. The entailed estate included the Hacienda La Asunción near Santa María del Tule, a trapiche near Teotitlán del Camino in the Mixteca Alta, and at least three houses in Antequera. The founder was succeeded by his son Pedro sometime between 1680 and 1683. The younger Pedro was followed by Joseph Joaquín de Guendulain (1707–12), Manuel de Guendulain (1712–33), Miguel de Guendulain (1733–50), and Manuel de Guendulain (mentioned in 1808 and 1819). The family owned several other estates apart from the mayorazgo, including the trapiche San José in the Valley of Nexapa, which was sold in 1683, and the Hacienda Aranjuez near Tlalixtac, bought and sold in the space of three years, 1710–12.

During the second half of the seventeenth century the Guendulain estate had enough liquid assets to loan 2,000 pesos to one Juan Rubén de Celi.[138] The estate also held a 12,000-peso mortgage on the trapiche San José. In the eighteenth century the situation took a decided turn for the worse. By 1727 the estate had acquired a debt of 1,000 pesos to an Antequera merchant; also some 6,000 pesos in back interest was due on a lien of 36,400 pesos held by the cathedral church at Antequera. In 1741 Miguel de Guendulain obtained an additional lien of 4,000 pesos on the pretext of repairing the Hacienda La Asunción. (The hacienda certainly needed repairs, judging from a 1741 description of it as "ruined and without equipment or provisions."[139]) The Guendulain mayorazgo had become land-poor. To meet personal expenses the Guendulains rented out much of the estate's rural land. A rancho appended to the Hacienda La Asunción was rented in 1734, followed by much of the hacienda's grazing land in 1743 and the trapiche at Teotitlán del Camino in 1750. The hacienda's arable lands were rented to the Indian community of Santa María del Tule in the 1790's.[140]

The two largest entails were located in the extreme southern portion of the Valley: the Mayorazgo de Bohórquez, founded in 1624, and the Mayorazgo de Maldonado, founded before 1623. The Mayorazgo de Bohórquez was established by Juan de Bohórquez, Oaxaca's bishop, on behalf of his nephew, José Ximeno de Bohórquez, the son of Diego Cataño de Bohórquez, a corregidor of Tlacolula. In addition to buildings in Antequera, the estate included the Hacienda Valdeflores, composed of five adjacent estancias north of Tlapacoya, which Juan de Bohórquez purchased between 1621 and 1623. At the time of its entailment, the hacienda had five Negro slaves, 17 teams of oxen, 470 head of cattle, and 3,500 sheep and goats.[141] Although a genealogy with dates of succession has not been found for this mayorazgo, various holders can be identified. Documents dated 1676 and 1710 indicate that Antonio de Bohórquez held the mayorazgo during this period.[142] He was apparently succeeded by a son, Juan, and a grandson, Joaquín, who died in 1792. Micaela Ximeno de Bohórquez managed the estate from 1792 until 1796, when she was succeeded by her son, José Varela Ximeno de Bohórquez.[143]

Several nearby rural properties were added to the Valdeflores hacienda during the late seventeenth century and the early eighteenth: a *labor* and an estancia east of Valdeflores in the 1690's, and the trapiche La Soritana in 1713. In 1717 La Soritana was returned to its former owner, the Convent of Santa Catalina de Sena, because of persisting land disputes with neighboring Indians; the estancia and the *labor* had been sold by 1713.[144] Although early-eighteenth-century records of the Valdeflores hacienda have not been located, later references indicate that the mayorazgo was affected by the regional economic problems of the time. Valdeflores was rented out rather than directly operated by the Bohórquez family during the 1770's.[145] In 1778 Valdeflores reached a rare boundary agreement with an adjoining mayorazgo estate, the Hacienda de Buenavista, which had been entailed in the 1620's by another prominent priest, Francisco Maldonado de Ovalle. The ostensible reason was that both parties were in financial difficulty and could ill afford to continue their boundary dispute, some 50 years old, in the courts. Another and perhaps more important reason for the agreement was the marriage of a son of the Bohórquez family to a daughter of the Maldonados.[146]

Another mayorazgo hacienda, located near San Sebastián Etla and known since the eighteenth century as Los Molinos de Lazo, also had a familial tie with the Bohórquez family. Rafael Pinelo, who founded the mayorazgo in 1591, was the brother-in-law of Diego Cataño de Bohórquez, the father of the first holder of the Mayorazgo de Bohórquez. The four mills and the adjoining arable land and pastureland that made up the rural holdings of the Pinelo estate were purchased from the Marqués del Valle in 1591.* The owners extended the hacienda's boundaries in the

---

* Among the holders of the Jaúregui Pinelo mayorazgo were Ana Pinelo, the wife of Rafael Pinelo (1634); Francisco Jaúregui Pinelo (1681) and his brother Lucas (1682); Francisca Jaúregui y Cataneo (1702); Antonio Llarena Lazo (1730); Joaquín Llarena Lazo (1781); and Francisco Jaúregui Pinelo (pre-1806) and his daughter Ana María (1806).

late seventeenth century by purchasing four tracts of Indian land totaling about a hundred acres and by renting the rancho Xabiogo and a millstone quarry from Francisco Ramírez de León, the cacique of Etla.[147] At the same time they took out liens totaling 9,000 pesos on the estate for the repair of houses in Antequera. More lands were added in the eighteenth century: the rancho Cerro Gordo, near San Pablo Etla, in 1730, and rentals near San Pedro Ixtlahuaca and San Agustín Etla in the 1740's. But by 1781 the mayorazgo was delinquent in paying the interest on these liens, and in the 1790's the hacienda was rented out.[148]

Spanish Landowners

The owners of rural estates in the Valley of Oaxaca were often prominent figures in the government and society of the Valley. But except for the few who came from the wealthiest or oldest families of colonial society and owned other property or productive capital, they were dependent for their prominence exclusively on the productivity of their land—a precarious resource indeed, as we have seen. With so many estates sold on the death of their owners, the prestige of a family was rarely ascendant for more than a generation or two.

Land ownership and political officeholding were intertwined in colonial Oaxaca from the sixteenth century. As early as the 1530's, members of the Antequera cabildo and corregidores and alcaldes mayores with jurisdictions in the Valley were landowners. Property-owning political officials in the sixteenth century included Cristóbal Gil, a regidor who owned a cattle ranch near Tlacochahuaya in the 1530's; Diego Hernández Calvo, a regidor who owned cattle estancias near Tlapacoya in the 1560's; Pedro Sánchez de Chávez, an *alcalde ordinario* of Antequera who owned an estancia east of Mitla in 1565; Luis and Cristóbal Ramírez de Aguilar, regidores with two estancias de ganado mayor near San Lorenzo Cacaotepec and Huitzo in 1582; Melchior Ruiz, an *alcalde ordinario* with two sitios de ganado menor near Ocotlán in 1590; and Cristóbal de Sala, the corregidor of Teitipac in the 1590's.[149]

Despite the obvious chance that conflicts of interest might

arise when landowning officials sat in judgment on boundary disputes and property rights, land ownership by local officials was encouraged by the Crown. Royal decrees of 1532, 1563, and 1596 stipulated that preference should be given to members of Spanish cabildos in the distribution of surrounding lands.[150] By 1600 the tie between land ownership and political office was a time-honored tradition in the Valley, and the resulting abuses were as evident there as they were elsewhere in the viceroyalty of New Spain. For example, Gaspar Asencio, the corregidor of Teotitlán, was found guilty of usurping Indian lands within his jurisdiction and forcing Indians to work these lands for his benefit without pay.[151]

Officials continued to hold land in the seventeenth and eighteenth centuries; including cabildo officials, who were frequently responsible for vistas de ojos, or boundary measurements, in the Valley. The potential for abuse of office was greatest when corregidores de indios wielding substantial judicial and fiscal authority owned lands within their own political jurisdiction. At least seven corregidores are known to have owned estates in the Valley. Cristóbal de Sala, corregidor of Teitipac, received a ranching grant in 1591; Luis de Moya, corregidor of the Cuatro Villas, owned a sheep ranch near Cuilapan in 1617; Francisco Ramírez de Torres, corregidor for the political jurisdiction of Antequera, owned a *labor* near the city in 1692; Miguel Ortiz, corregidor of Huitzo, owned lands near the town of Huitzo in 1682; Esteban García, corregidor of Tlacolula in 1694, owned lands near Mitla; Vicente de León, corregidor of Antequera in 1687, owned an hacienda near the city; and José Antonio de Larrainzán, corregidor of Antequera, owned the Hacienda San Antonio Buenavista in the 1770's.[152]

Unlike most Valley hacendados and their families, whose prominence in political affairs was at best transient, the holders of entailed estates remained in the political and social limelight even when their fortunes were in decline. Members of the Guendulain, Ramírez de Aguilar, and Bohórquez families in particular receive frequent mention in colonial documents as "leading citizens," thanks to their perpetual membership in the military

orders and the cabildo of Antequera. Not only did the mayorazgos of these families and that of the Lazo de la Vega family carry
with them the title of regidor perpetuo, but from time to time
individual holders of Valley mayorazgos secured other political
and religious offices as well. Some were positions of substantial
authority such as corregidor, *alguacil mayor, alcalde ordinario,
alguacil mayor del Santo Oficio,* and *promotor fiscal del obispado;* others, such as *alférez real,* were honorific. The social rank
of mayorazgo holders gave them a subtle influence in political
matters beyond their tenure in office. Their friendship and advice were frequently sought by political officials of lower social
standing. In 1711, for example, Teotitlán del Valle complained
that Joseph de Guendulain's favor with the Spanish alcalde
mayor had resulted in a faulty measurement of the boundary
between Teotitlán and the Guendulain hacienda.[153]

Owing to the frequent sale of estates owned by Spaniards, the
landowning class of Antequera was not a closed, homogeneous,
self-perpetuating group. Most new owners, like their predecessors, were not wealthy men. Their investment might be as little
as 1,000 pesos on a heavily mortgaged estate worth over 20,000
pesos;[154] and the estate was likely to be their only worldly possession, and its productivity their sole means of livelihood. Few
merchants and miners, the wealthiest citizens of Antequera, invested in Valley lands. Oaxaca's early-eighteenth-century mer-
chant-philanthropist Manuel Fernández Fiallo owned no lands
in the Valley, nor did such other wealthy merchants and notables
as Bartolomé Ruiz, Diego Martínez de Cabrera, and Pedro de
Godoy Ponze de León, a former governor of Honduras.[155] Merchants of the late eighteenth century acquired small *labores* and
haciendas on the outskirts of Antequera, but chiefly as country
houses rather than investments. We know of five such merchant-
owned *labores* and haciendas. Alvaro González de la Vega purchased the *labor* La Quinta south of Antequera in 1772; Gabriel
de Noriega owned the Hacienda de Noriega (San Nicolás Obispo) in the 1750's; Diego Joseph Seleri owned the Hacienda de
los Cinco Señores before 1762; and Diego de Benites Merino
and Phelipe de Mier each held a *labor* on the eastern outskirts

of the city in the late eighteenth century.[156] Secular priests, many the children of wealthy residents of Antequera, made up another transitory group of part-time owners of small estates in the late colonial period, as we shall see in the next chapter.

It is hard to trace the family backgrounds of most of the persons who suddenly appear as landowners in the records of the seventeenth and eighteenth centuries, only to disappear within a generation or two. Some were apparently new arrivals to Antequera. Of these, a number were peninsular Spaniards, notably José Martínez, Martín de Larralde, Antonio Vidal, Francisco Ibáñez, Andrés Fernández de Larrazábal, Cristóbal Angulo, Andrés de Montoya, and Gaspar Rodríguez de Montenegro; others were the younger sons of wealthy residents of Mexico City.[157] Still others may have been skilled craftsmen of some financial means or the children of merchants and owners of textile workshops (obrajes).[158] A key to the periodic disappearance of family names from the land records is found in the 1792 census of Antequera. Many of the sons of landowners listed in the census became lawyers, vendors, and craftsmen (bakers, tailors, tinsmiths, and so on), probably because they knew that the estates would eventually have to be sold anyway.*

Most of Oaxaca's hacendados and farmers were creoles. Of the 133 landowners and tenant farmers in Antequera in 1792, 88 were creoles, 34 were mestizos, 9 were peninsulars, and 2 were mulattoes. The predominance of creoles and mestizos suggests that landowners were not a uniform social and economic class in Oaxaca. As was probably true elsewhere in New Spain, the creoles were the most mobile group in colonial society, spanning the social spectrum from vagrants, beggars, and impoverished sharecroppers to the wealthiest landowners. Far from congregating in one barrio of the city, Antequera's landowning residents were spread out, some living in predominantly Indian and mulatto sections, others among artisans, still others in the most resplendent neighborhoods.

---

* AGN *Padrones* 13. Families owning entailed estates were apparently exceptions to this pattern. In the middle of the eighteenth century, for example, three sons of the Lazo de la Vega family acquired rural estates and the fourth became a priest.

As many of the Valley's haciendas began to deteriorate in the early eighteenth century or were sold to the Church, the owners found that by renting out their lands they could get a steady if small return on their investment. A substantial class of landless creoles and mestizos can be identified as the group that actually worked a number of Spanish-owned estates in the Valley during the eighteenth century.

Rentals of haciendas and *labores* to those without land were common by the 1690's and were especially numerous after 1740. Among the large haciendas rented out in the southern arm of the Valley, where rentals were particularly frequent, were Valdeflores, El Vergel, San Juan Bautista, and San Isidro.[159] Several large estates elsewhere in the Valley were also rented out: in the north, Santa Cruz and San José in the 1740's, Montoya, Santísima Trinidad, and Jalapilla in the 1770's, and Guadalupe in the 1790's; in the east, Aranjuez after 1799 and Santo Domingo Buenavista in the 1780's.[160] A number of much smaller properties were also rented to landless residents of Antequera, including at least ten *labores*—located near Zautla, Cuilapan (two), San Pedro Ixtlahuaca, Xoxocotlán, Etla, Zaachila, Coyotepec, Azompa, and Zegache—during the eighteenth century.[161]

In summary, a fixed pattern of Spanish land tenure in the Valley was not established in the colonial period. First, types of holdings were diverse and changing. The cattle ranches of the sixteenth century were largely replaced in the seventeenth century by haciendas that combined cattle raising and farming. *Labores*, or small estates mainly devoted to farming, also developed in the seventeenth century and increased in number during the eighteenth century as a result of purchases and rentals from Indian nobles and communities. Second, Spanish ownership was quite unstable. Haciendas and *labores* changed hands frequently, more often by sale than by inheritance. The six entailed estates, which maintained greater continuity of ownership through legal means, accounted for only a small portion, perhaps one-fourth, of Spanish lands in the Valley. The economic slowdown of the early eighteenth century made landhold-

ing even more unstable. Mortgages on rural estates increased
during this period, prompting more sales and rentals. Finally,
Spanish landholdings in the Valley were not consolidated and in
general remained small and widely dispersed. Few Spaniards
were able to acquire large areas of land surrounding their estates. In fact, it appears that individual Spaniards owned more
Valley lands in the seventeenth century than they did in the
eighteenth. At most, Spanish estates accounted for one-third of
the land in Oaxaca, and the largest holdings were suited only to
grazing.

V

CHURCH ESTATES

THE CONQUEST and colonization of Mexico were Christian as well as military ventures. Initially dedicated to converting Indians and establishing a Christian society, secular and regular clergymen reaped the material rewards of conquest as well. Only the Franciscans resisted the temptations of Mammon and remained true to their vow of poverty. Like a healthy plant the colonial Church grew in size and complexity. And as it grew it became increasingly preoccupied with economic affairs and displays of opulence. Throughout the colonial period a numerous, wealthy, and influential clergy did much to create the texture of life and land tenure in the Valley of Oaxaca. This chapter describes the acquisition and use of property by the Church and the changing pattern of land control by various Church groups in the seventeenth and eighteenth centuries.

Churchmen came early to the Valley of Oaxaca. A small group of Dominican friars established permanent residence in Antequera in 1528;[1] and the bishopric of Oaxaca was formally established in 1535, with Antequera as its center. Oaxaca's first bishop, Juan López de Zárate, was a man of considerable stature in the city, serving as its official spokesman in various petitions to the Crown in the 1530's and 1540's.[2] The Dominican Order was empowered to set up parishes throughout the bishopric of Oaxaca; and it concentrated most of its energy there because the Franciscans and Augustinians had already established spheres of influence in the core of the viceroyalty, in and around the Valley of Mexico.

Unlike the impoverished Spanish lay community of Antequera, whose population fluctuated drastically during the sixteenth century because of conflicts with the Marqués del Valle and a shortage of vacant land, the Church grew steadily and enjoyed the paternalistic support of both the Crown and the Marqués. Doctrinas, consisting of a religious head town (where the church and the priest's residence were located) and a group of smaller subject communities or *visitas*, were founded by the Dominicans at Etla, Cuilapan, and the Villa de Oaxaca in 1550, Huitzo in 1554, and Ocotlán in 1562.[3] By the end of the sixteenth century, Dominican doctrinas had been established in a number of other major towns: Zaachila, Santa Ana Zegache, Santa Cruz Mixtepec, Santa Catarina Minas, Santa Marta Chichicapan, San Miguel Tlalixtac, San Gerónimo Tlacochahuaya, San Juan Teitipac, Teotitlán del Valle, and Tlacolula.[4] In 1597 there were more than 70 Dominicans in the Valley, roughly one for every four households in Antequera.[5] Other religious orders penetrated the Dominican domain of central Oaxaca in the late sixteenth century. The Franciscan, Jesuit, Augustinian, Carmelite, and Mercedarian orders each established a house in Antequera. The following nunneries were also founded: Santa Catalina de Sena (an affiliate of the Dominican Order), Recoletas Agustinas (Nuestra Señora de la Soledad), La Concepción, Capuchinas Españolas, and Capuchinas Indias.

As elsewhere in New Spain the number of secular priests in Oaxaca increased considerably after the initial "spiritual conquest" by the regular orders. With the Dominicans in firm control of more than two-thirds of the bishopric's Indians by 1550, relations between the regular and secular clergies were periodically tense and abrasive. Trouble first surfaced in a heated quarrel between Bishop Zárate and the Dominicans in 1551. The bishop wrote:

They [the Dominicans] have informed the high Council that I do not treat them well. I reply, May God treat me as well as I have treated them; and likewise, May God treat them as they have treated me. I have permitted them to be virtual lords of the bishopric. I have neither powers nor possessions in the towns to which they minister. All their towns are populous, healthy, rich, and located on level ground. They have all of the Villa de Oaxaca; part of Cuilapan, one league away [from Antequera]; Tlacochahuaya, Macuilxóchitl, and Teotitlán, two leagues away; Teitipac, four leagues away; and Mitla and Tlacolula, seven leagues away. All these towns are in the Valley and are easily served. They have not wished to take charge of the many towns and provinces located in the tropics or on rough terrain.

They say that I treat them badly. The reverse is true, for I am the one who is mistreated. I have little, and have received little help from the aforesaid friars. The worst is that they do not respect my authority as bishop. The Indians and towns in their jurisdiction do not acknowledge my authority or treat me as a bishop; they do not dare do so for fear of being whipped and mistreated [by the Dominicans].[6]

The general climate of opinion in seventeenth-century Oaxaca was increasingly materialistic; this, coupled with the ambitions and limited vision of individual clerics, served to magnify tensions between the regular orders and secular priests. Sixteenth-century and seventeenth-century records are peppered with mutual accusations of cruelty to Indian neophytes and accounts of struggles for control of Indian alms.[7] Grasping bishops like Juan de Bohórquez, the founder of the largest entailed estate in the Valley, carried on running feuds with the Dominicans, their archrivals for wealth and influence.

In the early eighteenth century these tensions came to a head over the control of native parishes. Pointing to the poverty of the secular Church, Oaxaca's bishops sought the secularization of Dominican parishes. In 1702 Bishop Angel Maldonado urged the Crown to secularize ten Dominican districts, six located in the Valley: Santa Cruz Mixtepec, Santa Ana Zegache, Ocotlán, Zaachila, Tlalixtac, and Huitzo. In 1705 the Crown supported the secular clergy by ordering that the next ten Dominican parishes to fall vacant would pass to the secular hierarchy.[8] Enforcement of the royal order was slow, but Dominican parishes were reduced from 45 in 1705 to 23 in 1776. By 1760 the Dominicans had lost Etla, Zimatlán, Tlalixtac, Zaachila, and Cuilapan, five of their richest Valley parishes.[9] This intra-clerical strife did not result in a decline of the Church's strength in terms of wealth and numbers until the last quarter of the eighteenth century. In 1777 there were 742 churchmen living in Antequera, including 312 members of the regular orders. In 1792 there

TABLE 9

Regular Clergy in Antequera, 1777 and 1792

Institution	Number of residents	
	1777	1792
Monasteries:		
Santo Domingo (Dominican)	61	41
San Francisco, Descalzos	22	16
Del Carmen, Descalzos	19	13
San Agustín, Calzados	10	9
La Merced	9	13
San Pablo (Dominican)	9	10
Oratorio de San Felipe Neri	—	5
TOTAL	130	107
Convents:		
Santa Catalina de Sena	67	50
La Concepción	35	39
Capuchinas Españolas	32	35
La Soledad	26	27
Capuchinas Indias	—	26
TOTAL	160	177
Hospitals:		
Betlén	13	9
San Juan de Dios	9	8
Hospital Real de San Cosmé	—	0
TOTAL	22	17
Colleges:		
Niños de la Presentación	—	0
Seminario de Estudios	—	2
Infantes de Cristo	—	2
TOTAL	—	4
GRAND TOTAL	312	305

NOTE: Institutions for which no figures are given for 1777 were not mentioned in that year.

were still 305 regulars, but there were only 289 secular priests in a total population of 18,241 (see Table 9).[10]

Methods of Acquiring Property

Churchmen often spoke of benevolent reasons for acquiring and using land. In 1788 the Carmelites argued that if they built a wheat mill on their San Juan Bautista estate, they would charge nearby farmers lower prices and give better service than other mill owners in the Valley.[11] An eighteenth-century instruction to

Jesuit hacienda administrators stressed their obligation to treat their laborers well and to educate them in matters of the faith.[12] In the long run, however, good intentions did not prevent land and labor disputes between clerical estate owners and their Indian neighbors. In the eighteenth century Dominican hacendados in the eastern arm engaged in bitter, occasionally bloody disputes with the towns of Mitla, Matatlán, and Teotitlán del Valle.

The methods of acquiring land varied greatly both among the different orders and among different houses of the same affiliation. Donations and *capellanías* (grants to individual clerics or Church groups to support certain religious ceremonies, such as masses in honor of the donor) were an important source of rural land for urban convents and monasteries in New Spain.[13] In the Valley of Oaxaca most rural land acquired by the Church in this way came from Indians. Capellanías established by Spaniards and creoles generally consisted of a money grant of 2,000 to 3,000 pesos or a house in Antequera; only one example of a grant of land from a Spaniard has been found.[14] Occasionally a Spanish hacendado stipulated in his will that a part of his estate, usually 2,000 pesos, be set aside for a church or an individual priest.[15] Five per cent of this amount was to be paid annually to the beneficiary, as if a lien had been established on the hacienda. These voluntary liens were designed to provide a regular income for a priest, a church, or the residents of a monastery or a convent.

Dominican parish churches and monasteries received nearly all their landholdings through capellanías and gifts from Indian nobles and communities. Apparently some of these grants were voluntary donations from devout natives. The Cuilapan convent accumulated all its important holdings before 1644 in the form of gifts from childless caciques and *principales*.[16] Since these bequests generally involved small plots only an acre or two in size, the holdings of rural monasteries were often fragmented and dispersed.[17] Other native grants were the result of prodding and persuasion by the Dominicans. The Villa de Etla, for example, complained bitterly that nearly all its community land had been given away to the local Dominican monastery by gullible caciques and *principales*.[18] Still other grants were made by Indian communities desiring to form separate parishes. Zimatlán, seeking to become independent of the doctrina of Zaachila, turned over two estancias de ganado menor to the Dominicans.[19]

Cofradía lands provided another important source of rural lands for the parish curate, whether Dominican or secular. Cofradías were the religious brotherhoods responsible for staging various religious celebrations in a native village. Ernesto de la Torre Villar has described a broad range of activities carried out by colonial cofradías in Michoacán, from conducting funeral rites to running hospital facilities and other social welfare projects.[20] Documentation for Oaxaca, however, suggests that cofradía activities were confined to the celebration of certain annual religious festivities. The following is a composite list of all expenses recorded for Valley cofradías in a 1790 inspection report: candles and wine for mass throughout the year, oil for sacramental lamps, adornments for altars and images of saints, and physical maintenance of the churches. According to the same record the cofradías were responsible for the vespers, processions, masses, and sermons for Corpus Christi, Holy Week, Christmas, and the festivals of the visitas' patron saints. Judging from the treasuries of the cofradías, they could hardly afford to do more. The average cofradía in 1790 possessed slightly less than 32 pesos and 11 pounds of wax for the coming year.[21]

Much like the eighteenth-century cofradías of Yucatán described by Justo Sierra O'Reilly, those in the Valley supported themselves by raising small herds of livestock or by using lands legally belonging to the brotherhood. Such lands were sometimes covertly administered by the local priest rather than by native officials.[22] The cofradías of Etla and Zimatlán were reportedly "controlled by the parochial church and convent."[23] One colonial document calls the parish priest of Santa María Tenexpan the "owner" of cofradía land.[24] And the monastery at Cuilapan oversaw cofradía revenues in the visita of Azompa and received rent payments from various arable lands belonging to the cofradía. In short, cofradías may have served as a cover for clerical landholding in Indian communities, which was forbidden by law. An inspection was initiated in the Marqués del Valle's Cuatro Villas jurisdiction in 1760 specifically to investigate the suspected control of native communal property by the parish clergy.[25]

The convents and monasteries in Antequera acquired most of their rural lands by direct purchase and foreclosure.* The many bequests of money, gifts of urban property, and capellanías gave the regular orders a vast reserve of liquid assets, enabling them to become the principal source of credit very early in colonial Oaxaca. Interest-bearing loans and mortgages on urban and rural estates were an important source of income for the Church.[26] In 1597 the Convent of La Concepción had already accumulated 17,000 pesos in mortgages, the Jesuits 6,000, the Augustinians 7,000, Santa Catalina de Sena 1,400, and the cathedral in Antequera 16,000 to 17,000.[27] Although most of these mortgages were not explicitly granted in perpetuity, the clerical lender usually considered the annual interest of 5 per cent a perpetual income and willingly allowed the debt to pass from one estate owner to the next. The borrower could pay off the principal at his convenience. Occasionally, however, lenders foreclosed on estates whose owners had been delinquent in their interest payments. Most foreclosures took place when an estate was being transferred to a new owner. At this time the creditors had the option of declaring their loans payable in a lump sum. When the value of a mortgage equaled, or nearly equaled, the value of the estate, title to the property often passed to the lender. Fifteen cases of acquisition by foreclosure or debt, most in the eighteenth century, have been found. The fact that 12 of the 15 involved convents in Antequera does not necessarily mean that convents were more inclined to foreclose than other Church institutions. Rather, it results from the fact that three convents, Santa Catalina de Sena, La Concepción, and La Soledad, dominated the business of mortgaging rural estates in the Valley.[28]

Churchmen also acquired usufruct rights to Valley lands by means of land grants, rentals, and inheritance. Land grants by the cabildo of Antequera in the first half of the sixteenth cen-

---

* No land transactions in which Spaniards acted as intermediaries for the Church, a common practice in the Valley of Mexico in the late sixteenth century, have been found for Oaxaca. Gibson, *Aztecs Under Spanish Rule*, p. 126.

tury and by the Crown in the last half, although infrequent, do account for some Jesuit and Dominican holdings on the outskirts of Antequera.[29] Rentals were an important source of land for the Church. The Dominicans in particular increased the productive area of their estates in the eighteenth century by renting nearby Indian cattle ranches.[30]

Land Use

The Church in Oaxaca did not take a special interest in agricultural lands; cattle estancias were the most common type of Church estate. Probably this was due in part to the difficulty of acquiring large areas of arable land. Each regular order usually concentrated its attention on one fairly large estate in the Valley, renting out other lands or leaving them untended. The Carmelites owned and operated only one hacienda, San Juan Bautista, south of Antequera, which encompassed 21 caballerías of arable land. The Bethlemites confined their holdings to the ranching hacienda Santo Domingo Buenavista, near Teotitlán del Valle and Macuilxóchitl. The Jesuits' only estate in the Valley was a small *labor* and lime deposit adjacent to the town of San Antonio de la Cal, southeast of Antequera.

The problems of disputed boundaries and underused land faced by the Monastery of Santo Domingo in the eighteenth century underscore the wisdom of operating only consolidated holdings. Santo Domingo's large, dispersed holdings were hard to oversee, and the monastery did not use them effectively. The obscure boundaries of its estates in the Valley of Tlacolula led to countless controversies with, and incursions by, neighboring Indian towns. Santo Domingo ultimately limited its direct involvement to a few estates, allowing the Indians to graze their cattle on untended lands and converting agricultural lands into pastures on other properties, such as the rancho de Lope near Matatlán in the eastern arm.[31] As a result of the problems inherent in managing dispersed estates, Church landowners rented out many small tracts, usually for periods of seven or nine years, and let out other tracts to Indians in sharecropping arrangements.[32]

The direct sale of unwanted lands, almost always overlooked

by historians, was another way the Church disposed of property.[33]
In theory, all property accruing to Church bodies belonged to
the Church as a corporation and could be alienated only on in-
structions from the Pope himself; in fact, this principle was not
applied to all acquisitions. Capellanías, *obras pías* (charitable
funds), and the dowries of novices were treated as inalienable,

TABLE 10

Sales of Land by Regular Orders

Year	Property	Seller	Source
1610	H. de Escovar	Merced	AGNH 380, 9:69r
1629	Lands near San Felipe del Agua	Agus.	AGNH 163, 48:36r
1638	E. near Zaachila	Merced	AGNT 333, 2:17v
1638	E. de los Tres Ríos	SCdS	AGNT 333, 2:17v
pre-1641	E. near Azompa	Dominican mon- astery, Cuilapan	AGNH 69, bk. 2, fol. 66r–v
1666	H. San Joaquín	SCdS	AN 1707, fol. 253r
1666	EGM near Cuilapan	SCdS	CCGL, 1666
1667	EGM near Zimatlán	Merced	AGNT 333, 2:3v
pre-1682	H. Jalapilla	SCdS	AGNT 125, 4:1r
1708	San Roque	Agus.	AN 1708, fol. 175v
1714	H. de pan sembrar, Cuilapan	Conc.	CDChO, rollo 66
1715	*Labor* near Sola	SCdS	AN 1717, fol. 152v
pre-1717	E. Higonachada	Conc.	AGNG, exp. 326
1717	E. La Soledad	Conc.	AN 1717, fol. 98v
1717	HH. San Diego and Poblete	SCdS	AN 1717, fol. 107v
1748	H. Matagallinas	SCdS	AN 1749, fol. 238v
1753	Trapiche Santa Ana	Jesuit colegio	AN 1767, fol 32r
1758	H. Xaagá	Conc.	CCGL, 1758
1762	H. San Diego	SCdS	AN 1762, fol. 16r
1762	H. Cinco Señores	Conc.	AGNT 890
1768	Rancho Guegonivalle	Agus.	AN 1768
1769	H. Xuchitepec	Agus.	AN 1769, fol. 49v
1769	SGM near San Pedro Ixtlahuaca	SCdS	AN 1769, fol. 121r
1770	H. Jalapilla	Conc.	AN 1770, fol. 27v
1772	*Labor* La Quinta	Conc.	AN 1772, fol. 178v

NOTE: The following abbreviations are used in this table. In the Property column: E. = Es-
tancia, EGM = Estancia de ganado menor, H. = Hacienda, SGM = Sitio de ganado menor.
In the Seller column, Agus. = Agustinas (La Soledad), Conc. = La Concepción, SCdS = Santa
Catalina de Sena.

but these rarely involved rural lands.[34] Lands that the convents and monasteries of Oaxaca acquired by purchase, outright gift, or foreclosure, in contrast, were not considered entailed properties. Such lands could be and were sold. Table 10 lists the known sales of Valley lands by the regular orders.

As elsewhere in New Spain churchmen in the Valley of Oaxaca became increasingly preoccupied with economic affairs and property ownership in the seventeenth and eighteenth centuries. Urban property became a special interest of the regular clergy. In 1792 monasteries and convents owned 870 houses in Antequera, most of which were rented out (see Table 11).[35] But unlike convents in Mexico City, which dealt almost exclusively in urban real estate and land mortgages, the regular orders in Oaxaca also invested in rural lands. They, like individual secular priests, acquired numerous cattle ranches and agricultural

TABLE 11

Houses in Antequera Owned by Monasteries and Convents, 1792

Institution	Number of houses owned
Monastic Institutions:	
San Pablo	131
Santo Domingo	70
Oratorio de San Felipe Neri	68
La Merced	55
San Agustín	41
Del Carmen	32
San Juan de Dios	24
Colegio Seminario de Estudios	17
Betlén	7
Colegio de Infantes de Cristo	1
San Francisco	0
Conventual Institutions:	
Santa Catalina de Sena	210
La Concepción	113
Recoletas Agustinas (La Soledad)	64
Hospital Real de San Cosmé	22
Capuchinas Indias	8
Colegio de Niños de la Presentación	7
Capuchinas Españolas	0
GRAND TOTAL	870

holdings in the eighteenth century. Of the major owners of urban property, only the Monastery of San Pablo and the Oratorio de San Felipe Neri did not have rural estates.

The Spread of Church Lands

The growth of various Church estates will now be considered in detail. Whenever possible the regular orders and the secular clergy will be treated separately. Maps 5 and 6, which show identifiable Church estates in 1660 and 1760, provide a visual demonstration of growth during the late colonial period.

The Dominicans, whose colonial holdings in the Valley are shown on Map 7, were the first churchmen to take an active interest in land ownership. In fact, late-sixteenth-century records suggest that they were the first Spaniards to make a concerted effort to acquire land. As early as 1560 Spaniards from Antequera complained that the Dominicans had an unfair advantage because, unlike laymen, they were allowed to accept gifts of pastureland from Indians.[36] The Dominican order as a body did not own land; instead, individual monasteries scattered throughout the Valley held separate properties. The principal Dominican monastery, Santo Domingo at Antequera, was the major landowner in the bishopric at the end of the sixteenth century. According to a 1597 report on ecclesiastical properties, Santo Domingo owned four cattle ranches in Tehuantepec, worth over 33,000 pesos, and these properties in the Valley: two sheep ranches, worth between 11,000 and 16,000 pesos, various houses and lots in Antequera and liens on a number of others, two mills, a fishery, and a small farm.[37]

Total Dominican landholdings in the province of San Hipólito Mártir, which encompassed roughly the same area as the bishopric of Oaxaca, increased in the late seventeenth century and the eighteenth.* In 1713 the Dominicans owned 33 sitios de ganado, 21 caballerías, and "part of seven leagues" in these jurisdictions

---

* The bishopric of Oaxaca in the colonial period included all of the modern state of Oaxaca except Huajuapan, Xiuxtlahuacan, and Tzilacayoapan, which were attached to the bishopric of Puebla, and parts of Veracruz, Guerrero, and Tabasco. Francisco del Paso y Troncoso, "La división territorial de la Nueva España en 1636," in Lecturas históricas mexicanas (Mexico, 1966), 2: 582.

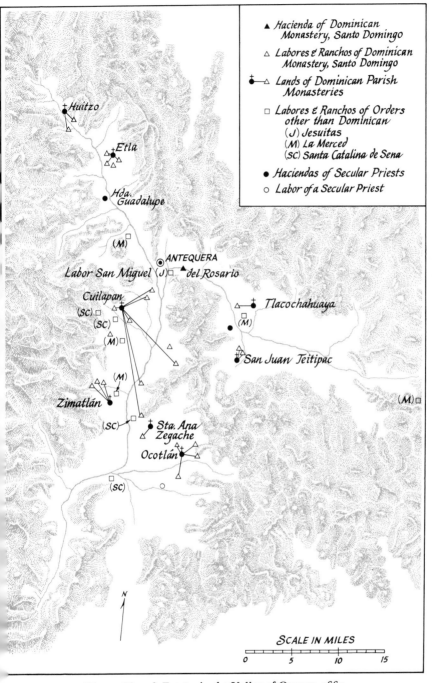

+Huitzo

Etla

Hda.
Guadalupe

(M)

ANTEQUERA

Labor San Miguel (J)□ ▲del Rosario

Cuilapan
(SC)□   △△ + Tlacochahuaya
  (SC)□   □
  (M)□   (M)

              ⁂San Juan Teitipac

    (M)□   (M)□

  (M)□
Zimatlán

(SC)□   + Sta. Ana
               △ Zegache
        Ocotlán△

(SC)□   ○

N

SCALE IN MILES

0   5   10   15

Map 5. Church Estates in the Valley of Oaxaca, 1660

KEY TO MAP 6

E1. Hacienda San Isidro
E2. Rancho San José
E3. *Labor* Santa Rita
E4. Hacienda Jalapilla
I5. Sitio Duhuatia
I6. *Labor* San Blas
I7. Rancho San Blas
I8. Hacienda San Francisco Xavier
I9. *Labor* Jesús Nazareno
I10. Hacienda San Isidro
I11. *Labor* San José
I12. Hacienda del Cacique
I13. Hacienda San Nicolás Obispo
I14. Hacienda de Zorita
I15. Hacienda Tlanechico
Z16. Hacienda de Ortega
Z17. Hacienda Quialana
Z18. Hacienda Xuchitepec
Z19. *Labor* San Isidro
Z20. Hacienda San Diego
Z21. Trapiche Santa Cruz
Z22. Hacienda Matagallinas
Z23. Trapiche Santa Ana and *Labor* San José
Z24. Hacienda El Vergel
Z25. *Labor* La Gachupina
Z26. Sitio El Capitán

Z27. *Labor* Guelavichigana
Z28. Rancho La Chilayta
Z29. Hacienda Santa Rosa
I30. Haciendas San Juan Bautista, San José, and Los Naranjos
I31. Hacienda San Miguel
I32. *Labor* Sangre de Cristo
I33. *Labor* La Quinta
I34. *Labor* San Miguel
I35. Rancho de la Noria
I36. *Labor* de la Palma
I37. Hacienda de los Cinco Señores
I38. *Labor* San Luis
I39. Hacienda Dolores
I40. Hacienda del Rosario
I41. *Labor* de Alfaro
T42. Hacienda Aranjuez
T43. Hacienda Santo Domingo Buenavista
T44. Hacienda San Francisco Buenavista
T45. Rancho Guadalupe
T46. *Labor* de Soriano
T47. Sitio de Don Pedrillo
T48. Rancho del Fuerte
T49. Rancho de Lope
T50. Hacienda Xaagá

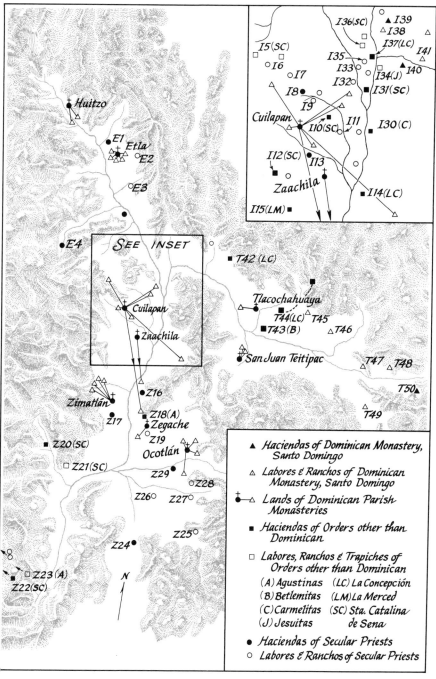

Map 6. Church Estates in the Valley of Oaxaca, 1760

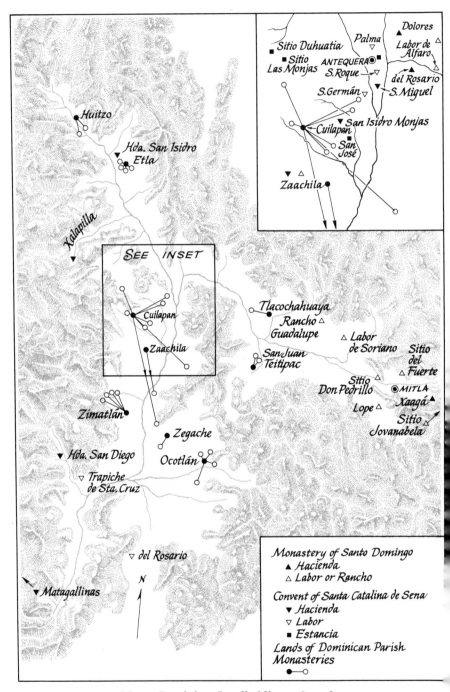

Map 7. Dominican Landholdings, 1600–1810

of the province: Las Cuatro Villas, Nochixtlán, Tehuantepec, Nexapa, Teotitlán del Valle, Yanhuitlán, Antequera, and Villa Alta.[38] Dominican holdings continued to grow to the end of the colonial period.

The parochial Dominican monasteries took an early interest in landholding. Nearly all their lands were obtained by capellanías or donations from Indian nobles and communities. Indians also supplied most of the labor on the estates. The Cuilapan monastery, apparently founded in 1555, was extremely rich by 1597, holding six sheep ranches, two of which together grazed 16,000 animals and were termed "the best sitios in the Valley," a small farm, and liens worth 8,000 to 13,000 pesos on property in Antequera.[39] It acquired at least eight other pieces of land before 1618.[40] The monastery preferred to derive rental income from its holdings rather than to work them directly, and by 1644 almost all had been rented out, most for a period of one or two generations. One exception was an "hacienda de ganado menor" near Xoxocotlán, where an unspecified number of sheep and goats were grazed. By 1659, however, it too was rented to a resident of Antequera. The lease was renewed in 1718, according to the latest known reference to the estate.[41] The monastery acquired two *labores*, one near Coyotepec and the other near Zaachila, as a result of debts. One was sold outright before 1641; the other was rented out in censo perpetuo before 1689.[42]

Other parochial Dominican monasteries also sought to acquire land, especially nearby grazing land. The monastery at Ocotlán owned at least four ranchos and estancias de ganado, two of them acquired before 1597.[43] All four were located in the general vicinity of Ocotlán, one near San Antonino, another near San Pedro Apostol, the third bordering on the Hacienda San José, and the fourth near Santa Catarina Minas.[44] The monastery at Zimatlán had only one sheep ranch in 1597, but by 1700 it owned three estancias northwest of town (one for ganado mayor) and one arable tract one-half caballería in size.* The houses at San Juan Teitipac, Huitzo, and Santa Cruz Mixtepec owned at least two estancias each before 1700, and those at Teotitlán del Valle,

---

* AGNT 241, 7:21r, 1689. Ownership of the estancia de ganado mayor, Lobaniza, was contested by the Indian cabildo of Zimatlán in 1740. AGNT 1460, exp. 7.

Tlacochahuaya, Zaachila, Santa Ana Zegache, and the Villa de Oaxaca at least one site each.[45] Arable lands held by Dominican monasteries appear less frequently in colonial records for the Valley. The monastery at Zaachila owned a small *labor*, and the one at Etla accumulated mostly arable land. In 1791 the Etla house owned the Hacienda del Rosario in the Etla arm as well as much good farm land near the Villa de Etla; most of this land was rented out. In addition to its emphasis on arable land, the Etla monastery was exceptional in another way. Most Dominican parish monasteries held land only in their immediate vicinities, but the Etla house owned two caballerías of land near Mitla at the far end of the eastern arm.[46]

Santo Domingo differed from its rural counterparts in that it actively sought property in all parts of the bishopric. It was already a significant landowner by the late sixteenth century. We know that Santo Domingo acquired stray pieces of land in the southern arm during the first half of the seventeenth century: an estancia near San Lucas Tlanechico, two caballerías near Coyotepec (both obtained in censo perpetuo from the Marqués del Valle), and grazing sites rented from the Indian community of Zimatlán. At the same time the monastery was developing the Hacienda Grande de Nuestra Señora del Rosario, southeast of Antequera. Until the eighteenth century Santo Domingo's major land interests were outside the Valley in the jurisdiction of Tehuantepec. By the mid-seventeenth century its four cattle ranches there, first mentioned in 1597, had grown into a large hacienda encompassing "twenty-two continuous leagues of land."[47]

From the late seventeenth century through the eighteenth, many new estates in the Valley fell to Santo Domingo. In contrast to the rural Dominican monasteries, which received most of their lands by donation, Santo Domingo acquired new properties by purchase. (Writing only occasional mortgages on Valley haciendas, Santo Domingo was apparently not a major creditor and did not acquire lands through foreclosure.) The monastery's attention was centered on the eastern arm of the Valley after 1700, and by 1750 it was the largest non-Indian landowner in the area. Its new holdings included the *labor* de Alfaro, bordering on

Santa Lucía, acquired about 1684; the Hacienda Dolores near
Ixcotel; the *labor* de Soriano, bordering on Teotitlán del Valle;
the rancho Guadalupe, also near Teotitlán; three cattle ranches
near Mitla, del Fuerte, Lope, and Don Pedrillo, acquired in the
1730's; and the Hacienda Xaagá east of Mitla, finally purchased
in 1758 after an unsuccessful attempt in 1747.[48]

As other monasteries and convents in the Valley also learned
by experience, Santo Domingo found that its newly acquired
estates were not always an asset. Neighboring Indian towns frequently encroached on the monastery's dispersed, poorly marked
haciendas. Disputes between Mitla and the Hacienda Xaagá
were chronic, despite several costly vistas de ojos that presumably
established definitive boundaries.[49] A pitched battle between the
residents of Mitla and Xaagá ensued after the hacienda began
to construct a fence along its boundary in 1792.[50] Santo Domingo
had acquired more land in the eastern arm than it could effectively use. Consequently, it left some parts of the Lope, del
Fuerte, and Xaagá estates untended, and in an attempt to promote amicable relations, allowed natives to graze their cattle
there. Farming was abandoned on the rancho de Lope in 1808
and the laborers dismissed.[51] In view of the monastery's limited
use of its estates, it is surprising that some of the haciendas were
not rented out.

The financial rewards of land ownership proved slim for Santo
Domingo in the late eighteenth century. Between 1764 and 1769
expenses on the monastery's Valley estates exceeded revenues by
6,000 pesos.[52] An 1814 report describes increasing debts and deteriorating properties:

From 1789 on the administrator of the monastery's rural properties
began to borrow sums of money at interest, mortgaging the aforesaid
properties in the belief that by spending heavily on new equipment
and supplies, the monastery would reap greater profits and would be
able to escape the difficulties in which it found itself. The administrator took out loans of nearly 70,000 pesos, and far from improving,
the monastery's situation became so adverse that he was able neither
to meet the interest payments nor to maintain the estates in their
former condition. . . . The lands have not yielded even what is spent
in production.[53]

The landholdings of other monasteries in the Valley of Oaxaca were considerably smaller than those of the Dominicans. The Valley's one Franciscan house, located in Antequera, adhered to the order's vow of poverty and its prohibition of property ownership. The 1792 census of the religious orders in Antequera notes that the Franciscans did not own any urban real estate, and no evidence has been found that they owned any rural property.

The Jesuit monastery and college at Antequera, established in 1576, owned a small wheat farm with a lime deposit southeast of the city. This property was valued at 7,000 pesos in 1769, two years after Charles III had expelled the order from the empire.[54] The Jesuits had traded a nearby cattle ranch and mill (obtained in 1580) to the cabildo of Antequera for the *labor* in 1607.[55] They relied heavily on Negro slaves to mine the lime and to work the land. In the 1770's there were six huts on the former Jesuit properties occupied by slaves.[56] The Jesuits invested heavily in urban property, paying out 9,600 pesos in 1718 alone to acquire houses in Antequera.[57] They also owned several rural estates on the periphery of the Valley: a trapiche at Nexapa, 40 miles to the southeast; another trapiche, Nuestra Señora del Rosario, located near Santa María Nativitas in the jurisdiction of Coatlán, southwest of the Valley; the Hacienda Santa Inés, in the vicinity of Ejutla in the south; and a rancho further south near Miahuatlán, which supplied food and hides to the trapiche del Rosario. A small packet of letters from the administrator of the hacienda to the rector of the Jesuit college in Antequera, dated 1717 and 1718, notes that the hacienda raised maize and beans for the trapiche and bred and sold some 410 sheep, 2,500 goats, and horses, mules, and burros.*

The Jesuits in New Spain generally appreciated the fact that the most profitable property investments were well-managed agricultural enterprises. Those in Antequera, however, devoted

---

* AGN *Archivo Histórico de Hacienda* 285, exp. 81. These letters are a unique source of information on weather conditions, crop yields, and the day-to-day problems of running a rural estate. During the period they cover, for example, many of the hacienda's cattle were killed by mountain lions. Also, a letter of March 20, 1717, complains of a shortage of farmhands, asserting that previously there was an abundance.

much attention to urban properties. Further, the remote locations of the college's sugar trapiches made efficient management difficult. Thus the Jesuits did not escape the economic decline in Oaxaca in the early eighteenth century. Even the cochineal boom beginning about 1740 apparently did not improve the Jesuits' situation, for they found it necessary to sell the Coatlán trapiche in 1753.[58] An undated report from the first half of the eighteenth century provides a picture of inactivity, overdue rents and interest payments, and a meager, dwindling income, despite capital investments in the bishopric of 238,000 pesos:

[The following is] an explanation of why the estates of the Colegio de Oaxaca have deteriorated so badly. First, the sugar mills are located at a great distance from Oaxaca over rough roads and through bad weather conditions, especially the Nexapa trapiche. . . . One can hardly find overseers or administrators for Nexapa, since they quickly die or become ill after going there. Furthermore, the mill's costs have exceeded revenues. Second, much capital was invested in houses that are not business establishments. The houses have run to waste. Not only are the rents unpaid, the principal has been lost as well, mainly because the commerce of this city has become so different over the last 30 years that one can hardly find properties free of debt. Those seemingly unencumbered are, in fact, rife with entanglements and cunning deceits, so that if one is not careful and vigilant in seeing to whom the money is lent and who the guarantors are, the entire sum will be lost. The capital of the Pious Fund, which is considerable, amounting to 238,000 pesos at present, is distributed throughout the city and the bishopric. Some of the debtors have died recently; and when their worldly goods were inventoried, it was found that they were almost penniless. The result has been 14 lawsuits. Special care must be taken, particularly with the inventories, sales, and accounts, in which hundreds of frauds are perpetrated, not only by debtors but also by the scribes and judges who sign their approval.[59]

The Carmelites had one large estate in the Valley, the Hacienda San Juan Bautista. Together with the adjoining estates Los Naranjos and San José, south of Antequera and east of Zaachila, the hacienda was acquired in 1745 from Juan Martínez de Antelo.[60] At that time it consisted of 21 caballerías of land valued at 34,250 pesos, the largest single tract of arable land owned by a non-Indian. Detailed account records for the late 1790's indi-

cate that San Juan Bautista was primarily an agricultural enterprise, cultivating wheat, corn, beans, and fodder.[61] As of 1790
the Carmelites also owned the small Hacienda del Espinar on
the southern edge of the Antequera ejido.[62]

Within 20 years after the Carmelites purchased San Juan Bautista, its value had risen to 60,000 pesos, the highest in the Valley.
The increase was not due to the acquisition of additional lands,
but to large investments by the Carmelites in new buildings,
irrigation works, and cattle and to a slight rise in prices. Despite
their investments the Carmelites found that upkeep and expenses
left them with either a deficit or an annual income less than the
reasonably secure 5 per cent to be gained from property mortgages. In 1748, only three years after acquiring San Juan Bautista, the Carmelites tried unsuccessfully to sell it. They put it
up for sale again in 1768, this time offering a 5 per cent discount,
but again no buyer could be found. The Carmelites retained a
precarious hold on San Juan Bautista into the nineteenth century. Annual expenditures near the end of the colonial period
were between 8,000 and 9,000 pesos and annual revenues about
9,500. The hacienda's revenues were not greatly supplemented
by revenues from urban property, since the Carmelites owned
only 32 houses at the end of the eighteenth century; but income
from the agricultural estate apparently increased after independence. In 1829 the order still owned San Juan Bautista and began to expand its boundaries by purchasing an adjacent *labor*
and other pieces of surrounding land.[63]

The Bethlemite hospital purchased its one rural estate in the
Valley, the Hacienda Santo Domingo Buenavista, later known
as Guadalupe, in 1738 for 29,083 pesos.[64] Located in the eastern
arm southeast of Tlacochahuaya, Santo Domingo Buenavista was
primarily a cattle estate; it included only a few small sections of
arable land, and these were suited only to the cultivation of
maize. The Bethlemites' belief that Santo Domingo Buenavista
was "the richest hacienda in the region" stemmed from the enthusiasm of owning an estate rather than from a true assessment
of its worth. After unsuccessful efforts to expand the hacienda's
activities by cultivating other properties and renting adjacent

lands from the Mayorazgo de Guendulain in 1743, the Bethlemites gradually allowed the estate to fall into disrepair. Liens of 16,400 pesos were accumulated on the hacienda between 1751 and 1765, when portions of the estate were rented out to the neighboring Indian communities of San Sebastián Teitipac and Santa Cruz Papalutla.* Under Bethlemite ownership the number of cattle on the estate fell from 11,479 in 1738 to 3,015 in 1777.[65]

The Monastery of La Merced, which owned 55 houses in Antequera at the end of the eighteenth century, showed only a marginal interest in rural properties in the Valley. In contrast to other houses it was most active in acquiring property in the seventeenth century. Between 1610 and 1667 the monastery purchased three cattle estancias near Azompa, Zimatlán, and Zaachila, the rancho Lachicocana in the mountainous area east of Mitla (later joined to the Hacienda San Bartolo), and two caballerías near Zaachila—all of which were sold before 1700.[66] The Mercedarians acquired a fourth estancia near Tlacochahuaya in the Valley of Tlacolula in 1638;[67] no record of sale by the monastery has been located for it. Apparently the Mercedarians did not buy new estates to replace those that they sold. As of 1792 the only rural estate known to belong to them was the Hacienda Tlanechico, west of Zaachila.[68]

Several of Antequera's nunneries became prominent landowners in the late colonial period, largely by purchase and foreclosure on unsettled debts. The Convent of Santa Catalina de Sena is especially notable for its aggressive, businesslike approach to land ownership in the seventeenth and eighteenth centuries. The convent was established at Antequera in 1576 with ten residents and an endowment of several buildings and one estancia de ganado mayor.[69] By 1597 two more estancias and 40 caballerías had been added by viceregal merced. The convent rented out all these lands rather than operating them directly.[70] By the late eighteenth century Santa Catalina had more members than

---

* The need for indebtedness was partially attributed to mismanagement: "Since the monastery experienced various financial setbacks in the calamitous times of former administrations, certain debts had to be assumed." BEOB, fol. 347r.

other houses in Antequera, more urban properties than any other regular order, and extensive rural estates.

Santa Catalina's interest in rural properties in the seventeenth century led to the following acquisitions: the estancia de los Tres Ríos and two adjoining caballerías, in the southern arm west of San Lucas Tlanechico (1611); grazing lands in the southern arm near San Gerónimo Zegache (1618); a wheat mill near Sola, southwest of the Valley (1639); an unspecified hacienda in the jurisdiction of Antequera (1651); the Hacienda del Rosario, south of the Valley near Miahuatlán (1662); an estancia de ganado menor in the jurisdiction of Cuilapan (1666); the Hacienda San Joaquín, just south of the Valley in the jurisdiction of Ejutla (1666); the Hacienda Jalapilla, northwest of Antequera (pre-1682); an estancia de ganado menor southwest of Cuilapan (1692); and a *labor* and an estancia de ganado mayor y menor east of the Mayorazgo de Valdeflores near Zimatlán.[71] Santa Catalina's lands were not restricted to the Valley and its environs. As of 1670 the convent owned an hacienda near Totomeguacán, Puebla, which was rented to a Spaniard from the city of Puebla.[72] The convent did not hold all these lands at the same time, as records of transfers indicate. The Hacienda Jalapilla was sold in 1682, the estancia de los Tres Ríos in 1638, the estancia de ganado menor near Cuilapan in 1666, the estancia and *labor* near Valdeflores in 1694, and the Hacienda San Joaquín in 1707.

In contrast to the acquisition of lands through dowries, capellanías, and donations, which was typical of convents in Mexico City, Santa Catalina de Sena secured most of her eighteenth-century properties by purchase or foreclosure. The dowries of Santa Catalina's novices were clearly an important source of capital, but they rarely included rural lands. According to a manuscript record of the convent's founding, which includes a list of novices and their dowries during the colonial period, nearly all dowries were in the form of cash payments of 1,500 pesos during the late sixteenth century, 2,000 pesos throughout the seventeenth, and 3,000 pesos in the eighteenth.[73] Even novices from prominent landowning families brought cash dowries: two daughters of Rafaela Pinelo in 1640 and 1642, a daughter of Gaspar de Espina

Calderón in 1656, and two daughters of Luis Ramírez de Aguilar in 1707. Houses in Antequera occasionally took the place of cash dowries, as in the case of the daughters of Fernando Méndez in 1642. Dowries and donations of urban property help explain Santa Catalina's commanding position in real estate in Antequera; the convent owned 210 houses in 1792.

Stores of ready cash made Santa Catalina an obvious source of credit for the debt-ridden lay haciendas of the early eighteenth century. The convent invested heavily in 5 per cent liens on real estate throughout the Valley. Nearly all the large haciendas, not to mention several *labores* and ranchos, held one or more liens from Santa Catalina, ranging from 300 to 6,000 pesos. (See Appendix F for a partial list of mortgages written by the convent.) Heavily mortgaged estates were often sold on the death of the owner to meet outstanding debts, and often they went to the principal creditor. Santa Catalina acquired at least seven properties this way: the estancia near Cuilapan in 1666, the Haciendas San Diego and Poblete in the Miahuatlán jurisdiction in 1717, a *labor* near Sola in 1717, the Hacienda Matagallinas in 1747 and again in 1757, the Hacienda San Diego near Zimatlán in 1756, and a *labor* near San Andrés Zautla in 1764.[74]

Santa Catalina took a remarkably practical attitude toward land ownership, disposing of lands that were of no long-range use or that could yield a quick profit by resale. The convent's transactions provide the clearest example in the Valley of unrestricted alienation of Church lands not acquired in arrangements specifically stipulating entailment. Twelve sales of rural estates by Santa Catalina are documented, and in most cases the convent owned these properties for only a short period of time. The sales of property acquired in the seventeenth century have already been mentioned. During the eighteenth century the convent sold the Hacienda San Diego near Zimatlán in 1762; the Hacienda Matagallinas in 1748 and again in 1786; and the Haciendas San Diego and Poblete, the two *labores* near Sola and Zautla, and an estancia de ganado menor near San Pedro Ixtlahuaca all within a year of acquiring them.

All of the properties that the convent held for more than one year were located in the southern arm of the Valley, where there was much good pastureland. Unlike Santo Domingo, however, Santa Catalina did not specialize in grazing sites. During the eighteenth century the convent owned a trapiche and a cane field near Santa Ana Tlapacoya, two *labores*, four small cattle ranches, some scattered plots of arable land along the border of Ante-quera's ejido, and six haciendas: San Isidro east of Cuilapan, San Diego near Zimatlán, San José near Cuilapan, San Miguel (also known as Careaga) adjoining the Jesuit *labor* San Miguel on the east, San Germán east of Xoxocotlán, and Matagallinas in the Mixtepec Valley. Of these properties six were acquired by foreclosure on outstanding debts, the rest by direct purchase. (See Appendix G for a summary of Santa Catalina's land transactions in the eighteenth century.) The Hacienda San Isidro, obtained in the early eighteenth century, was the largest of the convent's haciendas and received most of its administrative attention. Valued at 26,358 pesos in 1766, it was the one estate that Santa Catalina held continuously throughout the eighteenth and early nineteenth centuries.[75] The convent's other haciendas and *labores* were valued at less than 10,000 pesos apiece; for example, San Miguel was worth 7,000 pesos, Matagallinas 5,580 pesos (in 1749), San Joaquín 4,000 pesos, and Poblete 1,900 pesos.[76]

Santa Catalina rented out some of its properties and secured usufruct rights to other lands by rent. The estancia Las Monjas near San Pedro Ixtlahuaca was rented out in 1708, the Hacienda San Isidro in 1766 and again in 1786, and the estancia La Sole-dad in 1798.[77] Two ranchos were rented from Indian nobles of Cuilapan in 1753 and 1799.[78] Santa Catalina de Sena passed into the national period with its wealth nearly intact, and its assets continued to grow until the sales and confiscations of the late 1850's. The value of these assets at the time of the reform laws has been estimated at 500,000 pesos.[79]

The Augustinian convent Nuestra Señora de la Soledad also became an important landowner in the eighteenth century. It had held some land as early as the sixteenth century: a *labor* near San Antonio de la Cal in 1579 and two nearby cattle estancias obtained by mercedes in 1590.[80] One of the estancias was ceded to a local carpenter in 1606 in return for several years of unpaid service.[81] The convent also lost its other two sixteenth-century properties, since by 1750 they were part of the Hacienda San Miguel, owned by the Convent of Santa Catalina de Sena. In addition, several tracts of land bought during the seventeenth century were sold before 1700.[82] Soledad's eighteenth-century holdings included the rancho Guegonivalle and the Hacienda Xuchitepec in the southern arm, valued in the 1760's at 3,527 pesos and 4,883 pesos, respectively; the San Roque estate, composed of 24 separate pieces of land near the ejido lands of Antequera and sold for 500 pesos in 1708; the Hacienda San Guillermo in the jurisdiction of Miahuatlán, valued at 6,446 pesos in 1742; and the Hacienda de Montoya northwest of Antequera, which was acquired in the late eighteenth century.[83] Montoya, worth 30,000 pesos in 1805, was by far the most valuable of the Augustinians' investments.[84] The convent did not hold all these properties at one time. It sold Guegonivalle in 1768 after two years of ownership, Xuchitepec in 1769 after six years, and San Roque in 1708 after four years. The two largest haciendas were let out: rentals are recorded for San Guillermo in 1742 and 1778 and for Montoya in 1790 and 1805.[85]

The Convent of La Concepción in Antequera was second only to Santa Catalina de Sena among landowning convents in the Valley during the eighteenth century. Between 1700 and 1810 La Concepción owned at least seven haciendas, two *labores*, and one estancia in the Valley. The haciendas were Cinco Señores and Zorita, south of Antequera; San Bartolo, Xaagá, Aranjuez, and San Francisco Buenavista, all in the Valley of Tlacolula; and Jalapilla in the Etla arm.[86] (San Francisco Buenavista was divided into two sections, one south of Macuilxóchitl and the other in the mountainous area north of Teotitlán del Valle.) The *labores* were La Quinta, immediately southwest of Antequera, and an unnamed estate near Cuilapan, and the estancia was La Soledad near Zimatlan.[87]

Again land tenure was fluid, and not all these estates were held simultaneously. Only two, the Haciendas Zorita and Aranjuez, were long-term, directly managed investments. The other estates were sold after only short periods of ownership. The convent owned La Quinta from 1768 to 1772, Jalapilla from 1767 to 1770, and Xaagá from 1747 to 1763. The *labor* near Cuilapan was obtained and sold in the same year (1714), as were Cinco Señores (1762) and the estancia La Soledad (1717). The lands and buildings of the Hacienda San Bartolo passed to La Concepción in 1800 only to be reacquired shortly thereafter by the former owners, the Monterrubio family. This rapid transfer of landholdings is explained by the fact that the convent did not actively seek to acquire most of the estates in the first place; rather they fell to it by default. Like Santa Catalina de Sena, La Concepción was a principal creditor to Valley hacendados in the eighteenth century. Five estates that were sold had been obtained through unpaid debts: Cinco Señores, La Quinta, San Bartolo, the estancia La Soledad, and Jalapilla. In at least one case, La Quinta, the convent was able to turn a fine profit in the transaction, selling the estate for 4,460 pesos after receiving it by default on a 2,000-peso mortgage.

As well as a lack of interest in certain estates acquired by foreclosure, dwindling finances may have prompted La Concepción to sell land in the second half of the eighteenth century. A 1774 report on La Concepción's accounts revealed that the nuns were in debt to ten creditors for 29,630 pesos.[88] Although their total capital amounted to 224,231 pesos, their circumstances were described as "altogether miserable," since less than one-third of the capital produced any income. The sale of Xaagá, La Quinta, and Jalapilla between 1763 and 1772 seems to support this analysis. La Concepción's financial woes were not totally due to the mismanagement typical of Mexico City's nunneries in the eighteenth century. In part they were the result of circumstances beyond the convent's control. La Concepción was engaged in a prolonged and costly legal dispute with the Dominican monastery Santo Domingo over rights to the Hacienda Xaagá.[89] In addition, as of 1790, the royal government was 32 years in arrears in paying interest to La Concepción for its 30,000-peso investment in *juros*, a kind of royal annuity.[90] La Concepción's heavy investment in urban property (113 houses) probably brought the same problems as the Jesuits experienced in the eighteenth century, namely, unpaid rents and deteriorating houses.

Either La Concepción's poverty was exaggerated somewhat in the 1774 report to avoid the *vida común* reform, or conditions began to improve in the final years of the eighteenth century.* In 1799 the convent wrote a mortgage of 3,000 pesos on the Hacienda San Bartolo and in 1802 one of 8,000 pesos on land belonging to a resident of Orizaba.[91] The convent continued to own and operate the Hacienda de Zorita while renting out its other two estates, the Haciendas Aranjuez and San Francisco Buenavista.

Since the Dominicans had formed parishes in the wealthiest Indian areas before the bishopric of Oaxaca was established in 1535, secular priests sometimes turned to the land for support early in the colonial period. By law clergymen were not permitted to hold property in the early years of colonization, but the royal government apparently ignored most violations. In 1551 Bishop Zárate admitted establishing several cattle ranches for the cathedral. His explanation was that without the ranches, "I would not have been able to sustain myself and would have had to abandon the bishopric."[92] Zárate justified the commercial ventures of his priests on the same grounds. His complaints that the tithe brought in very little income reflected a chronic problem; in 1772 revenues from tithes in Oaxaca were less than those in the bishoprics of Durango, Guadalajara, Michoacán, Puebla, and Mexico.[93]

Seventeenth-century documentation provides more examples of secular clergymen who held rural estates. Oaxaca's bishop in the early 1600's, Juan de Bohórquez, bought five cattle ranches south of Zimatlán between 1621 and 1623, which he consolidated into the Mayorazgo de Valdeflores for his nephew José Ximenes de Bohórquez in 1624.[94] Other notable seventeenth-century landholding priests include Br. Andrés Sánchez de Ulloa, who owned

---

* Lavrín, p. 383. The aim of the vida común reform was to return to a simple, abstemious monastic life. One aspect of the attack on luxuries called for community meals rather than large cash allowances to monks and nuns for food. Bernard E. Bobb, *The Viceregency of Antonio María Bucareli in New Spain, 1771–1779* (Austin, Texas, 1962), chap. 3.

tracts of 2.5 and 4.5 caballerías in the Etla arm between 1619 and 1630; Br. Juan Barranco, who owned the Hacienda Guadalupe in the Etla arm in the 1680's; Br. Tomás Ruiz de Estrada, who owned the Hacienda de los Negritos (also known as San Antonio Buenavista) until 1689; and Br. Ignacio Ximeno de Bohórquez, who bought the Hacienda San Juan Bautista in 1694.[95]

Although the sparseness of documentation for the seventeenth century may exaggerate the contrast somewhat, it does seem clear that the number of estates owned privately by secular priests increased considerably in the eighteenth century. No less than 20 *labores*, 15 small haciendas, 7 ranchos, 3 trapiches, and a wheat mill belonged to priests in that century. Priests were increasingly preoccupied with the same economic concerns as most of the regular orders in the late colony. Priestly hacendados were in the habit of taking at least a weekly ride over their estates "in order to observe the work and supervise the workers."[96] One priest, Gerónimo Morales Sigala, the canon of the cathedral in the mid-eighteenth century, owned three of the Valley's largest estates simultaneously, Jalapilla in the north and San José and El Vergel in the extreme south.

The numerous clerical estates of the eighteenth century contributed to the fragmented and fluid pattern of land distribution in the Valley of Oaxaca. With some notable exceptions, including Morales Sigala's three haciendas, Br. Manuel de Llarena Lazo's Hacienda Guadalupe, and Br. Felipe Noriega's Hacienda San Nicolás Obispo, the holdings of secular priests were small estates, primarily *labores*, ranchos, and marginal haciendas. Such estates were usually owned for less than 25 years. Virtually all the documented eighteenth-century estates owned by priests were sold either by the priests themselves or by their executors on their death. Apparently few of the priests had relatives in the Valley of Oaxaca, or at least few cared to pass their lands on to relatives. In a rare exception Br. Juan Manuel de Maradona left the *labor* Santa Rita to his mother, who quickly sold it to meet her son's various debts.[97]

Secular priests acquired private estates mainly by inheritance or direct purchase. Sons of prominent landowning families in the Valley occasionally inherited haciendas or enough money to purchase separate estates. Br. Juan Barranco, for example, inherited the Hacienda Guadalupe from his father.[98] Bernardo and León Díaz, brothers who were parish priests in Sola and Zimatlán, inherited the rancho La Chilayta near Ocotlán from their father in 1768.[99] However, the great majority of estates owned by priests were acquired by purchase, as Appendix H, a summary of eighteenth-century land transactions involving secular priests, shows.* Rentals were another means by which secular priests gained the use of Valley lands. Seven rentals of *labores* by individual priests from Spanish and Indian owners are recorded between 1619 and 1789.[100] Aside from their personal holdings parish priests frequently had access to certain community lands. The secular priest residing in Zaachila in the 1780's, for example, used two caballerías of arable land belonging to the town.†

Conclusion

The Church was the leading Spanish landowner in the Valley of Oaxaca at the end of the colonial period, controlling perhaps one-fourth of the Valley's productive rural property. Together the various Church groups owned more Valley land than all other Spanish landholders combined. Of the ten most valuable rural estates after 1740, the regular orders owned six: San Isidro (Zimatlán), San Juan Bautista, Santo Domingo Soriano, Montoya, Santo Domingo Buenavista, and Xaagá. The Monastery of Santo Domingo was the largest single landowner, controlling seven estates with over 20,000 acres. Santo Domingo's sister convent, Santa Catalina de Sena, was the wealthiest property holder,

---

* Occasionally a Valley priest owned lands elsewhere; Br. Francisco Ordinia Sosa y Castilla, for example, owned property near Querétaro but none in the Valley. And at least one outside priest owned a Valley estate, the *cura* of Chacaltongo, who held the *labor* Jesús Nazareno near Cuilapan in the 1730's.

† Parish priests received other benefits from their doctrinas, such as annual tribute. In Zaachila the priest received one hundred pesos a year from the community, as well as fees for presiding over marriage and burial ceremonies and religious festivities. Juan Joseph de Guendulain, the priest at Zaachila in 1781, earned the enmity of his parishioners by charging 12 pesos rather than the usual seven for directing the religious holidays. AGNT 1063, exp. 4.

with 210 houses in Antequera and over 70,000 pesos' worth of the Valley's best grazing and arable land.

Clerical groups in the Valley, both monastic and secular, took a greater interest in owning land, especially grazing lands and urban real estate, during the eighteenth century. By 1750 one could hardly travel more than a few miles in the Valley without treading on ecclesiastical soil. The houses of Santo Domingo and Santa Catalina de Sena, as well as many secular priests, were the most active in expanding their estates. Other houses tended to concentrate their investments in one fairly large rural estate, occasionally acquiring smaller properties but usually selling them within a few years. With the exception of the Dominican monastery San Pablo, which owned houses in Antequera and no rural Valley lands, religious groups did not systematically limit their investments to one kind of real estate. In fact, the same houses—Santo Domingo, Santa Catalina de Sena, La Soledad, and La Concepción—were the major owners of both rural and urban properties. The frequently leveled charge that Church lands were underused does seem justified for the Valley of Oaxaca. Several houses, Santo Domingo and La Concepción in particular, were land-poor. Having acquired more productive land than they could effectively use, they neglected several of their estates and allowed them to deteriorate.

As an institution the Church could presumably maintain a firmer hold on its property than lay owners could. But the concept of ecclesiastical mortmain, which presumes that all property acquired by the Church remains in its possession forever, was not so encompassing as has been supposed. Not all lands acquired by various religious groups were inalienable. In particular, monasteries and convents sold estates acquired by purchase or foreclosure with considerable frequency during the colonial period, giving Church tenure a rather fluid and unsettled character. Nineteenth-century documentation does suggest, however, that much Church property remained intact in the 50 years after independence.

CONCLUSION

LAND TENURE, with all its implications for social organization, the distribution of wealth, and the use of natural resources, is one of the least understood topics in colonial Latin American history. Ignorance has preserved a variety of well-worn impressions about colonial land systems, generally emphasizing the Spaniards' greed and their cruelty to native Americans. The North Mexican hacienda—entailed, feudal in spirit, and relentlessly expanding onto the small holdings of Indian peasants—has come to serve as a model for colonial land tenure.

The history of land in colonial Oaxaca represents a significant departure from the North Mexican model. As elsewhere in the viceroyalty Spanish holdings in the Valley shifted from grazing lands in the sixteenth century to farms and haciendas in the seventeenth. But the degree of change in the Valley was different, and the effect of the rise of the hacienda on Indian tenure was less severe. In much of the viceroyalty Indians lost a good deal of land, as millions fell victim to epidemics and haciendas surrounded, and in some cases completely overran, their towns. In contrast, Valley caciques and pueblos retained a considerable amount of land, certainly more than enough to meet their basic needs and keep them independent of Spanish landowners.

Changes did take place in Indian society in the Valley over the three centuries of Spanish rule. The mayeque class slowly disappeared, and the lesser nobility frequently lost economic power. But the changes were not so drastic as in the regions farther north, especially the Valley of Mexico. There Indian lands proved quite vulnerable to Spanish encroachment.[1] The resulting redistribution of wealth tended to level Indian society into a fairly uniform, undifferentiated mass. Indian communities in Oaxaca were moving in the same direction but at a much slower pace. At the end of the colonial period the hereditary nobility was still distinguishable as the wealthiest social group.

Indians controlled a considerable portion of the Valley's pastures as well as its best farmland. Incomplete census figures from the early national period indicate that Indians owned 100,000 head of livestock and Spanish estates 60,000.[2] Only in the sixteenth century and the first half of the seventeenth is it likely that Spaniards owned more livestock than Indians owned. The *Relaciones Geográficas* for various Valley towns for 1579 to 1581 mention the large number of Spanish livestock;[3] but starting in the late sixteenth century, individual Indians and Indian communities received numerous grants for cattle and sheep ranches. Burgoa was impressed that most Indian families owned teams of oxen and a few horses, and that some had flocks of sheep and herds of goats.[4]

Many native communities had large holdings, and most had enough land to remain independent of outside landowners. These holdings tended to remain stable or to contract. Very few Indian communities expanded their territory in the colonial period except at the expense of smaller neighbors. Even when two or more small towns were threatened by an aggressive neighbor, they did not join forces, which suggests an inability to associate above the community level except in the marketplace.

Indian landholdings were quite fragmented. A resident of one community, for example, might work several small plots five kilometers from his home and completely surrounded by lands of another town. Cacicazgos were the most fragmented of all. Those of Etla, San Juan Guelache, Magdalena Apasco, and Cuilapan owned 20 or more pieces of land spread over distances of 10 to 30 kilometers. Life was not easy for Valley Indians in the colonial period. Land disputes were frequent and fluctuations in rainfall could spell drought and famine, but land ownership did bring with it a measure of social independence and community autonomy.

The monopoly of the Spanish corregidor de indios on the sale

of certain products in his jurisdiction (reparto de efectos) was
not so disruptive to Indian land tenure in Oaxaca as in other
parts of Latin America. Since the corregidores usually demanded
cash payment in the late colonial period, the reparto could force
Indians into a money economy. In highland Peru, for example,
Indians sold land and worked on rural estates to get the necessary
cash; thus the reparto contributed to the growth of haciendas at
the expense of Indian communities.[5] In Oaxaca, however, there
are very few cases in which Indians sold land to pay the corregidor. Though the reparto may have been somewhat less important as a source of goods for Valley Indians, the main reason it
did not affect them so severely is that they had other sources of
cash. The city of Antequera depended on Indians for pottery,
firewood, building materials, and various foodstuffs. Nearly every
town had a marketable specialty.

Indian landholding in the Valley of Oaxaca contradicts the
thesis that Indians retained land only in the isolated and mountainous reaches of the viceroyalty.[6] This thesis assumes that the
Indian was either completely passive or too weak to resist any
Spaniard who took an active interest in ownership. In fact, Valley Indians were quite aggressive in defending their lands by
litigation and by force, though other local studies may show
they were not typical in this respect. Their aggressiveness helps
explain the survival of their lands and institutions. A century
after the end of Spanish rule in Mexico, Emilio Rabasa found
the attitude of Oaxaca's Indians unchanged. After considering
the long history of boundary encroachments and legal actions by
local Indians, he concludes that "foreign capital does not dare
engage in agriculture in Oaxaca because its lands cannot be
guaranteed; even oaxaqueños prefer to invest in other endeav-
ors."[7]

The persistence of Indian tenure in Oaxaca throughout the
colonial period surely is related to the strength of community
life there at the time of the Spanish conquest. But this alone
does not explain the obvious differences between the pattern of
landholding in the Valley and the land regime that developed
in the Valley of Mexico, the cultural and political center of pre-

Columbian civilization. The nature of the Spanish presence in each area in the formative sixteenth century had much to do with the differences. The conquest itself was much more violent and destructive in the Valley of Mexico. The Aztec capital, Tenochtitlán, was the focal point of the military conquest and was virtually leveled. In contrast, the conquest of Oaxaca was nearly bloodless. There was no strong need to destroy Indian culture as in the center of Aztec hegemony. Further, there was little political power above the community level in Oaxaca that required obliteration. After the conquest the Valley of Mexico quickly became the primary area of Spanish settlement and the capital of colonial life. Since Oaxaca had relatively few Spaniards in the sixteenth century, royal laws intended to protect Indian communities were more readily enforced there. Certainly the number of royal confirmations of Indian holdings, reflecting actual land distribution as well as legal rights, is impressive. The Spaniards' indifference to agriculture in sixteenth-century Oaxaca was essential to the special patterns of land tenure described in this study. In the Valleys of Mexico, Atlixco, and Cuernavaca, where many Spaniards settled early in the colonial period, the declining Indian population was unable to meet the demand for European grains. As a result Spanish-owned wheat farms and sugar-cane fields developed earlier and on a larger scale than in Oaxaca. The earlier Spanish interest in land ownership near Mexico City inevitably meant a loss of first-rate land to Indian communities.

Indian tenure has a great deal to do with Oaxaca's peculiar history since independence and the state's reputation as provincial, backward, and resistant to change. The frustrated hacendado Jose María Murguía y Galardi remarked in 1826 that "the poverty of agriculture in the Valley is due to the intransigence of the Indian landholders in failing to diversify their crops."[8] Since most communities were nearly self-sufficient in food, the community was the only important social entity above the family. Oaxaca remained a distinctive regional center in the nineteenth century, and although it supplied several famous national leaders, including Benito Juárez and Porfirio Díaz, it was only marginally involved in national affairs. True to form, Oaxaca had little to do with the Revolution of 1910. The Revolution in the countryside was essentially a struggle for land and economic independence, not for political freedoms. Valley towns, firmly rooted in the land, had never really lost what Zapata and his followers were fighting for. Thus they showed relatively little interest in the revolutionary cause.* The obvious exception, the community of Zaachila, proves the rule; it was one of the few large Valley towns chronically short of land. Valley communities are still agriculturally self-sufficient and continue to show distinctive local and regional characteristics.

In tracing the history of Spanish land ownership in the Valley, we find that at first the Spaniards were interested only in raising livestock. Spanish estancias were in evidence as early as the 1520's, especially in the Valley of Tlacolula and the southern part of the Valley of Zimatlán. In a pattern familiar throughout New Spain, ranches gradually gave way to more complex rural estates, the hacienda and the *labor*, in the late sixteenth and seventeenth centuries. The Valley estates referred to as haciendas in the colonial period engaged in the same kinds of economic activities and aspired to the same degree of labor control and political autonomy as the huge rural estates of northern Mexico. They had a mixed economic base of ranching and agriculture and relied on debt peonage for laborers.

But despite these general similarities Spanish estates in the Valley were very different from the conventional hacienda, which was as much a form of social organization as a type of landholding. In two areas of the New World that have been studied in detail, the Ameca Valley in the state of Jalisco (Mexico) and the Puangue Valley (Chile), a few entailed haciendas gradually took over an entire region, establishing quasi-judicial authority and driving Indians off the land or incorporating them into the hacienda economy.[9] We can hardly speak of such a "creeping paralysis of the hacienda system" in the Valley of Oaxaca.[10] Spanish estates

---

* Two apologists for the Porfiriato, Toribio Esquivel Obregón and Emilio Rabasa, argue that the Revolution was unjustified because Mexico did not have a land problem: the rural, largely Indian population owned more than enough land to support itself. Significantly, they use examples from Oaxaca to substantiate their argument.

in the Valley were generally small and fragmented. There were as many farms as haciendas. Most haciendas were less than 3,000 acres in size, and few were able to expand their holdings in the late colonial period. Further, they were politically and economically tied to Antequera and nearby cabeceras. In Oaxaca, unlike northern Mexico, the pattern of land distribution did not crystallize after the composiciones de tierras of the 1640's with Spaniards in control of immense rural estates.[11] Nor does the Valley's colonial history support the proposition that families, not individuals, owned rural estates. Aside from the six entailed haciendas, ownership was rarely continuous in one family for more than two or three generations. As mortgages accumulated on rural Valley estates in the seventeenth and eighteenth centuries, transfer by sale rather than by inheritance predominated.

It is more accurate to view large size, economic and political self-sufficiency, and continuity of ownership as nineteenth-century developments for the hacienda in southern Mexico. An examination of hacienda transfers in the Valley of Oaxaca for the late eighteenth century and the first half of the nineteenth indicates that a new pattern of transfer by inheritance was emerging. Of the eight Valley haciendas with complete transfer records, six were acquired in the eighteenth century by private families and Church groups who held them well into the nineteenth: Santo Domingo Buenavista was acquired by the Bethlemite hospital in 1738, San Juan Bautista and San Jacinto by the Carmelite monastery in 1745, Xaagá by the Monastery of Santo Domingo in 1758, San José by the Mimiaga family in 1766, and San Bartolo by the Monterrubios in 1778. The seventh, San Nicolás Obispo, was acquired by the Murguía y Galardi family in 1807. Only the ownership of Guadalupe was still unstable as of 1810.

The striking contrast between Oaxaca's small, unstable Spanish estates and the huge, semi-independent haciendas of the north suggests significant differences between the northern and southern portions of Mesoamerica. Chevalier recognizes that geographic differences accounted for a densely settled, seden-

tary native peasantry in the south; but he assumes that geographic
and native cultural factors had no important effect on colonial
land tenure. He regards the development of the hacienda as
uniform throughout New Spain. Spaniards did settle throughout the viceroyalty; thus the superficial similarity among regions.
But the large and numerous Indian settlements in the Valley of
Oaxaca played a major role in the land system there, frequently
frustrating Spanish efforts at expansion. Other areas of dense
native settlement in southern Mesoamerica, such as central Veracruz and highland Guatemala, probably had a greater similarity
to Oaxaca in terms of land tenure than to the area north of
Mexico City.

In conclusion, the eighteenth century does not seem to be the
great age of haciendas in southern Mexico. At the end of the
colonial period, non-Indians held less than half the land in the
Valley, primarily grazing land. A large number of small ranches
and farms account for most of the land controlled by Spaniards.
Spanish landowners, many of whom were creoles, were numerous
and generally not wealthy. Political officeholders and merchants
rather than hacendados made up the wealthiest class in Antequera. Few non-Indian estates were entailed, and the rate of turn-
over, usually by sale, was high. The priesthood made the most
significant gains in land ownership during the late colonial
period, usually at the expense of local Spaniards rather than Indians. Secular priests and the regular orders acquired many of
the best haciendas and *labores* in the Valley between 1680 and
1770. About one estate in ten owned by a Church group was resold before the end of the colonial period, suggesting that the
principle of "ecclesiastical mortmain" was not always followed.
Only Indian holdings in the late eighteenth century can be
called stable. Individual Indians and Indian communities controlled about two-thirds of the Valley's agricultural land during
the last hundred years of Spanish rule. Most towns also had several grazing sites, and Indian nobles owned some of the largest
private estates in the region.

As one of the first studies of local land tenure in colonial Latin
America, this work raises many questions for research. Was the

sale of Church lands a common pattern elsewhere in Spanish America? Were there more cacicazgo estates in the late colonial period than is generally supposed? Did mortgages on haciendas in the eighteenth century generally lead to transfers by sale? Was the *labor* a viable unit in other parts of Mexico? Did a pattern of land distribution really crystallize in the colonial period? For these and other questions the Valley of Oaxaca can serve as a reference point for other parts of Spanish America. Certainly  Oaxaca's history suggests that the North Mexican hacienda is not a very satisfying model for land use and distribution in all of New Spain. A number of models will probably be needed. The Valley of Oaxaca and northern Mexico may well represent the extremes.

APPENDIXES

Appendix A

Lands Rented Out by Indian Nobles

Date	Noble and lands	Valley[a]	Source
1593	*Principal* of Zaachila, unspecified lands	Zim.	AGNI 6, primera parte, exp. 6
1639	*Principal* of Cuilapan, suerte for eight years at 35 pesos a year	Zim.	AGNI 11, exp. 233
1640	*Principal* of Cuilapan, unspecified lands	Zim.	AGNI 12, segunda parte, exp. 33
1640's	Cacique of Etla, 2.5 caballerías near San Sebastián Etla	Etla	AGNH 69, bk. 1, fol. 475v
pre-1664	Cacique of Cuilapan, unspecified lands	Zim.	AGNI 19, exp. 725
1667	Cacique of Etla, plot four medidas in size	Etla	AGNT 113, 2:1r
1684	Cacique of Etla, plot 30 fanegas de sembradura in size	Etla	AN 1684, fol. 111r
1690	Cacique of Etla, rancho Xabiogo, nine years at 30 pesos a year	Etla	CDChO, rollo 10
1690	Cacique of Etla, lands near Santiago Etla, nine years at 20 pesos a year	Etla	AGNMer 62, fol. 118v
1690	Cacique of Etla, unspecified rancho	Etla	AGNMer 62, fol. 113v
1691	Cacique of Etla, plot 12 fanegas de sembradura in size, nine years at 21 pesos a year	Etla	CDChO, rollo 8
1691	Cacique of Etla, Lachivigia site, nine years at 15 pesos a year	Etla	CDChO, rollo 8
1692	Cacique of Etla, an unspecified *labor*	Etla	CDChO, rollo 10
1692	Cacique of Etla, rancho Pájaro Bobo near San Pablo Etla, nine years at 30 pesos a year	Etla	CDChO, rollo 10

Date	Noble and lands	Valley[a]	Source
1692	Cacique of Etla, two small pieces totaling six fanegas de sembradura, nine years at 12 pesos a year	Etla	CDChO, rollo 10
1692	*Principal* of Cuilapan, sitio Chiltetela, nine years at eight pesos a year	Zim.	CDChO, rollo 9
1693	*Principal* of Cuilapan, canyon and piedmont Cuatizaquaha, nine years at 12 pesos a year	Zim.	CDChO, rollo 9
1693	Cacique of Etla, *labores* Xanabitobi and Xaguanigola	Etla	CDChO, rollo 9
1693	Cacique of Etla, quarry near San Agustín Etla, nine years at 25 pesos a year	Etla	CDChO, rollo 9
1707	Cacique of Etla, unspecified lands	Etla	AN *Loose papers*
1707	Cacique of Etla, various lands near Soledad Etla	Etla	AGNH 307, 11:1r.
1708	Cacique of San Juan Chapultepec, estancia Cacalutla, five years at 40 pesos a year	Zim.	AN *Loose papers*
1708	Cacique of San Juan Chapultepec, estancia de ganado menor, nine years at eight pesos a year	Zim.	AN *Loose papers*
1708	Cacique of Zimatlán, estancia de ganado menor	Zim.	AGNT 241, 7:59r–61v
1708	Cacique of Etla, two *labores*, a rancho, and quarries	Etla	AN 1708, fols. 192r, 273v
1712	*Principal* of Zaachila, two plots at 33 pesos a year	Zim.	CCGSNO, fol. 81r
1712	*Principal* of Cuilapan, several pieces at 80 pesos a year	Zim.	CCGSNO, fol. 81r
1712	Cacique of Huitzo, sitio de *labor* near Magdalena Apasco at 40 pesos a year	Etla	AGNT 2958, exp. 153
1714	Cacique of Magdalena Apasco, farming plots, nine years at 30 pesos a year	Etla	AGNI 47, exp. 44
1718	*Principal* of Santo Domingo Etla, three tracts 15 fanegas de sembradura in size	Etla	AN 1718, fol. 89r
1718	Cacique of Etla, *labor* Xaguee, nine years at 50 pesos a year	Etla	AN 1718, fol. 15v
1718	Cacique of Etla, tract near San Sebastián Etla, 200 medidas in size, nine years at 150 pesos a year	Etla	AN 1718, fol. 20r

Date	Noble and lands	Valley[a]	Source
1723	Cacique of Magdalena Apasco, unspecified rancho	Etla	AGNI 50, exp. 124
1724	Cacique of Etla, rancho and quarry Xanavidovi, nine years at 55 pesos a year	Etla	AGNH 348, 7:1v
1726	Cacique of Etla, *labor* five to six fanegas de sembradura in size, nine years at 80 pesos a year	Etla	AGNH 348, 7:1v
1727	Cacique of Etla, lands near Hacienda Montoya in censo perpetuo	Etla	AGNH 85, exp. 2
1728	Cacique of Etla, unspecified lands	Etla	AGNH 348, 7:1v
1729	Cacique of Huitzo, unspecified hacienda	Etla	AGNI 52, exp. 25
1734	Cacique of Etla, four caballerías	Etla	AGNH 85, 1:4r
1734	Cacique of Cuilapan, various lands near Hacienda San Nicolás Obispo	Zim.	CCGSNO, cuaderno 2
1735	*Principal* of Etla, labor near Azompa, nine years at 60 pesos a year	Etla	AGNH 348, 7:1v
pre-1736	Cacique of Cuilapan, lands near *labor* San Blas, nine years at 100 pesos a year	Zim.	AN 1736, fol. 182r
1737	Cacique of Etla, *labores* Roaguichi and Santaella, nine years at 200 pesos a year	Etla	AN 1737, fol. 57v
1737	Cacique of Cuilapan, two caballerías in San Blas Canyon, nine years at 40 pesos a year	Zim.	AGNH 348, 7:1v
1738	Cacique of Etla, unspecified lands	Etla	AGNH 307, exp. 23
1739	Cacique of Cuilapan, *labor* Lichigueya near San Agustín, nine years at 8o pesos a year	Zim.	AGNH 348, exp. 7
1739	Cacique of Cuilapan, Duazadi, one caballería in size, nine years at 25 pesos a year	Zim.	AGNH 348, exp. 7
1739	*Principal* of Cuilapan, unspecified tract at three pesos a year	Zim.	CCGSJB 11
1740	Cacique of Cuilapan, *labor* Jague, nine years at 200 pesos a year	Zim.	AGNH 348, 7:1v
1740	Cacique of Etla, three tracts	Etla	AN 1740
1742	Cacique of Cuilapan, unspecified sitio de ganado menor	Zim.	CCGSJB
1746	Cacique of Cuilapan, unspecified lands	Zim.	AN 1746, fol. 102v

Date	Noble and lands	Valley[a]	Source
1746	Cacique of Cuilapan, unspecified lands	Zim.	AN 1746, fols. 102v–106r
1746	Cacique of Cuilapan, unspecified lands	Zim.	AN 1746, fols. 162v–166r
pre-1748	Cacique of Cuilapan, sitio de ganado menor near Hacienda San Isidro	Zim.	AN 1748, fol. 138v
pre-1749	Cacique of Cuilapan, lands near *labor* Jesús Nazareno, nine years at 25 pesos a year	Zim.	AN 1749, fol. 281r
1749	Cacique of Oaxaca, sitio de ganado menor near San Pedro Ixtlahuaca	Zim.	AN 1749, fol. 238v
1751	Cacique of Cuilapan, *labor* Suchiaya, nine years at 65 pesos a year	Zim.	AN 1751, fol. 102r
1753	*Principal* of Cuilapan, irrigated lands, nine years at 20 pesos a year	Zim.	AN 1753, fol. 19v
pre-1765	Cacique of Cuilapan, unspecified lands	Zim.	AGNT 910, exp. 1
1765	Cacique of Etla, Panzacola Canyon, nine years at 35 pesos a year	Etla	AGNT 910, 1:62v
1784	Cacique of Cuilapan, *labor* San José, nine years at 25 pesos a year	Zim.	AGNH 118, exp. 2
1790	Cacique of Cuilapan, rancho Tiracoz, nine years at 60 pesos a year	Zim.	AN 1790, fol. 32r
1792	Cacique of Tlacolula, estancia Teoquitlatengo	Tlac.	AGNT 1225, exp. 3
1799	Cacique of Cuilapan, *labor* San José	Zim.	AN 1799, fol. 22v
1799	Cacique of Etla, unspecified lands, nine years at 18 pesos a year	Etla	AN 1799, fol. 60v
1804	Cacique of Tlacolula, rancho de Doña Gracia	Tlac.	AGNT 354, exp. 6
?	*Principal* of Santiago Guaxolotitlán, 2.5 caballerías near Azompa	Etla	AGNT 221, 1:3v

NOTE: In all there were 68 rentals, of which 62 were to Spaniards, two to Indian communities, two to individual Indians, one to the Church, and one unknown.

[a] Zim = Zimatlán and Tlac. = Tlacolula.

Appendix B

Land Disputes Among Indian Towns

Date	Litigants	Source
1586	Cuilapan, Santa María Peñoles	AGNT 2941, exp. 96
1676–1802	San Juan Teitipac, San Marcos Tlapazola, Macuilxóchitl	AGNT 185, exp. 16
1680–1817	Tlacochahuaya, Santa María Guelaxe	AGNT 1206, exp. 1
1682	San Marcos Tlapazola, San Juan Guelavia	AGNT 182, exp. 6
1690–1705	Tlacolula, Teotitlán del Valle	AGNT 148, exp. 3
1690–1705	Macuilxóchitl, Teotitlán del Valle	AGNT 148, exp. 3
1705	Tlacolula, San Juan Guelavia	AGNT 148, exp. 3
1691–1720	Santa Cruz Papalutla, San Sebastián Teitipac	AGNT 387, exp. 4; AGNT 388, exp. 1
1695–1704	Nazareno Etla, Guadalupe Etla	AGNT 211, exp. 2; AGNH 119, exp. 5
1697	San Sebastián Teitipac, Coyotepec	Local record from San Sebastián
1700	San Antonino, Lareche	AGNT 1058, exp. 1
1705	San Juan Guelavia, San Marcos Tlapazola	AGNT 223, exp. 4
1706	San Pablo Etla, San Agustín Etla	AGNH 307, exp. 7
1710	Jalatlaco, Santa Lucía	AGNH 348, exp. 11
1717–1805	Santa Cecilia Jalieza, Santo Domingo Jalieza	AGNT 1864, exp. 2; AGNT 1231, exp. 2
1720	San Sebastián Tutla, Santa Cruz Amilpas, Santa Lucía	AGNT 360, exp. 1; AGNT 384, exp. 3
1720	San Francisco Tutla, San Sebastián Tutla	AGNT 381, exp. 5
1733–1814	Tlacolula, San Juan Guelavia	AMT, doc. 12

Date	Litigants	Source
1743	San Pedro against San Martín Ocotlán and Santa Lucía	AGNT 646, exp. 1
1744– 1797	Santo Domingo Ocotlán, Santa Catarina Minas	AGNT 990, exp. 2
1744– 1807	Tlalixtac, Tomaltepec	AGNT 2384, exp. 1
1744	Teotitlán del Valle, Santiago Ixtaltepec	AGNT 2384, exp. 1
1755	San Juan Teitipac, Magdalena Teitipac	AGNT 842, exp. 6
1760	San Jacinto Amilpas, Xochimilco	AGNH 119
1760	San Pedro Ixtlahuaca, San Andrés Ixtlahuaca	AGNH 119
1760	San Juan Chapultepec, San Martín Mexicapan	AGNH 119
1771– 1807	Macuilxóchitl, Santiago Ixtaltepec	AGNT 937, exp. 1
1774	San Juan Teitipac, San Jacinto	AGNT 999, exp. 13
1780	Cuilapan, San Lucas Tlanechico	AGNH 118, exp. 24
1782	Teotitlán del Valle, Macuilxóchitl	AGNT 148, exp. 3
1788	Ocotlán, Santa Catarina Minas	AGNT 867, exp. 2
1796– 1803	Tlacolula, Santa Ana del Valle	AGNT 1268, exp. 1
1802	San Pablo Huistepec, Guelatoba	AGNT 1343, exp. 4
1803	Zimatlán, Magdalena Ocotlán, Santa Inés Yatzechi	AGNT 1351, exp. 6
1803	Tlacochahuaya, San Sebastián Teitipac	AGNT 1351, exp. 1
1811– 1815	Taviche, San Juan Lachigalla	AGNT 1414, exp. 1
1816	Tlacochahuaya, San Francisco Lachigolo	AGNT 1206, exp. 1

Appendix C

An Emphiteutic Grant by the
Marqués del Valle, 1618

Sepan quantos esta carta de poder vieren como yo D. Pedro Cortés, Marqués del Valle de Oaxaca, Señor de las Villas de Toluca y Cuernavaca, patrón y administrador perpetuo deel Hospital de Nuestra Señora de la Limpia Consepción de esta ciudad, Cavallero deel hávito de Santiago deel consejo de su Magestad digo que por quanto en la jurisdición de las Villas de Oaxaca están yermo y despoblados algunos pedasos de tierra valdíos y eriasos que son en la jurisdición y mayorasgo deel dicho estado y a la buena administración de sus rentas combiene y es nessessario se den a sensso perpetuo para que su prossedido entre y se comprehenda en las rentas que tiene y para que se cumpla y tenga efecto en la via y forma que mejor aya lugar de derecho otorgo mi poder cumplido quan vastante se requiere a Luis de Moya Alcalde Mayor de las quatro villas del dicho valle de Oaxaca para que precediendo las diligencias necessarias de la utilidad que se requiere y que no viene daño ni perjuicio alguno al dicho estado antes la utilidad y provecho que se pretende pueda dar y de a senso perpetuo o redimible todos los pedasos de citios de estancia y cavallerías de tierra que hubiere valdíos y eriasos en toda la dicha juridición anexos y pertenecientes al dicho estado a las personas y por el precio que justo fuere y más abentajados hallare haciendo y otorgando las scripturas que para su balidación se requieren con la obligación de que serán ciertos y seguros que no les serán quitado en manera alguna cumpliendo por su parte lo que se obligare en que para todo ello y ponerles en la possesión utilidad y señorío que yo e y tengo a las dichas tierras y constituirme por su tenedor y poseedor en su nombre con las demás cláusulas que para su balidación se requieran aunque aquí no bayan declaradas le otorgo este dicho poder con facultad de enjuiciar y jurar y sustituir y le relebo en forma y otorgo este dicho poder con calidad que fechas las dichas escripturas se an de traer ante mi para las ver y haser la aprovación de ellas con lo qual a de tener perpetuidad y cumplido efecto lo que en virtud de este dicho poder se hiziere y para su cumplimiento obligo mis bienes y rentas y doy poder a los jueses y justicias que de mis causas puedan y devan conoser para que me apremien al cumplimiento de lo que dicho es como por definitiva de jues competente pasada en cosa jusgada renuncio las leyes de mi favor y la general del derecho que dise que general renunciación fecha de leyes nonvala en testimonio de lo qual lo otorgué ante el presente escrivano y testigos que es fecha a la carta en la ciudad de México a tres días de el mes de nobiembre de mill y seiscientos y diez y ocho anos . . .

PEDRO CORTÉS

[Conditions of the grant as appended.] Primeramente que dicho don Andrés de Mendosa y León y sus sucesores en las dichas dos cavallerías y media de tierra sean obligados a las tener cultivadas y labradas de suerte que bayan en augmento y no en diminución y estén seguros los beinte pesos del dho tributo y senso perpetuo cada un año donde no que quien por el dho Sr. Marqués fuere parte lo mande hazer a su costa y execute por lo que se gastare y debiere de corridos.

y con condición que si lo que Dios no quiera algún caso fortuito susediere en las dichas tierras de fuego, agua, eladas y otro qualquier no se pueda pedir descuento deste dicho senso sino que se pague llana y enteramente a los dichos plasos y según dicho es.

y con condición que el dicho D. Andrés de Mendosa y León y sus erederos y subsesores no puedan vender ni traspasar las dichas tierras a ninguna de las personas en derecho prohibidas salvo a persona legal llana y abonada con el cargo de este dicho senso y condiciones de esta escriptura y antes y primero lo hagan saver a quien por el dicho Sr. Marqués fuere parte dentro de treinta días declarando con juramento el precio cierto para que si las quisiere por el tanto las tome y prefiera donde no dé licensia para ello y lo que de otra manera se hisiere sea en sí ninguno y no valga ni pase derecho a tercero y caigan en comiso las dichas tierras con lo en ellas edificado y labrado.

y con condición que el sucsesor en las dichas tierras dentro de otros treinta días sea obligado a su reconosimiento deste dicho senso en favor del dicho Sr. Marqués y de sus susesores en su estado y dar la escriptura sacada a su costa. . . .

SOURCE: CCGG, fols. 2v–4r, 8v–9r.

Appendix D

Viceregal Land Grants to Spaniards

Date	Type of grant	Valley	Source
1549	Estancia	Etla	CCGG
1555	Estancia	Zim.	AGNMer 4, fol. 112v
1561	E. de ganado menor	Zim.	CCGSJ
1561	E. de ganado menor	Zim.	AN 1707
1563	E. de ganado menor	Zim.	CCGSJ
1563	Estancia	Zim.	AGNT 241, exp. 7
1563	Estancia	Zim.	AGNMer 6, fol. 32
1564	E. de ganado mayor	Tlac.	CCGL
pre-1565	E. de ganado menor	Tlac.	AGNMer 8
1565	E. de ganado menor	Tlac.	AGNMer 8, fol. 38r–v
1566	Two caballerías	Zim.	AGNMer 9, fol. 98r–v
1571	Estancia	Tlac.	CCGL
pre-1576	Estancia	Tlac.	CCGL
1583	Estancia	Tlac.	CCGL
1590	Estancia	Zim.	AGNMer 16
1591	E. de ganado mayor	Tlac.	CCGS
1592	E. de ganado menor	Tlac.	AGNI 6, segunda parte, exp. 726
1594	Two caballerías	Tlac.	CCGL
1596	One caballería	Zim.	AGNT 1877, exp. 9
1596	E. de ganado mayor	Tlac.	CCGS
1599	E. de ganado menor	Zim.	AGNT 333, exp. 2
1590's	E. de ganado menor	Zim.	AGNT 104, exp. 12
1604	E. de ganado mayor	Tlac.	AGNT 35, exp. 7
1607	E. de ganado mayor	Tlac.	AGNT 73, exp. 4
1613	Four caballerías	Tlac.	CCGS

NOTE: In the Grant column, E. = Estancia. In the Valley column, Zim. = Zimatlán and Tlac. = Tlacolula.

Appendix E

Hacienda Transfers

An asterisk before a date in this appendix means that the estate was sold at that time.

Hacienda San José:

1615   Juan Valeriano, cacique of Ocotlán, sells two sitios de ganado menor to Capt. Francisco Suárez de Herrera.

1616   License issued for mass to be said in the hacienda chapel.

*1651   Widow of Francisco Suárez de Herrera sells the two sitios to Lucas de Silva. He consolidates them with four other properties (an adjacent *labor* and three sitios de ganado), originally granted in mercedes of 1544, 1571, and 1592 and purchased by his father, Juan de Silva, before 1606.

1660   Silva purchases an adjacent estancia de ganado menor from Juan de Villalva.

*1673   Executors of Silva's estate sell the hacienda to Antonio de Avellán y Carrasco for 17,312 pesos. Mortgages on the estate amounted to 8,000 pesos; thus Avellán paid only 9,312 pesos in cash.

1675   Avellán purchases an adjacent *labor* and an estancia near Zaachila (sold separately before 1683).

1683   Avellán receives a merced for an adjacent sitio de ganado mayor.

*1701   As of this date the hacienda is owned by Pedro Núñez Villavicencio, who purchased it from the executors of Avellán's estate. Mortgages: 13,000 pesos.

1701   Núñez Villavicencio buys Garzona, an adjacent sitio.

*1721   Núñez Villavicencio sells the hacienda to Lic. Rodrigo Ortís de Acuña for 29,752 pesos. Mortgages: 23,000 pesos.

*172?   Sold by Ortís de Acuña to Juan de Pasqua Obrien.

*1730   Sold by Pasqua Obrien to Alonso Téllez for 42,096 pesos. Mortgages: 26,000 pesos.

*1738   Sold by Alonso Téllez to Br. Gerónimo Morales Sigala, who also owns Hacienda El Vergel.

*1742   Sold by Morales Sigala to Capt. Antonio de Echeverría for 33,968 pesos. Mortgages: 32,710 pesos.

*1745   Sold by Echeverría to Guillermo de San Germán and Antonio de Vera for 38,085 pesos. Mortgages: 30,040 pesos.

 1747   Vera sells his interest to San Germán.

 1755   Inherited by Thomás de San Germán, son of Guillermo.

*1766   Sold by San Germán to José Mariano de Mimiaga for 38,662 pesos. Mortgages: 30,040 pesos. The Mimiagas retain possession of the hacienda well into the nineteenth century and reduce the debts to 21,929 pesos as of 1808.

Hacienda San Nicolás Obispo:

 1615   Convent of Cuilapan leases a *labor* "for two lifetimes" to Pedro Pérez de Salazar.

*162?   Pérez de Salazar sells his rights to the *labor* to Alonso de Castellanos.

*163?   Castellanos sells his rights to Rodrigo de Olivera.

*1650   Olivera sells his rights to Capt. Juan de los Reyes; convent agrees to lease the *labor* "for an additional lifetime."

*1664   Convent sells the *labor* "a censo perpetuo" to Gaspar Díaz Jurado.

 168?   Inherited by Br. Gaspar Díaz Jurado, hijo.

*1705   Sold by Díaz Jurado to Lucía de Munar for 7,159 pesos.

*1708   Sold by Munar to Rodrigo de Olivera Pimentel for 12,893 pesos.

 1708   Olivera Pimentel buys the adjacent *labor* Santa Marina.

 1711   Olivera Pimentel buys an adjacent sitio de ganado menor from a *principal* of Cuilapan.

*1712   Olivera Pimentel sells the estate to Ana de Olivera, widow of Capt. Sebastián Varela Moreno.

 1717   Ana de Olivera transfers the estate to her son, Francisco Varela.

 1719   Varela buys the adjacent sitio Los Reyes.

*1722   Sold by Varela to his brother Manuel Varela for 17,329 pesos.

*1727   Sold by Manuel Varela to Lt. Col. Francisco López Varaona for 20,630 pesos. Mortgages: 9,200 pesos.

*1752   Sold by the executors of López Varaona's estate to Gabriel de Noriega for 20,030 pesos.

 1776   Inherited by Gabriel's son, Joseph Noriega.

1782   Inherited by Joseph's son, Br. Felipe Noriega; valued at 24,257 pesos.

*1790   Sold by the executors of Felipe Noriega's estate to Agustín Antonio Vidal for 17,140 pesos. Mortgages: 10,800 pesos.

*1799   Sold by Vidal to Br. José Guerrero for 17,534 pesos. Mortgages: 16,140 pesos.

*1807   Sold to Manuel Murguía y Galardi.

Hacienda San Juan Bautista:

1616   Juan de Zúñiga, barrio cacique of Cuilapan, sells a piece of land to Alonso de Tarifa.

*1641   Tarifa sells the tract and adjoining lands to Gaspar de Espina.

1645   License issued for mass to be said in the hacienda chapel.

*1670?   Sold by Espina to Lic. Miguel de Saavedra.

*1694   Sold to Br. Ignacio Ximeno de Bohórquez, who apparently resells it to Saavedra before 1712.

*pre-   Sold by Saavedra to Thomás Varela de Figueroa.
1712

*pre-   Sold by Varela de Figueroa to Marzial de Espina.
1725

*1725   Sold by Espina to Juan Martínez de Antelo.

1741   Abortive sale to Juan de Pasqua.

*1745   Sold by Martínez de Antelo to Carmelite monastery in Antequera for 59,062 pesos. Mortgages: 16,000 pesos.

1748   Offered for sale by the Carmelites; no buyer.

1768   Again offered for sale, at a discount of 5 per cent off the value (ca. 60,000 pesos); no buyer. Mortgages: 22,000 pesos.

1836   Monastery purchases the adjacent *labor* de San Juan Bautista. The Carmelites own the estate until the 1850's.

Hacienda San Jacinto:

1623   Gerónimo de Lara, cacique of Cuilapan, sells a plot of land near San Agustín to Nicolás Muñoz de Alarcón.

1633   Rented to Francisco Maldonado Zárate.

1644   Rented to Convent of Nuestra Señora de la Concepción.

1654   Inherited by the widow of Muñoz de Alarcón.

*1655   Sold to Juan de Almogabar, who founds the hacienda.

*1695   Sold on death of Almogabar. Sold again before 1734.

*1734   Sold to Juan Martínez de Antelo.

1741 Abortive sale to Juan de Pasqua.

*1745 Sold to the Carmelite monastery in Antequera.

Hacienda Valdeflores:

1528 Merced for an estancia de ganado menor by the Marqués del Valle to Don Martín, *principal* of Tlapacoya.

*1529 Sold by Don Martín to Diego de Guinea.

*1555 Sold by Guinea's executors to Diego Hernández Calvo and Cosmé de Larauz. Now described as an estancia y *labor*.

1564 Larauz sells his share to Calvo.

1577 Calvo gives two of his daughters, Cathalina and Francisca, each a dowry of one estancia.

1583 Calvo wills the estate to his five children: Diego Calvo, Cathalina Rendón, Francisca Rendón, Juana Rendón, and Alonso Calvo.

1584 Cathalina sells the estancia received as dowry to her brother Diego.

1615 The hacienda, which had been sequestered by the Convent of Santa Catalina de Sena for the payment of back interest, is now returned to its owners.

1617 Diego and Alonso Calvo will their three sitios to the Monastery of La Merced in Antequera.

*1621 Cathalina and Francisca sell the estancia willed to them jointly in 1583 to Juan de Bohórquez, bishop of Oaxaca.

*1622 Br. Juan de Mora, Juana Rendón's heir, sells his estancia to Bohórquez.

*1623 Monastery of La Merced sells the remaining three estancias to Bohórquez.

1624 After paying off all mortgages on the hacienda, Bohórquez entails it. He later passes it on to his nephew. The estate remains in the Bohórquez family into the nineteenth century.

VALLEY OF TLACOLULA

Hacienda San Bartolo:

1591 Merced for an estancia de ganado mayor to Pedro de Espina.

pre- Inherited by Elena de Espina. Later inherited by Gaspar de Espina.
1652 Five estancias and two *labores* added to the original merced. Mortgage: 1,000 pesos.

1652 Gaspar de Espina establishes a capellanía on the hacienda.

*pre- Sold by Espina's executors to Gabriel de Achica and José Martínez
1693 de la Sierra for 5,300 pesos. Mortgages: 5,300 pesos.

*1693   Sold by Achica's widow to Antonio Somoza y Lozada.

*1694   Sold by Somoza y Lozada's executors to Capt. Manuel Fernández del Rincón for 7,179 pesos. Mortgages: 5,300 pesos.

*1701   Fernández del Rincón's widow cedes the hacienda to the Convent of La Concepción in Antequera to cancel debts.

*1705   Sold by the convent to Manuel de Figueroa.

1707   Mortgage of 300 pesos added.

*1712   Sold by Figueroa to Bartolomé de Torres for 6,600 pesos. Mortgages: 5,000 pesos.

*1723   Sold by Torres to Br. Juan de Quintana for 7,200 pesos. Mortgages: 3,500 pesos (1,500-peso debt transferred to another hacienda owned by Torres.)

*173?   Sold by Quintana to Andrés Mariano de Quintana for 7,240 pesos. Mortgages: 3,500 pesos.

*1745   Sold by Quintana to Vicente Molano for 7,990 pesos. Mortgages: 3,500 pesos.

1752   Vicente Molano adds a 500-peso mortgage.

*1758   Sold by widow of Vicente Molano to an unknown buyer for 7,314 pesos. Mortgages: 4,000 pesos.

*1778   Sold to Ignacio Monterrubio. Owned by the Monterrubios into the twentieth century.

Hacienda Santo Domingo Buenavista (alias Guadalupe):

1523   Cristóbal Gil establishes an estancia de ganado mayor y menor.

1538   Gil's holding is formalized by a merced from the cabildo of Antequera.

pre-   Owned by Gaspar Calderón.
1566

*1588   Merced of estancia de ganado menor to the community of Macuilxóchitl. Later sold to Juan de Vitoria, who had already purchased the other estancia from Calderón.

*1601   Sold by Vitoria to his son-in-law, Manuel de Cepeda.

*1609   Sold by Cepeda to Andrés de la Sierra, along with two adjacent caballerías.

1630   License issued for mass to be said in the hacienda chapel.

*1630   Sold by the widow of Andrés de la Sierra, who had inherited the estate, to her son Domingo and her two sons-in-law.

1643   Owned by Juan de Quevedo Alvarado.

*1657   Sold to Joseph de Cepeda.

pre-
1675
Inherited by Manuel Cepeda Medinilla.

pre-
1738
Inherited by Manuel Cepeda Medinilla, hijo.

*1738   Sold by Manuel Cepeda Medinilla's widow to the Bethlemite hospital of Antequera for 29,083 pesos. Mortgages: 20,618 pesos. Owned by Bethlemites for the rest of the colonial period.

Hacienda Xaagá:

1564   Merced for a sitio de ganado menor to María de la Cueva. She receives mercedes for two more sitios in 1571 and 1583.

1586   María de la Cueva cedes the estancias as a dowry to Fernando de Salas and Leonor de Padilla.

*1589   Sold to Pedro de Espina.

1695   Owned by Capt. Pedro de Espina Pacheco y Quiñones.

*1728   Sold to Juan de Quintana.

*pre-
1758
Sold to the Convent of La Concepción in Antequera.

*1758   Sold by La Concepción to the Dominican monastery Santo Domingo (Antequera). Owned by the Dominicans until the 1850's.

VALLEY OF ETLA

Hacienda Guadalupe:

1618   Marqués del Valle sells 2.5 caballerías "a censo perpetuo" to Andrés de Mendoza y León, Indian gobernador of Etla.

*1619   Sold with two additional caballerías to Andrés Sánchez de Ulloa, canon of La Santa Iglesia de Antequera for 485 pesos.

1621   Merced from the Marqués del Valle for ganado menor on the 4.5 caballerías.

*1630   Sold by Sánchez de Ulloa to Juan de Porras y Canseco for 6,000 pesos. Transaction includes a second sitio de ganado menor later separated from the estate.

1655–
1687
Small adjacent plots acquired.

*1665   The original 4.5 caballerías sold by Porras's widow to Antonio Delgado for 1,600 pesos. Mortgages: 700 pesos.

*1667   Sold, along with "*labor* despoblado a su linde," by Delgado to Lorenzo Pérez de la Peña for 1,700 pesos. Mortgages: 700 pesos.

*1673   Sold by Pérez de la Peña to Juan López de Silva for 5,465 pesos. Mortgages: 3,400 pesos.

*1674   Sold by López de Silva to Juan Cavallero de Carrión for 5,770 pesos. Mortgages: 3,400 pesos.

*1678   Sold by Cavallero de Carrión to Sebastián Barranco for 6,000 pesos. Mortgages: 3,400 pesos. Now termed "una hacienda de ganado menor y pan llevar."

168?   Inherited by Sebastián's son, Juan Barranco.

*169?   Sold to the cathedral at Antequera.

*1699   Sold by the cathedral to Francisco Fernández y Barreros for 9,868 pesos. Mortgages unknown.

*1728   Sold by Fernández y Barreros to Pedro Joseph García del Barrio for 20,700 pesos. Mortgages unknown.

*1735   Sold by García del Barrio to Br. Manuel de Llarena Lazo for 19,500 pesos. Mortgages: 13,500 pesos.

*1737   Sold to Capt. Ignacio de la Serrán.

1738–   Various small plots acquired.
1739

*pre-   Sold to Vicente Rafael de Pasqua.
1757

1757   Pasqua adds a 2,000-peso capellanía. Total debts are now 18,000 pesos.

*1761   Sold by Pasqua's widow to Juan Labariega.

*1764   Sold by Labariega's widow to Joseph Antonio Moreno for 18,769 pesos. Mortgages: 18,000 pesos.

*1793   Sold by Moreno to Sebastián González Romero for 24,300 pesos. Mortgages: 10,800 pesos.

*1796   Sold by González Romero to Juan María Ibáñez for 24,385 pesos. Mortgages: 10,800 pesos.

1797   Owned by Joseph Moreno Villafañe.

*1808   Sold to Juan de Dios Alarcón for 24,385 pesos. Mortgages: 10,800 pesos.

*1818   Sold by Dios Alarcón to Juan José Serrano.

Hacienda Santa Rita (partial):

*1740   Sold by Gaspar Miguel de Castro to Pedro de Rivera.

*1743   Sold by Rivera to José de Segura.

*1765   Sold by Segura to Br. Juan Manuel de Maradona.

*1780   Sold.

Appendix F

Mortgages of the Convent of Santa Catalina de Sena

Date	Amount in pesos	Estate	Source
1668	300	Hacienda Guadalupe	CCGG, fol. 38v
1705	800	Hacienda Jalapilla	AN 1705, fol. 37r
1707	3,750	Hacienda San Joaquín	AN 1707, fol. 253r
1717	700	*Labor* near Sola	AN 1717, fol. 152v
1717	1,900	Hacienda San Diego	AN 1717, fol. 107v
1727	6,000	Ranchos near Antequera owned by the cacique of Zapotitlán	CCGSNO, 1727
1749	500	Sitio Duhuatia, San Pedro Ixtlahuaca	AN 1749
1761	1,000	Rancho El Capitán	AN 1761, fol. 30v
1764	1,200	*Labor* near San Andrés Zautla	AN 1764, fol. 23v
1766	5,000	Hacienda San José	CCGSJ, 1766
1766	5,000	Hacienda San Juan Bautista	CCGSJB, 1766
1772	700	Rancho Guegonivalle	AN 1772, fol. 190v
1786	16,000	Hacienda Matagallinas	AN 1786, fol. 241v

Appendix G

Eighteenth-Century Land Documents of the Convent of Santa Catalina de Sena

Date	Description	Source
1708	Santa Catalina rents out the estancia Las Monjas, which it had owned "for many years."	AN 1708, fol. 240r
1713	Acquires the trapiche Santa Cruz near Tlapacoya.	CCGL, 1713
1715	Sells a *labor* near Sola to Br. Manuel de Morales for 700 pesos. In 1717 the *labor* is returned to Santa Catalina.	AN 1717, fol. 152v
1717	Sells two haciendas near Miahuatlán, San Diego and Poblete, which had been obtained by foreclosure from Joaquín Díaz de Ordaz in 1717.	AN 1717, fol. 107v
1747	Purchases the Hacienda San José near Cuilapan and immediately rents it to Vicente de Ossorio y Merecilla for 365 pesos a year.	AN 1747, fol. 43
1748	Sells the Hacienda Matagallinas to Jorge González for 5,580 pesos.	AN 1749, fol. 238v
1749	Purchases the sitio de ganado menor Duhuatia, east of San Pedro Ixtlahuaca, for 700 pesos.	AN 1749
1753	Rents "tierras de riego, humedad y temporal" from Manuel de Velasco, *principal* of Cuilapan, at 20 pesos a year for nine years.	AN 1753, fol. 19v
1762	Sells the Hacienda San Diego near Zimatlán, obtained by foreclosure in 1756.	AN 1762, fol. 16r
1764	*Labor* near San Lorenzo Cacaotepec ceded to the convent for debts after the death of the owner, Juan de Santaella.	AN 1764, fol. 23v
1766	Rents out the Hacienda San Isidro (Zimatlán), valued at 26,350 pesos, to Agustín de Achutigui y Gandarillas for three years at 1,092 pesos, 7 *reales* a year.	AN 1766, fol. 26v

Date	Description	Source
1769	Sells the sitio Duhuatia for 1,050 pesos.	AN 1769, fol. 121r
1775	Buys the Hacienda San Germán near Xoxocotlán.	AGNT 1064, exp. 13
1779	Sells the Hacienda San Miguel near San Antonio de la Cal. Reclaimed shortly thereafter and held continuously into the 1820's.	AGNT 2386, exp. 1; Murguía y Galardi, "Extracto general," parte 2, fol. 36r
1786	Rents Hacienda San Isidro to Juan Bautista Santa Cruz de Zaragoza for nine years at 1,166 pesos a year.	AN 1786, fol. 121r
1786	Sells the Hacienda Matagallinas.	AN 1786, fol. 241v
1798	Rents out the estancia La Soledad.	AN 1798, fol. 22v
1799	Rents the rancho San José from Manuel José de Mendoza Cortez y Lara, *cacique* of Cuilapan.	AN 1799, fol. 22v
1836	Still owns the Hacienda San Isidro.	CCGSJB 1836

Appendix H

Eighteenth-Century Land Transactions Involving Secular Priests

Date	Description	Source
1701	Executors of Br. Antonio de Grado sell an hacienda in the Valley of Zimatlán near the Hacienda San José.	CCGSJ, fol. 13r
1705	Br. Gaspar Díaz Jurado sells the Hacienda San Nicolás Obispo.	CCGSNO, fol. 14r
1711	Br. Francisco Ordinia Sosa y Castilla inherits lands near Querétaro from his father.	Van de Velde Papers, Univ. of New Mexico
1717	Br. Manuel de Morales, who had bought a *labor* near Sola from Santa Catalina, returns it to the convent because he cannot pay the interest on the mortgage.	AN 1717, fol. 152v
1718	Br. Joseph Sarmiento sells a *labor* near Mitla for 2,150 pesos, 440 pesos less than he paid for it.	AN 1718, fol. 50v
1719	Executors of Br. Miguel de Saavedra sell his *labor* near Zaachila for 3,500 pesos.	CCGSJB
1720	Executors of Br. Juan Antonio Díaz sell the Hacienda Taniche near Ejutla.	AN 1737
1725	Br. Fernando Manuel de Elorsa buys Hacienda Lachigobana near Matatlán.	AN 1725
1729	Br. Silvestre Muñós de Acuña sells the Hacienda San Francisco Xavier near Cuilapan to another priest, Martín Rodríguez de Medina, for 11,000 pesos.	AN 1729, fol. 5r
1730	Br. Enrico Buenaventura y Angulo sells the Hacienda La Soledad for 12,000 pesos.	AN 1737, fol. 371
1734	Francisco de Merezilla Zota, parish priest of Chacaltongo, buys the *labor* Jesús Nazareno.	AN 1734, fol. 345r
1735	Cacique of Cuilapan rents a *labor* near Azompa to Br. Benito de Montoya Maldonado.	AGNH 348, 7:4

Date	Description	Source
1737	Br. Manuel de Llarena Lazo sells the Hacienda Guadalupe, which he bought in 1735 for 19,500 pesos.	AN 1737, fol. 227r
1738	Br. Ignacio Castellanos buys lands near Santa Catalina Quiané; resells them in 1742.	AN 1754, fol. 162v
1738	Br. Gerónimo Morales Sigala buys the Hacienda San José.	CCGSJ, fol. 109r
1744	Br. Antonio González de Llano sells the Hacienda Maia near San Baltazar Chichicapa for 9,590 pesos, some 400 pesos less than he paid for it in 1735.	AN 1744, fol. 9v
1748	Br. Juan Antonio Macaya buys the trapiche San Joseph (Teotitlán del Valle jurisdiction).	AN 1748, fol. 123r
1744	Br. Juan de Carrión owns the Hacienda San Isidro (Etla).	AGNH 348, 7:6r
1749	Br. Francisco de Valencia y Aragón, owner of the *labor* Jesús Nazareno, rents lands from the cacique of Cuilapan.	AN 1749, fol. 281r
1752	Br. Vicente de Ossorio sells the sitio y tierras de pan sembrar La Noria, which he had bought in 1749, for 3,220 pesos.	AN 1752, fol. 65r
1760	Br. Manuel Joseph de Veytia owns the *labor* San Blas near San Pedro Ixtlahuaca.	AGNH 306, 1:12r
1760	Br. Gerónimo Morales Sigala owns the Hacienda Jalapilla.	AGNH 306, 1:14v
1760	Br. Pedro de Carrión owns the *labor* La Quinta.	AGNH 306, 2:21v
1761	Br. Manuel Vasques Latatua buys the rancho El Capitán for 1,000 pesos.	AN 1761, fol. 30v
1765	Br. Manuel Joseph de Veytia rents the Rancho San Blas, adjoining his *labor*. Document terms the rental a renewal.	AN 1765, fol. 35v
1767	Br. Guillermo Martínez buys the trapiche Santa Ana and the *labor* San Joseph near Sola.	AN 1767, fol. 32r
1767	Br. Lásaro de Olivera buys the *labores* Guelavichigana and La Gachupina near Ocotlán for 5,147 pesos.	AN 1767, fol. 78v
1767	Br. Juan Joseph de Quintana buys an estancia de ganado mayor near San Pedro Ixtlahuaca.	AGNT 1049, exp. 1
1767	Executors of Gerónimo de Morales Sigala cede the Hacienda Jalapilla, valued at 5,400 pesos, to the Conceptionist convent.	AN 1770, fol. 27v

Date	Description	Source
1768	Bernardo and Leon Díaz, brothers who are both priests, inherit the rancho La Chilayta near Ocotlán. León sells his half to Bernardo.	AN 1768, fol. 101r
1770	Br. Juan Leonardo Fernández buys the *labor* Jesús Nazareno for 8,200 pesos.	AN 1770, fol. 9r
1772	Br. Joseph Ruiz buys the rancho Guegonivalle for 4,722 pesos.	AN 1772, fol. 190v
1772	Executors of Br. Mariano Carrión sell the Hacienda San Nicolás Tolentino for 16,000 pesos.	AN 1772, fol. 27
1774	Br. Juan Joseph Quintana rents out the *labor* San Blas, valued at 14,670 pesos.	AGNT 1048, exp. 11
1775	Br. Angel Remigio Briones sells the rancho San Joseph near San Gabriel Etla, valued at 3,981 pesos.	AN *Loose papers*, 1775
1780	Executor of Br. Juan Manuel de Maradona sells the *labor* Santa Rita for 7,600 pesos.	AN 1780, fol. 109r
1782	Br. Felipe Noriega inherits the Hacienda San Nicolás Obispo, valued at 24,257 pesos.	CCGL, 1782
1789	Br. Fernando Callexas rents the *labor* San Joseph near Cuilapan from José Agustín Contreras.	AN 1789, primera parte, fol. 71v
1789	Br. Joachín Agustín de la Vega rents out the *labor* San Isidro near Santa Ana Zegache.	AN 1789, primera parte, fol. 77v
1789	Br. José Gabriel María de Contreras y Burgoa rents out the *labor* La Preciosíssima Sangre de Cristo near Xoxocotlán.	AN 1789, primera parte, fol. 113r
1790	Executors of Br. Juan José Quintana rent his estancia Duhuatia to San Pedro Ixtlahuaca.	AN 1790, fol. 104v
1790	Executors of Br. Felipe Noriega sell the Hacienda San Nicolás Obispo for 17,140 pesos.	CCGL, 1790
1790	Br. Juan Manuel de Ortega rents out the *labor* de la Soledad near Santa Catalina Quiané.	AN 1790, fol. 146r
1798	Br. Miguel Andrés de Aguilar owns the Hacienda Cantove (also known as the Hacienda de la Soledad).	AN 1798, fol. 38r
1808	Br. Joachín Agustín de la Vega rents out the Hacienda de la Zoritana near Ejutla.	AN 1808, fol. 152r
1816	Br. Francisco Núñez Carrión owns the Hacienda del Dulce near San Felipe Tejalapan.	AGNT 1419, exp. 4

NOTES

NOTES

Complete authors' names, titles, and publication data for books and articles cited in the Notes are given in the Bibliography, pp. 267–78; the archives cited are discussed in the introduction to the Bibliography, pp. 265–67. The following abbreviations are used in the Notes:

ADAA	Archivo del Departamento de Asuntos Agrarios, Mexico City
AEO	Archivo del Estado de Oaxaca
AGI	Archivo General de las Indias, Seville
AGII	AGI *Indiferente General*
AGIJ	AGI *Justicia*
AGIM	AGI *Audiencia de México*
AGN	Archivo General de la Nación, Mexico City
AGNC	AGN *Ramo de Civil*
AGNG	AGN *Ramo de General de Parte*
AGNH	AGN *Ramo de Hospital de Jesús*
AGNI	AGN *Ramo de Indios*
AGNMer	AGN *Ramo de Mercedes*
AGNT	AGN *Ramo de Tierras*
AGNTr	AGN *Ramo de Tributos*
AMT	Archivo Municipal de Tlacolula, Oaxaca
AN	Archivo de Notarías, Oaxaca
BEOB	Biblioteca del Estado de Oaxaca, *Hacienda Buenavista Papers*
BN	Biblioteca Nacional, Madrid, *Sección de Manuscritos*
CCG	Lic. Luis Castañeda Guzmán Collection
CCGG	CCG *Hacienda Guadalupe Papers*
CCGL	CCG *Loose Papers*
CCGS	CCG *Hacienda San Bartolo Papers*
CCGSJ	CCG *Hacienda San José Papers*
CCGSJB	CCG *Hacienda San Juan Bautista Papers*
CCGSN	CCG *Hacienda San Nicolás Papers*
CCGSNO	CCG *Hacienda San Nicolás Obispo Papers*
CDChO	Centro de Documentación del Museo Nacional, Chapultepec, Mexico City, *Serie Oaxaca*
CDII	*Colección de documentos inéditos para la historia de Ibero-América*

CDIU   *Colección de documentos inéditos relativos al descubrimiento, conquista, y organización de las antiguas posesiones españolas de Ultramar*

ENE   Francisco del Paso y Troncoso, ed., *Epistolario de Nueva España, 1505–1818*

MNM   Archivo Histórico del Museo Nacional, Chapultepec, Mexico City

RAHM   Real Academia de Historia, Madrid, *Muñoz Collection*

Citations from AGN are in condensed form: thus "AGNT 211, 2:15r" stands for "Archivo General de la Nación, Mexico City, *Ramo de Tierras*, tomo 211, expediente 2, folio 15 recto." In citations from AGI and BN, the number immediately following the abbreviation is the legajo number. The AMT documents are numbered according to their order when studied in May 1968. AN volumes are numbered by year. When sources are grouped together in a note and are not labeled, they are in the same order as the text examples they document.

INTRODUCTION

1. Borah and Cook, *Aboriginal Population of Central Mexico.*
2. AGIM 357; AGI *Casa de Contratación* 197.
3. AGIM 357 and 1088.
4. Borah, *Silk Raising.*
5. BN 2449–50, eighteenth-century *Relaciones Geográficas* for Oaxaca.
6. Chevalier, *La formation*, p. 185.
7. *Ibid.*, pp. 406–409; Algiers.
8. Mathieu de Fossey, *Le Mexique* (Paris, 1857), p. 342.
9. González Sánchez, pp. 9–26. See also Chevalier, *La formation*, pp. 282–83; Marion Clawson, *Man and Land in the United States* (Lincoln, Neb., 1964), pp. 102–104; Tannenbaum, p. 7.

CHAPTER ONE

1. BN 2450, fol. 12r: "The head town of the parish of Ayoquesco, nine leagues [south] from the city of Antequera, is the last parish in the valley known as the Great Valley of Oaxaca."
2. Lorenzo, p. 56.
3. Flannery et al., p. 4.
4. Lorenzo, pp. 53–56.
5. AGNT 211, 2:15r.
6. Iturribarría, *Oaxaca en la historia*, p. 68.
7. Méndez, p. 182; CCGSJB, Aug. 1648; AGNH 119, 2:14v; *Gacetas de México*, Aug. 25, 1789.
8. Barlow, "Dos relaciones," pp. 26–27.
9. Murguía y Galardi, "Extracto general," primera parte, fol. 4r; AMT, doc. 2, 1807; Paso y Troncoso, *Papeles*, 4: 112.
10. Brioso y Candiani, p. 21; AGNI 42, exp. 104.
11. Paso y Troncoso, *Papeles*, 4: 146, 190; AGNH 306, 1:20v; Méndez, p. 182; Barlow, "Dos relaciones," pp. 26–27; Burgoa, 1: 395, 2: 46, 116.

12. Flannery et al., p. 4.
13. Barrera, pp. 55–56.
14. CCGG, bk. 3, fol. 41v.
15. Tamayo, *Geografía*, p. 91.
16. ENE, 4: 141–42.
17. Motolinía (Toribio de Benavente), p. 31.
18. Thièry de Menonville, p. 822.
19. AGNT 1864, exp. 2.
20. Murguía y Galardi, "Extracto general," *passim*.
21. See Zárate's description in ENE, 4: 141.
22. AGNH 102, 6:8r, 1617.
23. Archivo Histórico del Instituto Nacional de Antropología e Historia, legajo 99 de la antigua colección, número 39, fols. 329–32.
24. AGNT 2696, 8:7v, 1643.
25. Murguía y Galardi, "Extracto general," partido de Tlacolula, fols. 1–23; Villaseñor y Sánchez, 2: 115.
26. Paddock, p. 241; Paso y Troncoso, *Papeles*, 4: 103, 113.
27. Spores, p. 8; Paso y Troncoso, *Papeles*, 4: 112, 149.
28. AGNC 822, fol. 217r–v.
29. See Paso y Troncoso, *Papeles*, 4: 103, 107, 113, 146–47, 150, 181, 194 for the southeast and Zaachila, and Barlow, "Dos relaciones," pp. 27–28 for Cuilapan.
30. AGNH 432, 5:1; *Instrucciones que los vireyes*, p. 237.
31. AGNH 404, exp. 2.
32. Murguía y Galardi, "Extracto general," *passim*. Figures for Indian and Spanish cattle add up to considerably less than the total number of livestock in the political jurisdictions of the Valley, since some non-Valley towns are included in the 260,000 total and since the figures from the jurisdiction of Ocotlán do not distinguish between Indian and Spanish livestock.
33. Paso y Troncoso, *Papeles*, 4: 107, 113, 146, 150; Murguía y Galardi, "Extracto general," partido de Zimatlán, fol. 9v.
34. AGNH 293, exp. 133; ENE, 4: 141.
35. Villaseñor y Sánchez, 2: 121; Gamboa, p. 504.
36. Borah and Cook, *Aboriginal Population of Central Mexico*, p. 83; AGIM 357. This figure (actually 367,038) is obtained by solving the following equation for x:

$$\frac{(1569 \text{ tributaries} \div 1.17) \, 3.3}{1{,}598{,}096} = \frac{x}{10{,}672{,}316}$$

At present this is our most reliable estimate of the pre-conquest population. The real figure is likely to be somewhat lower since the 1569 figure includes a few towns outside the Valley. Also the population of the Valley probably did not decline so dramatically between 1519 and 1548 as the population of the central plateau (Borah and Cook's area 1), where the violent conquest took place.
37. Tamayo, *Oaxaca*, pp. 13–31.
38. Villaseñor y Sánchez, 2: 123.
39. *Ibid.*, p. 114; AMT, doc. 25, 1826 population records.

40. AGNTr 34, 7:51.
41. Villaseñor y Sánchez, 2: 114, 123; AGII 107, fols. 386v, 389r; Burgoa, 2: 55.
42. AGIM 2589, cuaderno 38; AGIM 2590, cuaderno 34.
43. AGNH 163, 48:46r.
44. AGIM 355.
45. *Ibid.*
46. AGIM 2589, cuaderno 38.
47. AGNC 822, fols. 90v–91v. Domingo de Mendoza, the cacique of Tlacolula, owned a twenty-four-year-old Negro slave in 1576.
48. AGNTr 43, 9:1–8.
49. AGNH 163, 48:46r–47r.
50. Burgoa, 1: 398.
51. Paso y Troncoso, *Papeles*, 4: 196–205.
52. According to Villaseñor y Sánchez, 2: 119–21, Mixtec and Nahuatl were spoken in the jurisdiction that included the following communities: Cuilapan, Xoxocotlán, San Lucas Tlanechico, San Raimundo Xalpa, San Agustín de la Cal, San Andrés Huayapan, Santa Lucía, San Sebastián Tutla, Santo Domingo Tomaltepec, Santa Ana Zegache, San Juan Chilateca, San Pedro Guegorexe, Santa Catarina Minas, Santa Marta, San Martín Yachila, San Miguel de las Peras, San Pablo Cuatro Venados, Santa María Azompa, and San Pablo Etla.
53. Burgoa, 1: 395, 397, and 2: 60; AGNH 63, *passim*, Santa Ana Zegache, 1804.
54. Burgoa (1: 278 and 2: 12) says the Huitzo had "forasteros terrasguerros," which probably included Mixtecs. In 1654 the Villa de Etla reported three Mixtec couples (AGNI 17, exp. 29).
55. Schmieder, p. 24.
56. Salazar, p. 112; AGNI 43, exp. 79; AGNH 380, 9:41; AGNT 997, 1:35r–v. Without noting his source Brioso y Candiani (p. 12) says that only 400 Aztec allies settled in the Valley.
57. Gay, tomo 1, vol. 2, p. 448.
58. AGNI 43, exp. 79. Another document identifies the founders of Jalatlaco as "the Mexican and Tlaxcalan conquerors who came with Cortez." AGNT 997, 1:35r.
59. Andrés Cavo, *Historia de México* (Mexico, 1949), p. 90.
60. AGNH 146, 430:335v.
61. Burgoa, 2: 29.
62. *Ibid.*, p. 103.
63. AGNI 41, exp. 25.
64. AGNT 71, exps. 9, 5.
65. AGNT 64, exp. 5; AGNH 380, 9:36v, 37r, 58r, 75r; AGNT 1231, 2: 2v; AGNI 30, exp. 66.
66. AGNI 51, exp. 246.
67. AGNT 1268, 1:33–44.
68. Cline discusses the administrative motive in "Civil Congregations."
69. AGNT 71, 5:488.
70. AGNH 380, 9:55r.

TABLE FOR NOTE 78

Population Figures for Three Valley Towns

Year	Tributaries	Population estimate	Year	Tributaries	Population estimate
		ZAACHILA			
1568	——	3,594	1734	500 ca.	——
1570	1,300	3,770	1760	600 ca.	——
1593	800 ca.	2,320	1826	——	3,804
1623	512½	——			
		TEITIPAC			
pre-1579	3,000–4,000[a]	——	1623	581½	——
1568	——	2,948	1670	40[b]	——
1570	1,000	2,900	1826	——	1,325
1580	——	2,822			
		TLACOCHAHUAYA			
1568	——	1,552	1743	367	——
1570	500	1,450	1748	370	——
1595	——	1,050	1759	507	——
1597	373	1,079	1815	——	1,400
ca. 1670	300	——	1826	——	1,362

[a] Number of households.   [b] Married couples only.

71. Spores, pp. 90–109.

72. AGNI 39, fol. 218r; AGNH 380, 9:37r, 58r, 75r; CCGG, fol. 14v; AGNI 51, exp. 246.

73. AGNT 867, 9:5; AGNT 2412, 1:3r.

74. AGNH 119, 3:19r–20r.

75. AGNI 35, fol. 68r; AGNI 3, exp. 160; AGNI 33, exp. 194; AGNI 7, exp. 268; AGNI 11, exp. 160.

76. AGNT 2386, 1:54r; AGNT 1343, 4:4r; AGNI 34, exps. 113, 166, 223; AGNI 35, exp. 33; AGNI 41, exp. 220; AGNH 85, exp. 5. Four other Valley towns may have been established after 1521. *Colección de cuadros sinópticos de los pueblos, haciendas y ranchos*, compiled by Manuel Martínez Gracida (Oaxaca, 1883), lists three towns: San Dionicio Ocotlán, 1526, San Sebastián Ocotlán, 1599, and San Antonio, 1649. Santa Catarina de Sena may have been a sixteenth-century congregación. Esteva, *Elementos*, p. 80. I have not found colonial documentation for these towns.

77. AGNI 15, exp. 2; AGNI 34, exp. 37; AGNI 39, exp. 61. By the 1660's there was a popular movement in the Etla arm among small communities seeking to become their own cabeceras. Burgoa, 2: 6–7.

78. For other figures of interest, see the accompanying table.

79. Borah and Cook, *Population of Central Mexico in 1548*, p. 75.

80. *Ibid.*

TABLE FOR NOTE 81

Multiplying Factors for Seven Marquesado Communities in 1804

Community	Tributaries	Population	Multiplying factor
Cuilapan	321½	1,397	4.35
Azompa	199½	916	4.59
Etla	132	571	4.33
San Lucas Tlanechico	106½	514	4.83
San Pablo Peras	67	300	4.47
Asunción Etla	46	214	4.65
San Pablo de la Raya	31	128	4.3
TOTAL	903½	4,040	4.48 (avg.)

81. See the accompanying table.

82. This figure is probably somewhat high, since the Antequera jurisdiction included pueblos outside the Valley's limits. The 4.48 multiplying factor is probably too low for the Valley as a whole. It does not include any of the southeastern pueblos, which may have had a larger tributary-population ratio.

CHAPTER TWO

1. Gibson, *Aztecs Under Spanish Rule*; López Sarrelangue, *La nobleza indígena*.

2. Cuilapan, 1717–28 and 1776–93, see AGNT 34, exp. 3, and AGNH 119, exp. 7; for Etla, 1692, and Magdalena Apasco, 1680's, see CDChO, rollo 9.

3. Salazar, p. 103; Manuel Martínez Gracida, "La conquista de Oaxaca," *Lecturas Históricas Mexicanas*, 2: 621–28.

4. López Sarrelangue, *La nobleza indígena*, pp. 92–93; Solórzano Pereira, *Política Indiana*, libro 2, capítulo 27, par. 14. Solórzano quotes a 1603 cédula that banned the appointment or election of caciques by Spaniards. This law, repeated in 1619, affirmed hereditary succession to cacicazgos.

5. Several cacicazgo titles attest to the loyalty of the native nobility: Santo Domingo Etla, AGNI 36, exp. 349; Cuilapan, AGNT 1016, exp. 5; San Juan Chapultepec, AGNT 236, exp. 1.

6. Burgoa, 2: 29.

7. *Ibid.*, p. 8.

8. AGIJ 117.

9. AGIJ 231, fol. 316r–v.

10. AGNH 102, 6:8v, 16r; AGNG 2, exps. 718, 1138.

11. AGNT 1016, 5:10r.

12. AGNI 10, exp. 134.

13. AGNT 1058, 1:98r, cacique of Santa Cruz Mixtepec; CDChO, rollo 7, cacique of Macuilxóchitl, rollo 10, nobles of San Juan Chapultepec, and rollo 11, nobles of Huitzo; AN 1740, fol. 124r, nobles of Etla; AN 1747, fol. 139v, nobles of San Pedro Guaxolotitlán. AGNG 19, exp. 240 (1709), records that the Etla cacique acquired houses in Antequera for his children and nephews who were studying there.

14. Luis Chávez Orozco, *Indice del Ramo de Indios del Archivo General de la Nación* (Mexico, 1953); AGNG 1, exps. 737, 815, 818, 820, 858, 856, 1065.

15. AN 1734, fols. 77r–79r.

16. *Ibid.*; AN 1747, fol. 139v; AN 1749, fol. 238v.

17. Mörner, "La infiltración mestiza," p. 160.

18. AGNG 19, exp. 337; AGNT 1016, exp. 5; AGNI 54, exp. 31; AGIM 2859, cuadernos 45 and 41.

19. Esquivel Obregón, p. 303.

20. The following nobles received mercedes (all grants were for one sitio de ganado menor except those specifically labeled otherwise): 1551, the cacique and *principales* of Santo Domingo Tomaltepec, one sitio de ganado menor and one sitio de ganado mayor (AGNT 2384, 8:28r); 1553, various nobles of Mitla and Tlacolula, two sitios de ganado menor (AGNT 485, primera parte, 1:104r); 1564, the cacique of San Felipe del Agua, monte y aguas (AGNI 34, exp. 91); 1564, the cacica of Mitla (CCGL); 1566, the cacique of Coyotepec (AGNMer 9, fol. 26r); 1570, a *principal* of Ocotlán (CCGSJ, fol. 66r); 1571, a *principal* of Ocotlán *(ibid.)*; 1571, the cacica of Mitla (CCGL); 1575, the cacique of Tlacolula, one sitio de ganado menor y mayor (AGNT 2721, 5:1r); 1578, a *principal* of Ocotlán (CCGSJ, fol. 62r); 1581, the cacique of Ocotlán (AGNH 85, 5:1–10); 1582, a *principal* of San Pablo, sujeto of San Juan Teitipac (AGNI 2, exp. 235); 1583, the cacica of Mitla (CCGL); pre-1584, a *principal* of Huitzo (AGNI 2, exp. 541); 1587, the cacique of Huitzo (AGNT 415, exp. 3, primera numeración, fols. 69r–72r); 1588, two *principales* of Tlacolula (AMT, doc. 43); 1591, a *principal* of Etla, sitio y herido de molino (CCGL); 1591, a *principal* of Cuilapan (CCGSN, fol. 65r); 1592, a *principal* of Ocotlán (CCGSJ, fol. 69r); 1599, the cacique of Cuilapan (AGNI 15, exp. 36); 1599, a *principal* of San Lorenzo Cacaotepec (CCGG, fol. 13r); 1618, the cacique of Etla (AGNH 102, segundo atado, exp. 7); undated, a *principal* of Tlacochahuaya (AGNI 2, exp. 865, document dated 1583); undated, a *principal* of Tlacolula, one sitio de ganado mayor (AGNI 6, primera parte, exp. 137, document dated 1593); undated, the cacique of Cuilapan, one sitio de ganado mayor (AGNT 1016, 5:10r, document dated 1685); undated, *principales* of Santo Domingo Etla, unspecified lands (AGNI 36, exp. 349, document dated 1706).

21. Spores, p. 126, Tlalixtac; AGNT 485, primera parte, exp. 1, Mitla and Tlacolula; AGNT 1016, exp. 5, Cuilapan; AGNI 52, exp. 89, Jalatlaco; AGNT 2384, exp. 2, Santo Domingo Tomaltepec; AGNT 1026, exp. 1:5v, Tlacochahuaya.

22. AGNT 236, 1:8v.

23. AGNI 19, exp. 597.

24. AGNT 2384, 2:28r.

25. AGNI 52, exp. 89.

26. AGNI 6, primera parte, exp. 174.

27. AGNH 118, unnumbered exp., 1717.

28. AGNH 69, bk. 1, fols. 419–29, 1644.

29. AGNI 23, exp. 211, 1658; CCGSN, fol. 56r.

30. AGNG 2, exp. 1142, 1581.

31. AGNT 645, primera parte, exp. 3.

32. AGNG 2, exps. 623, 625.

33. Zavala and Castelo, 2: 271–72; AGNI 12, segunda parte, exp. 42, 1640. There are other examples of terrasguerros on the Etla cacicazgo: CDChO, rollo 8, 1689, Guadalupe Etla; AGNT 268, exp. 3, 1711, Soledad Etla; AGNT 495, exp. 4, 1730. Resident terrasguerros were also found on cacicazgos at Huitzo (1553) and San Lorenzo Cacaotepec (1635). CDII, 1: 203; CCGG, bk. 3, fol. 41v.

34. AGNI 3, exp. 528, 1591; AGNI 19, exp. 600, 1663. A detailed record of the cacicazgo of Tlacolula in 1576 does not mention terrasguerros. AGNC 822.

35. AGNT 2386, 1:54r.

36. AGNI 27, exp. 139, 1681.

37. AGNI 43, exp. 16, 1716; AN 1771, fol. 44r.

38. AGNI 43, exp. 16.

39. Chevalier, *La formation*, p. 60.

40. AGNC 822, fols. 223r–27r.

41. The following examples of probable usurpation have been located: in 1576 the cacique of Tlacolula was accused of stealing Indian lands (AGNC 822, fol. 275r); in 1590 a *principal* of Tlacochahuaya took lands from heirs of a deceased native, claiming that they were intestate property (AGNI 3, exp. 264); complaints were lodged against the cacique of Etla in 1711 by the community of Soledad Etla and in 1740 by a neighboring hacienda (AGNT 268, exp. 3, and AGNT 702, exp. 4); in 1725 the Cuilapan barrio of Anaa claimed that the cacique had sequestered its lands (AGNT 1449, exp. 6); and in 1648 Juan de Zúñiga, a *principal* of Cuilapan, was ordered to restore two caballerías that he had taken from a native of San Lorenzo Guaxolotitlán (AGNI 15, exp. 69). Zimatlán provides the most blatant example of usurpation. Over a 15-year period, the cacique, Hipólito Vásquez, accumulated two estancias and three caballerías of communal property, as well as many smaller tracts belonging to individual townsmen. AGNI 39, exp. 146, Zimatlán.

42. Solórzano Pereira, libro 2, capítulo 27, par. 19. López Sarrelangue, *La nobleza indígena*, p. 106, also describes the connection between mayorazgo and cacicazgo.

43. AGNT 415, exp. 3, tercera numeración, fols. 45–48.

44. AGNH 85, exp. 1, 1734.   45. AGNT 256, 2:121v, 1599.

46. AGNT 1016, 5:6r.   47. AGNT 125, 4:18v.

48. AGNT 645, primera parte, exp. 3; AGNT 310, exp. 2; CCGG, bk. 2, fol. 46r; AGNT 415, exp. 3, tercera numeración, fols. 45r–48r; AGNT 125, exp. 4; AGIJ 117.

49. AN 1749, fol. 238v; AGNT 1016, 5:2v.

50. AGNT 1016, 5:2v.

51. AGNT 395, exp. 2, 1721.

52. AMT, doc. 6.

53. AGNT 256, 2:128r, 1698. See the accompanying table. AGN *Tierras* contains other wills of Valley *principales* with equally complicated divisions of property: AGNT 256, 2:136r, six wills for the period 1607–76 from San Sebastián Teitipac; AGNT 350, exp. 4, 1707, Andrés Martín of San Felipe Tejalapan; AGNT 956, 3:63–69, 1724, Micaela de la Cruz y Zárate of Huitzo.

TABLE FOR NOTE 53
Division of a Principal's Estate

Tract (and no. of medidas)	Inheritor					
	First son	Second son	Third son	Fourth son	Grand-son	Church
1 (15 m.)	1/3	1/3	1/3	—	—	—
2 (1 m.)	—	—	—	—	All	—
3 (15 m.)	—	—	1/2	1/2	—	—
4 (15 m.)	1/3	1/3	—	—	1/3	—
5 (4 m.)	—	—	1/2	1/2	—	—
6 (4 m.)	—	—	1/2	1/2	—	—
7 (4 m.)	All	—	—	—	—	—
8 (5 m.)	—	All	—	—	—	—
9 (4 m.)	—	1/2	—	1/2	—	—
10 (15 m.)	All	—	—	—	—	—
11 (15 m.)	—	—	—	—	—	All
TOTAL MEDIDAS	29	17	16½	13½	6	15

54. AGNT 236, exp. 1, San Juan Chapultepec; CCGSN, fol. 56r, Cuilapan.

55. AGNI 15, exp. 36, 1599; AGNMer 9, fol. 26r, 1566.

56. CCGL, 1659.

57. CDChO, rollo 11, San Juan family; AN *Loose Papers*, 1708, and CDChO, rollo 10, Cruz y Fonseca family.

58. CCGG, fols. 35r–40r.

59. AN 1705, fol. 54r.

60. AN 1771, fol. 44r; AGNT 956, 3:63–69, 1724; AGNT 350, 5:225r; AGNG 2, exp. 1051.

61. AGNI 2, exp. 235, 1582, Martín, a *principal* of San Pablo, sujeto of San Juan Teitipac; exp. 254, 1582, Juan de Zárate, a *principal* of Mitla; exp. 255, 1582, Diego Hernández, Luis de Velasco, and Domingo López, *principales* of Mitla.

62. CCGSJ, fol. 69r.

63. AGNT 415, exp. 3, tercera numeración, fols. 20v–25v.

64. AGNI 61, fol. 139r, Santo Domingo Ocotlán, 1764.

65. AN 1708, fol. 273v.

66. AGNT 34, 91:97r.

67. AGNI 19, exp. 553, 1662, and AGNI 24, exp. 319, Sebastián Ramírez I and Sebastián Ramírez II, caciques of Etla; AGNH 69, bk. 1, Jacinto Hernández de Yllescas, a *principal* of San Juan Guelache; AGNT 110, exp. 4, 1669, Gregorio de la Cruz, a *principal* of San Miguel Etla; CCGL, 1591, Domingo de San Gabriel, a *principal* of the Villa de Etla.

68. AN 1705, fol. 54r; AGNT 415, exp. 3, tercera numeración, fol. 12v.

69. AGNH 85, exp. 2, Etla, 1727.

70. López Sarrelangue, *La nobleza indígena,* pp. 116, 124, 126–27.
71. AGNI 36, exp. 448.
72. AGNI 34, exp. 191.
73. AGNI 41, exp. 56, Teotitlán del Valle, 1715.
74. Aguirre Beltrán, *Formas,* p. 49.
75. AGNI 60, exp. 13; AGNI 12, segunda parte, exp. 110; AGNI 34, exp. 42.
76. Aguirre Beltrán, *Formas,* p. 49.
77. AGNI 39, exp. 39.
78. AGNI 60, exp. 13; AGNI 37, exp. 8.
79. Bentura Beleña, 1: 206; AGNT 1854, exp. 5, 1676.
80. For other examples, see AGNI 43, exp. 159, and AGNI 41, exp. 56.
81. AGNI 6, segunda parte, exp. 311, 1591, Domingo de la Cruz, gobernador of Zaachila; AGNI 10, exp. 134, 1631, Felipe Garcés, gobernador of Huitzo; AGNI 10, exp. 181, 1629, Juan de Chábez, gobernador of Teotitlán del Valle.
82. AGNI 60, exp. 13.
83. AGNI 12, segunda parte, exp. 110.
84. AGNI 54, exp. 31, 1734.
85. AGNI 51, exp. 26, Coyotepec.
86. Burgoa, 2: 14.
87. AGNI 33, exp. 162, 1697; AGNI 52, exp. 84.
88. AGNI 37, exp. 175.   89. AMT, doc. 35, 1722.
90. See the accompanying table.   91. See the accompanying table.
92. CDChO, rollo 8.
93. AGNT 645, primera parte, exp. 3.
94. AGNH 118, unnumbered exp., 1717.
95. AGNI 19, exp. 600.
96. AGNI 15, exp. 39, 1649.
97. A 1635 survey of such censos perpetuos lists 22 separate pieces of land in the Cuatro Villas jurisdiction. AGNH 69, bk. 1, fols. 367–69.
98. AGNH 69, bk. 2, fols. 654r–59r.
99. CCGG, fol. 81r, 1682, two caballerías with a mortgage of 200 pesos; BEOB, fol. 222r, 1660, one-half sitio with a mortgage of 300 pesos; CCGSN, fol. 110r, 1722, a *labor* with a mortgage of 300 pesos; AGNT 221, fol. 3v, no date, two and one-half caballerías with a mortgage of 143 pesos; CDChO, rollo 11, 1694, mortgage of 918 pesos; CDChO, rollo 9, 1692, mortgage of 1,000 pesos.
100. AGNI 33, exp. 344, 1698.
101. CCGSJ, fol. 2r, 1615.
102. Here are some of the reasons nobles gave for renting land: "The aforementioned land is of no use to us because we do not cultivate it. We own better lands which are also closer to our community"; "To repay debts that we accumulated in various land disputes, I must rent [a sitio de ganado menor]"; "We find ourselves in extreme need." AN *Loose Papers,* Cuilapan, Dec. 24, 1707, and San Juan Chapultepec, 1708; CDChO, rollo 9, Cuilapan, 1692.
103. AGNT 1449, exp. 6.
104. AGNT 34, exp. 3.

TABLE FOR NOTE 90
Political Disputes Between Caciques and Townspeople

Date	Location	Source
1582	Mitla	AGNI 2, exp. 256
1590	Zaachila	AGNI 3, exps. 161–63
1594	Ocotlán	AGNI 6, primera parte, exp. 867
1607	Tlacolula	AGNI 2956, exp. 103
1616	Etla	AGNI 7, exp. 29
1670	Macuilxóchitl	AGNT 2951, exp. 38
1676	Zimatlán	AGNT 1854, exp. 5
1699	Santiago, Ocotlán jurisdiction	AGNI 34, exp. 42
1700	Zaachila	AGNI 34, exp. 191
1705	Tlacochahuaya	AGNI 36, exp. 448
1707	Tlacochahuaya	AGNI 36, exp. 448
1713	Macuilxóchitl	AGNI 38, exp. 116
1714	Santiago, Ocotlán jurisdiction	AGNI 39, exp. 39
1719	Zaachila	AGNI 43, exp. 159
1729	Santa María Lachixio	AGNI 52, exp. 84
1734	Tlalixtac	AGNI 54, exp. 31
1735	Coyotepec	AGNI 54, exp. 82
1762	Zimatlán	AGNI 60, exp. 13

TABLE FOR NOTE 91
Land Disputes Between Caciques and Townspeople

Date	Location	Source
1576	Tlacolula	AGNC 822
1591[a]	Tlalixtac	AGNI 3, exp. 574
1591[a]	Tlacochahuaya	AGNI 3, exp. 528
1632[a]	Huitzo	CCGG, bk. 2, fol. 13r
1654–70	Cuilapan	AGNI 17, exp. 13
1658[a]	Cuilapan	AGNI 23, exp. 211
1663[a]	Tlalixtac	AGNI 19, exp. 588 bis.
1698	Zimatlán	AGNI 33, exp. 311
1714	Etla	CCGL, 1714
1726[a]	Soledad Etla	CCGL, 1714
1731	Tlacolula	AMT, doc. 43
1814[a]	Guelavia	AMT, doc. 31

[a] Disputes due to macehual encroachment.

105. These lands were alienated from the estate prior to 1717:
(1) 1577 sale of an estancia de ganado menor to the Convent of Cuilapan. AGNH 69, bk. 1, fol. 245v.
(2) Pre-1634 sale of 11 caballerías, which later formed the Hacienda San Juan Bautista. CCGSJB.
(3) 1637 sale of an estancia de labor y ganado menor for 2,000 pesos. CCGSJB.
(4) Pre-1644 sale of one caballería. AGNH 69, bk. 2, fol. 214r.
(5) 1618 sale of a suerte of unspecified size. AGNH 69, bk. 1, fols. 521–48.
(6) 1618 sale of an estancia and two caballerías. AGNH 69, bk. 2, fols. 419–29.
(7) 1658 sale of "la hazenduela," three caballerías. AGNT 412, 6:10r.
(8) 1690's sale of "el sitio savicu." AGNT 1016, 5:3v.
(9) Pre-1717 sale of 4.5 caballerías. AGNT 412, 6:10r.
106. AGNT 1016, 5:9v; AGNH 118, unnumbered exp., 1717.
107. Miguel de los Angeles y Lara used cacicazgo lands as collateral during the 1720's and 1730's for cash loans from various creditors. CCGSN, 1734. See the accompanying table.
108. AGNH 50, exp. 3, unpaginated, 1581; AGNT 241, 7:34r, 1563.
109. AGNT 1854, exp. 5; AGNI 33, exp. 180.

TABLE FOR NOTE 107
Rentals of Cuilapan Cacicazgo Lands

Date	Description	Source
pre-1664	Not specified	AGNI 19, exp. 725
1734	Various lands surrounding the Hacienda San Nicolás Obispo	CCGSNO, cuaderno 2
pre-1736	Lands adjoining the *labor* San Blas near San Pedro Ixtlahuaca	AN 1736, fol. 182r
1737	Two caballerías near San Pedro Apostol	AGNH 348, 7:1v
1739	*Labor* Lichigueya near San Agustín	AGNH 348, 7:1v
1739	One caballería, Duazadi	AGNH 348, 7:1v
1740	*Labor* Jague	AGNH 348, 7:1v
1742	Sitio de ganado menor adjoining Hacienda San Juan Bautista	CCGSJB
1746	Not specified	AN 1746, fols. 102v–106r
1746	*Labor* (not located)	AN 1746, fols. 162v–66r
pre-1748	Sitio de ganado menor	AN 1748, fol. 215v
pre-1749	Lands adjoining *labor* Jesús Nazareno	AN 1745, fol. 281r
1751	*Labor* Suchaiya	AN 1751, fol. 102r
pre-1765	Additional lands adjoining *labor* Jesús Nazareno	AGNT 910, exp. 1
1784	*Labor* San José	AGNH 118, exp. 2
1790	Rancho Tiracoz	AN 1790, fol. 32r
1799	*Labor* San José	AN 1799, fol. 22v

110. AGNT 241, 7:1r, 14r.
111. AGNI 39, exp. 146.
112. *Ibid.*; see also AGNT 42, exp. 81.
113. AGNT 1422, exp. 8. 114. CCGSJ, fols. 66–69.
115. AGNI 37, exp. 60. 116. AGNT 125, exp. 4.
117. AGNH 69, bk. 1, fol. 138r.
118. Lands of the Etla cacicazgo are described in the following sources: AGNH 69, bk. 1, fols. 471–508; AGNH 85, exp. 1; AGNH 102, exps. 7, 14; CCGG, fol. 2r; AN 1684, fol. 111r; AN 1689, fol. 3v; AN 1740, exp. 124; AGNT 155, exp. 2; AGNT 211, exp. 2; AGNT 350, exp. 4; AGNT 911, exp. 1; AGNT 1877, exp. 2; CDChO, rollo 10; AGNI 33, exp. 344; AGNI 36, exp. 226.
119. AGNH 307, 4:13r.
120. *Ibid.*, fol. 13v.
121. AGNT 211, 2:39r.
122. CDChO, rollo 9, 1692; AGNT 113, 2:1r.
123. AGNH 102, 14:1r. 124. AGNG 19, exp. 240.
125. AGNH 307, 4:13r. 126. CDChO, rollo 8.
127. AN 1708, fol. 273v; AGNI 46, exp. 6; AGNT 415, exp. 3.
128. CDChO, rollo 9.
129. AGNT 155, exp. 2, 1690; AGNT 268, exp. 3, 1711.
130. Strife between the cacique and community of Etla was evident as early as 1620. AGNH 102, exp. 10.
131. CDChO, rollo 8, 1633.
132. AGNH 348, exp. 7, 1744.
133. AGNT 1877, exp. 2, 1796.
134. AN 1749, fols. 198v–218r, describes the holdings and gives these totals: 98 medidas, 17.5 fanegas de sembradura de maíz, and 60 almudes de sembradura. Since 98 medidas is equivalent to 28.75–57.7 acres, 17.5 fanegas to 154.35 acres, and 60 almudes to 8.8–35.20 acres, the total acreage was between 191.90 and 247.25. The following equivalents for colonial units of measurement were used in making the conversions:
1 medida = 0.2934–0.5867 acre
1 fanega de sembradura de maíz = 8.82 acres
1 almud de sembradura de maíz = 0.5–1 medida
These equivalents are based on measurements found in AGNT 129, 4: 241r; CCGSNO, fol. 35r; AGNH 118, unnumbered exp., fol. 1r–v; Carrera Stampa, p. 19.
135. AGNT 415, exp. 3.
136. AGNI 47, exp. 44; AGNI 50, exp. 124.
137. AGNT 867, 9:6r, 1760.
138. AGNC 822; AGNT 2956, exp. 103.
139. AGNT 485, primera parte, 1:104r, 1553.
140. AMT, doc. 43.
141. CCGS (typescript), p. 31; BEOB, fols. 222–55.
142. AMT, doc. 43. 143. AGNT 1354, exp. 6.
144. AMT, doc. 29. 145. AGNI 19, exp. 597.
146. AMT, doc. 6.
147. BN 2450, fol. 3r, *Relación de Ayoquesco.*

CHAPTER THREE

1. *Recopilación de leyes*, libro 4, capítulo 12, ley 5.
2. Martínez Báez, pp. 112–17.
3. Bentura Beleña, 1:208.
4. AGNH 85, 5:1–5.
5. Chevalier, *La formation*, pp. 257–58.
6. AGNT 512, 3:6r–9r.
7. Mendieta y Núñez, *El problema agrario*, p. 37. Copies of the 1567 and 1687 laws may be found in AGNH 408, exp. 1.
8. Phipps, pp. 26–28.
9. Mendieta y Núñez, *El problema agrario*, p. 37; see also AGNH 408, exp. 1.
10. AGNH 119, exps. 1–3, and AGNH 306, exp. 1, 1760; CCGG, 1818; AGNT 997, exp. 1, 1776.
11. AGNH 119, exp. 1.
12. AGNT 360, exp. 1; AGNT 358, exp. 2; AGNT 939, exp. 1; AGNT 512, exp. 3; AGNT 186, exp. 8; AGNT 867, exp. 9; AGNT 2783, exp. 5; AMT, doc. 17.
13. AGNH 163, 48:12r.
14. AGNT 129, 4:240r–v.
15. AGNT 358, 2:15r.
16. AGNI 10, exp. 117, 1631.
17. López Sarrelangue, "Las tierras comunales indígenas," p. 133.
18. *Ibid.*, p. 134.
19. Martin, p. 156.
20. *Recopilación de leyes*, libro 6, capítulo 4, ley 31.
21. López Sarrelangue, "Las tierras comunales indígenas, p. 135.
22. AGNT 512, 3:6r–9r; AGNH 119, 3:20r.
23. AGNT 956, exp. 3; AGNT 742, exp. 3; AGNT 2384, exp. 2; AGNI 33, exp. 304; AGNI 42, exp. 67; AGNI 61, fol. 139r–v; AN 1708, fol. 38r.
24. AGNT 956, exp. 3; AGNH 69, bk. 1, fol. 160; AGIM 2588, 1780 visita; AGN *Cofradías y Archicofradías* 18, 4:113–39.
25. Phipps, p. 28, Indian use of tierras realengas; Miranda, "Orígenes," p. 787, 1551 cédula.
26. The calpullalli is discussed in Gibson, *Aztecs Under Spanish Rule*, Chap. 10.
27. AGNI 37, exp. 157.
28. AGNI 34, exp. 84; AGNT 490, primera parte, 1:41r–44r.
29. AGNT 256, 3:122r–v (1624). See fols. 133r (1614) and 134r (1616) for two other examples.
30. AGNT 512, 3:6r–9r.
31. AGNMer 68, fols. 49v–50r.
32. AGNH 69, bk 1, fol. 251; AGNMer 17, fol. 184v; AGNH 50, exp. 3, capítulo 34, num. 1.
33. Aguirre Beltrán, *El señorío de Cuahtochco*, p. 196; Rabasa, p. 306.
34. CCGL, 1529.
35. AGNH 102, exp. 14, 1619.
36. AGNH 380, 9:46v.
37. AGNT 1425, exp. 1, 1818.
38. AGNI 42, exp. 34.
39. *Ibid.*
40. CDChO, rollo 11, Oct. 11, 1694.
41. AGNT 1099, exp. 2.

42. AGNT 742, exp. 3.
43. Tamayo, p. 169. There were 82 plots totaling 1,064 medidas, or 312.18–624.36 acres, 36 plots totaling 42 fanegas de sembradura de maíz, or 370.44 acres, and 6 plots totaling 99 almudes de sembradura de maíz, or 14.52–58.08 acres. Adding these figures together, we get 124 plots totaling 697.14–1,052.88 acres, for an average of 5.6–8.5 acres per plot. See Chap. 2, note 134 for values of medidas, fanegas, and almudes.
44. AGNT 939, exp. 1.
45. Santa Ana is one example. AGNT 997, 1:58.
46. Murguía y Galardi, "Extracto general," fol. 4v, Zaachila; AGNH 163, 48:41v, Santa María.
47. AGIM 1088, libro 2, fol. 69r.
48. RAHM, vol. 111, fols. 122v–24.
49. AGNMer 44, fol. 167v, 1643.
50. AGNT 2385, exp. 1, última numeración, fols. 1–5, Tlalixtac; AGNH 69, bk. 1, fols. 245v, 251v; Cuilapan; AGNH 85, exp. 5, Zimatlán and San Pedro Apostol; AGNH 69, bk. 1, fols. 1–6, San Juan Guelache; AGNI 34, exp. 84, Santa Catalina Quiané; AMT, doc. 43, Tlacolula; AGNG 24, exp. 326, San Andrés Ixtlahuaca; AN 1799, fol. 23v, San Pedro Ixtlahuaca. The Mitla and San Sebastián purchases are mentioned in records of colonial litigation located in these two communities. The San Sebastián document was transcribed by Scott Cook.
51. Burgoa, 2: 103.
52. Six Valley nobles are known to have possessed estancias de ganado mayor: 1593, a *principal* of Mitla (AGNI 6, primera parte, exp. 137); 1673, a *principal* of San Pablo Huistepec (AGNT 2384, 2:28r); 1551, nobles of Santo Domingo Tomaltepec (AGNI 25, exp. 457); 1705, the cacique of Etla (AGNI 36, exp. 226); 1611, the cacique of Tlacolula (CCGS, p. 31); 1570, the cacique of Ocotlán (CCGSJ, fol. 65r). In several other cases nobles were permitted to graze small numbers of ganado mayor, usually 50 to 100 head, on their estancias de ganado menor; 1583, a *principal* of Huitzo (AGNI 2, exp. 541); 1583, a *principal* of Tlacochahuaya (AGNI 2, exp. 865); 1708, the gobernador of Ocotlán (AGNI 37, exp. 60); 1680's, the cacique of Magdalena Apasco (AGNT 415, exp. 3, tercera numeración, fol. 12r).
53. Miranda, "Orígenes," p. 788.
54. AGNG 1 and 24 give examples of licenses to own mules and horses.
55. AGNG 4, exp. 1.
56. AGNI 33, exp. 304, 1698; AGNI 61, fol. 139r–v, 1761; AGNI 42, exp. 67, 1718.
57. AGNI 61, exp. 2, 1764.
58. Miranda, "Orígenes," p. 787.
59. Murguía y Galardi, "Extracto general," fol. 1ff.
60. Burgoa, 1: 272.
61. AMT, doc. 26, Quialana, 1826.
62. BN 2450, fols. 7r, 19v, 37r, 225v, 315r, 317v, 320v.
63. AGNT 2922, 1:9r.
64. AGNT 1216, 1:1v–2r, Etla, 1791; AGNI 54, exp. 359, Zimatlán, 1735.
65. AGNT 1225, exp. 19.

66. AGNI 88, fols. 118.
67. López Sarrelangue, "Las tierras comunales indígenas," p. 141.
68. AGNT 1864, exp. 2, segunda numeración, fol. 30r.
69. AGNT 1414, exp. 1, 1811.
70. AGNH 307, 4:5r, 1725.
71. AGNT 381, 5:1r–v.
72. AGNT 186, 8:2v; AGNT 1206, 1:8r; AGNT 223, 4:1r–2r; AGNI 37, exp. 190; AGNT 335, exp. 1; AGNH 307, 4:5r; AGNT 1460, 7:1r–14r; BEOB, unnumbered folio before 385; CCGL, Nov. 12, 1792; AGNT 1877, 2:10.
73. BEOB, fol. 394.
74. AGNT 148, 3:116; AGNH 50, 3:5r.
75. CCGSJ, fol. 21r.
76. AGNT 853, 3:4–12; AGNT 148, 3:116.
77. AGNT 867, 9:1r; AGNT 1206, 1:14r, 1788.
78. AGNT 867, 9:1r, 1760; ADAA, exp. 276.1, p. 908.
79. AGNT 867, 9:1r; AGNT 1206, 1:14r.
80. AGNT 867, exp. 9, the suits with the padres betlemitas; AGNT 981, exp. 3, and AGNT 2412, exp. 1, disputes with the Hacienda de los Negritos; AGNT 867, 9:1r, the litigation with San Francisco. ADAA, exp. 276.1, p. 1370, contains titles and boundary surveys for Tlacochahuaya in 1712.
81. ENE 8: 228–29, San Juan Teitipac; AGNT 1417, exp. 11, and AGNG 2, exps. 143, 147, Macuilxóchitl.
82. AMT, doc. 42, 1816.
83. AGNT 1351, 3:3r–4v, 1800–1803; ADAA, exp. 276.1, p. 2234, documents the barrio problems and the origins of the town of Abasolo.
84. AGNT 2384, exp. 2, 1801–1809.
85. AGNT 2386, 1:86v.
86. AGNT 185, exp. 16; AGNT 186, exp. 8; AMT, doc. 7; AGNT 1351, exp. 6.
87. AGNI 11, exp. 152, Ocotlán, 1639; AGNI 24, exp. 465, Coyotepec, 1664.
88. The birthrate may have been higher in the larger towns. When we compute the multiplying factor for converting hypothetical tributaries to total population for ten southeastern towns whose tributaries and population in 1826 are known, we find that the factor is generally larger for the more populous towns. AMT, doc. 26. See the accompanying table.
89. AGNT 867, 9:6v.
90. AGNH 163, 48:8v, 1686.
91. AGNH 307, 4:14r.
92. AGN *Cofradías y Archicofradías* 18, 11: 113–39.
93. Murguía y Galardi, "Extracto general," segunda parte, fols. 16v and 13v.
94. AGNI 43, exp. 53, San Pedro Ixtlahuaca; Murguía y Galardi, "Extracto general," segunda parte, fols. 13v, San Andrés Ixtlahuaca, and 14r, San Pablo Guaxolotitlán; AGNG 2, exp. 618, San Andrés Zautla.
95. AGNT 113, 2:1r; AGNMer 4 and 18; Cruz Caballero; AGNI 24, exp. 319; *ibid.*; CDChO, rollo 64; AGNT 110, 4:1r; AGNI 22, exp. 64.

Multiplying Factors for Ten Towns in the Valley of Tlacolula, 1826

Town	Hypo-thetical tribu-taries[a]	Popu-lation	Multi-plying factor	Town	Hypo-thetical tribu-taries[a]	Popu-lation	Multi-plying factor
San Francisco Lachigolo	86	365	4.23	San Bartolomé Quialana	70½	263	3.73
Santa Cecilia Jalieza	66	234	3.55	San Juan Teitipac	308	1,384	4.49
San Baltazar Guelavia	79½	315	3.97	Santo Domingo del Valle	218	927	4.25
Magdalena Teitipac	141	501	3.55	San Sebastián Teitipac	187	729	3.89
Santiago Matatlán	289½	1,266	4.37	Mitla	253½	1,029	4.05

[a] Computed on the basis of one unit for a married male, one-half unit for each bachelor and widower.

96. AGNI 3, exp. 612.

97. Genaro V. Vásquez, *Doctrinas*, pp. 462–64.

98. AGNH 163, 48:12r–v.

99. CDChO, rollo 64, Dec. 10, 1686; ADAA, exp. 276.1, p. 690.

100. AGNT 310, 1:1v, San Pablo; CCGL, Aug. 14, 1781, San Gabriel.

101. AGNH 348, 7:1v, Etla; CCGL, Aug. 14, 1781, San Agustín; AGNH 69, bk. 1, fols. 1–5, Guelache; Burgoa, 2: 16, Huitzo.

102. AGNT 211, exp. 2, Soledad Etla; AGNT 113, 2:18r–19r, 110r–11r, and AGNH 69, bk. 1, fols. 1–10, San Juan Guelache.

103. AGNH 163, 48:12r–v, Etla; CCGL, Aug. 14, 1781, San Agustín Etla; AGNI 24, exp. 44, Santo Domingo Etla.

104. Quotation from Juan de Matienzo, *Gobierno del Perú*, ca. 1570, in Ots Capdequí, p. 101.

105. AGNT 211, 2:48r.

106. AGNI 11, exp. 313. There are two other recorded examples of water disputes between Indian communities in the Valley of Etla, although the towns involved have not been positively identified. In 1662 two communities, known as Lachivise and San Sebastián, barrios within the jurisdiction of the Villa de Etla, argued over the right to irrigate their fields with water from "a big river that flows to the city of Oaxaca," presumably the Atoyac. In this case the judge distributed water to the two communities in proportion to their populations: since Lachivise had 60 families and San Sebastián 20, Lachivise was awarded 30 days of water for irrigation to every 10 days for San Sebastián. AGNT 2963, exp. 109. In the second case, dated 1661, two "barrios of Etla," Logotao and Lachiuexi, were ordered to share an irrigation channel. Logotao was to receive 10 days of water to every 14 for Lachiuexi. AGNI 19, exp. 460.

107. Cruz Caballero; CDChO, rollo 7, fol. 376r.

108. Arroyo, 2: 87.
109. References to sources of water for irrigation: AGNT 64, 5:3v, Tepe-zimatlán, 1599; AGNH 360, exp. 1, San Pedro Ixtlahuaca, 1760; AGNH 119, 1:14v, San Jacinto Amilpas, 1760.
110. AGNI 35, exp. 33. In 1597 Cuilapan was described as "the greatest community in these valleys." AGIM 357.
111. Steininger and Van de Velde, pp. 100–104; AGNT 395, exp. 1, 1721. AGNT 2941, exp. 96, describes land disputes between Cuilapan and Santa María Peñoles in 1586.
112. AGNI 35, exp. 33.
113. Burgoa, 1: 399–400; Barlow, "Dos relaciones," pp. 26–27.
114. AGNH 307, 4:5r, 1725.
115. AN 1786, fol. 176v.
116. AN 1799, fol. 66r; CCGSNO, May 31, 1615; AGNH 102, 42:1–6; AGNT 1048, 11:18–21; AGNH 69, bk. 1, fol. 251.
117. Murguía y Galardi, *Apuntamientos estadísticos*, p. 20.
118. AGNT 1045, 5:1v; AGNT 2784, 1:1r–v.
119. Burgoa, 1:395.
120. AGNI 11, exp. 152; AGNI 24, exp. 465; AGNT 2959, exp. 103.
121. AGNT 2784, 1:1v.
122. Bustamante, p. 5.
123. Velasco, p. 133.
124. AGNI 39, fol. 218r; AGNI 40, exp. 145.
125. AGNI 45, exp. 40; AGNT 241, 7:19–21; AGNT 266, 1:6v; AGNH 85, exp. 5.
126. AGNH 50, exp. 3, sec. 33; AGNT 997, 1:11r.
127. Méndez, p. 54.
128. AGNT 359, 3:1–6; AGNI 43, exp. 221.
129. AGII 107, fol. 389, maize, beans, and corn; AGNH 380, 9:32r, and AGNH 432, 2:6r, 1551, wheat and sugar cane.
130. Villaseñor y Sánchez,2: 121.
131. AN 1725, fol. 29v; AGNH 380, 9:79; AGNT 1222, primera parte, 4: 1–5; AGNT 2952, exp. 66.
132. AGNT 203, 6:121–30; AN 1708, fol. 38r.
133. AGII 107, fol. 388v, cotton; Arroyo, 2: 155.
134. AGNT 2934, exp. 67.
135. AGII 107, fol. 389r.
136. Burgoa, 2: 46; Villaseñor y Sánchez, 2: 116.
137. AGNI 11, exp. 152; AGNI 61, fol. 139r.
138. AGNI 53, exp. 171; Méndez, p. 183.
139. AGNI 42, exp. 121; AGNH 50, exp. 3, secs. 9–10; AGNH 85, exp. 5; ADAA, exp. 276.1, p. 2075.
140. Esteva, *Elementos*, pp. 70–72; BN 2450, fol. 11v.
141. AN 1799, fol. 7v. Oaxaca received a merced for an estancia de ganado menor that I have not been able to find in later records.
142. Murguía y Galardi, "Extracto general," primera parte, fol. 58r.
143. AGNH 119, exp. 2.
144. AN 1724, fol. 33r. According to AN 1799, fol. 50r, San Martín owned the rancho Espina.

145. AGI *Escribanía de Cámara* 1045, fol. 7v.
146. BN 2450, fol. 316v. 147. *Ibid.*, fols. 5v, 6v, 10–12.
148. AGNT 129, 4:241v, 1682. 149. AGNT 1064, 13:1–11.
150. AGII 107, fol. 387v.
151. See AGNT 485, primera parte, fol. 104, 1556, for the boundary document. For estancias in the Teotitlán-Mitla area, see AGNT 35, exp. 7, 1604; AGNT 148, exp. 3, 1690; AGNT 485, primera parte, exp. 1, 1625. AGNT 148, exp. 3, documents the land disputes.
152. Murguía y Galardi, "Extracto general," partido de Tlacolula, fols. 1r–11r.
153. CDChO, rollo 66, "Instrucción para los visitadores de magueyes de la comprehensión de la Receptoria de Teotitlán del Valle," 1806.
154. AMT, doc. 42, 1816. "La república y común del pueblo de San Francisco Lachigolo, jurisdicción de Teotitlán del Valle sobre despojo de tierras de que se hallan en posesión por la república y natural del pueblo de Tlacochahuaya de este corregimiento."
155. Murguía y Galardi, "Extracto general," partido de Tlacolula, fols. 1r–14r.
156. *Ibid.*; Villaseñor y Sánchez, 2: 115–17.
157. AGNI 41, exp. 159, Mitla: AGII 107, fol. 391v, San Andrés Huayapan. Colonial references to the Sunday market at Tlacolula, so important today, have not been located. San Sebastián's *metate* (grinding stone) industry is not mentioned by Murguía y Galardi, who identifies local industries for a number of towns in the Valley.
158. Murguía y Galardi, "Extracto general," partido de Oaxaca, fol. 31v, and partido de Tlacolula, fols. 1r–21r; a 1697 document from San Sebastián Teitipac brought to my attention by Scott Cook; AGNG 1, exp. 815; AGNG 2, exp. 147.
159. AGNI 24, exp. 508.
160. Bustamante, p. 5.
161. CDChO, rollo 11, fol. 191r; AGNG 23, exp. 82.
162. AGNT 387, 4:1–6; ADAA, exp. 276.1, p. 691.
163. AGNT 186, 8:2r–v.
164. Documents from San Sebastián Teitipac, 1691 and 1781, transcribed by Scott Cook.
165. CDChO, rollo 66, "Instrucción para los visitadores de magueyes," fol. 20v.
166. AGNT 388, 1:127–41; AGNT 256, 2:119–38.
167. AGNT 485, primera parte, 1: 104; AGNMer 15, fol. 316v, 1561; AGNMer 8, fol. 209v, 1565.
168. AGNT 148, 3:1–8.
169. AMT, doc. 43, June 25, 1712; AGNT 1868, exp. 8.
170. AMT, doc. 2, 1807, "Se libró mandamiento para que la República dé el agua a José Martín y Antonio Martín"; ADAA, exp. 276.1, p. 1370.
171. Paso y Troncoso, *Papeles*, 8: 148–50.
172. AMT, doc. 1, Ixtaltepec; Burgoa, 2: 127–41, Teotitlán del Valle; BEOB, fols. 31–40, Macuilxóchitl.
173. AGNH 163, 48:11v, 1686. 174. AGNT 2934, exp. 67, 1647.
175. AGNT 1901, 11:58v–59r. 176. Gay, tomo 1, vol. 2, p. 497.

CHAPTER FOUR

1. AGNH 293, exp. 133; Gay, tomo 1, vol. 2, pp. 389, 468; Iturribarría, *Oaxaca en la historia*, p. 56.
2. AGIJ 224, 1531.
3. Chevalier, *La Formation*, p. 107; *Colección de documentos para la historia de Oaxaca*, pp. 9–37.
4. AGNH 293, exp. 133, 1531.
5. Arteaga Garza and Pérez San Vicente, pp. 238–40; ENE, 3: 25.
6. AGNH 102, segundo atado, exp. 24.
7. CDChO, rollo 64, Molinos de Lazo, libro 1, cuaderno 1.
8. AGNH 287, 1:7v, abasto; AGNH 146, 430:335–45, trees. Borah, *Silk Raising*, contains a good discussion of the silk industry in Oaxaca.
9. AGNH 287, exp. 1.
10. CDChO, rollo 64, Molinos de Lazo, libro 1, cuaderno 2.
11. AGNH 50, 3:1–5.
12. AGIM 256.
13. AGIM 256 and 678.
14. AGNT 236, *passim*.
15. Alexander Marchant, *From Barter to Slavery: The Economic Relations of Portuguese and Indians in the Settlement of Brazil, 1500–1580* (Baltimore, Md., 1942).
16. AGNH 69, bk. 1, fol. 475v.
17. Berthe.
18. See AGNH 69, bk. 1, fols. 331v, 367–69, and bk. 2, fols. 654–59, for material on censos perpetuos in the Valley.
19. Chevalier, *La formation*, p. 247; Puga, 2: 185; Brioso y Candiani, p. 14.
20. *Instrucciones que los vireyes*, p. 239.
21. García Pimentel, 2: 61; AGIM 355.
22. AGIM 1088; RAHM, vol. 113, fols. 135–36.
23. Gay, tomo 1, vol. 2, p. 497.
24. Cuevas, p. 181.
25. AGNMer 4, fol. 112v; AGNMer 6, fol. 32.
26. Gage, pp. 113–14.
27. AGNMer 70, fols. 116v–17v.
28. BEOB, fol. 1r–v.
29. AGNT 2386, exp. 1, primera numeración, fols. 20–22, 1539, and segunda numeración, fols. 1r–9r, 1544; BEOB, fol. 1r–v, 1541.
30. Silvio Zavala, "De encomiendas y propiedad territorial," pp. 263–65.
31. *Instrucciones que los vireyes*, p. 239.
32. Zavala and Castelo, 2: 380.
33. AGI *Escribanía de Cámara* 1047; AGNG 2, exp. 9.
34. AGI *Escribanía de Cámara* 1045; AGIM 1088.
35. AGI *Escribanía de Cámara* 1045.
36. AGI *Escribanía de Cámara* 1047.
37. AGNT 2696, 8:8r–v, lists 23 haciendas in the Antequera jurisdiction and five in the Tlacolula jurisdiction in 1643; AGNH 380, 9:97r, lists 13 in the Cuilapan jurisdiction for the same year.
38. Romero de Terreros, *passim*.
39. Priestley, p. 25; Phipps, p. 40. See also Carrera Stampa, p. 19 (21,690 acres).

40. Wolf and Mintz.

41. CCGSJ, Sept. 6, 1610; BEOB, fols. 259–69. The right to say mass might profitably be used as a criterion in studying the development of the hacienda in other parts of New Spain.

42. AGNH 330, 1:7r, 1699.   43. *Ibid.*, fols. 22r–23r.

44. CCGL, Feb. 18, 1782.   45. CCGL, 1791.

46. AGNT 2696, 8:7v; CCGS, p. 94.   47. AGNT 213, 1:2r–12r.

48. CCGSJB, 1694; CCGSNO, fol. 27v; AGNT 266, 1:34r.

49. AN 1786, fol. 88v; AGNT 2764, exp. 31.

50. The Haciendas San José and San Guillermo near Miahuatlán, for example, had 20 tracts and five tracts, respectively, in the eighteenth century. AN 1742, fol. 268r; AN 1717, fol. 94v.

51. These are the Valley estates where sugar cane was grown as of 1901. Centro: Aguayo, Arrazola, Candiani, El Carmen, Cinco Señores, La Concepción, Mantecón, Montoya, La Noria, El Rosario, San Isidro (Monjas), San Isidro (Prío), San José, La Sangre de Cristo, Nazareno, Dolores, San Javier, Guadalupe, Aragón, and San Isidro. Etla: Las Bocas, Alemán, Viguera, and Blanca. Zimatlán: Valdeflores, Mejía, La Soleada, La Labor, Tlanechico, San Nicolás, and Santa Gertrudis. Belmar, p. 82.

52. CCGSJ; CCGL; CCGS; BEOB, fol. 1r–v; AN 1707, fol. 253r.

53. AGNT 485, primera parte, 1:104; AGNH 50, exp. 3, sec. 9; AN 1767, fol. 56r; AGNT 2922, exp. 1; AN 1808, fol. 152r.

54. AN 1734, fol. 347r; AN 1743, fol. 356v.

55. AGNH 102, exp. 24; CCG *Molinos de Lazo*, libro 1, cuaderno 1; AGNH 85, exp. 2.

56. AGNH 69, bk. 2, fols. 654r–59r.

57. AN 1747, fol. 139v; AN 1780, fol. 109ff; AGNH 118, exp. 6; CCGG, fols. 34v–42r, 107r–14r.

58. AGNT 2958, exp. 153, 1712.

59. AGNT 1045, 5:1–19; AGNT 1901, 11:2v.

60. AN 1693, fol. 49r–v.

61. AGNH 118, 15:9r.

62. AN 1748, fol. 362, Guendulain; CCGSNO, Jan. 8, 1650, Church rental; AGNH 118, 15:9r, San José.

63. AN 1780, fol. 110r; CCGG, fols. 34v–42r, 107r–14r. For other examples, see CCGSNO, four plots, 1676–1707; CCG *Molinos de Lazo*, an unknown number of plots equaling one-fourth caballería in 1675 and another one-fourth caballería in 1699.

64. AGNH 118, exp. 6.

65. CCGSJ; CCGSNO.

66. For the Espina holdings, see AN 1707, fol. 43v; AGNT 2764, exp. 31; CCGS, p. 7ff; CCGSJB, Oct. 2, 1725.

67. AN 1761, fol. 30v, San Cristóbal and El Capitán; AN 1772, fol. 190v, Guegonivalle.

68. For transfers of Duhuatia, see AN 1749, Feb. 19, unpaginated; AN 1769, fol. 121r; AN 1770, fol. 220v; AN 1790, fol. 104v; AN 1799, fol. 23v. For del Fuerte and Lope, see CCGL, March 20, 1763. Rancho Blanco is another example of a ranch that was attached to a large nearby estate, the Hacienda Tanibé.

69. Rippy; Priestley, p. 98. Chevalier, *La formation*, pp. 68–71, discusses sixteenth-century wheat farms in central Mexico.

70. AN 1733, fol. 54r.

71. The following sources for *labores* in the vicinity of Antequera are listed chronologically: AN 1684, fols. 18r, 56r; AN 1692, fol. 348r; AN 1694, fol. 287r; AN *Loose Papers*, Jan. 12, 1708; AN 1708, fols. 339r, 536r; AN 1710, fol. 235r; AN 1717, fol. 94v; AN 1718, fols. 50v, 89r; AN 1724, fol. 69r; AN 1725, fols. 13r, 24v; AN 1733, fol. 54r; AN 1740, fol. 100v; AN 1742, fol. 200r; AN 1744, fol. 115r; AN 1749, fols. 227r, 281r; AN 1749, Feb. 19; AN 1751, fol. 102r; AN 1752, fol. 65r; AN 1761, fol. 9v; AN 1764, fols. 23v, 26r; AN 1769, fol. 121r; AN 1770, fols. 9r, 220v; AN 1776, fol. 191v; AGNH 50, exp. 3, sec. 9, 1778; AN 1786, fols. 56r, 229v; AN 1799, fol. 23v.

72. CCGL, Jan. 7, 1744.

73. AN 1710, fol. 235r; AN 1718, fol. 89r; AN 1725, fol. 13r; AN 1764, fol. 23v; AN 1780, fol. 109.

74. The following sources for *labores* in the Zimatlán arm are listed chronologically: AN 1708, fol. 339r; AN 1717, fol. 94v; AN 1724, fol. 69r; AN 1740, fol. 100v; AN 1742, fol. 200r; AN 1749, fol. 227r; AN 1751, fol. 102r; AN 1761, fol. 30v; AN 1764, fol. 26r; AN 1786, fol. 229v; AN 1792, segunda parte, fol. 40v; AN 1790, fol. 146v.

75. AGNT 919, 3:35–43.

76. AN 1737, fol. 76r; AGNT 146, 3:18r–v.

77. AN 1767, fol. 78v.

78. AN 1780, fol. 109, Santa Rita; AN 1712, fol. 216v, Aranjuez. For Duhuatia see AN 1749, Feb. 19; AN 1769, fol. 121r; AN 1770, fol. 220v; AN 1790, fol. 104v; AN 1799, fol. 23v.

79. Borde and Góngora, App. I.

80. We know of six haciendas that were mortgaged in the seventeenth century. The total mortgages amounted to 20,760 pesos, or 46.4 per cent of the estates' total value of 44,719 pesos. For the years 1700 to 1750 we know of nine mortgaged haciendas, whose total mortgages (122,910 pesos) were 74.7 per cent of their total value (164,430 pesos). For the years 1750 to 1810 we know of 14 mortgaged haciendas, whose mortgages (160,295 pesos) were 71.6 per cent of their total value (223,752 pesos). See the accompanying table for the mortgages on each hacienda and the market value of each.

81. The total value of the 27 estates was 346,456 pesos; the mortgages on them amounted to 231,855 pesos. Dividing the second figure by the first gives us a mean average of 66.92 per cent. For 25 estates (excluding Santa Cruz and San Juan Bautista), the total value was 252,711 pesos and the total mortgages 194,057 pesos, for a mean average of 76.79 per cent.

82. CCGSJ, Feb. 22, 1806, and Nov. 15, 1808; AN 1786, fol. 200r.

83. *Recopilación de leyes*, libro 6, capítulo 12, ley 19; AMT, doc. 15, April 24, 1787; BEOB, fols. 155–59; AGNI 22, exp. 87; AGNI 31, exps. 207, 227.

84. AGNH 146, 430:335v.

85. AGNI 11, fols. 114v–15v; AGNH 85, exp. 4; BEOB, fols. 155r, 430r.

86. CCGL, Nov. 23, 1554; AGNT 2386, exp. 1. Other colonial estates known to have used Negro slaves are Xaagá (CCGL, April 15, 1666); the

TABLE FOR NOTE 80

Mortgages Relative to the Market Value of Valley Haciendas
(in pesos)

Seventeenth century		1700–1750		1750–1810	
Market value	Mortgages	Market value	Mortgages	Market value	Mortgages
6,000	360	12,000	11,000	12,000	10,800
5,770	3,400	30,000	14,000	18,015	13,950
6,000	3,400	4,490	3,500	11,300	8,000
2,450	300	29,752	23,000	7,600	3,000
7,187	5,300	33,986	32,710	7,314	4,000
17,312	8,000	17,500	13,600	13,149	5,885
		17,329	11,100	38,663	30,000
		18,037	12,700	17,543	16,140
		1,336	1,300	60,000	42,000
				8,200	4,200
				20,000	16,000
				3,220	2,320
				4,460	2,000
				2,308	2,000

estancias of the Marquesado del Valle, 1561 (AGNH 85, exp. 4); El Vergel, 1676 (AGNT 919, 3:9–14); San José, 1686 (CCGSJ, fol. 76r); *Labor* San Miguel, 1579 to 1767 (AGNT 2386, exp. 1, segunda numeración, fol. 27v); La Concepción, 1693 (AN 1693, fol. 323v); Santo Domingo Buenavista, 1720 (BEOB, fol. 58r); Jalapilla, 1736 (AN 1736, fol. 121r); and an unnamed *labor* near Antequera, 1711 (AGNT 266, 1:22v–23r).

87. AGNT 212, 7:21–26.

88. Zavala, *Contribución*, p. 95; Fals Borda, p. 78.

89. AGNI 14, exp. 114.

90. José Miranda, "La función económica," p. 423; AGNT 2782, 6:1–4. The 1578 mining repartimiento included the following towns: Mitla, Tlacolula, Teotitlán del Valle, Tlalixtac, Tlacochahuaya, Coyotepec, Zaachila, Cuilapan, Ocotlán, Macuilxóchitl, and Chichicapa.

91. AGNI 14, exp. 94.

92. *Recopilación de leyes*, libro 6, capítulo 12, ley 19.

93. AGNI 31, exps. 207, 227; Zavala and Castelo, 1: 141.

94. AGNI 7, exp. 119; AGNI 12, primera parte, exp. 86, and segunda parte, exp. 106; AGNI 14, exps. 94, 95, 114.

95. CDChO, rollo 64, Molinos de Lazo, libro 4, cuaderno 9.

96. AGNI 3, exp. 596; AGNI 4, exp. 884; AGNI 14, exp. 114.

97. AGNI 14, exp. 114.

98. AGNI 12, primera parte, exp. 86, and segunda parte, exp. 106.

99. AGNI 22, exp. 87; BEOB, fols. 171, 202, 206.

100. Silvio Zavala, "Orígenes coloniales," p. 321.

101. CCGSJ, fol. 28v, 1648; AGNI 31, exps. 207, 227, 1694; AGNT 2958,

exp. 105, 1710; AGNI 22, exp. 87, 1714; CCGL, June 3, 1732, and Feb. 6, 1772.

102. AGNI 31, exp. 227.

103. See AGNT 2958, exp. 105, for an order formally ending a repartimiento from Zegache in 1712.

104. CCGL, June 3, 1732, "Digo que por falta de operarios . . ."

105. AMT, doc. 15, April 24, 1787.

106. AGNI 22, exp. 87.

107. Genaro V. Vásquez, *Doctrinas,* p. 440.

108. AGNI 3, exp. 516.

109. AGNI 17, exp. 287. See also AGNI 3, exp. 156; AGNI 6, primera parte, exp. 136; AGNI 11, exp. 160; AGNI 10, exp. 2.

110. Zavala, "Orígenes coloniales," p. 331.

111. AGIM 2589–91.

112. Zavala, "Orígenes coloniales," p. 331.

113. Genaro V. Vásquez, *Doctrinas,* p. 286; CCGSJB, 1793, financial records.

114. Bentura Beleña, 1: 15; AGNT 1216, 1:27v.

115. AGNT 1216, 1:1r–2r; Bentura Beleña, 1: 15.

116. Figures from the sample: 1–6 pesos, 97 laborers; 7–30 pesos, 170 laborers; 31–60 pesos, 112 laborers; 61–90 pesos, 56 laborers; over 91 pesos, 40 laborers.

117. AGNI 37, exp. 146; AGNH 118, 15:1–24; AGNT 1216, 1:1–5.

118. In 1710 the Audiencia recognized that a local hacendado, Simón de Salvatierra, had forced debts on laborers from Xoxocotlán, but it ordered the debtors to repay Salvatierra by working on his hacienda. AGNI 37, exp. 146. AGNT 1216, exp. 1, describes a similar case for Etla in 1791.

119. AGNI 29, exp. 121.

120. AN 1786, fol. 121r; AGNT 2784, 1:1–3.

121. CCGSJB, Feb. 18, 1745, inventory.

122. AGNH 118, 15:9r; AMT, doc. 9, 1808, "expediente promovido por Fray Juan María Sierra religioso lego del orden de Santo Domingo de Oaxaca como administrador del Rancho de Lope."

123. AGNT 1216, 1:11v.

124. AGNI 17, exp. 81; AGNI 29, exp. 121.

125. AGNI 37, exp. 146.

126. AGNT 2784, 1:1–3.

127. AGNT 1271, exp. 2.

128. Chevalier, *La formation,* p. 391.

129. AGNC 1934, 4:1–6.

130. AGN *Vínculos* 147, 1:32v; AN 1734, Dec. 9, unpaginated; AN 1776, fol. 40v.

131. *Cedulario americano del siglo XVIII* (Seville: 1956), p. 352.

132. AGNT 2693, 12:1r–v, 1727; CCGL, vista de ojos of Dominican haciendas around Mitla, Oct. 1782.

133. AGIM 638.

134. AGNH 136, 430:61–86.

135. *Ibid.*

136. CCGL, copy of a document dated Aug. 30, 1632.

137. See these sources for the Ramírez de Aguilar mayorazgo: AGNH 146, 430:61–86; AN 1684, fol. 83r; AN 1712, fol. 33r; AN 1725, fol. 24v; AN 1733, fol. 54r; AGN *Vínculos* 147, 1:1–32; AGNT 2386, 1:55r; AGNT 890, fols. 29–33; AGNT 449, 4:5–9, 42–47; AGNT 485, primera parte, 1:114r; AN 1693, fol. 281r; CCGL, July 23, 1716, July 13, 1630, and Aug. 30, 1632.

138. AGNT 212, 7:6r–7r; AGNG 24, exp. 245.

139. AGN *Vínculos* 51, 10:15r.

140. Only two livestock inventories have been located for the Guendulain hacienda. In 1655 it had 2,100 sheep, 1,700 goats, and 46 horses; in 1826, 189 ganado mayor and 1,000 ganado menor. For general information on the Guendulain mayorazgo, see AGNT 212, exp. 7; AGNT 2693, 12:1r–v; AGN *Vínculos* 51, 10:1–9; Burgoa, 2: 504; AMT, doc. 26, 1826 inventory of cattle; AMT, doc. 36, 1808 testimony by Manuel de Guendulain; AGNT 387, 4: 6r–v; AGNT 2922, exp. 1; AN 1712, fol. 216v; AN 1734, fol. 347v; AN 1743, fol. 356v; AN 1750, fol. 26v; AN 1794, fol. 526r; AGNT 1063, 4:3–13; AGNT 2952, 1:1–4.

141. Fernández de Recas, *Mayorazgos*, p. 456.

142. AGNT 112, exp. 3.

143. Fernández de Recas, *Mayorazgos*, p. 458.

144. CCGL, April 5, 1713.

145. AN 1776, fol. 40v.

146. Zimmerman Library, University of New Mexico, Special Collections, "En la ciudad de Antequera, valle de Oaxaca a veinte días del mes de julio de mil setecientos setenta y ocho ante mi . . . don Joachín Ximeno Bohórquez. . . ." Also see AGNT *Tierras* 535, primera parte, 2:1r.

147. CCGL, Dec. 30, 1682.

148. *Ibid.*

149. BEOB, fol. 1r–v; CCGL; CCGL, a 1782 copy of the 1565 document; AGNI 3, exp. 544; AGNI 3, exp. 154; AGNI 6, segunda parte, exp. 317.

150. *Recopilación de leyes*, libro 4, capítulo 12, ley 5.

151. Zavala and Castelo, 2: 232.

152. AGNI 6, segunda parte, exp. 317; AGNH 69, bk. 1, fol. 251; AN 1692, fol. 348r; CCGG, bk. 4, fol. 143r; AGNT 159, 7:64v; AGNT 186, exp. 2; AGNT 981, 3:1–6.

153. AGNT 273, 2:1–3.

154. CCGSJ, April 22, 1743.

155. AN 1687, fols. 323–24; AN 1692, fol. 400r; AGNG 18, exp. 79.

156. AN 1772, fol. 178v; CCGSNO, Dec. 7, 1752; AGNT 889, fols. 43–55; AN 1725, fol. 24v; AN 1769, fol. 152v. Seleri also owned an hacienda in the Mixteca Alta and mills near Teposcolula. AGNT 889, fols. 43–55. Sebastián Labairu, a merchant involved in the repartimiento de mulas in the southern arm during the 1770's, may have owned a cattle estancia somewhere near the Valley. AGNT 1037, 2:1925.

157. Landholding peninsular Spaniards are mentioned in AGNT 911, 1:128–36; AGNT 266, 1:1–3; AGNT 890, fols. 29–33; AN 1772, fol. 178v.

158. AGNC 1601, exp. 20. The Monterrubios were prominent obraje-owners in the eighteenth century.

159. AN 1776, fol. 40v; AGNT 2784, exp. 2; AN 1736, fol. 382; AN 1786, fol. 121r.

160. AN 1748, fols. 60r, 215v; AN 1790, fol. 159r; AGNT 1274, exp. 2; AN 1770, fol. 27v; CCGG, 1798; AN 1808, fol. 170r; AGNT 1268, exp. 1.

161. CCGG, fols. 80–86; AN 1790, fol. 33r; AN 1789, primera parte, fol. 71v; AGNT 911, 1:62v; AN 1789, primera parte, fol. 113r; AN 1780, fol. 155; AGNT 1209, exp. 12; AN 1726, fol. 382r; AN 1708, fol. 12v; AN 1786, fol. 229v.

CHAPTER FIVE

1. Iturribarría, *Oaxaca en la historia*, p. 73.
2. AGIM 357; AGIM 1088, libro 3.   3. Galaviz de Capdevielle.
4. Arroyo, 2: 84; AGIM 357.   5. AGIM 357.
6. AGIM 357, 1:1r–v.
7. AGIM 357 (1551, 1597, 1602, 1614, 1631), 358 (1560, 1562), 887 (1650).
8. AGIM 879, 881.   9. AGIM 881.
10. AGNTr 34, 7:50.   11. AGNH 307, 15:1r.
12. François Chevalier, ed., *Instrucciones a los hermanos jesuitas administradores de haciendas* (Mexico, UNAM, 1950), p. 35.
13. Lavrín, p. 372.
14. AN 1688, fol. 499r, the estancia San Antonio de Padua, jurisdiction of Chichicapa, established in 1688 by Br. Tomás Ruiz de Estrada for his nephew Pedro Manso de Contreras.
15. CDChO, rollo 7, 1688, 2,000-peso capellanía on the Hacienda de los Negritos (San Antonio Buenavista).
16. AGNH 69, bk. 1, fol. 258r–v, 1644.
17. For example, the parochial church of Tlalixtac owned four pieces of land each containing less than one fanega de sembradura. AN 1786, fol. 114v.
18. AGNH 380, 9:85r, 1644.
19. AGNT 241, 7:21r.
20. Torre Villar.
21. AGN *Cofradías y Archicofradías* 18, 11:113–39.
22. Ernesto de la Torre Villar, ed., *Lecturas históricas mexicanas* (Mexico, 1966), 2: 285.
23. AGNH 69, bk. 1, fol. 160r, 1618; AGNT 241, 7:21r, 1689.
24. AGNT 956, 3:34r, 1772.
25. AGNH 306, exp. 1, 1760, San Pedro Ixtlahuaca; AGNH 119, exps. 1–3, 1760, San Jacinto de las Amilpas, Villa de Oaxaca, and San Juan Chapultepec.
26. Lavrín; Michael Costeloe, *Church Wealth in Mexico: A Study of the "Juzgado de Capellanías" in the Archibishopric of Mexico, 1800–1856* (Cambridge, Eng., 1966).
27. AGIM 357, "Rentas de los religiosos del obispado de Oaxaca."
28. See the accompanying table.
29. AGNMer 16, fol. 114r, 1590 merced for an estancia de ganado menor to the Cuilapan monastery; AGNT 2386, exp. 1, 1578 and 1580 mercedes for a mill and grazing land to the Jesuits.

TABLE FOR NOTE 28
Church Lands Acquired by Debts and Foreclosures

Year	Recipient	Source
pre-1641	Cuilapan monastery	AGNH 69, bk. 2, fol. 66r–v
1666	Santa Catalina de Sena	CCGL, 1666
1684	Cofradía of Villa de Oaxaca	AN 1684, fol. 56r
pre-1689	Cuilapan monastery	CDChO, rollo 7, 1689
1708	La Soledad	AN 1708, fol. 175v
1717	Santa Catalina de Sena	AN 1717, fol. 152v
1717	Santa Catalina de Sena	AN 1717, fol. 107v
1762	Santa Catalina de Sena	AN 1762, fol. 16r
1762	La Concepción	AGNT 890
1764	Santa Catalina de Sena	AN 1764, fol. 23v
1768	La Soledad	AN 1768
1770	La Concepción	AN 1770, fol. 27v
1772	La Concepción	AN 1772, fol. 178v
1786	Santa Catalina de Sena	AN 1786, fol. 241v
1800	La Concepción	AMT, doc. 25

30. AGNT 241, 7:19–21, 1702; AGNH 85, exp. 4, 1602; AGNH 50, exp. 3, sec. 26, 1778.

31. AMT, doc. 8.

32. AGNT 203, 6:132r, 1736; AGNH 380, 9:97r, 1644; CCGSNO, 1656.

33. Phipps, p. 43; Chevalier, *La formation*, p. 179.

34. Fals Borda, p. 71.

35. AGNC 1935, exp. 3, 1670, Santa Catalina de Sena; AGN *Archivo Histórico de Hacienda* 325, 6:1r, Jesuits.

36. AGIM 358.

37. AGIM 357.

38. CCGL, 1713. The "seven leagues" probably refers to the hacienda that grew from Santo Domingo's four cattle ranches in Tehuantepec.

39. AGIM 357.

40. AGNMer 16, fol. 114r, 1590; AGNI 43, exp. 84, 1718.

41. AGNT 129, 4:15r, 1659; AGNI 43, exp. 84, 1718.

42. AGNH 69, bk. 2, fol. 66r–v, 1641; CDChO, rollo 7, 1689.

43. AGIM 357.

44. AGNT 990, 2:6r, 1788; CCGSJ, fols. 28r (1660), 73r (1651); AN 1725, fol. 29v.

45. AMT, doc. 43, 1712, San Juan Teitipac, Teotitlán del Valle, Tlacochahuaya; AGNT, 415, exp. 3, tercera numeración, fols. 1–16, 1690, Huitzo; AGNH 50, exp. 3, sec. 34, para. 1, 1734, Santa Cruz Mixtepec; AGNT 203, 6:1r, Santa Ana Zegache; AN 1684, fol. 56r, Villa de Oaxaca; AN 1754, fol. 162v, Zaachila.

46. AGNT 481, primera parte, 1:1r, 1717. Held for only a short time, these lands are not shown on Map 7.

47. Burgoa, 2: 395.

48. CCGL, 1758.

49. A 1783 vista de ojos of the Hacienda Xaagá was located among the municipal records of Mitla. I am indebted to the town officials for permission to use these records. AGNT 1225, exp. 19, and AMT, doc. 34, describe friction between Mitla and Xaagá in 1792 and 1814.

50. AGNT 1225, exp. 19.

51. AMT, doc. 8.

52. AGIM 2586.

53. AGNT 2788, 3:3r.

54. AGNT 1064, exp. 13.

55. AGNT 2386, exp. 1.

56. *Ibid.*

57. AGNT 355, exp. 5. Early-eighteenth-century letters in AGN *Archivo Histórico de Hacienda* 325, exp. 6, lament the heavy urban investment.

58. AN 1767, fol. 32r.

59. AGN *Archivo Histórico de Hacienda* 325, exp. 6. This report appears to date from the late 1740's or early 1750's. Since the document mentions the trapiche near Coatlán, which was sold in 1753, it could not have been written after that year; it was not written before 1722, since 1721 is used with the past tense. The text is very similar to other documents in the same legajo dating from the 1750's and 1760's.

60. CCGSJB. In 1705 Pedro de Espina Pacheco willed eight caballerías of land near Coyotepec to his son, Br. Agustín de Espina, on the condition that the land would pass to the Carmelite monastery on Agustín's death. No subsequent reference to this land has been found. AN 1707, fol. 43v.

61. CCGL, 1798.

62. AGNT 1209, exp. 12.

63. CCGSJB, 1790–1800.

64. BEOB, fol. 275v.

65. BEOB, fol. 288r.

66. AGNH 300, 9:69r, 1610 sale; AGNT 333, 2:3v, 1667 sale; CCGS, p. 83, pre-1693 sale.

67. AGNT 333, 2:17v.

68. AGNT 2784, exp. 1.

69. Arroyo, 2: 129; Barlow, "Descripción," pp. 136–37.

70. AGNG 4, exp. 1; AGIM 357.

71. AGNT 333, 2:17r; AGNH 69, bk. 1, fols. 266r–67v; AGNMer 41, fol. 18r–v; AGNMer 51, fols. 2v–3v; AGNT 2963, exp. 50; CCGL, Oct. 2, 1666; AN 1707, fol. 253r; AGNT 125, 4:1r; CCGL, 1692; CDChO, rollo 11.

72. AGNC 1935, exp. 3.

73. CDCHO, rollo 67. From the private collection of Jorge Fernando Iturribarría.

74. CCGL, Oct. 2, 1666; AN 1717, fol. 107v; AN 1717, fol. 152v; AN 1749, fol. 238v, and AN 1786, fol. 241v; AN 1762; AN 1764, fol. 23v.

75. CCGSJB. Santa Catalina still owned the San Isidro estate in 1836.

76. AGNT 2386, exp. 1, segunda numeración, fol. 1r; AN 1749, fol. 238v; AN 1707, fol. 253r; AN 1717, fol. 107.

77. AN 1708, fol. 240r; AN 1766, fol. 26v; AN 1786, fol. 121r; AN 1798, fol. 181.

78. AN 1753, fol. 19v, several tracts of land rented from Manuel de Velasco, a *principal* of Cuilapan; AN 1799, fol. 22v, rancho San José rented from the cacique of Cuilapan.

79. Torres, p. 8.

80. AGIM 357; AGNT 2386, exp. 1, tercera numeración, fols. 19v, 48v.
81. AGNT 2386, exp. 1, tercera numeración, fol. 56r.
82. AGNH 163, exp. 48, 1629.
83. AN 1768; AN 1769, fol. 42v; AN 1708, fol. 175v; AN 1742, fol. 224r; AN 1790, fol. 159r.
84. CDChO, rollo 103.
85. AN 1742, fol. 224r; AN 1778, fol. 263v; AN 1790, fol. 159r; CDChO, rollo 103.
86. AGNT 890, 1762; AGNT 2784, exp. 1, 1792; AMT, doc. 25, 1800; CCGL, 1763; AN 1808, fol. 170r; AGNT 1268, 1:12r–24r, 100r–104r, 1803; AN 1770, fol. 27v.
87. AN 1772, fol. 178v; CDChO, rollo 66, 1714; AN 1717, fol. 94v.
88. Lavrín, p. 386.
89. CCGL, 1743–58.
90. Lavrín, p. 381.
91. AMT, doc. 25; Van de Velde Collection, *Loose Papers*, University of New Mexico Library, Albuquerque.
92. AGIM 357.
93. AGII 191.
94. Fernández de Recas, *Mayorazgos*, p. 455.
95. AGNH 135, 1:1v; CCGG, fols. 12r, 102r; AN 1689, fol. 371r; CCGSJB.
96. AGNT 1048, 11:81r–94r.   97. AN 1780, fol. 109ff.
98. CCGG, fol. 102r.   99. AN 1768, fol. 101r.
100. AGNH 102, 14:2r, 1619; CDChO, rollo 10, 1693; AGNT 395, 4:6r, 1696; AN 1729, fol. 1r; AGNH 348, 7:1v, 1735; AN 1765, fol. 35v; AN 1789, segunda parte, fol. 40v.

CONCLUSION

1. Gibson, *Aztecs Under Spanish Rule*, Chap. 10.
2. Murguía y Galardi, "Extracto general," *passim*.
3. Paso y Troncoso, *Papeles*, 4: 103, 106, 110, 113, 119, 129, 146, 149, 179, 194, 202.
4. Burgoa, 1: 272.   5. Spalding.
6. Tannenbaum, p. 7.   7. Rabasa, p. 291.
8. Murguía y Galardi, "Extracto general," primera parte, fol. 60r.
9. Amaya Topete; Borde and Góngora.
10. Crist, p. 17.
11. Chevalier, "Le grand domaine," pp. 400–401.

GLOSSARY

Abasto de Carne. Monopoly on a local meat supply
Alcalde mayor. Spanish official in charge of a district
Almud. Unit of dry measure; one-twelfth of a *fanega*
Bando. Proclamation
Barrio. Neighborhood in a community; sometimes composed of one lineage or a small number of lineages in Indian towns
Braza. Unit of measure; two *varas*
Caballería. Unit of agricultural land; roughly 105 acres
Cabecera. Head town
Cabildo. Municipal council
Cacica. Female Indian chieftain
Cacicazgo. Estate of a *cacique*
Cacique. Hereditary Indian chieftain or local ruler
Capellanía. Ecclesiastical benefice; a grant to support certain ceremonies of the Church, such as the periodic celebration of mass in honor of the donor
Casco. Compound or permanent buildings of an *hacienda*
Cédula real. Royal order
Censo. Mortgage or loan
Censo perpetuo. Emphiteutic grant; a kind of perpetual rent
Cofradía. Sodality; a lay brotherhood responsible for financing a community's religious services and maintaining the local church
Composición de tierras. Legalization of land title
Congregación. Congregation or concentration of scattered settlements into one community
Corregidor de indios. Spanish officer in charge of a local Indian district
Corregimiento. Jurisdiction of a *corregidor*
Cura. Parish priest
Doctrina. Parochial jurisdiction or its head town
Dueño. Owner
Ejido. Type of community land
Encomendero. Possessor of an *encomienda*
Encomienda. Grant of an Indian town or towns, carrying the right to assess tribute
Entrada. Rapid invasionary thrust of a Spanish expedition of conquest
Estancia de ganado mayor. Cattle ranch; theoretically about 6.76 square miles

Estancia de ganado menor. Sheep or goat ranch; theoretically about three square miles

Fanega. Unit of dry measure; about 1.5 bushels

Fanega de sembradura. Area planted with one *fanega* of seed; roughly 3.5 acres

Fundo legal. Townsite to which every community was entitled; 600 varas by 600 varas in the late colonial period

Ganado mayor. Cattle, horses, and mules

Ganado menor. Sheep, goats, and pigs

Hacendado. Owner of an *hacienda*

Hacienda. Landed estate with a mixed economic base of ranching and agriculture

Herido de molino. Mill site

Labor. Small landed estate devoted largely to agriculture

League. Distance traversed by a mule in one hour; widely accepted to be 2.6 miles

Macehual. Indian commoner

Maguey. Agave; the source of *pulque*

Mayeque. Indian of a subordinate class, below a *macehual* and usually dependent on an Indian noble

Mayorazgo. Entailed estate

Medida. Unit of agricultural land; roughly one-half acre in the Valley of Oaxaca

Merced. Royal or viceregal grant

Mestizo. Person of mixed white and Indian ancestry

Mezcal. Liquor obtained from a narrow-spined species of *maguey*

Minifundio. Division of agricultural land into tiny plots

Obraje. Workshop, especially for textiles

Obra pia. Charitable fund or establishment

Paraje. Boundary marker

Peso de oro común. Monetary unit; eight *reales*

Pregón. Public announcement of the sale of private property

Primitivo patrimonio. Indian ownership of land at the time of the Spanish conquest

Principal. Member of the Indian upper class; a hereditary status

Pueblo. Town or village; usually refers to small and medium-sized Indian communities

Pulque. Liquor obtained from *maguey*

Rancho. Ranch

Real. Monetary unit; one-eighth of a *peso*

Repartimiento. Labor draft

Salina. Salt deposit

Sementera. Plot of cultivated land

Señor. Lord

Serape. Woolen cloak

Sitio. Site

Solar. House plot

Suerte. Plot of land

Sujeto. Subject town

Temporal. Unirrigated cropland

Terrasguerro. Subordinate Indian, especially a sharecropper

Tianguis. Indian market

Tierras de humedad. Moist bottomlands

Tierras realengas. Royal lands, including woodlands, rivers, hunting preserves, and lime deposits

Toma de agua. Water source

Trapiche. Sugar mill

Vara. Unit of measure; roughly 33 inches

Veintena. A 5 per cent tax on lands transferred to a new owner

Villa. Municipal corporation one level below the city

Visita. Small community subject to a religious head town

Vista de ojos. Boundary inspection

Vocales. Electors in a *cabildo* election

Zontle. Four hundred (bundles)

BIBLIOGRAPHY

BIBLIOGRAPHY

This study relies heavily on unpublished materials for documentation. The archives that proved most valuable for colonial Oaxaca are the Archivo General de la Nación (AGN) in Mexico City, the Archivo General de las Indias (AGI) in Seville, the Archivo de Notarías (AN) in Oaxaca, the private collection of Licenciado Luis Castañeda Guzmán (CCG), and the microfilm collection of the Centro de Documentación del Museo Nacional (CDCh) in Mexico City's impressive museum of anthropology.

Of the 47 colonial sections of the Archivo General de la Nación, the *Tierras, Indios, Hospital de Jesús, General de Parte, Mercedes*, and *Civil ramos* are especially useful on land tenure, local economy, and the social history of the sixteenth and seventeenth centuries. With the exception of *Civil* these sections are at least partially indexed. *Tierras*, with over 3,000 volumes of land-related documents, is especially rewarding to use. Because colonial titles still serve as the basis of many community land rights, *Tierras* is well inventoried and carefully maintained. Since 1931 the *Boletín del Archivo General de la Nación* has listed volume-by-volume sections of the *Tierras* inventory, citing entries by place name and subject matter. (The subject headings are usually drawn from the title pages of the expedientes rather than from a survey of the contents, and are occasionally inaccurate.) The *Tributos, Padrones, Vínculos, Congregaciones, Archivo Histórico de Hacienda*, and *Cofradías y Archicofradías* sections of AGN provide additional information on special subjects.

Most of the material on Oaxaca in the Archivo General de las Indias is concentrated in the *Audiencia de México* section, which includes numerous church records and special reports. Wills of early Spanish residents of Antequera appear in *Casa de Contratación*. The *Indiferente General, Justicia, Papeles de Estado, Contaduría*, and *Patronato* sections provide a small body of documents on Oaxaca.

Skeleton manuscript inventories of these sections are the logical starting point for this valuable collection.

Oaxaca's notarial records, continuous from 1689, supply wills of
landowners, inventories of estates, and crucial information on land
transactions. Another especially useful source in Oaxaca is the Castañeda Guzmán collection, which contains complete land records for
eight colonial haciendas in the Valley and important records relating to the Church in Oaxaca.

The microfilm collection of the Centro de Documentación contains a variety of local materials, including parish records for Zaachila, several documents from the Castañeda Guzmán collection,
notarial papers for the 1690's, and a set of documents on the Hacienda de Buenavista from the Biblioteca del Estado de Oaxaca.

A number of other archives in Mexico, Spain, and the United
States have materials of value. In Mexico, I used the Archivo Histórico del Museo Nacional (MNM), the Archivo del Estado de Oaxaca (AEO), and the Archivo del Departamento de Asuntos Agrarios
(ADAA). The Asuntos Agrarios archives house copies of colonial records gathered from communities throughout Mexico as part of the
agrarian reform program of the Revolution, and some of the original documents as well. Worth special mention are the municipal archives of Tlacolula (AMT), a colonial cabecera. The archives amount
to heaps of old papers stored under the town bandstand. In addition
to information on Indian land tenure that is hard to obtain in national archives, the Tlacolula materials include local census data and
a variety of civil and criminal records, some of which deal with
drunkenness, an important Indian response to cultural shock. Records kept in colonial head towns remote from the large Spanish cities
are perhaps the greatest untapped source for the social history of the
colonial period. In Madrid, I used the Muñoz collection of the Real
Academia de Historia (RAHM) and the manuscript collection of the
Biblioteca Nacional (BN) for background material on Oaxaca. In
the United States the libraries of the University of New Mexico and
the University of Texas contain documents that filled in small but
important gaps.

Published material on colonial Oaxaca is rather sparse. The great
multivolume collections (especially CDII, CDIU, and ENE) contain
some important items. The *Colección de documentos para la historia
de Oaxaca* is a slim volume of documents on the early history of An-

tequera. *Para la historia del terruño* by Genaro V. Vásquez is less
well known but contains a number of interesting colonial documents
on Oaxaca. The sixteenth-century *Relaciones Geográficas* are published in Paso y Troncoso's *Papeles de Nueva España*. Nine eighteenth-century *Relaciones Geográficas* for the Valley will appear in
a 1972 number of *Mesoamerican Notes*. Time and again I turned to
Burgoa's *Geográfica descripción* for a firsthand account of the seventeenth century. There are a number of local histories for Oaxaca,
but all rely almost exclusively on Burgoa for the colonial period.
The best local histories are José Antonio Gay's *Historia de Oaxaca*
and Jorge Fernando Iturribarría's *Oaxaca en la historia*. Steininger
and Van de Velde's *Three Dollars a Year* documents the long and
bitter land disputes between Cuilapan and San Pablo Cuatro Venados. Woodrow Borah's works on Oaxacan archives and the Mixteca Alta are the most useful secondary sources dealing directly with
Oaxaca.

On the general subject of land and society in colonial Latin America, the works of Charles Gibson, Mario Góngora, François Chevalier, Orlando Fals Borda, Silvio Zavala, and Delfina López Sarrelangue are especially valuable. *Evolución de la propiedad rural en
el valle de Puangue* by Góngora and Juan Borde is the only con-
vincing treatment of colonial land tenure in a regional setting.

The following Bibliography consists of published books and articles I have found useful, as well as a few unpublished manuscripts.
It is arranged in a single alphabetical list to facilitate the use of short
forms in the Notes.

Acosta, José de. *Historia natural y moral de las Indias*. Mexico, 1940.
*Advertimientos generales que los virreyes dejaron a sus sucesores para el
gobierno de Nueva España, 1590–1604*. Edited by France V. Scholes and
Eleanor B. Adams. Documentos para la historia del México colonial, vol.
2. Mexico, 1956.
Aguirre Beltrán, Gonzalo. *Formas de gobierno indígena*. Mexico, 1953.
———. *El señorío de Cuahtocho: Luchas agrarias en México durante el
virreinato*. Mexico, 1940.
Aiton, Arthur Scott. *Antonio de Mendoza: First Viceroy of New Spain*. Dur-
ham, N.C., 1927.
Alamán, Lucas. *Historia de México*. 5 vols. Mexico, 1883–85.
Alegría, Ricardo E. "Origin and Diffusion of the Term 'Cacique,'" in *Ac-
culturation in the Americas*, Proceedings and Selected Papers of the 29th
International Congress of Americanists (1952), pp. 313–15.
Algiers, Keith Wayne. "Feudalism on New Spain's Northern Frontier: Valle

de San Bartolomé, a Case Study." Unpublished Ph.D. dissertation, University of New Mexico, 1965.

Alzate [y Ramírez], José Antonio. *Gacetas de literatura de México.* 4 vols. Puebla, Mexico, 1831.

Amaya Topete, Jesús. *Ameca, protofundación mexicana: Historia de la propiedad del valle de Ameca, Jalisco y circunvecindad.* Mexico, 1951.

Arcila Farías, Eduardo. *El régimen de la encomienda en Venezuela.* 2d ed. Caracas, 1966.

Armillas, Pedro. "Land Use in Pre-Columbian America," in *A History of Land Use in Arid Regions,* Arid Zone Research, UNESCO (Paris, 1961), 17: 255–76.

Arroyo, Esteban. *Los dominicos, forjadores de la civilización oajaqueña.* 2 vols. Oaxaca, 1957.

Arteaga Garza, Beatriz, and Guadalupe Pérez San Vicente, comps. *Cedulario cortesiano.* Mexico, 1949.

Bancroft, Hubert Howe. *History of Mexico.* 6 vols. Hubert Howe Bancroft, *Works,* vols. 9–14. San Francisco, 1886–88.

Barlow, Robert H., ed. "Descripción de la ciudad de Antequera," *Tlalocan,* vol. 2, no. 2 (1946), pp. 134–37.

———. "Dos relaciones de Cuilapa," *Tlalocan,* vol. 2, no. 1 (1945), pp. 18–28.

———. "The Periods of Tribute Collection in Moctezuma's Empire," *Notes on Middle American Archaeology and Ethnology,* 23 (1943): 152–54.

Barrera, Tomás. *Guía geológica de Oaxaca.* Mexico, 1946.

Beals, Ralph. "Algunos aspectos de la agriculturación mixe," *Revista mexicana de estudios antropológicos,* 16 (1960): 227–30.

El Becerro. Libro famoso de las behetrías de Castilla, que se custodia en la real chancillería de Valladolid. Santander, Spain, 1866.

Belmar, Francisco. *Breve reseña histórica y geográfica del Estado de Oaxaca.* Oaxaca, 1901.

Benítez, José R. *Los catedrales de Oaxaca, Morelia y Zacatecas.* Mexico, 1934.

Bentura Beleña, Eusebio. *Recopilación sumaria de todos los autos acordados de la real audiencia y sala del crimen de esta Nueva España, y providencias de su superior gobierno.* 2 vols. Mexico, 1787.

Berthe, Jean-Pierre. "Xochimancas: Les travaux et les jours dans une hacienda sucrière de Nouvelle-Espagne au XVIIᵉ siècle," *Jahrbuch für Geschichte von Staat, Wirtschaft und Gesellschaft Lateinamerikas,* 3 (1966): 88–117.

Bishko, Charles J. "The Peninsular Background of Latin American Cattle Ranching," *Hispanic American Historical Review,* 32 (1952): 491–515.

Bloch, Marc. *French Rural History.* Translated by Janet Sondheimer. Berkeley, Calif., 1966.

Borah, Woodrow. "The Cathedral Archive of Oaxaca," *Hispanic American Historical Review,* 28 (1948): 640–45.

———. "The Collection of Tithes in the Bishopric of Oaxaca During the Sixteenth Century," *Hispanic American Historical Review,* 21 (1941): 386–409.

———. *Early Colonial Trade and Navigation Between Mexico and Peru.* Ibero-Americana: 38. Berkeley, Calif., 1954.

———. *New Spain's Century of Depression.* Ibero-Americana: 35. Berkeley, Calif., 1951.

———. "Notes on Civil Archives in the City of Oaxaca," *Hispanic American Historical Review,* 31 (1951): 723–49.

———. *Silk Raising in Colonial Mexico.* Ibero-Americana: 20. Berkeley, Calif., 1943.

———. "Sources and Possibilities for the Reconstruction of the Demographic Process of the Mixteca Alta, 1519–1895," *Revista mexicana de estudios antropológicos,* 16 (1960): 159–72.

Borah, Woodrow, and Sherburne F. Cook. *The Aboriginal Population of Central Mexico on the Eve of the Spanish Conquest.* Ibero-Americana: 45. Berkeley, Calif., 1963.

———. *The Population of Central Mexico in 1548: An Analysis of the Suma de visitas de pueblos.* Ibero-Americana: 43. Berkeley, Calif., 1960.

———. *Price Trends of Some Basic Commodities in Central Mexico, 1531–1570.* Ibero-Americana: 40. Berkeley, Calif., 1958.

Borde, Juan, and Mario Góngora. *Evolución de la propiedad rural en el valle de Puangue.* Santiago, Chile, 1956.

Bradomín, José María. *Toponimia de Oaxaca.* Mexico, 1955.

Bravo H., Helia. "Algunos datos acerca de la vegetación del Estado de Oaxaca," *Revista mexicana de estudios antropológicos,* 16 (1960): 31–48.

Brioso y Candiani, Manuel. *La evolución del pueblo oajaqueño de la conquista hasta la consumación de la Independencia.* 2d ed. Tacubaya, D. F., 1943.

Burgoa, Francisco de. *Geográfica descripción de la parte septentorial del polo ártico de la América y nueva iglesia de los indias occidentales, y sitio astronómico de esta provincia de predicadores de Antequera, valle de Oaxaca . . . .* 2 vols. Mexico, 1934.

Bustamante, Carlos María de. *Memoria estadística de Oaxaca y descripción del valle del mismo nombre.* Edición facsimilar de la Secretaría del Patrimonio Nacional. Mexico, 1963.

Carrasco, Pedro. "El barrio y la regulación del matrimonio en un pueblo del Valle de México en el siglo XVI," *Revista mexicana de estudios antropológicos,* 17 (1961): 7–26.

———. "The Civil-Religious Hierarchy in Mesoamerican Communities: Pre-Spanish Background and Colonial Development," *American Anthropologist,* 63 (1961): 483–97.

Carrera Stampa, Manuel. "The Evolution of Weights and Measures in New Spain," *Hispanic American Historical Review,* 29 (1949): 2–24.

Caso, Alfonso. "Land Tenure Among the Ancient Mexicans," *American Anthropologist,* 65 (1963): 863–78.

Chevalier, François. *La formation des grands domaines au Mexique: Terre et société aux XVIᵉ–XVIIᵉ siècles.* Paris, 1952.

———. "Le grand domaine au Mexique du XVIᵉ au debut de XIXᵉ siècle," in *Contributions à la Première Conférence Internationale d'Histoire Economique* (Stockholm, 1960), pp. 399–407.

————. "The North Mexican Hacienda," in Archibald R. Lewis and Thomas F. McGann, eds., *The New World Looks at Its History*. Austin, Texas, 1963.

————. "Noticia inédita sobre los caballos en Nueva España," *Revista de Indias* (Madrid), 16 (1944): 323–26.

Cline, Howard F. "Civil Congregations of the Indians in New Spain, 1598–1606," *Hispanic American Historical Review*, 29 (1949): 349–69.

————. "Mexican Community Studies," *Hispanic American Historical Review*, 32 (1952): 212–42.

————. "Native Pictorial Documents of Eastern Oaxaca, Mexico," in *Summa Antropológica en homenaje a Roberto J. Weitlaner* (Mexico, 1966), pp. 101–20.

Colección de documentos inéditos para la historia de Ibero-América. 14 vols. Madrid, 1927–32. Title varies.

Colección de documentos inéditos relativos al descubrimiento, conquista, y organización de las antiguas posesiones españolas de América y Oceania, sacados de los archivos del reino, y muy especialmente del de Indias. 42 vols. Madrid, 1864–84.

Colección de documentos inéditos relativos al descubrimiento, conquista, y organización de las antiguas posesiones españolas de Ultramar. 25 vols. Madrid, 1885–1932.

Colección de documentos para la historia de Oaxaca. Mexico, 1933.

Colección de leyes y decretos del estado libre y soberano de Oaxaca formada por el C. Juan Nepomuceno Cerqueda. 2 vols. Oaxaca, 1861.

Conzatti, Cassiano. *El estado de Oaxaca y sus recursos naturales.* Oaxaca, 1920.

Cook, Sherburne F. *Soil Erosion and Population in Central Mexico.* Ibero-Americana: 34. Berkeley, Calif., 1949.

Cook, Sherburne F., and Woodrow Borah. *The Indian Population of Central Mexico, 1531–1610.* Ibero-Americana: 44. Berkeley, Calif., 1960.

————. *The Population of the Mixteca Alta, 1520–1960.* Ibero-Americana: 50. Berkeley, Calif., 1968.

Córdoba, Juan de. *Relación de la fundación, capítulos y elecciones, que se han tenido en esta provincia de Santiago de esta Nueva España, de la Orden de Predicadores de Santo Domingo, 1569 . . . .* Mexico, 1944.

————. *Vocabulario Castellano-Zapoteco, 1578.* Edited by Wigberto Jiménez Moreno. Facsimile edition. Mexico, 1942.

Cossío, José L. *¿Cómo y por quienes se ha monopolizado la propiedad rústica en México?* 2d ed. Mexico, 1966.

Cravioto, Rene O. "Valor nutritivo de los alimentos mexicanos," *América indígena*, 11 (1951): 297–309.

Crist, Raymond E. *The Cauca Valley, Colombia: Land Tenure and Land Use.* Baltimore, Md., 1952.

Cruz Caballero, Miguel. *Huitzo.* Mexico, n.d.

Cuevas, Mariano, ed. *Documentos inéditos del siglo XVI para la historia de México.* Mexico, 1914.

Dahlgren de Jordán, Barbro. *La grana cochinilla. Nueva Biblioteca Mexicana de Obras Históricas*, no. 1. Mexico, 1963.

————. *La Mixteca, su cultura e historia pre-hispánicas*. Mexico, 1954.

Dessaint, Alain Y. "Effects of the Hacienda and Plantation Systems on Guatemala's Indians," *América indígena*, 22 (1962): 323–54.

Díaz del Pino, Alfonso. *El maíz: Cultivo, fertilización, cosecha*. Mexico, 1954.

Diguet, Léon. "Histoire de la cochenille au Mexique," *Journal de la Société des Américanistes de Paris*, n.s., 6 (1909): 75–99.

Disposiciones complementarias de las leyes de Indias. 3 vols. Madrid, 1930.

"División de la raya marquesana en tierras de la antigua Antequera," *Boletín del Archivo General de la Nación* (Mexico), vol. 3, no. 4 (1932), pp. 488–511.

División territorial del estado de Oaxaca y datos recopilados para la campaña de la división "veintiuno." Oaxaca, 1916.

Dusenberry, William H. *The Mexican Mesta: The Administration of Ranching in Colonial Mexico*. Urbana, Ill., 1963.

————. "The Regulation of Meat Supply in Sixteenth-Century Mexico City," *Hispanic American Historical Review*, 28 (1948): 38–52.

————. "Woolen Manufacture in Sixteenth-Century New Spain," *The Americas*, 4 (1947–48): 223–34.

Esesarte, Juan A. de. *Geografía del estado de Oaxaca*. Oaxaca, 1909.

Esquivel Obregón, Toribio. *Influencia de España y los Estados Unidos sobre México*. Madrid, 1918.

Esteva, Cayetano. *Elementos de geografía del distrito del centro . . . .* Oaxaca, 1911.

————. *Noticias elementales de geografía histórica del estado de Oaxaca*. Oaxaca, 1913.

Esteva, Constantino. "Copias de documentos originales en la biblioteca del Lic. Constantino Esteva." Oaxaca, 1937. Typewritten manuscript, Zimmerman Library, University of New Mexico.

Fals Borda, Orlando. *Hombre y tierra en Boyacá-Bogotá, Colombia*. Bogotá, 1957.

Fernández de Recas, Guillermo. *Cacicazgos y nobiliario indígena de la Nueva España*. Mexico, 1961.

————. "Descendientes de tres conquistadores de Chiapas," *Estudios de historia Novohispana*, 1 (1966): 157–86.

————. *Mayorazgos de la Nueva España*. Mexico, 1965.

Flannery, Kent V., et al. "Farming Systems and Political Growth in Ancient Oaxaca," *Science*, vol. 158, no. 3,800 (October 27, 1967), pp. 445–54.

Florescano, Enrique. "El abasto y la legislación de granos en el siglo XVI," *Historia mexicana*, 14 (April–June 1965), pp. 567–630.

————. *Precios del maíz y crisis agrícolas en México (1708–1810)*. Mexico, 1968.

Fonseca, Fabián de, and Carlos de Urrutia. *Historia general de la real hacienda*. 6 vols. Mexico, 1845–53.

Ford, Thomas R. *Man and Land in Peru*. Gainesville, Fla., 1955.

Friede, Juan. "Proceso de formación de la propiedad territorial en la América Intertropical," *Jahrbuch für Geschichte von Staat, Wirtschaft und Gesellschaft Lateinamerikas*, 2 (1965): 88–105.

Gacetas de México. Mexico, 1949– .

Gage, Thomas. *Travels in the New World.* Edited by J. Eric Thompson. Norman, Okla., 1958.

Galaviz de Capdevielle, María Elena. "Los dominicos," in *Homenaje a Rafael García Granados.* Mexico, 1960, pp. 195–203.

Galván Rivera, Mariano. *Ordenanzas de tierras y aguas o sea formulario geométrico judicial.* 2d ed. Mexico, 1844.

Gamboa, Francisco Xavier. *Comentarios a las ordenanzas de minas.* Madrid, 1761.

García Martínez, Bernardo. *El Marquesado del Valle: Tres siglos de régimen señorial en Nueva España.* Mexico, 1968.

García Pimentel, Luis. *Relación de los obispados de Tlaxcala, Michoacán, Oaxaca y otros lugares en el siglo XVI.* Mexico, 1904.

Gay, José Antonio. *Historia de Oaxaca.* 3d ed., 4 vols. Mexico, 1950.

Gibson, Charles. "The Aztec Aristocracy in Colonial Mexico," *Comparative Studies in Society and History,* 2 (1960): 169–96.

————. *The Aztecs Under Spanish Rule: A History of the Indians of the Valley of Mexico, 1519–1810.* Stanford, Calif., 1964.

Gillow, Eulogio. *Apuntes históricos.* Mexico, 1889.

Góngora, Mario. *Origen de los inquilinos de Chile central.* Santiago, 1960.

————. "Régimen señorial y rural en la Extremadura de la orden de Santiago en el momento de la emigración a Indias," *Jahrbuch für Geschichte von Staat, Wirtschaft und Gesellschaft Lateinamerikas,* 2 (1965): 1–29.

————. "Vagabondage et société pastorale en Amérique Latine," *Annales: économies, sociétés, civilisations,* 21 (1966): 159–77.

González de Cossío, Francisco. *Historia de la tenencia y explotación del campo desde la época precortesiana hasta las leyes del 6 de enero de 1915.* 2 vols. Mexico, 1957.

González Navarro, Moisés. "Indio y propiedad en Oaxaca," *Historia mexicana,* 8 (1958): 175–91.

González Sánchez, Isabel, ed. *Haciendas y ranchos de Tlaxcala en 1712.* Mexico, 1969.

Guthrie, Chester L. "Colonial Economy, Trade, Industry, and Labor in Seventeenth-Century Mexico City," *Revista de historia de América,* 7 (1939): 104–34.

Hamnett, Brian R. "Obstáculos a la política agraria del depotismo ilustrado," *Historia mexicana,* 20 (1970): 55–75.

Handbook of Middle American Indians. 11 vols. to date. Austin, Texas, 1964– .

Harris, Charles H. "A Mexican Latifundio: The Economic Empire of the Sánchez Navarro Family, 1765–1821." Unpublished Ph.D. dissertation, University of Texas, 1968.

————. *The Sánchez Navarros: A Socio-Economic Study of a Coahuilan Latifundio, 1846–1853.* Chicago, 1964.

Humboldt, Alexander de. *Political Essay on the Kingdom of New Spain.* Translated by John Black. 4 vols. London, 1822.

Icaza, Francisco A. de. *Diccionario autobiográfico de conquistadores y pobladores de Nueva España.* 2 vols. Madrid, 1923.

Indice de documentos de Nueva España existentes en el Archivo de Indias de Sevilla. 4 vols. Monografías bibliográficas mexicanas, vols. 12, 14, 22, 23. Mexico, 1928–31.

Instrucciones que los vireyes de Nueva España dejaron a sus sucesores. Mexico, 1867.

Iturribarría, Jorge Fernando. "Alonso García Bravo, trazador y alarife de la villa de Antequera," *Historia mexicana,* 7 (1957): 80–91.

———. Oaxaca en la historia. Mexico, 1955.

———. "Oaxaca, la historia y sus instrumentos," *Historia mexicana,* 2 (1953): 459–76.

Kirchhoff, Paul. "Land Tenure in Ancient Mexico: A Preliminary Sketch," *Revista mexicana de estudios antropológicos,* vol. 14, part 1 (1954–55), pp. 351–61.

Konetzke, Richard, ed. *Colección de documentos para la historia de la formación social de Hispanoamérica, 1493–1810.* 3 vols. Madrid, 1953–62.

Lavrín, Asunción. "The Role of the Nunneries in the Economy of New Spain in the Eighteenth Century," *Hispanic American Historical Review,* 46 (1966): 371–93.

Lee, Raymond L. "American Cochineal in European Commerce, 1526–1625," *The Journal of Modern History,* 23 (1951): 205–24.

———. "Cochineal Production and Trade in New Spain to 1600," *The Americas,* 4 (1947–48): 449–73.

———. "Grain Legislation in Colonial Mexico, 1575–1585," *Hispanic American Historical Review,* 27 (1947): 647–60.

Lewis, Oscar. "Plow Culture and Hoe Culture: A Study in Contrasts," *Rural Sociology,* vol. 14, no. 2 (June 1949), pp. 116–27.

"Libro de ordenanzas y medidas de tierra y aguas, vista de ojos con el modo de medir las minas, y necesidad que hay de su inteligencia, y otras cosas mui curiosas y necesarias, que en él se contienen. . . ." N.d. Unpublished manuscript. Special Collections, Zimmerman Library, University of New Mexico.

El libro de las tasaciones de pueblos de la Nueva España, siglo XVI. Edited by France V. Scholes and Eleanor B. Adams. Mexico, 1952.

López Rayón, Ignacio, ed. *Sumario de la residencia tomada a D. Fernando Cortés, gobernador y capitán general de la Nueva España, y a otros gobernadores y oficiales de la misma.* 2 vols. Mexico, 1852–53.

López Sarrelangue, Delfina Esmeralda. *La nobleza indígena de Pátzcuaro en la época virreinal.* Mexico, 1965.

———. "La población indígena de la Nueva España en el siglo XVIII," *Historia mexicana,* 12 (1962–63): 515–30.

———. "Las tierras comunales indígenas en la Nueva España en el siglo XVI," *Estudios de historia Novohispana,* 1 (1966): 131–48.

Lorenzo, José L. "Aspectos físicos del Valle de Oaxaca," *Revista mexicana de estudios antropológicos,* 16 (1960): 49–64.

McBride, George McCutchen. *The Land Systems of Mexico.* American Geographical Society Research Series, no. 12. New York, 1923.

McGreevey, William P. "Tierra y trabajo en Nueva Granada, 1760–1845," *Desarrollo económico,* vol. 8, no. 30–31, pp. 263–91.

Maniau, Joaquín. *Compendio de la historia de la real hacienda escrito en el año de 1794.* Mexico, 1914.

Martin, Norman F. *Vagabundos en la Nueva España.* Mexico, 1957.

Martínez Báez, Antonio. "El ejido en la legislación de la época colonial," *Universidad de México,* vol. 2, no. 8 (June 1931), pp. 112–17.

Martínez Cosío, Leopoldo. *Los caballeros de las órdenes militares en México.* Mexico, 1946.

Martínez Gracida, Manuel. *Colección de cuadros sinópticos de los pueblos, haciendas y ranchos, estado libre y soberano de Oaxaca.* Oaxaca, 1883.

Martínez Ríos, Jorge. *Bibliografía antropológica y sociológica del estado de Oaxaca.* Mexico, 1961.

Maza, Francisco F. de la. *Código de colonización y terrenos baldíos de la república mexicana.* Mexico, 1893.

Méndez, Andrés. "Relación de la vicaria y partido de Santa Cruz que en mexicano se dize Ixtepec y en zapoteco Quialoo," *Revista mexicana de estudios históricos,* 2 (1928): 180–84.

Mendieta y Núñez, Lucio. *El problema agrario de México.* 5th ed. Mexico, 1946.

———. "El régimen de la tierra en México en el siglo XIX," in *Proceedings of the First Congress of Historians from Mexico and the United States Assembled in Monterrey, Nuevo León, Mexico, September 4–9, 1949* (1950), pp. 209–22.

———, ed. *Los zapotecos: Monografía histórica, etnográfica y económica.* Mexico, 1949.

Miranda, José. "La función económica del encomendero en los orígenes del régimen colonial, Nueva España, 1525–1531," *Anales del Instituto Nacional de Antropología e Historia,* 2 (1941–46): 421–62.

———. "Notas sobre la introducción de la Mesta en la Nueva España," *Revista de historia de América,* 17 (June 1944): 1–26.

———. "Orígenes de la ganadería indígena en la Mixteca," *Miscelánea Paul Rivet, octogenario dicata,* 2 (1958): 787–96.

———. "La población indígena de México en el siglo XVII," *Historia mexicana,* 12 (1962–63): 182–89.

———. *El tributo indígena en la Nueva España durante el siglo XVI.* Mexico, 1952.

Moreno Toscano, Alejandra. *Geografía económica de México (siglo XVI).* Mexico, 1968.

Mörner, Magnus. "La infiltración mestiza en los cacicazgos y cabildos de indios (siglos XVI–XVIII)," in 36th Congreso Internacional de Americanistas, *Actas y Memorias,* 2 (1964): 155–60.

———. *Race Mixture in the History of Latin America.* Boston, 1967.

Morrisey, Richard J. "Colonial Agriculture in New Spain," *Agricultural History,* 31 (1957): 24–29.

———. "The Northward Expansion of Cattle Ranching in New Spain, 1550–1600," *Agricultural History,* 25 (1951): 115–21.

Motolinía (Toribio de Benavente). *History of the Indians of New Spain.* Translated by Elizabeth A. Foster. Berkeley, Calif., 1950.

Murguía y Galardi, José María. *Apuntamientos estadísticos de la provincia de Oaxaca en esta Nueva España.* Oaxaca, 1861.

———. "Extracto general que abraza la estadística toda en su primera y segunda parte del estado de Guaxaca y ha reunido de orden del Supremo Gobierno y yntendente de provincia en clase de los cesantes José María Murguía y Galardi." 1827. Unpublished manuscript. University of Texas Manuscript Collection.

Navarrete, Demetrio M. *Lecciones de nomenclatura geográfica de la ciudad de Oaxaca y del distrito del centro, para texto de las escuelas primarias de la capital.* Oaxaca, 1889.

Navarro y Noriega, Fernando. "Memoria sobre la población del reino de Nueva-España," *Boletín de la Sociedad de Geografía y Estadística de la República Mexicana,* época 2, vol. 1 (1869), pp. 281–91.

Nolasco Armas, Margarita. *La tenencia de la tierra en el municipio de San Juan Teotihuacán, estado de México. Acta Antropológica,* época 2, vol. 2, no. 3. Mexico, 1962.

Orozco, Wistano Luis. *Legislación y jurisprudencia sobre terrenos baldíos.* 2 vols. Mexico, 1895.

Ots Capdequí, José María. *El régimen de la tierra en la América española durante el período colonial.* Ciudad Trujillo, 1946.

Paddock, John, ed. *Ancient Oaxaca: Discoveries in Mexican Archeology and History.* Stanford, Calif., 1966.

Páez Courvel, Luis E. *Historia de las medidas agrarias antiguas: Legislación colonial y republicana y el proceso de su aplicación en las titulaciones de tierras . . . .* Bogotá, 1940.

Parry, J. H. *The Audiencia of New Galicia in the Sixteenth Century.* Cambridge, Eng., 1948.

Parsons, Kenneth H., et al., eds. *Land Tenure.* Madison, Wis., 1956.

Paso y Troncoso, Francisco del, ed. *Epistolario de Nueva España, 1505–1818.* 16 vols. Mexico, 1939–42.

———. *Papeles de Nueva España.* 9 vols. Madrid, 1905–48.

Phipps, Helen. *Some Aspects of the Agrarian Question in Mexico.* University of Texas Bulletin, no. 2515. Austin, 1925.

Ponce, Alonso. *Relación breve y verdadera de algunas cosas de la Nueva España . . . escrita por dos religiosos.* Madrid, 1873.

Portillo, Andrés. *Oaxaca en el centenario de la independencia nacional.* Oaxaca, 1910.

Pous Angeles, Guillermo. *El latifundio en el derecho mexicano.* Tesis elaborada en el Seminario de Derecho Agrario, UNAM. Mexico, 1963.

Priestley, Herbert I. *The Coming of the White Man, 1492–1848.* New York, 1929.

Puga, Vasco de. *Provisiones, cédulas, instrucciones para el gobierno de la Nueva España.* Colección de incunables americanos, vol. 3. Madrid, 1945.

Rabasa, Emilio. *La evolución histórica de México.* Mexico, 1920.

Recopilación de leyes de los reynos de las Indias. Edición facsimilar de la cuarta impresión hecha en Madrid el año 1791. 3 vols. Madrid, 1943.

Relación de las encomiendas de indios hechas en Nueva España a los con-

quistadores y pobladores de ella, año de 1564. Documentos para la historia de México colonial, vol. 1. Mexico, 1955.

Rippy, Merrill. "Land Tenure and Land Reform in Modern Mexico," *Agricultural History*, 27 (1953): 55–61.

Rodríguez San Miguel, Juan. *Pandectas hispano megicanas* . . . . 3 vols. Mexico, 1839.

Romero, Emilio. *Historia económica del Perú*. Buenos Aires, 1949.

Romero, Matías. *El estado de Oaxaca*. Barcelona, 1886.

Romero de Terreros, Manuel. *Antiguas haciendas de México*. Mexico, 1956.

Salazar, Francisco. *Compendio de la historia de Oaxaca*. Oaxaca, 1917.

Sandoval, Fernando B. *La industria del azúcar en Nueva España*. Mexico, 1951.

Schmieder, Oscar. *The Settlements of the Tzapotec and Mije Indians, State of Oaxaca, Mexico*. Berkeley, Calif., 1930.

Schulman, Sam. "Land Tenure Among the Aborigines of Latin America," *The Americas*, 13 (1956): 43–67.

Silva Herzog, Jesús. *El agrarismo mexicano y la reforma agraria, exposición y crítica*. Mexico, 1959.

Simpson, Lesley Byrd. *Exploitation of Land in Central Mexico in the Sixteenth Century*. Ibero-Americana: 36. Berkeley, Calif., 1952.

———. *Studies in the Administration of the Indians in New Spain*. Part 3. *The Repartimiento System of Native Labor in New Spain and Guatemala*. Ibero-Americana: 13. Berkeley, Calif., 1938.

Smith, T. Lynn. *Colombia: Social Structure and the Process of Development*. Gainesville, Fla., 1967.

Sobre el modo de tributar los indios de Nueva España a su magestad, 1561–1564. Edited by France V. Scholes and Eleanor B. Adams. Documentos para la historia del México colonial, vol. 5. Mexico, 1958.

Solórzano Pereira, Juan de. *Política Indiana*. Amberes, 1703. Facsimile edition. 5 vols. Madrid, 1930.

Spalding, Karen. "Tratos mercantiles del Corregidor de Indios y la formación de la hacienda serrana en el Perú," *América indígena*, 30 (1970): 595–608.

Spores, Ronald. *The Mixtec Kings and Their People*. Norman, Okla., 1967.

Steininger, George Russell, and Paul Van de Velde. *Three Dollars a Year*. New York, 1935.

Strickom, Arnold. "Hacienda and Plantation in Yucatan: An Historical-Ecological Continuum in Yucatan," *América indígena*, 25 (1965): 35–63.

Tamayo, Jorge L. *Geografía de Oaxaca*. Mexico, 1950.

———. *Oaxaca: Breve monografía geográfica anexa a la carta municipal*. Mexico, 1960.

Tannenbaum, Frank. *The Mexican Agrarian Revolution*. New York, 1929.

Tarcena, Angel. *Apuntes históricos de Oaxaca*. Oaxaca, 1941.

———. *Efemérides oajaqueñas*. Oaxaca, 1941.

Teixidor, Felipe. *Bibliografía del agrarismo en México hasta 1930*. Boletín de la Biblioteca Nacional, 2d época. Vol. 6. Mexico, 1955.

Thièry de Menonville, Nicolas Joseph. "Travels to Guaxaca . . . ," in *A Gen-

eral Collection of the Best and Most Interesting Voyages and Travels ..., 13 (1912): 753–876.

Torre Villar, Ernesto de la. "Algunos aspectos acerca de las cofradías y la propiedad territorial en Michoacán," *Jahrbuch für Geschichte von Staat, Wirtschaft und Gesellschaft, Lateinamerikas,* 4 (1967): 410–39.

Torres, Gilberto. "La ciudad de Oaxaca y sus principales edificios." Oaxaca, 1889. Typewritten manuscript, Zimmerman Library, University of New Mexico.

Toscano, Salvador. "Una empresa renacentista de España: La introducción de cultivos y animales domésticos en México," *Cuadernos americanos,* 25 (Jan.–Feb. 1946): 143–58.

"Unpublished Letters of the First Bishop of Mexico and Oaxaca," *The Americas,* 1 (1944): 104–7.

Valderrama, Jerónimo. *Cartas del licenciado Jerónimo Valderrama y otros documentos sobre su visita al gobierno de Nueva España, 1563–1565.* Edited by France V. Scholes and Eleanor B. Adams. Documentos para la historia del México colonial, vol. 7. Mexico, 1961.

Vásquez, Genaro V., ed. *Doctrinas y realidades en la legislación para los indios.* Mexico, 1940.

———. *Para la historia del terruño.* Mexico, 1931.

Vásquez, Mario C. *Hacienda, peonaje y servidumbre en los Andes Peruanos.* Lima, 1961.

Vásquez de Espinosa, Antonio. *Descripción de la Nueva España en el siglo XVII.* Mexico, 1944.

Velasco, Adolfo. "Semblanza de la villa de Zaachila, Oaxaca, antigua capital del reino de los zapotecos," *Boletín de la Sociedad Mexicana de Geografía y Estadística,* vol. 41, no. 2 (1929), pp. 131–71.

Verdiga, Pedro. *Descripción de Antequera por Pedro de Verdiga (1580).* Mexico, 1957.

Villarraza Ribera, Francisco Antonio. "Fundación de la Iglesia de San José de la ciudad de Oaxaca." 1796. Unpublished manuscript. Special Collections, Zimmerman Library, University of New Mexico.

Villaseñor y Sánchez, José Antonio de. *Theatro Americano, descripción general de los reynos, y provincias de la Nueva España y sus jurisdicciones ....* 2 vols. Mexico, 1746–48.

Viñas y Mey, Carmelo. "La sociedad americana y el acceso a la propiedad rural," *Revista internacional de sociología,* vol. 1, no. 1, pp. 103–48; nos. 2–3, pp. 257–84; no. 4, pp. 159–78.

Weeks, David. "Land Tenure in Bolivia," *The Journal of Land and Public Utility Economics,* vol. 23, no. 3, pp. 321–36.

West, Robert C. *The Mining Community in Northern New Spain: The Parral Mining District.* Ibero-Americana: 30. Berkeley, Calif., 1949.

Whetten, Nathan. *Rural Mexico.* Chicago, 1948.

Wolf, Eric R. *Peasants.* Foundations of Modern Anthropology Series. Englewood Cliffs, N.J., 1966.

Wolf, Eric, and Sidney Mintz. "Haciendas and Plantations in Middle America and the Antilles," *Social and Economic Studies,* 6: 380–412.

Zavala, Silvio. *Contribución a la historia de las instituciones coloniales en Guatemala.* 2d ed., vol. 5. Guatemala City, 1967.

———. *La encomienda indiana.* Madrid, 1935.

———. "De encomiendas y propiedad territorial en algunas regiones de la América española," in *Estudios indianos,* 1948, pp. 207–305.

———. "Orígenes coloniales del peonaje en México," in his *Estudios indianos.* Mexico, 1948.

Zavala, Silvio, and María Castelo, eds. *Fuentes para la historia del trabajo en Nueva España.* 8 vols. Mexico, 1939–46.

INDEX

Communities are alphabetized under their distinctive last names rather than under the names of their patron saints (e.g., Zautla, San Andrés), except when the last name is a description in Spanish (e.g., San Felipe del Agua).

Abajo, hacienda, 140
Abasto de carne, 113, 117
Abellán, Dionicio de, 64
Abellán y Carrasco, Antonio de, 62
Adamni, barrio of Cuilapan, 42
Agriculture, 3f, 10–17 *passim*, 80, 91–105 *passim*, 120f, 127, 137, 184, 196ff
Aguirre Beltrán, Gonzalo, 50, 68n, 73
Albarradas, San Lorenzo, 23, 103
Albarradas, Santa María, 70
Albuquerque, Fray Bernardo, 117
Alcalde mayor, 28, 73
Alemán, hacienda, 132
Alfaro, *labor*, 180
Almógabar, Juan de, 139
Amatengo, San Agustín, 69, 100
Ameca, Valley of, 199
Amilpas, San Jacinto, 10, 23, 26, 69, 71, 95
Amilpas, Santa Cruz, 70, 105, 209
Angeles Aguilar y Velasco, Diego de los, 52
Angeles y Lara, Miguel de, 45
Angulo, Cristóbal, 161
Antequera, 11, 23, 69, 79, 100, 110, 138, 160f, 164; population of, 18–21, 34, 38f, 62, 165; *cabildo* of, 20, 109, 116f, 119, 158f, 170; and Indian labor, 101f, 117, 197; early history of, 111–12, 112n, 116f, 121, 184; owners of property in, 153–58 *passim*, 168, 173–74, 182ff, 186, 190–91
Apasco, Magdalena, 80, 94
Aragón, Juan de, 139
Aranjuez, hacienda, 141, 156, 189, 191
Arriba, hacienda, 140
Asencio, Gaspar, 158

Asunción, La, hacienda, 133, 155f, 253
Atepec, 37n
Atlixco, Valley of, 198
Atoyac, 37n
Atoyac River, 9f, 60, 93f, 98, 100f
Audiencia: Indian appeals to, 45, 53f, 112; on Indian lands and labor, 70, 74–75, 82, 108, 147, 149
Augustinians, 164f, 170. *See also* Soledad, Nuestra Señora de la
Ayoquesco, 19, 94n, 99–100, 119, 230
Azompa, 20, 23, 80, 94n, 169, 234
Aztecs, *see* Nahuas

Barranco, Br. Juan, 192f
Barranco, Juan, 139
Barrio, 21, 72, 89
Benites Merino, Diego de, 138f, 160
Bethlemites, 131, 171, 173, 184–85, 185n, 200
Bishopric of Oaxaca, 164, 174n, 191
Bohórquez, Juan de, 156, 166, 191, 217
Bohórquez family, 134, 153, 156–57, 159, 166, 191
Borah, Woodrow, 30
Bourbon reforms, 50
Buenaventura de Angulo, Enrico, 155
Buenavista, hacienda (Valley of Zimatlán), 157
Burgoa, Francisco de, 26, 51–52, 81, 107, 127
Bustamente, Carlos María, 97, 104

Cabeceras, 21, 49, 200
Cacicazgos, *see* Nobility, Indian
Cacique, *see* Nobility, Indian
Calpullalli, 72

Capellanías, 52, 168, 172, 179, 186
Capitán, El, rancho, 135, 221
Capuchinas Españolas, convent, 165, 173
Capuchinas Indias, convent, 165,
Carmelites, 134, 148, 165, 171, 173, 183–84, 200, 216f
Carrasco, Pedro, 52n
Casa grande, 122, 126
Casco, 122, 126
Castillo, Joseph del, 137ff
Cathedral of Oaxaca, 82, 154, 156, 170, 220
Cattle: Indian-owned, 47, 72, 81, 243; Spanish-owned, 114f, 128–31 *passim,* 137f, 156, 174, 184
Cédula real, see Laws
Censos perpetuos, see under Marqués del Valle
Cerro Gordo, rancho, 158
Céspedes, Alonso de, 54
Chapultepec, San Juan, 23, 40–41, 69f, 101, 115
Chevalier, François, 6, 43, 200–201
Chichicapa, 15, 17, 19, 28, 39, 112n, 119
Chichicapa, San Baltazar, 19, 103
Chichicapa, Santa Marta, 165
Chichimec frontier, 2
Chilateca, 26f, 99
Chilayta, La, rancho, 193, 226
Chile, 153, 199
Church, 59, 75, 147; as creditor, 141–42, 170, 179f, 187, 190f; acquisition of property by, 167–71, 180, 186–87, 192–93, 255; uses of land by, 171–74, 179f, 184, 193; sales of land by, 173, 186–94 *passim,* 201
Cinco Señores, hacienda, 148, 160, 172, 189f
Climate, 9f, 12
Coatlán, 182f
Cochineal, 14, 14n, 47, 94, 94n, 98, 146f, 183
Cofradía, 71, 98, 169–70
Coixtlahuaca, 37n
Colegio de Infantes de Cristo, 173
Colegio de Niños de la Presentación, 173
Colegio Seminario de Estudios, 173
Comitlán, hacienda, 140
Composiciones de tierras, 6f, 61, 79, 102
Concepción, La, convent, 165, 170, 172f, 189–91, 194, 216, 218f, 226
Congregaciones, 21, 26–27, 37
Cook, Sherburne, 30
Coronación, hacienda, 97

Corregidor, 49, 70, 82, 108, 147, 158f, 197
Cortabarría, hacienda, 97
Cortez, Fernando, 1, 22f, 36, 111ff, 115, 163
Cortez, Martín, 113
Cortez, Pedro, 54–55, 115
Cortez Dhahuyuchi, Diego, 40–41
Coyotepec, 20, 36, 50f, 112n, 239; lands of, 80, 88, 97, 99, 104n, 108, 209
Creoles, 135, 161f, 201
Cruz, Domingo de, 38n
Cruz y Fonseca family, 46
Cuatro Villas, 13, 21, 30–34, 36, 61, 69, 112. *See also* Marqués del Valle; Cuilapan; Etla, Villa de; Oaxaca, Villa de; Tlapacoya
Cuernavaca, Valley of, 198
Cuicatlán, 37n
Cuilapan, 11, 20, 28n, 29, 102, 112, 165f, 168; population of, 20, 22f, 27, 31f, 234; lands of, 78f, 80f, 88, 95–96, 209, 239

Delgado, Matheo, 137, 139
Depression, in early eighteenth century, 16, 130, 142, 153, 155, 157, 162, 183
Díaz, Br. Bernardo, 193
Díaz, Br. León, 193
Díaz, Porfirio, 198
Díaz de Ordaz, Diego, 140
Doctrina, 123, 165
Dolores, hacienda, 180
Dominicans, 23, 26, 37, 164, 165–66; parish churches of, 87, 92, 99, 165–74 *passim,* 179–80; estates of, 168ff, 174–81
Donatarios, 115
Don Pedrillo, estancia, 106, 123n, 154f, 181
Dowries, 186–87
Duhuatia, rancho, 135, 141, 221ff, 226
Dulce, del, hacienda, 226

Ejido, 67, 72f, 75, 117, 121, 138
Ejutla, 28, 37n
Encomienda, 5, 28, 36–37, 112, 120, 143
Enríquez, Martín, 83, 114
Entailed estates: of Indian nobles, 44–45, 56–65; of Spaniards, 152–58, 161n, 173
Epidemics, 28, 28n, 31f, 90, 195
Escovar, hacienda, 132, 172
Escovar, Pedro de, 139
Espina, Gaspar de, 99, 128, 139, 186, 216f
Espina family, 134, 217, 219, 256

Espinar, del, hacienda, 184
Esquivel, Obregón, Toribio, 199
Estancias, see Ranching and individual
    estates listed by name
Estayula, 37n
Etla, Asunción, 63, 234
Etla, Guadalupe, 30, 60, 70, 77, 93, 209
Etla, Nativitas, 42, 54, 93
Etla, Nazareno, 10, 60–61, 77, 93, 209
Etla, Reyes, 93
Etla, San Agustín, 63, 91ff, 93n, 209
Etla, San Gabriel, 91f
Etla, San Miguel, 63, 91
Etla, San Pablo, 16, 29f, 91f, 209
Etla, San Pedro (Villa de), 9f, 20, 33, 39,
    70, 112, 165–69 passim, 232, 239; lands
    of, 80, 90–93 passim, 102, 109, 239
Etla, Santa Marta, 47, 133
Etla, Santo Domingo, 47, 63, 93, 93n
Etla, Soledad, 10, 54, 60–61, 70, 77, 92f,
    152, 239
Etla, Valley of, 9–16 passim, 84, 89, 90–
    94, 111, 119f, 129, 134f, 145

Feria, Nicolás, 139
Fernández de Larrazábal, Andrés, 161
Fernández Fiallo, Manuel, 160
Franciscans, 164f, 173, 182
Fuerte, del, rancho, 106, 137, 181
Fundo legal, 8, 68ff, 89f, 100, 104f

Gachupina, La, labor, 140, 225
Gage, Thomas, 117
Ganado mayor, see Cattle; Horses
Ganado menor, see Goats; Sheep; Swine
Garcés, Felipe, 37–38
García, Esteban, 159
Garzona, La, estancia, 133
Geography, 1f, 9–17, 201
Gibson, Charles, 66
Gil, Cristóbal, 117, 158, 218
Goats, 47, 72, 99, 128, 138, 156, 182
Gobernador, 49, 51–52
Godoy Ponze de León, Pedro de, 160
Góngora, Mario, 141
González Cataneo, Diego, 133
González de la Vega, Alvaro, 160
Guadalcázar, Marqués de, 149
Guadalupe, hacienda, 28, 123–35 passim,
    140–41, 149ff, 162, 192f, 200, 219–20,
    221
Guadalupe, rancho, 139, 181
Guatemala, 3, 66, 144, 201
Guaxolotitlán, San Felipe, 74

Guaxolotitlán, San Pablo, 71f
Guaxolotitlán, San Pedro, 70
Guegonivalle, rancho, 172, 189, 221, 226
Guegorexe, 99
Guelache, San Juan, 63, 79, 91ff
Guelatoba, 29
Guelavia, San Baltazar, 245
Guelavia, San Juan, 11f, 85, 87f, 106,
    147, 209, 239
Guelavichigana, labor, 140, 225
Guelaxe, Santa María, 14, 70, 87–88, 89,
    104, 209
Guendulain, mayorazgo, 102, 104n, 131,
    133, 152, 185
Guendulain family, 134, 153–60 passim,
    185, 193n
Guinea, Diego de, 113

Hacendado: powers of, 7, 123; position
    in colonial society, 158–62, 201
Hacienda, 5f, 121–35, 174–93 passim,
    248; in northern Mexico, 6ff, 78, 83–
    84, 122, 148, 195, 199f; unstable own-
    ership of, 133, 140–42, 158–63, 200.
    See also Labor; Ranching; individual
    estates listed by name
Heras y Thorres, Antonio de las, 139
Hernández Calvo, Diego, 158
Higonachada, estancia, 172
Hijo, El, hacienda, 134
Horses, 47, 81f, 114, 128, 137f, 138n, 182
Hospital Real de San Cosmé, 173
Huayapan, San Andrés, 26f, 68n, 103
Huichilobos, lands of, 78
Huistepec, San Pablo, 29, 80, 100, 210
Huitzo, 15, 19, 23, 29, 91f, 112n, 165f
Huitzo, Santiago, 50
Hunting, 15

Ibáñez, Francisco, 161
Indians, see Society, Indian; Nobility,
    Indian
Irrigation, 10ff, 60, 63, 91–96 passim,
    104, 106
Ixcotel, Santa María, 23, 30, 69, 78, 112
Ixtaltepec, Santiago, 80, 103, 107, 210
Ixtlahuaca, San Andrés, 23, 60, 69, 79f,
    91, 94n, 100, 100n
Ixtlahuaca, San Pedro, 11, 23, 26f, 30,
    42, 69, 95; lands of, 79, 85, 91, 94n,
    101

Jalapilla, hacienda, 135, 142, 162, 172,
    186, 189f, 192, 221, 226

Jalatlaco, 19, 20–21, 69, 101, 112, 209, 232
Jalatlaco River, 11, 101, 137
Jalieza, Santa Cecilia, 26, 76, 103, 105, 209, 245
Jalieza, Santa Domingo, 27, 76, 209
Jalpan, San Raimundo, 42, 100
Jaúregui Pinelo, Francisco de, 145, 153, 157–58
Jaúregui Pinelo, mayorazgo, see Molinos de Lazo, Los
Jesuits, 88, 144, 165, 168, 170ff, 182f
Jesús Nazareno, labor, 132, 139, 193n, 224ff
Juárez, Benito, 198
Juros, 190
Juzgado de Indios, 53, 108

Labor, 41–43, 53f, 182n; on haciendas, 100, 121–22, 143–52, 179. See also Peonage; Repartimiento
Labor: Indian-owned, 47, 55, 60, 63; Spanish-owned, 100, 122f, 131–34 passim, 135–40, 148, 157, 160ff, 199; Church-owned, 88, 171, 179–92 passim. See also individual estates listed by name
Lachicocana, rancho, 185, 224
Lachigalla, San Juan, 84, 210
Lachigolo, San Francisco, 14, 29, 87–88, 103f, 210, 245
Lachigubicha, rancho, 99
Lachixio, Santa María, 239
La Chizalana, Santa Cruz, 29
Land grants, 114, 116; to Indians, 40, 74, 79ff, 91, 96, 235; to Spaniards, 119f, 170–71, 185, 188
Landholdings, Indian; in early laws, 4, 67–73 passim, 116; size and distribution of, 7–8, 89–107, 196–97, 201; sources of, 40, 70–71, 74, 79ff, 96, 235; transfers of, 63, 72–79 passim, 95, 98, 105ff, 131–33, 168, 180; types of, 67–75; communal, 68–73 passim, 89; privately owned, 68, 73ff, 89, 103; use of, 71–73, 79, 81–82, 89–107 passim; defense of, 82–89, 151, 197; obtained by encroachment, 85, 87–89, 96f, 100, 104
Landholdings, Spanish, 69, 84, 111, 113–21, 124, 175–76, 178; bought or rented from Indian nobles, 48, 55–56, 62, 96; obtained by encroachment on Indian land, 54, 91f, 97–101 passim, 119, 132; worked by sharecroppers, 78, 100, 102,

104n, 131; attempted expansion of, 97, 132–34, 138, 162–63, 201; nineteenth-century consolidation of, 128, 184, 194, 200; unstable ownership of, 140–43, 162, 192. See also Hacienda; Labor; Ranching; individual estates listed by name
Lara, Francisco de, 139
Lara, Gerónimo de, I, 55, 216
Lara, Gerónimo de, II, 38, 45
Lara, Juana de, 42, 45, 56–57
Larrainzán, José Antonio de, 159
Larralde, Martín de, 161
Laws: on Indian landholding, 4, 67, 198; on Indian nobility, 44, 232; on Spanish estates, 112, 154, 169–70, 191; on ranching, 114, 120; on repartimientos, 145; on debt peonage, 148–49, 150
Lazo de la Vega family, 153, 157–58, 160, 161n
León, Vicente de, 159
Lime deposits, 17, 61, 182
Litigation: by Indians, 44, 53f, 65, 78, 82–109 passim; by Spaniards, 116, 157, 168, 171, 181, 183, 190
Llarena Lazo, Br. Manuel, 192, 220, 224
Lobenisa, rancho, 98
Lope, rancho, 137, 171, 181
López, Juan, 72
López Sarrelangue, Delfina, 66
Lorenzo, José L., 10, 12
Lubixui, rancho, 98

Macehual, 49–54 passim, 64, 74f
Macuilxóchitl, 15, 28, 36n, 50n, 53, 104, 112n, 239; lands of, 80f, 88, 102f, 106f, 119, 209f
Magdalena River, 93
Maguey, 47, 82, 91, 99, 102f, 105, 137
Maia, hacienda, 225
Maldonado, Angel, 166
Maldonado family, 153, 156–57
Maldonado de Ovalle, Francisco, 157
Manzano, rancho, 95
Maradona, Br. Juan Manuel de, 192
Markets, 47, 81, 91, 99, 103, 165, 152, 247
Marqués de Falcés, 68
Marqués del Valle, 90, 114–15, 143, 157; landholdings of, 29, 44, 78, 100, 113ff, 119; administration of, 36, 43, 60, 108–15 passim, 170; and censos perpetuos, 48, 54, 115–16, 131–32, 180, 211–12. See also Cortez, Fernando; Cortez, Martín; Cortez, Pedro

Martínez, José, 161
Martínez de Antelo, Juan, 183, 216
Martínez de Cabrera, Diego, 160
Mass, celebration of: in development of haciendas, 125–26
Matagallinas, hacienda, 172, 187f, 221ff
Matatlán, 65, 103, 168, 245
Mayeques, 41–43, 195
Mayorazgos, see Entailed estates
Mayordomo, 122
Melgar, Esteban, 147
Méndez, Fernando, 187
Mendieta y Núñez, Lucio, 68
Mendoza, Alonso de, 51
Mendoza, Andrés de, 74
Mendoza, Antonio de, 15, 114
Mendoza, Domingo de, 64, 232
Menonville, Thièry de, 12
Merced, La, monastery, 165, 167, 172f, 185
Mercedarians, see Merced, La
Mercedes, 40, 79. See also Land grants
Merchants: Indian, 100n, 103–4; Spanish, 156, 160f, 201, 253
Mesillas, Las, hacienda, 114
Mestizo, 5, 19ff, 34, 48, 51, 131, 148, 161f
Mexicapan, San Martín, 23, 70, 101, 112, 115
Mexico, Valley of, 20, 66, 164, 196–97
Mexico City, 3, 173, 190, 198
Mezcal, 14, 103
Miahuatlán, 37n, 94n
Michoacán, 66
Mier, Phelipe de, 160
Mimiaga family, 142, 200, 215
Minifundio, 77
Mining, 15, 17, 19, 28, 111f, 144f, 160
Miniyuu, barrio of Cuilapan, 42
Miranda, José, 80
Mitla, 15f, 36n, 71, 104, 112n, 145, 168, 239, 245; population of, 20n, 39; lands of, 75, 79ff, 102–7 passim, 119
Mixteca Alta, 38, 80, 154
Mixtecs, 22f, 40, 232
Mixtepec, Asunción, 26
Mixtepec, Magdalena, 26f
Mixtepec, San Miguel, 17, 100
Mixtepec, Santa Catalina, 26
Mixtepec, Santa Cruz, 15, 36n, 82, 94n, 100n, 112n, 165f
Mixtepec, Santiago, 30
Molinos, Los, hacienda, 114
Molinos de Lazo, Los, 92f, 93n, 113, 131, 157–58, 157n

Molongos, 37n
Monjas, Las, estancia, 188, 222
Monjas, Las, hacienda, 140
Monterrey, Conde de, 149
Monterrubio family, 190, 200, 218, 253
Montezuma, lands of, 79
Montoya, Andrés de, 161
Montoya, hacienda, 131, 148, 162, 189, 193
Morales Sigala, Br. Gerónimo, 192, 215, 225f
Mörner, Magnus, 39
Mortgages: on Indian land, 75n, 132; on Spanish estates, 138, 141–42, 153n, 154–58 passim, 250; by the Church, 170, 179ff, 185–91 passim, 221
Motolinía, 12
Moya, Luis de, 159
Mulattoes, 39, 51, 63, 148, 161
Murguía y Galardi, José María, 94, 96, 198, 200

Nahuas, 22f, 79, 96, 111, 115. See also Mexico, Valley of
Nahuatl, 22, 232
Naranjos, Los, hacienda, 134, 183
Negritos, de los, hacienda, 87, 134f, 159, 192
Negroes, 19, 21, 34, 47f. See also Slavery
New Granada, 144, 153
Nexapa, 37n, 182f
Nobility, Indian, 2, 15, 41–43, 48–49, 66, 101, 131, 195–96, 236; wealth and status of, 35–38, 39, 43–66 passim; and land titles, 39–40, 41; use of land by, 40, 47f, 52, 56f, 59ff, 63ff, 66, 75; entailed estates of, 44–45, 56–65; alienation of land by, 44–47, 55–56, 61, 74, 92f, 105, 168, 236, 240; political role of, 48–56
—individual nobles by location: Acatlán and Teposcolula, 38; Apasco, Magdalena, 16, 35, 45, 47, 61, 63, 196, 206f; Cacaotepec, San Lorenzo, 45; Chapultepec, San Juan, 29, 40–41, 43, 46, 206; Coyotepec, 59–60; Cuilapan, 35–46 passim, 54–57 passim, 65, 96, 101, 196, 205ff, 208, 225, 238, 240; Etla, 35, 38, 42–56 passim, 60–63, 65, 90, 92f, 196, 205ff, 208; Etla, San Miguel, 48; Etla, Santo Domingo, 46–47, 206; Guaxolotitlán, San Pablo, 38, 46; Guaxolotitlán, Santiago, 208; Guelache, San Juan, 48, 63, 196; Huitzo, 38, 38n,

41, 51–52, 63, 132, 206f; Ixtlahuaca, San Andrés, 45; Jalatlaco, 23, 40f; Matatlán, 45, 52; Mitla, 40, 64; Mixtepec, Santa Cruz, 39; Oaxaca, Villa de, 38, 42, 45, 54, 208; Ocotlán, 47, 51, 53, 55, 59, 214; Ocotlán, Santiago, 53; San Pedro Apostol, 43; Teitipac, San Sebastián, 43, 45f, 72, 105; Tejupan, 38; Teotitlán del Valle, 51, 64; Tlacochahuaya, 29, 40, 43; Tlacolula, 15, 40, 47, 64, 106, 208; Tlalixtac, 39ff, 43, 65; Tlapacoya, 74; Tomaltepec, 40f; Tutla, San Sebastián, 38; Zaachila, 53, 205f; Zimatlán, 52, 59, 206. See also individual nobles listed by name
Noria, La, rancho, 139, 225
Noriega, Br. Felipe, 192, 216, 226
Noriega, hacienda, see San Nicolás Obispo
Novices, 186–87

Oaxaca, Santa María (Villa de), 20, 23, 33, 39, 50, 69f, 111f, 165; lands of, 80, 94n, 100–101, 116
Obrajes, 161
Obra pía, 172
Ocotlán, Magdalena, 9, 88, 210
Ocotlán, San Dionicio, 233
Ocotlán, San Jacinto, 100
Ocotlán, San Sebastián, 233
Ocotlán, Santo Domingo, 88, 97, 210
Ocotlán, Villa de, 9, 11, 36, 39, 112n, 145, 165f, 239; lands of, 80f, 98f, 119, 210
Oratorio de San Felipe Neri, 173f
Orchards, 11, 95, 117, 138
Ordinia Sosa y Castilla, Br. Francisco, 193n, 224
Orozco, Francisco de, 36, 111
Ortiz, Miguel, 159
Oxen, 72, 81f, 130, 137f, 138n, 156

Pacheco, Rodrigo, 117–18
Pacheco family, 134, 134n
Papalutla, Santa Cruz, 30, 103, 105, 185, 209
Parajes, 84
Peláez de Berrio, Juan, 37
Peñoles, Santa María, 95, 112n, 209
Peonage: on Spanish estates, 5f, 102, 122, 138, 147–52, 199; to Indian nobles, 43, 47, 63
Peru, 197
Petapec, 37n

Philip II, King of Spain, 81
Phipps, Helen, 73
Pimentel, Juana Faustina, 63
Pinelo, Rafael, 114, 157, 186
Poblete, hacienda, 172, 187f, 222
Population: Indian, 2, 5, 17f, 21–34, 90, 117, 145, 231, 245; non-Indian, 5, 18–21, 34, 38f, 62, 165
Porras, Diego de, 112
Pozo, Clemente del, 139
Pregón, 44, 73
Priests, secular, 161, 169, 173, 191–93, 194, 224–26
Primitivo patrimonio, 73, 78
Principales, see Nobility, Indian

Quarries, 17, 47, 63
Quelobigoa River, 100
Quiabejo, rancho, 154f
Quialana, hacienda, 98
Quialana, San Bartolomé, 14, 81, 245
Quiané, Santa Catalina, 72, 79
Quiavini, San Lucas, 103, 119
Quiechapa, 94n
Quinta, La, labor, 160, 172, 189f

Rabasa, Emilio, 73, 197, 198n
Racial mixing, 19f, 31, 39. See also Mestizo; Mulattoes
Ramírez de Aguilar, Luis, 139, 155, 187
Ramírez de Aguilar family, 56n, 134, 153–59 passim, 187
Ramírez de León, Francisco, 53, 55, 61–62, 158
Ramírez de León, Isabel, 62–63
Ramírez de León, Sebastián, 61
Ramírez de Torres, Francisco, 159
Ramos, Joseph, 138f
Ranching: in early colonial period, 3, 15f, 69, 112f, 116–21, 145, 231; by Indian nobles, 40, 47, 52, 57, 59f, 64; by Indian communities, 71ff, 79, 81, 93–107 passim, 196; by Spaniards, 113–23 passim, 128f, 131, 135–37, 154; by the Church, 179ff, 184–85, 186
Rancho, see Ranching; individual estates listed by name
Recoletas Agustinas, see Soledad, Nuestra Señora de la
Recopilación, 82
Relaciones Geográficas: for years 1579–81, 12, 14, 16, 22, 31, 95, 107, 196; for 1777, 82, 94n, 101, 138n
Rentals: by Indian nobles, 48, 54, 57,

238, 240; by Indian communities, 94, 96, 98, 104f, 113n; by and to Spanish estates, 113, 131ff, 135, 156, 158, 162; by the Church, 170–71, 179f, 184f, 188, 193
Repartimientos, 5, 26, 28, 37, 42, 120, 143–47 *passim*
Reparto de efectos, 152, 197
Revolution of 1910, 107, 199
Rodrígues de Montenegro, Gaspar, 161
Rojas, Diego de, 63
Rosario, del, hacienda, 180, 186
Rosario, del, trapiche, 182
Ruiz, Joseph, 45
Ruiz, Melchior, 158
Ruiz de Estrada, Br. Tomás, 192

Sala, Cristóbal de, 158f
Salado River, 11, 106
Salt deposits, 16, 16n, 41, 47, 63
San Agustín de las Juntas, 10–11, 17, 29f
San Antonio, *labor*, 139
San Antonio Buenavista, hacienda, 159
San Antonio de la Cal, 17, 20, 29, 43, 100
San Bartolo, hacienda, 127f, 134f, 140ff, 185, 189ff, 200, 217–18
San Blas, barrio of San Pedro Ixtlahuaca, 72
San Blas, *labor*, 225f
San Blas, rancho, 16, 148
Sánchez, Bartolomé, 119
Sánchez, Cosmé, 132
Sánchez de Chávez, Pedro, 158
Sánchez de Ulloa, Br. Andrés, 191–92
San Cristóbal, rancho, 95, 135
San Diego, hacienda (Miahuatlán jurisdiction), 172, 187, 221f
San Diego, hacienda (near Zimatlán), 172, 187f, 222
Saneya, Santa Catarina, 26
San Felipe del Agua, 11, 103
San Francisco Buenavista, hacienda, 189, 191
San Germán, hacienda, 188, 223
Sangre de Cristo, *labor*, 139, 226
San Guillermo, hacienda, 189
San Hipólito Mártir, 174
San Isidro, hacienda (Valley of Etla), 123, 133, 225
San Isidro, hacienda (Valley of Zimatlán), 123, 128, 131f, 140, 162, 188, 193, 222f
San Isidro, *labor*, 140

San Jacinto, hacienda, 134, 140–41, 200, 216–17
San Jacinto, town, 70, 105, 210
San Javier, hacienda, 132, 134
San Joaquín, hacienda, 128, 172, 186, 188, 221
San José, hacienda (near Zaachila), 128, 132, 183, 188, 222
San José (Progreso), hacienda, 84, 109, 123, 133, 135, 142, 162, 192, 221; transfers of, 140f, 200, 214–15
San José, *labor*, 139, 225f
San José, rancho, 226
San José, trapiche, 155f, 225
San José Guelatoba, hacienda, 128, 140
San Juan, *labor*, 140
San Juan Bautista, hacienda, 127f, 132, 135, 140–41, 148, 162, 192, 216; 221; under Carmelite ownership, 167, 171, 183f, 193, 200
San Juan de Dios, monastery, 173
San Juan del Estado, 16, 91
San Juan family, 46
San Luis, *labor*, 139
San Miguel (Careaga), hacienda, 101, 132, 188f, 223
San Miguel, *labor*, 88, 139, 188
San Miguel de la Sierra, 107
San Miguel de las Peras, 57, 95, 234
San Nicolás, *labor*, 139
San Nicolás Obispo (Noriega), hacienda, 97, 127f, 132ff, 140–41, 147, 160, 192, 215–16, 224
San Nicolás Tolentino, hacienda, 134, 226
San Pablo, monastery, 173f, 194
San Pablo Cuatro Venados, 95, 96n
San Pablo de la Raya, 234
San Pedro Apostol, 69, 79, 85f, 98, 119
San Pedro Mártir, 100
San Roque, *labor*, 172, 189
Santa Ana, trapiche, 172
Santa Ana del Valle, 26, 106, 210
Santa Anita, barrio of San Juan Chapultepec, 101
Santa Catalina de Sena, convent, 157, 165, 170, 172f, 185–88, 189, 193–94, 221–23, 224
Santa Catalina de Sena, town, 107, 233
Santa Catarina, sujeto of Mitla, 107
Santa Catarina Minas, 26, 80, 98–99, 119, 165, 209
Santa Cruz, hacienda, 135, 162
Santaella, Juan de, 139, 222

Santa Gertrudis, hacienda, 148
Santa Inez, hacienda, 182
Santa Inez del Monte, 59
Santa Lucía (Valley of Tlacolula), 70,
    78, 85, 105, 209
Santa Lucía (Valley of Zimatlán), 100
Santa Marina, *labor*, 133
Santa Rita, hacienda, 132f, 141, 220
Santa Rita, *labor*, 139, 192, 226
Santa Rosa, hacienda, 140
Santa Rosa Buenavista, hacienda, *see*
    Negritos, de los
Santa Rosa del Peñol, *labor*, 140
Santiago, Order of, 134
Santiago Apostol, Sujeto of Ocotlán, 50f,
    100, 119, 239
Santísima Trinidad, hacienda, 135, 162
Santísima Trinidad, town, 29f, 69, 100
Santo Domingo, monastery, 154, 171,
    173f, 180–81, 187–94 *passim*, 200, 219
Santo Domingo Buenavista, hacienda,
    16, 88, 123, 128–34 *passim*, 140ff, 162,
    218–19; under Bethlemite ownership,
    171, 184–85, 193, 200
Santo Domingo del Valle, 80, 103, 245
Santo Domingo Soriano, hacienda, 193
Sarmiento, José, 139
Segoba, rancho, 98
Seleri, Diego Joseph, 160
Sharecroppers, 29, 47f, 57, 82, 93, 102,
    131, 161, 171. *See also Terrasguerros*
Sheep, 15, 47, 72f, 174; Indian-owned,
    79, 82, 95–106 *passim*; Spanish-owned,
    114f, 128–31 *passim*, 137f, 156, 182
Sierra O'Reilly, Justo, 169
Silk, 3, 113f, 116
Slavery: Negro, 21, 63, 144, 154, 156, 182,
    232, 250–51; Indian, 23, 143, 151
Society, Indian, 37, 48f, 52n, 132, 152,
    195–96; pre-conquest, 1f, 4, 15f, 21–22,
    27, 35, 40–45 *passim*, 72f, 78–79; accul-
    turation of, 4f, 35, 38, 81f; and re-
    settlement, 21f, 27–29, 37, 233; gov-
    ernment of, 29f, 37, 39, 48–56
Society, Spanish, *see* Antequera; *Ha-
    cienda*; *Labor*; Landholdings, Span-
    ish; Ranching
Sola, 37n
Solariego, 42
Soledad, hacienda, 135, 224, 226
Soledad, *labor*, 140, 226
Soledad, La, estancia, 135, 172, 188ff, 223
Soledad, Nuestra Señora de la, convent,
    165, 167, 170, 172f, 188–89, 194

Solórzano Pereira, Juan de, 44
Soriano, rancho, 139
Soritana, La, trapiche, 128, 131, 157
Spanish conquest, 36, 164, 198
Suaina, Santo Domingo, 27, 104
Suchilquitongo, 23, 47
Sugar cane, 14, 91, 98, 102, 127–28, 188,
    198
Sujetos, 21, 29f, 49
Swine, 82, 99, 114

Tamazulapan, 37n
Tanibé, hacienda, 106, 131, 154f, 249
Taniche, hacienda, 140, 224
Tehuacán, 37n
Tehuantepec, 14, 16, 16n, 174
Teitipac, Magdalena, 103, 210, 245
Teitipac, San Juan, 19, 28, 36n, 50n,
    112n, 165, 233, 245; economy of, 11,
    16, 104, 145; lands of, 85, 88, 103, 105f,
    105n, 209f
Teitipac, San Sebastián, 72, 79, 103, 105,
    185, 209f, 245
Tejalapan, San Felipe, 30
Tejupan, 37n
Tenexpan, 23, 36n, 169
Teocuicuilco, 37n
Teotitlán del Valle, 15f, 34, 80f, 112n,
    160, 165, 168; lands of, 85, 102ff, 107,
    119, 210
Teposcolula, 37n, 38
Terrasguerros, 41–43, 48, 54, 64, 78, 82,
    101, 131, 236. *See also* Sharecroppers
Tierras de humedad, 11, 95, 97, 105
Tierras realengas, 72
Tilquiapan, San Miguel, 80f
Tithe, 82, 191
Tititlán, San Gerónimo, 26
Tlacochahuaya, San Gerónimo and San
    Sebastián, 11, 14, 28, 30, 36n, 50f, 112n,
    165, 233, 239; expansion of, 27, 87–88,
    104; lands of, 85–87, 88, 103, 105, 105n,
    119, 209f, 239
Tlacolula, 9ff, 14, 19, 28, 39, 104, 112n,
    147, 239; lands of, 79ff, 102f, 105f, 209,
    239
Tlacolula, Valley of, 9–15 *passim*, 43,
    63–64, 84, 120, 128–29, 145; lands in,
    89, 102–7, 119f, 128–29, 134f, 171,
    180–81
Tlalixtac, 11, 14, 26, 36n, 41, 50f, 165f,
    239; lands of, 79f, 88, 103, 104–5, 119,
    210, 239
Tlanechico, hacienda, 97, 185

Tlanechico, *labor*, 140
Tlanechico, San Lucas, 23, 29, 95, 100, 210, 234
Tlapacoya, 10, 19f, 23, 98–99, 112, 112n, 119
Tlapazola, San Marcos, 14, 85, 87f, 103, 106, 209
Tlaxcala, 7, 23, 111
Tomaltepec, Santo Domingo, 26, 88, 103f, 210
Toribio de Benavente, 12
Torre Vilar, Ernesto de la, 169
Torres, Nicolás de, 139
trapiche, 127–28, 134, 155, 182f, 188
Tribute, 17n, 41, 70f, 79, 82, 108, 143f, 146, 193n
Trinidad de la Huertas, 69
Tres Ríos, estancia, 172, 186f
Tule, Santa María del, 43, 69, 80, 82, 102, 104, 104n
Tutla, San Francisco, 26, 209
Tutla, San Sebastián, 26f, 105, 209

Valdeflores, hacienda, 29, 100, 123, 131, 135, 144, 148, 156f, 191, 217
Varela de Figueroa, Tomás, 139, 216
Vásquez, Bernardo, 59
Vásquez, Hipólito, 52, 59
Veintena, 115
Velasco, Clemente, 64
Velasco, Gerónimo de, 64
Velasco, Luis de, I, 112n, 114
Veracruz, 201
Veracruz, Juan de, 54
Vergel, El, hacienda, 109, 123, 132, 162, 192
Vida común, 191, 191n
Vidal, Antonio, 161
Villaseñor y Sánchez, José Antonio de, 94
Visita, 165, 169
Vista de ojos, 84–85, 159
Vocales, 49

Wheat, 3, 13f, 13n, 91, 98, 103, 127, 145;

grown by Indians, 4, 82, 116–17, 143; grown by Spaniards, 5, 120, 145, 198; mills, 48, 61, 63, 79, 91ff, 113, 134f, 145, 157, 186
Wolf, Eric, 123
Wood products, 17, 91, 95–96, 99, 100n, 103, 105, 197

Xaagá, hacienda, 87, 106, 123, 128, 134f, 140–41, 154n, 219; Church ownership of, 172, 181, 189f, 193, 199
Xabiogo, rancho, 16, 158
Xaguia Abilana, barrio of Quiané, 72
Ximeno de Bohórquez, Br. Ignacio, 192
Xochimilco, San Sebastián, 91
Xochimilco, Santo Tomás, 112
Xoxocotlán, 20, 23, 30, 42, 46, 54, 75, 101–2
Xuchitepec, hacienda, 123n, 155, 172, 189

Yatzechi, Santa Inéz, 88, 210
"Y" River, 9

Zaachila, 11, 20–28 *passim*, 53, 57, 78, 112n, 152, 233; lands of, 88, 96–97, 119, 199, 239; Dominicans in, 165, 166, 169, 193, 193n
Zamora, Diego de, 131
Zapata, Emiliano, 199
Zapotecs, 22, 26, 96
Zárate, Juan López de, 79, 116, 164, 165–66, 193
Zautla, San Andrés, 29f, 81, 91
Zegache, San Gerónimo, 26f
Zegache, Santa Ana, 23, 26, 51, 80, 98–99, 119, 166
Zimatlán, 9ff, 19, 26, 34, 36n, 50f, 112n, 179n, 239; lands of, 79ff, 88, 98, 119, 210, 239; Dominicans in, 165f, 169, 180
Zimatlán, Valley of, 9, 12f, 16, 84, 94, 102, 119f, 128–29, 134f
Zorita, hacienda, 97, 132, 189, 191
Zoritana, hacienda, 226
Zúñiga-Guzmán family, 46